Quantum-Driven Financial Intelligence:

Innovations in Predictive Analytics and Autonomous Trading Systems

Mohammad Irfan
https://orcid.org/0000-0002-4956-1170
Chandigarh University, Unnao, India

Gilney Figueira Zebende
https://orcid.org/0000-0003-2420-9805
State University of Feira de Santana, Brazil

Adel Sarea
https://orcid.org/0000-0001-6154-4261
Ahlia University, Bahrain

Muhammad Shahbaz
Beijing Institute of Technology, China

IGI Global
Scientific Publishing
Publishing Tomorrow's Research Today

Vice President of Editorial	Melissa Wagner
Director of Acquisitions	Mikaela Felty
Director of Book Development	Jocelynn Hessler
Production Manager	Mike Brehm
Cover Design	Jose Rosado

Published in the United States of America by
IGI Global Scientific Publishing
701 East Chocolate Avenue
Hershey, PA, 17033, USA
Tel: 717-533-8845 | Fax: 717-533-7115
Website: https://www.igi-global.com E-mail: cust@igi-global.com

Library of Congress Cataloging-in-Publication Data

LCCN: 2025029109 (CIP Data Pending)
ISBN13: 9798337328935
Isbn13Softcover: 9798337328942
EISBN13: 9798337328959

British Cataloguing in Publication Data
A Cataloguing in Publication record for this book is available from the British Library.

Table of Contents

Detailed Table of Contents

This chapter introduces the revolutionary potential of quantum computing in finance, referencing its promise to revolutionize risk management, portfolio optimization, market forecasting, and data protection. It describes key quantum algorithms such as Grover's and Shor's, and technologies such as quantum annealing and quantum machine learning, while illustrating how the advances dramatically decrease computational complexity and improve decision-making efficiency. The research also includes the limitations of classical financial models and describes how quantum approaches bridge these limitations via superior stochastic modelling, real-time rebalancing, and high-level cryptographic systems. The paper also addresses challenges to implementation, including hardware constraints, high implementation costs, regulatory complexity, and the need for immediate interdisciplinary expertise. The paper lastly prescribes strategic imperatives for financial institutions, policymakers, and investors in preparation for an impending future enabled by quantum technology.

Quantum-driven brings the new innovation in the financial sectors and "predictive analytics, portfolio optimization, and autonomous" trading systems. Quantum computing's is the complex, high-dimensional data sets at unprecedented speed, financial institutions envision more accurate forecasting models and decision-making. It is the one of the foremost barriers is the immaturity of current quantum hardware, instability, and scalability limitations. On the other hand integration of quantum systems with existing classical infrastructures require "hybrid architectures, specialized algorithms, and substantial investment" in infrastructure and training. Quantum-enhanced models create opaque decision-making processes, amplifying risks of market exploitation, data privacy violations, or systemic vulnerabilities. Collaborative ecosystems involving academia, industry, and regulators are expected to accelerate the development of standards and best practices.

"Quantum age" is the name given to the new era when quantum technologies will start shifting out of laboratory research into real-world usage that can potentially data scientist, various areas and aspects of society change drastically (Possati, 2024). It is required to know about the potential uses of quantum computing in financial services because it is a developing technology that can potentially revolutionize the industry.It has the promise of accessing the Power of Quantum Computing for Enhanced Forecasting, Portfolio Optimization, etc. Likewise, the exponential acceleration of computation promised by quantum computers has potential benefits in fraud detection (Zhou, 2025). For instance, quantum-enabled anomaly detection which enables the identification of anomalous transaction patterns in real-time, could possibly lower false positives and improve the efficacy of fraud prevention when monitoring credit card and other banking transactions.

The convergence of financial technology (fintech) and sustainable finance represents a transformative paradigm in contemporary financial markets. This paper examines how digital platforms are democratizing access to green finance through comprehensive empirical analysis and econometric modeling. Our study employs a Fintech

Democratization Index (FDI) and panel data regression covering 25 countries from 2018-2023. Results demonstrate that fintech adoption increases green investment penetration by 84.7% (p<0.001), with minimum investment requirements falling by 96% and management fees declining by 67%.

Quantum Finance is a transformative field merging quantum computing, finance, and computer science to tackle complex financial challenges. As classical models face limits in scalability and optimization, quantum algorithms like Monte Carlo, Amplitude Estimation, and Grover's Search offer promising solutions. This study analyzes 54 articles from Scopus to trace the field's evolution in publication trends, vocabulary, sentiment, and modality. Using text normalization, tokenization, and domain-specific filtering, the study examines yearly output, lexical patterns, sentiment via VADER, and rhetorical framing. Results show a post-2022 surge in publications, with 2024 peaking. Sentiment fluctuates, with optimism in early and recent years, and caution in 2013 and 2023. Modality analysis reveals a shift from tentative to assertive claims. Thematic clustering highlights growth in quantum risk modeling, machine learning, cryptography, and hybrid systems.

Institutions — banks, insurers, hedge funds, and asset managers — are central to fueling the quantum revolution. They supply the capital necessary for research and development as principal investors in quantum startups and partnerships. As early movers, they pilot practical applications such as portfolio optimization, derivatives pricing, and catastrophe modeling, demonstrating quantum's real-world utility. They're also leading in quantum-safe security, advocating for higher encryption to keep valuable transactions secure from coming quantum attacks. By using quantum computing in risk management and product development, they can create more effective financial products, enhance lending and insurance precision, and facilitate better fraud detection. Briefly: Financial institutions drive, experiment with, secure, and amplify the quantum revolution, and profit from it as well. Finance and quantum are symbiotic — each propels the other.

Ruchika Rastogi, Pranveer Singh Institute of Technology, Kanpur, India
Sandeep Kumar, Institute of Business Management, GLA University, Mathura, India
Rui Dias, Universidade Europeia, Portugal

Green finance helps in climate change adaptation, biodiversity protection, managing sanitation, pollution control, managing renewable energies, and waste recycling and processing hence it is a broader term. Climate related investments are not the only one advantage of green finance rather other advantages are indirectly contributing in the carbon emission reduction. Green finance as important for everyone as it leads to low carbon emission for the society. Money landed by banks leads to make economy greener in terms of creating jobs, creating sustainable environment and reducing carbon emission.This study analyzes the relationship among green finance, ESG performance and carbon emission intensity in the countries like USA, Japan and Europe. This study checks the role of green finance in the overall improvement of ESG with carbon emission intensityIn this analysis it is seen that there is no significant relationship found in ESG and carbon emission intensity in USA.

Mohamed Ismail Mohamed Riyath, South Eastern University of Sri Lanka, Sri Lanka
Nagham Aldabbous, The Public Authority for Applied Education and Training, Kuwait
Mohammed Jaboob, Dhofar University, Oman
Mohammad Irfan, Chandigarh University, Unnao, India

This chapter synthesizes the state of quantum computing for finance through a task-first lens and a systems-aware stance. We begin by motivating quantum routines as specialised kernels embedded in classical workflows, then formalise foundations across gate and annealing paradigms, the finance-specific taxonomy (pricing/Greeks and risk aggregation; portfolio/ALM; anomaly/credit analytics; practice-facing benchmarking), and the translation of asymptotic advantage into implementable pipelines. Mapping algorithms to roles, we show how amplitude-estimation–based quantum Monte Carlo provides the cleanest pathway for pricing and risk under disciplined state preparation and depth control; how variational and annealer–gate

optimization, fraud detection, and risk assessment. Despite hardware limitations and regulatory challenges, the growth of quantum cloud services and tools like Qiskit and PennyLane is accelerating adoption. Cross-sector collaboration will be key in shaping ethical, transparent, and effective quantum finance systems. This shift signals a future of faster, smarter, and more adaptive financial technologies.

The swift progress of quantum computing is set to revolutionize the financial sector, especially in the fields of risk management and portfolio optimization. Existing financial models, though effective in some measure, are unable to handle the huge complexities of today's markets, where high-frequency trading, nonlinear interdependencies, and complex risk factors require advanced computational capabilities. Quantum finance, a new multidisciplinary research area, uses quantum computing concepts to improve financial decision-making, investment strategy optimization, and risk reduction more effectively than traditional techniques. This chapter discusses how quantum computing is revolutionizing risk management and portfolio optimization using quantum mechanics-based algorithms like quantum annealing, quantum Monte Carlo simulations, and variational quantum eigensolvers (VQEs). These methods enable financial institutions to resolve high-dimensional optimization problems exponentially quicker, detect more optimal risk-adjusted portfolios, and build predictive models with higher accuracy.

Quantum computing is poised to revolutionize financial intelligence by offering unprecedented computational power for solving complex problems in portfolio optimization and risk assessment. As financial markets become increasingly data-driven and interconnected, classical computational methods struggle to handle the exponential growth of financial data and the complexity of optimization challenges. Novel quantum algorithms, such as quantum approximate optimization algorithm,

Preface

Quantum computing is transforming financial systems, enabling advanced predictive analytics, portfolio optimization, and strategic decision-making. These innovations empower institutions, investors, and policymakers to navigate complex markets with greater efficiency, precision, and sustainability.

This volume of the edited book ***Quantum-Driven Financial Intelligence: Innovations in Predictive Analytics and Autonomous Trading Systems*** presents cutting-edge research and practical insights on quantum finance and fintech innovations. Contributions from global scholars explore key topics, including quantum-enhanced risk management, sustainable investment strategies, digital platforms for democratizing finance, and data-driven approaches to financial forecasting.

The chapters examine foundational principles, emerging challenges, and practical applications in quantum finance. Early contributions, such as Quantum Finance Unleashed and Challenges and Future Directions in Quantum-Driven Financial Innovation, provide a framework for understanding the evolving landscape. Other chapters, including Fintech Innovation in Green Finance and Impact of Green Finance on Carbon Footprint, emphasize sustainability, while Quantum Computing and Algorithms in Financial Applications and Smart Trading Systems in the Quantum Age explore technical applications. Institutional perspectives, highlighted in The Role of Financial Institutions in Driving the Quantum Revolution and Pioneering Quantum Computing in Financial Services, reveal global trends shaping financial systems.

CHAPTER OVERVIEW

Chapter 1 explores quantum computing's potential to revolutionize finance through enhanced risk management, portfolio optimization, market forecasting, and data security. It covers key algorithms like Grover's and Shor's, quantum annealing, and machine learning, addressing limitations of classical models and implementation challenges such as hardware, costs, regulations, and expertise needs, while offering strategic recommendations for stakeholders.

Focusing on quantum-driven innovations in predictive analytics, portfolio optimization, and autonomous trading, chapter 2 highlights quantum computing's ability to process complex data rapidly. It discusses barriers like hardware instability and scalability, the need for hybrid architectures and investments, risks of opaque models, and the role of collaborative ecosystems in developing standards and best practices.

Chapter 3 discusses the "quantum age" and its shift from research to real-world applications in finance, emphasizing enhanced forecasting, portfolio optimization, and fraud detection via quantum-enabled anomaly identification. It addresses potential benefits like real-time transaction monitoring to reduce false positives and improve fraud prevention efficacy.

Examining the intersection of fintech and sustainable finance, chapter 4 uses empirical analysis and econometric modeling, including a Fintech Democratization Index and panel data from 25 countries (2018-2023), to show how digital platforms boost green investment penetration by 84.7%, reduce minimum investments by 96%, and lower fees by 67%.

Chapter 5 analyzes 54 Scopus articles on quantum finance, tracing trends in publications, vocabulary, sentiment, and modality. It notes a surge post-2022, fluctuating sentiment with recent optimism, a shift to assertive claims, and thematic growth in quantum risk modeling, machine learning, cryptography, and hybrid systems.

Highlighting banks, insurers, hedge funds, and asset managers as key drivers, chapter 6 covers their investments in quantum startups, pilots for applications like portfolio optimization and catastrophe modeling, quantum-safe security, and innovations in risk management, fraud detection, and product development, emphasizing a symbiotic relationship between finance and quantum tech.

Chapter 7 defines green finance broadly, encompassing climate adaptation, biodiversity, and renewable energy, and its indirect role in reducing carbon emissions through job creation and sustainable environments. It analyzes relationships between green finance, ESG performance, and carbon intensity in the USA, Japan, and Europe, finding no significant link in the USA.

Adopting a task-first approach, chapter 8 motivates quantum routines in classical workflows, covering gate and annealing paradigms, a finance taxonomy (e.g., pricing, portfolio, anomaly detection), and algorithm mappings like quantum Monte Carlo for risk, hybrids for portfolios, and kernels for credit tasks, focusing on practical pipelines.

Chapter 9 examines using tools like Power BI, Excel, and R for forecasting revenue, profits, and expenses in the automobile industry. It emphasizes combining these for trend analysis, risk assessment, and decision-making, with ARIMA models showing superior accuracy for improved precision and competitiveness.

Exploring quantum's impact on complex financial systems, chapter 10 discusses algorithms like QAOA, Grover's Search, and quantum Monte Carlo for better forecasting and autonomous trading via pattern recognition and reinforcement learning. It covers hybrids for optimization, fraud, and risk, noting challenges, cloud services, and the need for collaboration.

Chapter 11 addresses quantum computing's revolution in banking, particularly risk management and portfolio optimization, using algorithms like quantum annealing, Monte Carlo simulations, and VQEs to handle market complexities faster, enabling optimal portfolios and accurate predictive models beyond classical capabilities.

Focusing on quantum's power for data-driven finance, chapter 12 covers algorithms like QAOA, VQE, and quantum-enhanced Monte Carlo for asset allocation, risk modeling, and analytics. It discusses improvements in portfolio tradeoffs, credit analysis, liquidity forecasting, and volatility modeling amid growing data complexity.

Chapter 13 examines quantum's transformation in financial services via risk assessment, optimization, fraud detection, and trading. It analyzes strategies of early adopters like JPMorgan Chase, Goldman Sachs, and HSBC, using algorithms like quantum annealing and Shor's, while addressing challenges in hardware, regulations, cybersecurity, and the role of quantum cloud and AI integration.

I extend my heartfelt gratitude to my parents, my beloved wife, and my children; without their unwavering support, love, and encouragement, this book would not have been possible.

Mohammad Irfan
Chandigarh University, Unnao, India

Gilney Figueira Zebende
State University of Feira de Santana, Brazil

Adel Sarea
Ahlia University, Bahrain

Muhammad Shahbaz
Beijing Institute of Technology, China

Chapter 1
Quantum Finance Unleashed:
Transforming Risk, Portfolios, and the Future of Financial Strategy

Nitesh Behare
https://orcid.org/0000-0002-9338-8563
Balaji Institute of International Business, Sri Balaji University, Pune, India

Bhagyashri Sahebrao Patil
https://orcid.org/0009-0001-2949-4871
School of Business, MBA Indira University, Pune, India

C. S. Yadav
Banarsidas Chandiwala Institute of Professional Studies, Dwarka, India

Syed Muhammad Abdul Rehman Shah
Allama Iqbal Open University, Islamabad, Pakistan

ABSTRACT

This chapter introduces the revolutionary potential of quantum computing in finance, referencing its promise to revolutionize risk management, portfolio optimization, market forecasting, and data protection. It describes key quantum algorithms such as Grover's and Shor's, and technologies such as quantum annealing and quantum machine learning, while illustrating how the advances dramatically decrease computational complexity and improve decision-making efficiency. The research also includes the limitations of classical financial models and describes how quantum approaches bridge these limitations via superior stochastic modelling, real-time rebalancing, and high-level cryptographic systems. The paper also addresses chal-

DOI: 10.4018/979-8-3373-2893-5.ch001

lenges to implementation, including hardware constraints, high implementation costs, regulatory complexity, and the need for immediate interdisciplinary expertise. The paper lastly prescribes strategic imperatives for financial institutions, policymakers, and investors in preparation for an impending future enabled by quantum technology.

1. INTRODUCTION: THE DAWN OF QUANTUM FINANCE

Finance is on the cusp of revolutionary transformation with the advent of quantum computing—a transformation that can redefine the cornerstones of modern finance. Even though conventional computational methods and algorithms are very strong (Eswaran et al., 2025), they are increasingly limited by the size and complexity of modern financial systems. Tasks like risk modelling, portfolio optimization, asset pricing, and market forecasting require computational powers that frequently surpass the power of classical models of computation. Here, quantum finance comes as a response to the growing need for greater speed, accuracy, and multi-dimensional analysis (Khang et al., 2025).

With the quantum mechanical concepts of superposition, entanglement, and quantum parallelism as its foundation, quantum computing enables parallel processing of enormous amounts of information and the concurrent exploration of numerous outcomes (Natraj et al., 2025). This has extremely important ramifications for financial usage, where uncertainty, probability, and responsiveness in real time are of most concern. From improved optimization of high-dimensional portfolios and systemic risk simulation under the presence of market volatility, quantum algorithms hold radical performance and analytical depth improvements (Vashishth et al., 2025), (Irfan, Mohammed, Kassim, & Ofori, 2024).

The quantum finance theory is moving from a theoretical model to an emerging field of research and study. As the financial institutions begin to explore solutions enabled by quantum technology, a new era of innovation is beginning—a one that has the potential to revolutionize strategic decision-making, enhance computational power, and redefine competitive advantages.

1.1. Fundamentals Quantum Finance

Quantum finance refers to the application of quantum computing to solve complex, computationally intensive financial problems beyond the reach of conventional methods. By leveraging quantum algorithms alongside financial modelling, it delivers unprecedented precision, scalability, and efficiency (Zhou, 2025). Unlike classical computing, which encodes information in binary bits, quantum computing employs qubits that exploit superposition and entanglement, allowing them to represent multiple states simultaneously. This property enables quantum systems to process vast calculations in parallel, accelerating simulations and enhancing predictive accuracy. Applications in finance include asset pricing, portfolio optimization, and risk assessment, particularly in scenarios involving high-dimensional data and stochastic modelling (Claudiu et al., 2024).

The importance of quantum finance lies in its ability to overcome the limitations of traditional methods such as Monte Carlo simulations, Black-Scholes models, and Markowitz portfolio theory. These classical approaches are computationally burdensome when addressing interconnected, real-time challenges in volatile markets. Quantum computing, by efficiently scanning immense solution spaces, offers improvements in systemic risk analysis, optimization of advanced portfolios, and detection of market anomalies. Its potential spans investment banking, algorithmic trading, asset management, and regulatory compliance, signaling a fundamental shift toward data-driven financial systems (Choi et al., 2023). Despite challenges—hardware maturity, algorithmic complexity, and regulatory gaps—quantum finance represents more than technological progress as it signals a paradigm shift in how financial markets will be structured, managed, and governed in the quantum era (Kedia et al., 2025).

1.2. Paradigm shift from Classical to Quantum Models

Traditional financial models have long been the required basis for decision-making in finance, employing common tools like the Capital Asset Pricing Model (CAPM), the Black-Scholes model, and various linear regression methods. While these common models have performed well enough in relatively stable market environments, they no longer suffice in today's volatile, data-rich environment. New financial systems generate enormous amounts of real-time data from an enormous number of sources globally, such as international markets, social media, geopolitics, and economic statistics (Koc et al., 2025), Irfan et al. (2024). Classical computing with its binary-based processing and sequential calculation paradigm cannot effectively analyse such high-dimensional, complex data sets. In addition, most financial phenomena exhibit non-linear, chaotic, and probabilistic behaviour that common models cannot handle easily. These limitations provide time-lagged insight, misleading risk estimation, and missed opportunities—problems no longer tolerable in the fast-evolving, networked world of finance (Walker et al., 2022).

Quantum models provide a compelling alternative in terms of exponential computational power and the ability to examine multiple variables and scenarios simultaneously. Unlike classical models, which often require simplifications and assumptions to be computationally feasible, quantum computing allows for more realistic models of financial systems. Quantum algorithms, such as quantum annealing and amplitude estimation (Gabor et al., 2020), can potentially outperform traditional optimization and forecasting functions—two hallmarks of financial strategy. This revolution is not so much technological as it alters the means of quantifying and managing uncertainty, correlation, and risk. As markets continue to grow in complexity and the margin for error shrinks, quantum models provide a framework ideally positioned to capture the dynamic, interdependent nature of financial ecosystems (Komiyama & Suzuki, 2024). The transition from classical to quantum should not be taken as an attempt to replace old tools, but an amplification of financial intelligence through more profound, faster, and more responsive insights—allowing for a new strategic precision and resilience.

1.3. Purpose and Scope of the Chapter

The underlying purpose of this chapter is to examine how quantum computing will revolutionize the domain of financial strategy by having a profound impact on risk management, portfolio optimization, and innovation in financial modelling. Today's financial markets are characterized by their complexity, uncertainty, and high-speed generation of data—factors that challenge the predictive power and responsiveness of traditional models severely. This chapter aims to examine how quantum principles of superposition and entanglement offer new possibilities of overcoming these challenges by facilitating more precise, multi-dimensional analyses. From an academic point of view, the chapter aims to conceptualize the term quantum finance, examine its pertinence, and identify certain areas where quantum algorithms can have a real impact. These problems directly relate to the larger objective of determining the applicability and potential of the quantum paradigm to modern financial systems.

This chapter strongly focuses on risk management, particularly under market volatility and systemic uncertainty. Previous risk models are prone to normal conditions and linear correlation assumptions, which lead to the inability to capture extreme events and correlated failures effectively. Quantum computing advancement offers new techniques for simulating risk events through probabilistic means closer to real-world complexity. Quantum algorithms, including quantum Monte Carlo simulations and quantum walks, improve sensitivity analysis and stress testing, allowing financial institutions to detect vulnerabilities more quickly and respond more effectively. This meets the research purpose of determining the extent to which quantum approaches can transform practices of classical risk assessment and directly answers the research question of how quantum computing is different from classical models in managing financial uncertainty (Irfan, Mohammed, Kassim, & Ofori, 2024).

This chapter explores portfolio optimization and strategic innovation, fields in which quantum computing will have a revolutionary influence. Classic models like mean-variance optimization are plagued by high-dimensional data sets and exponentially increasing constraints by portfolio size. Quantum optimization techniques, like quantum annealing and variational algorithms, allow the simultaneous testing of complex decision variables, leading to a more responsive and efficient asset allocation process. Beyond optimization, the chapter considers the influence of quantum innovation on more general financial strategy, like derivative pricing and the creation of next-generation trading algorithms. It similarly considers institutional readiness and the ethical, regulatory, and operational issues that will impede take-up. This analysis is in line with the overall objective of considering implementation challenges and provides context on the manner in which financial institutions can position themselves strategically for a quantum future. Finally, the chapter sets out a framework for understanding not just the technical potential but the strategic and organizational implications of quantum finance.

1.4. Objectives and Research Questions

1.4.1. Objectives of the Study

The aim of this chapter is to examine the revolutionary potential that quantum computing possesses in the field of finance. The following high-level aims are focused on understanding its application in financial modelling, portfolio optimization, and the challenges that are likely to be faced when transitioning from conventional to quantum finance practices.

- To understand the basic premises of quantum computing and evaluate their applicability and viability in revolutionizing financial modelling, risk assessment, and decision-making methodology.
- To evaluate the ability of quantum computing to enhance portfolio optimization, most notably in such fields as real-time asset allocation, reallocation, and investment efficiency.
- To investigate the underlying technological, institutional, and strategic challenges preventing widespread application of quantum finance in mainstream financial systems.

1.4.2. Research Questions

In order to direct this research, the chapter provides basic research questions that investigate the contrasts between quantum computing and the conventional models, its efficiency in optimizing portfolios, and the issues that limit its application. The questions provide the analytical framework and facilitate further investigation of quantum finance as a new strategy. The below are the primary research questions in the study:

- How does quantum computing distinguish itself from classical computing in the use of solving intricate financial issues, including risk calculation and modelling volatility?
- What are the benefits of quantum computing for portfolio optimization, and how might it redefine long-term financial plans?
- What are the underlying challenges — technological, institutional, or ethical — to the development of quantum finance, and how can financial institutions strategically surmount them?

2. QUANTUM COMPUTING: THE CATALYST FOR FINANCIAL TRANSFORMATION

Quantum computing is increasingly being touted as a rich source of innovation in finance, capable of solving problems that are impossible for classical computers. Central to this revolution are fundamental quantum concepts—superposition, entanglement, and quantum parallelism—which allow for the processing of vast financial data sets in parallel. Quantum algorithms like Grover's and Shor's augment computational power, resulting in quicker data searching, more secure encryption methods, and effective problem-solving methodologies (Zhou, 2025). These attributes greatly lower the time needed for intricate calculations of risk modelling, derivative valuation, and portfolio optimization, thereby making quantum computing a force of change in financial strategy and operations (Irfan, Dias, Rastogi, & Zebende, 2025).

2.1. Core Principles of Quantum Computing

Quantum computing is rapidly emerging as a paradigm shift in financial markets, offering computational advantages that transcend the limits of classical systems. Anchored in the principles of superposition, entanglement, and quantum parallelism, quantum technologies provide enhanced capacity for modeling complexity, managing interdependencies, and delivering precision at unprecedented speed. In finance, where investment strategies hinge on predictive modelling, real-time data analysis, and multi-variable optimization, these quantum properties unlock transformative possibilities (Orús et al., 2019). They enable institutions to reconfigure risk assessment frameworks, construct more resilient portfolios, and design proactive strategies that respond to evolving global financial conditions with greater sophistication.

Superposition allows qubits to exist in multiple states simultaneously, in contrast to the binary restrictions of classical bits. Applied to finance, this principle enables the evaluation of thousands of potential asset allocations or economic scenarios concurrently. In portfolio optimization, quantum systems dramatically reduce computational time, facilitating real-time selection of optimal investment mixes (Saito et al., 2023). Similarly, in risk management, superposition allows simultaneous simulation of diverse market shocks, strengthening institutional preparedness for volatility while enhancing the scalability and accuracy of decision-making under uncertainty.

Entanglement, another defining quantum property, mirrors the interconnectedness of global financial systems. When qubits are entangled, the state of one directly influences another, regardless of spatial distance. This interdependence is particularly relevant for pricing derivatives or aggregating risk exposures across correlated parameters such as credit spreads, interest rates, and volatility indices. By capturing these interrelationships holistically, entanglement supports more nuanced and realistic financial models, offering deeper insights into systemic vulnerabilities and inter-market contagion effects (Wilkens & Moorhouse, 2023). For financial managers, this translates into improved capacity for strategic foresight in highly complex environments (Irfan, Kadry, Sharif, & Khan, 2023).

Quantum parallelism, derived from the synergy of superposition and entanglement, enables simultaneous execution of vast computational tasks. This principle is especially impactful in Monte Carlo simulations, widely used in derivative valuation and scenario testing, where quantum systems significantly reduce resource intensity. In algorithmic trading, parallelism accelerates pattern recognition and decision-making across large-scale datasets, while in portfolio optimization, it enables continuous real-time recalibration. By shifting financial strategies from reactive to proactive modes, quantum parallelism signals a fundamental reorientation of financial management, reinforcing resilience, adaptability, and competitive performance in digital finance (Shunza et al., 2023).

2.2. How Quantum Algorithms Work

Quantum algorithms are potent instruments that enable quantum computation to break computationally hard problems more quickly than traditional computation methods. Some of the most important ones are Grover's algorithm and Shor's algorithm, which highlight the capabilities of quantum computation to break computationally hard problems. Grover's algorithm is specifically tailored to unstructured search problems, which yield quadratic improvement over traditional techniques. For instance, while a classical computer would take N steps to locate a target object, Grover's algorithm can accomplish it in about $\sqrt{N}$ steps. Shor's algorithm, in contrast, addresses the factorization of large numbers, which has far-reaching applications to the field of cryptography (Khurana & Nene, 2023). Classical computers need exponential time to factor large numbers, whereas Shor's algorithm accomplishes it in polynomial time. These quantum computation findings pose enormous challenges to established computational paradigms and are of special relevance to finance, specifically to fields such as data mining, cryptographic security, and algorithmic optimization.

2.2.1. Grover's algorithm

Grover's algorithm is a quantum computational algorithm to enable unstructured search operations to be carried out much faster than classical methods. Unlike classical algorithms, which in $O(N)$ linear time find a specific element in an unsorted database, Grover's algorithm accomplishes this in $O(\sqrt{N})$ time via the use of quantum superposal and amplitude amplification (Malhotra et al., 2025). In finance, such a quadratic speedup is extremely relevant in scenarios where large amounts of data are involved, like processing millions of market indications, transaction records, or customer account data for fraud detection or determining best investment models. Being able to compare multiple alternatives in parallel has enormous gains in terms of computational efficiency, especially when speed of decision is critical (Thakkar et al., 2024).

In addition to basic search, Grover's algorithm has been generalized to solve difficult optimization problems of much relevance in finance. For example, it improves global optimization by searching large, high-dimensional solution spaces more efficiently than traditional approaches. This is especially useful in portfolio optimization, where one must find the global minimum of a risk-return function (Leclerc et al., 2023). Furthermore, Grover-based quantum Monte Carlo approaches can decrease the sample size requirements and enhance the rate of convergence in simulations applied in risk modelling and derivative pricing. Such improvements result in more accurate and quicker financial analysis, providing firms with a useful competitive advantage. With emerging quantum hardware, Grover's algorithm is increasingly being considered an executable algorithm for early quantum advantage in financial application (Zhou, Quantum Finance: Exploring the Implications of Quantum Computing on Financial Models, 2025).

Figure 1. Quantum Algorithms- Types and application in Finance (Source: ScopusAI)

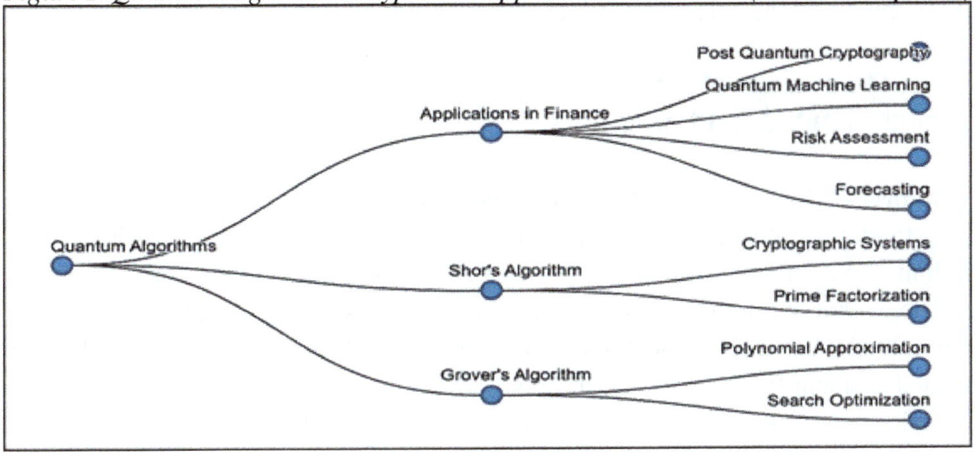

2.2.2. Shor's algorithm

Shor's algorithm is a milestone of quantum world that offers an exponential speedup for factoring big numbers—problems at the core of modern cryptographic infrastructures. Sub-exponential or exponential time is consumed by classical algorithms, however, to factor big numbers, which are the basis of popular cryptographic schemes like RSA and ECC. Shor's algorithm, on the other hand, factors numbers in polynomial time, i.e., $O((\log N^3))$, which basically erodes today's encryption methods in a post-quantum era (Mishra et al., 2024). This circumstance poses a grave threat to financial institutions where data integrity and transaction security take top priority. Additionally, the ability of the algorithm in efficiently solving the discrete logarithm problem poses another threat to elliptic curve cryptography, and thus necessitates the migration to quantum-resistant cryptographic protocols (de Lima Marquezino et al., 2019).

In finance, the effect of Shor's algorithm is not merely a theoretical speculation. The rapid factorization of cryptographic keys means that as soon as quantum computers are large enough, encrypted communication, customer data, and digital assets are vulnerable. This theoretical danger has already launched worldwide initiatives to develop and deploy post-quantum cryptography standards that protect sensitive financial information (Vashishth et al., 2025). Even though widespread use of Shor's algorithm is currently held back by hardware constraints, strides in quantum error correction and hybrid quantum-classical architectures mean that practicality is just around the corner. Financial institutions must therefore begin future-proofing their infrastructures and investing in quantum-safe solutions to mitigate the system risks of this revolutionary algorithm (Sabani et al., 2021).

2.2.3. Relevance of Grover's algorithm, Shor's algorithm in the field of finance

Grover's algorithm provides a quadratic speedup in searching unsorted databases, a fundamental operation in many financial applications. Financial firms deal with massive datasets—such as customer transactions, market feeds, and credit risk profiles—that require constant pattern recognition and anomaly detection (Chung et al., 2022). Grover's algorithm can dramatically reduce the computational effort needed to identify specific data points within these vast pools, enhancing fraud detection systems, accelerating portfolio rebalancing decisions, and improving data-mining efficiency. In particular, applications such as option pricing using quantum-enhanced Monte Carlo simulations benefit from Grover's algorithm to amplify high-probability samples, reducing the required simulation runs and yielding faster results (Ajagbe et al., 2025).

Grover's algorithm application comes from LuxProvide, Luxembourg's high-performance computing center. They have simulated the algorithm's utility in fraud detection for financial transactions (Khurana & Nene, 2023). *Shor's algorithm* poses a paradigm shift in financial cybersecurity. It can factor large integers exponentially faster than classical algorithms, threatening the foundation of widely used encryption systems such as RSA and ECC (Prodan et al., 2021). Since global financial infrastructure relies heavily on secure cryptographic protocols for online transactions, digital signatures, and data privacy, the feasibility of Shor's algorithm mandates an urgent transition to quantum-resistant encryption standards. Financial institutions must therefore preemptively adapt to post-quantum cryptography to safeguard data integrity in a future where quantum hardware may scale (Mina & Simion, 2022).

Prominent financial players and government bodies are already responding. For example, Visa and Mastercard are members of the Global Financial Innovation Network, which explores quantum-safe security frameworks. For the time being, IBM has partnered with financial institutions through its Quantum Network, allowing companies like Goldman Sachs to explore how Shor's algorithm may compromise traditional encryption and accelerate the shift to quantum-safe systems. These real-world efforts reflect the pressing impact Shor's algorithm has on financial cryptography and risk preparedness (Fu et al., 2024).

2.3. Quantum Speed and Complexity Reduction

Quantum computing represents a paradigm shift in financial analysis, enabling simultaneous processing of vast datasets and stochastic models beyond classical capabilities. By leveraging qubits in superposition, quantum systems accelerate tasks such as Monte Carlo simulations for option pricing and risk analysis. Techniques like quantum amplitude estimation (QAE) further enhance probabilistic forecasting by reducing runtime complexity, supporting faster decision-making in predictive analytics and high-frequency trading (Griffin & Sampat, 2021). Portfolio optimization also benefits, as quantum annealing and Variational Quantum Eigen-solvers (VQEs) allow parallel exploration of asset combinations. Initiatives by D-Wave, Goldman Sachs, and IBM demonstrate quantum computing's potential to enhance allocation efficiency and integrated investment planning (Koc et al., 2025).

Risk management and financial planning stand to gain significantly from quantum advances. Quantum entanglement enables efficient modelling of complex, interdependent market variables, reducing the burden of high-dimensional stochastic processes such as nested Monte Carlo simulations for derivatives. JPMorgan Chase has already demonstrated how quantum algorithms accelerate stress testing, improving responsiveness in volatile environments. Similarly, quantum techniques applied to path-dependent decision trees—like sequential hedging or multi-stage capital allocation—offer scalability with logarithmic growth. Collaborative initiatives, including the IBM Quantum Network and European Horizon 2020, highlight industry-wide momentum. As hardware matures, quantum computing will shift financial strategies from reactive to predictive and ultimately prescriptive approaches. (Liu et al., 2025)

3. REDEFINING RISK MANAGEMENT WITH QUANTUM TECHNOLOGY

The dynamic nature of modern financial markets demands adaptive and stable risk management systems. Traditional models such as Value-at-Risk (VaR), Black-Scholes, and Monte Carlo simulations, while essential, are not scalable and accurate in high-dimensional, fast-changing environments. Quantum technology brings a paradigm shift by enabling more profound stochastic modelling, rapid scenario simulations, and extensive multi-factor risk analysis (Irofti et al., 2021). Besides analytics, quantum cryptography offers means for secure safeguarding of sensitive financial data with quantum-resistant encryption. As quantum computing advances, financial risk management will be revolutionized by enabling unparalleled speed, accuracy, and security in complex decision-making scenarios.

3.1 Traditional Risk Models and Their Limitations

Traditional financial risk measurement models such as Value-at-Risk (VaR), the Black-Scholes model, and Monte Carlo simulations usually formed the center piece of quantitative finance. Value-at-Risk provides a statistical approximation of likely losses over a pre-specified time and at a specified level of confidence. The Black-Scholes model, widely used for pricing options, is based on certain assumptions that include constant volatility and log-normality of asset prices. Monte Carlo simulations generate a large number of scenarios for approximating the behaviour of financial instruments under uncertainty (Prasad et al., 2024). These models offer systematic solutions to the assessment of risk and valuation in instances of relative market calmness. These, however, are heavily dependent on historical data and assumptions about the behaviour of markets, which are found wanting in instances of high-volatility periods or market shocks. In addition, as financial instruments become increasingly sophisticated, these traditional models are inclined to have difficulty with multidimensional interdependencies and nonlinear relations between different factors.

In spite of ubiquitous use, these classic models have some fundamental flaws in today's data-intensive and dynamic financial environment. VaR, for example, is not sub-additive and does not capture tail risks, resulting in underestimation of extreme losses. Black-Scholes is based on the efficiency hypothesis of markets and does not incorporate sudden asset price jumps or time-varying volatility, making it less useful in real-world applications (Tao & Chao, 2023). Although Monte Carlo methods are general-purpose, they are computationally expensive and need high resources to tackle high-dimensional problems or extremely volatile markets. With markets still grappling with big data and complicated interactions, the inflexibility and computational nature of these models can delay timely and well-informed decisions. These shortcomings point to the requirement of alternative methods—such as quantum computing—that can handle complexity, increase the precision of modelling, and offer faster, scalable solutions for current financial risk management.

3.2 Quantum Risk Modelling

Quantum risk modelling is a remarkable leap beyond traditional approaches by leveraging the computational capability of quantum mechanics to simulate financial risks with greater speed and precision. Compared to classical models, which are constrained by linear approximations and single-path simulation, quantum computing can examine multiple risk situations in parallel through processes like superposition and entanglement. Through parallel processing, quantum computing allows real-time simulation of many stochastic processes and therefore significantly accelerates complex risk calculations (Woerner & Egger, 2019). For example, quantum-aided Monte Carlo simulations dramatically reduce the number samples needed to generate accurate estimates, thereby allowing faster and more efficient pricing of complex financial derivatives. Quantum algorithms also allow for greater precision in simulating tail-risk events through the use of non-Gaussian distributions and dynamic correlations, aspects that are commonly underrepresented in classical models. Such capabilities make quantum computing especially useful in environments characterized by high volatility and non-linearity, such as during times of market stress or when working with exotic financial derivatives.

Moreover, quantum technology enables a more extensive analysis of multi-factor risks by effectively processing large datasets with intricate interdependencies. Conventional approaches are likely to be challenged by dimensionality and interconnectedness of risk factors, especially when assessing portfolios composed of several asset classes and cross-market risks (Dri et al., 2023). Quantum algorithms, however, can navigate these multi-dimensional frameworks effectively and discover latent concentrations of risk and co-movement patterns that are not discoverable with conventional approaches. This is especially beneficial for global portfolio-managing financial institutions, where macroeconomic, geopolitical, and sectoral risks cross with complicated interactions. Firms like JPMorgan Chase and Goldman Sachs are already testing quantum applications with the intention of creating sophisticated risk engines that can model systemic risks in more integrated ways. The shift to quantum risk modelling is an important step ahead in financial analytics, enabling institutions to actively manage uncertainty, minimize exposure, and enhance strategic decision-making in a rapidly declining global financial system (Wilkens & Moorhouse, 2023).

3.3 Quantum Cryptography for Financial Security

Quantum cryptography is the key advancement in safeguarding financial systems against the threats of quantum computing. As quantum algorithms like Shor's have the potential to crack heavily used encryption schemes like RSA and ECC with efficient factoring of large prime numbers, the financial industry is at risk of likely data theft and insecure transactions (Szczesny & Gryncewicz, 2023). In order to overcome this threat, quantum cryptography draws upon the principles of quantum mechanics—most notably, quantum key distribution (QKD)—to create secure channels of communication. QKD allows two parties to share encryption keys with absolute security; any attempt at eavesdropping destroys the quantum state of the key, making such a discovery easily detectable. This feature makes quantum communication inherently secure, thus creating an impenetrable layer of security for sensitive financial data, client information, and high-value transactions. Financial institutions are now more and more recognizing the urgent need to deploy quantum-resistant cryptographic approaches to secure their systems before the post-quantum era (Capellaro et al., 2025).

In anticipation of these new threats, governments, technology companies, and financial institutions are investing in quantum-resistant encryption techniques. Companies like JPMorgan Chase are launching quantum key distribution pilot projects with IBM and Toshiba to secure inter-bank messaging. Similarly, the Bank of England and the European Central Bank are funding research on post-quantum cryptography standards to make digital payment infrastructures more resilient. These efforts also align with the call from the U.S. National Institute of Standards and Technology (NIST), which itself is actively developing new cryptographic algorithms designed to be quantum-resistant (KPMG, 2022). By integrating quantum cryptographic protocols into existing cybersecurity ecosystems, banks and financial institutions can build strong defence systems to secure real-time payments, digital identities, and trading algorithms. As quantum computing capabilities advance, quantum cryptography will become a fundamental component of financial security, defending data integrity, confidentiality, and trust in a rapidly changing digital world (Zafar, 2025).

4. QUANTUM-DRIVEN PORTFOLIO OPTIMIZATION

Quantum-Driven Portfolio Optimization is a leap beyond the limitations of classical models of finance. Although Markowitz's modern portfolio theory laid down the basic principles of optimal asset allocation, it suffers from the limitation of scalability and real-time responsiveness in the present day and age of high-volatility markets (Vashishth et al., 2025). Quantum computing, using techniques like quantum annealing and the Quantum Approximate Optimization Algorithm (QAOA), enables significantly faster and more precise optimization of intricate portfolios. These algorithms traverse huge investment space cost-effectively to locate the best asset allocations under multiple constraints. Moreover, quantum technology enables real-time adaptive rebalancing, enabling financial institutions to quickly react to market changes, maximizing returns and minimizing risk exposure (Rath & Date, 2025).

4.1 Classical Portfolio Theory Revisited

Modern Portfolio Theory (MPT), or Harry Markowitz's theory of 1952, is still one of the cornerstone theories of finance for designing the optimal portfolios through risk and return optimization. MPT promotes diversification to reduce portfolio variance for the attainment of a target return. With the quantification of expected returns, variances, and covariances of the assets (Claudiu et al., 2024), MPT enables the creation of an efficient frontier—a collection of portfolios with the maximum expected return for a specified level of risk. Rational investors, normally distributed returns, and constant relations among assets are the assumptions of the theory. Such assumptions gave portfolio selection a formal, quantitative framework and significantly impacted investment practice and academic finance (Kuo et al., 2025).

However, MPT has its limitations, especially in the current complex and dynamic financial environment. Its use of past returns to estimate future returns consistently breaks down in the event of regime changes or market shocks. Also, simplifying assumptions such as constant correlations and normally distributed returns do not hold well with actual market behaviour. Even the optimization problem itself becomes computationally complex as the number of assets is increased, resulting in inefficiencies and suboptimal solutions (Khang et al., 2025).

Real-world conditions such as transaction costs, regulatory requirements, and integer-based unit quantities of assets are not inherently part of the MPT framework. These limitations have created the quest for more flexible and scalable solutions. Quantum computing, with its capacity to solve multi-dimensional optimization problems and simulate realistic market behaviour, is about to be a powerful new tool to complement and redefine traditional portfolio management methods.

4.2 Quantum Portfolio Optimization

Quantum portfolio optimization applies the principles in quantum mechanics—i.e., via quantum annealing and the Quantum Approximate Optimization Algorithm (QAOA)—to address complex asset allocation problems better than conventional approaches. Quantum annealing is well suited for combinatorial optimization in problems, i.e., finding the best combination of assets in a portfolio to maximize return while simultaneously minimizing risk under given constraints. Unlike classical solvers that have to try all possible combinations sequentially, quantum annealers, e.g., D-Wave, can try a number of possible portfolio configurations in parallel through quantum superposition and tunnelling (Sindayigaya, 2025). This feature yields significant time savings, especially as portfolio size and complexity rise. Financial institutions increasingly leverage experimental uses of quantum annealing to improve portfolio optimization in real-world applications, solving constraints such as risk levels, capital constraints, and sector exposure in ways computationally infeasible for classical systems (Zafar, 2025).

The Quantum Approximate Optimization Algorithm (QAOA) is a quantum-classical hybrid that further optimizes portfolios by applying parameterized quantum circuits that attempt to find an approximation of the solution to hard optimization problems. QAOA is best suited to near-term quantum hardware and has promise to outperform classical algorithms in certain circumstances involving high-dimensional risk-return trade-offs (Mazumder et al., 2024). The algorithm allows for dynamic parameter adaptation during its execution, thus facilitating adaptive optimization that responds according to real-time market movement. Financial institutions like Goldman Sachs and JPMorgan Chase are actively seeking QAOA-based approaches to optimizing trading strategies and portfolio construction. QAOA's ability to handle real-world constraints, as well as its suitability with noisy intermediate-scale quantum (NISQ) hardware, makes it an attractive tool for financial practitioners. By explicitly incorporating risk functions and transaction costs in the quantum cost function, QAOA allows for more robust and realistic portfolio solutions to be built, which can potentially alter the speed, accuracy, and responsiveness of investment decision-making in the quantum era (Capellaro et al., 2025).

4.3 Real-Time Adaptive Portfolio Rebalancing

The process of real-time adaptive portfolio rebalancing is a key building block of contemporary asset management, where portfolios remain in sync with their financial objectives amidst turbulent markets. Rebalancing based on scheduled past time slots or trigger points linked with bounded thresholds is likely to be sluggish in responding to abrupt market changes or miss out on transient opportunities. Quantum algorithms introduce a revolutionary paradigm by providing real-time dynamic rebalancing using live market data (Shi et al., 2025). With the quantum superposition and entanglement capability, financial models can concurrently analyze multiple rebalancing alternatives over different risk-return profiles, asset correlations, and liquidity constraints. Investors can make more rapid and precise portfolio weight adjustments, thereby improving performance and refining risk management strategies (Wilkens & Moorhouse, 2023).

Firms like IBM and Fidelity have started venturing into quantum-based adaptive rebalancing systems that employ quantum-influenced heuristics and machine learning integration. For example, machine learning algorithms fuelled by quantum can more accurately predict asset volatilities and correlations, which can be fed into quantum optimization engines to provide real-time portfolio rebalances. Techniques like QAOA and quantum annealing enable the implementation of such rebalances by solving complex problems under time-limited scenarios (Ajagbe et al., 2025). The actual value comes in the form of the capability to evaluate and respond to multiple scenarios simultaneously, making portfolios shock-proof and responsive to short-term goals. With continued advancements in quantum technology, adaptive rebalancing can be shifted from an interval-based mechanism to an intelligent, continuous process, effectively redefining how investment portfolios are governed in volatile financial markets.

5. STRATEGIC INNOVATIONS IN FINANCIAL MARKETS

Strategic innovations in financial markets are increasingly driven by the confluence of quantum computing and advanced financial modelling. As markets grow more complex and data-heavy, traditional tools come to fall short of delivering the speed and precision required for good decision-making. Quantum technologies possess revolutionary potential across a variety of spheres. Quantum machine learning is capable of making more precise predictions of market direction and facilitating quicker, more intelligent high-frequency trading (Choi et al., 2023). Quantum game theory offers new paradigms for strategic decision-making, reshaping models of competition and negotiation. Furthermore, quantum computing revolutionizes liquidity management and derivative pricing through the ability to perform faster, more precise valuation of intricate financial products under conditions of turbulence.

5.1 Quantum Machine Learning for Financial Forecasting

Quantum Machine Learning (QML) combines the strength of quantum computing and machine learning techniques to significantly enhance predictive capability in financial markets. Traditional machine learning models, as efficient as they are, are typically at a disadvantage when dealing with the vast quantities of high-dimensional and unstructured data generated in real-time trading systems. QML leverages the quantum superposition and entanglement capability to investigate multiple states of data in parallel, resulting in accelerated and more efficient pattern and correlation discovery (Irofti et al., 2021). In market prediction, QML models are capable of identifying non-linear patterns and latent variables in vast datasets as well as improving asset price, volatility, and trading volume forecasts. Such capability is particularly important in identifying market mood, regime shift, and predicting black swan events with greater accuracy than traditional models (Komiyama & Suzuki, 2024).

In high-frequency trading (HFT) systems, QML enhances algorithmic trading strategies by optimizing trading decisions on nanosecond timescales. Quantum algorithms can dynamically adjust to real-time market dynamics by processing complex inputs such as order book depth, transaction latency, and price movement correlations. For instance, QML-powered reinforcement learning models can run thousands of parallel trading simulations to determine best entry and exit points. Additionally, quantum-uptick clustering and classification algorithms help detect financial instruments based on microstructural behaviours to help HFT systems respond more intelligently to market anomalies (Irofti et al., 2021). Large financial firms such as Goldman Sachs and JPMorgan are already exploring QML to gain trading performance edge. With the development of quantum hardware, the application of QML in live trading systems can revolutionize market prediction accuracy, reduce risks, and maximize returns in highly complex financial systems.

5.2 Quantum Game Theory

Quantum Game Theory is a new field generalizing classical game theory by using concepts from quantum mechanics such as superposition, entanglement, and quantum interference. Classical game theory relies on deterministic or probabilistic outcome-based strategies in which players decide within a specified set. Quantum game theory, on the other hand, supports richer strategy sets of quantum bits (qubits) so that players can take into account simultaneous strategies in superposed states (Prodan et al., 2021). This contributes immensely to strategic depth and richness, formulating a new paradigm for modelling competitive interaction in financial markets. For example, in auction design, pricing strategy, or adversarial market games, quantum game theory supports more advanced modelling of player payoffs and behaviour to achieve more efficient equilibria.

In finance, quantum game theory has the potential to revolutionize fields like market design, negotiation modelling, and behaviour prediction. By casting interactions between traders, institutions, and regulators in the form of quantum games, financial systems will have the ability to forecast strategic moves and counter-moves in situations of uncertainty (Capellaro et al., 2025). Quantum strategies will prevail over classical mixed strategies in repeated games and coalition building, and facilitate best negotiation and decision-making in high-stakes financial situations like mergers, acquisitions, and intricate contract negotiations. Additionally, entangled strategies permit market players to keep correlated decision-making structures intact even in decentralized and noisy environments. Leading academic institutions and fin-tech research institutions are applying quantum game theoretic models for financial simulations actively. With increasingly available quantum computers, these models will soon be incorporated into strategic planning tools, which will allow firms to respond wiser to competitive forces and regulatory conditions in changing markets (Liu et al., 2025).

5.3 Liquidity Management and Derivatives Pricing

Two of the most computationally demanding domains of finance in markets are derivatives pricing and liquidity management, and quantum computing has transformative potential in both domains. Traditional approaches to pricing advanced derivatives—exotic derivatives, options, and interest rate swaps—relate heavily to models such as Black-Scholes, binomial trees, or Monte Carlo simulations. These models, while fundamental, do not scale and are inaccurate when dealing with multi-factor risks, path dependencies, and high-dimensional data. Quantum algorithms, particularly quantum Monte Carlo and quantum amplitude estimation, have quadratic or exponential speedup over classical, allowing for more efficient and more accurate valuations of derivatives. This is highly relevant to pricing under illiquid or uncertain markets where accurate and timely decision-making is critical (Kuo et al., 2025).

Quantum computing also brings a new liquidity risk management paradigm through advanced forecasting and optimization. Liquidity risk models will encompass enormous, dynamic data sets and necessitate real-time management of asset allocation, funding strategy, and capital buffer. Quantum optimization algorithms like quantum annealing and the Quantum Approximate Optimization Algorithm (QAOA) can solve computationally intractable, complex liquidity constraint problems efficiently, which classical systems cannot. These technologies allow institutions to stress-test ahead of time, estimate exposures to counterparties, and manage intraday liquidity with greater accuracy. For instance, JPMorgan Chase and Goldman Sachs have started to investigate quantum computing platforms to optimize derivatives pricing and liquidity planning. With advancing quantum technology, their usage in treasury and trading operations will be crucial, which will allow financial institutions to remain solvent, comply with regulations, and maximize the deployment of capital under uncertainty (Fu et al., 2024).

6. CHALLENGES OF QUANTUM ADOPTION IN FINANCIAL MARKETS

The quantum computing potential for finance is transformative but is weighed down by a number of key issues in its adoption. Beyond algorithmic and optimization challenges, the field is hamstrung by technology challenges such as quantum de-Coherence, qubit stability constraints, and the requirement for effective errors correction methods. The cost of quantum hardware, infrastructure, and expert talent also remains a major barrier to financial institutions adopting quantum solutions. The talent deficit is also an urgent issue—finance professionals need to be upskilled to be able to understand and employ quantum technologies. In order to realize the full strategic value of quantum computing for finance, these barriers need to be addressed.

6.1 Technological Limitations

Technological limitations remain the most formidable barrier to the large-scale adoption of quantum computing in finance. Current machines suffer from quantum de-coherence, noise, and limited qubit stability, which undermine computational reliability and scalability. These noisy intermediate-scale quantum (NISQ) devices cannot yet provide the precision required for high-stakes applications such as real-time risk management or dynamic portfolio optimization. Equally pressing is the absence of robust quantum error correction, making accurate calculations infeasible at commercial scale (Dri et al., 2023). Until hardware advances deliver stable, noise-immune, and scalable architectures, financial applications of quantum computing will remain experimental, limiting their integration into mission-critical operations.

Beyond hardware, the lack of mature software ecosystems poses another obstacle. While ground-breaking algorithms such as Shor's and Grover's highlight quantum potential, most quantum programming tools remain underdeveloped, slowing deployment of advanced financial models. Developers face challenges of hardware compatibility, finite coherence times, and connectivity constraints, all of which restrict algorithm design (Kuo et al., 2025). Legacy infrastructure in banks further complicates integration, requiring costly reconfigurations and middleware to bridge classical-quantum workflows. Security risks also loom, as quantum capabilities threaten classical encryption, accelerating the need for quantum-resistant cryptography. Without breakthroughs in hardware, software, and secure integration frameworks, quantum finance will remain aspirational rather than transformative.

6.2 High Implementation Costs

Application of quantum computing in banking is a formidable economic challenge, primarily due to its very high upfront cost. Establishing a quantum infrastructure demands enormous investments in application-specific hardware, cryogenic coolers, quantum error correction technologies, and very highly skilled personnel. In contrast to economically matured classical computing systems scaled up to economically viable levels, quantum computing is still in a development stage with tailored configurations costing millions of dollars (Irofti et al., 2021). Moreover, the unavailability of commercial quantum technologies further exacerbates the situation, with financial institutions having to collaborate with third-party quantum providers or invest in Quantum-as-a-Service (QaaS) solutions. Such financial outlays have doubtful short-term paybacks since most quantum applications remain at proof-of-concept levels. Financial executives find it difficult to justify such investments against short-term share price profitability pressures from shareowners, regulatory pressures, and ongoing digital transformation projects already straining budgets.

Nonetheless, long-term value to finance from quantum computing is a strong business case for investment. Quantum technology holds the promise of exponential speedup on hard problems like portfolio optimization, risk modelling, fraud detection, and derivative pricing. This, long term, could translate into enormous cost savings, better decision-making, and competitive advantage (Shunza et al., 2023). Finance early adopters who start investing today can establish pioneer expertise and intellectual property that puts them at the forefront when commercial quantum systems are mature. In addition, as the technology matures, the cost of deployment should decrease, fuelled by innovation, standardization, and economies of scale. Strategic alliance with quantum start-ups and cloud-based quantum service providers can even amortize capital outlay while enabling firms to pilot use cases and develop quantum literacy internally. A phased, research-driven approach to adoption, balancing exploratory investment with scalable returns, therefore, can assist organizations to steer the cost-benefit equation while strategizing for a quantum-enabled financial future (Mazumder et al., 2024).

6.3. Knowledge Transfer and Collaboration

The uptake of quantum technology in the financial sector is significantly hindered by the lack of interdisciplinary competencies and formal collaboration between the main players. Quantum finance is a meeting ground for two extremely sophisticated disciplines—quantum computing and financial engineering—where a specific blend of competencies is in short supply in the international talent pool (Woerner & Egger, 2019). Financial professionals have minimal technical knowledge of quantum mechanics, while quantum physicists have minimal financial modelling or risk management competencies. The lack of matching skills inhibits innovation and keeps practical, application-oriented quantum solutions to asset pricing, algorithmic trading, and portfolio optimisation out of reach. Without specially designed education courses, cross-disciplinary training courses, and industry-sponsored upskilling, businesses are not able to create the quantum-proficient talent required for long-term technological integration and competitiveness (Szczesny & Gryncewicz, 2023).

Apart from manpower limitations, unstandardized platforms and collaborative spaces also hold back quantum adoption. Quantum finance innovation requires intense collaboration between academic scholars, financial institutions, regulators, and technology creators. However, the stand-alone nature of initiatives, lack of open-source development guidelines, and shortage of policy directives interfere with best-practice sharing and prevent scalable solutions. Institutional initiatives in silos duplicate efforts and overlook system-level concerns such as ethical use, security features, and market preparedness (Mina & Simion, 2022). Strategic collaboration—via consortia, shared research centers, and regulatory sandboxes—can facilitate knowledge sharing, improve innovation, and ensure policy consistency. Furthermore, international standard-setting bodies must coordinate in formulating quantum-specific benchmarks, quality assurance guidelines, and legal frameworks to facilitate safe and inclusive technology diffusion. By creating an integrated, knowledge-sharing ecosystem, the finance industry can prepare itself for the quantum era, ensuring not merely technological advancement but also responsible and equitable adoption (Prasad et al., 2024).

6.4. Regulatory and Ethical Issues

The incorporation of quantum computing into financial infrastructure is a nexus of elaborate ethical and regulatory challenges. As quantum technologies drive technological advancement, remaining compliant is getting more challenging. Regulators have yet to come up with general standards applicable to quantum-enabled financial products, and there is a gray area for using them in high-stakes applications such as credit scoring, automated trading, and fraud detection. In addition, ethical issues of algorithmic bias in quantum machine learning algorithms can result in discriminatory or unfair outcomes, and processing sensitive financial information raises significant issues of privacy and data ownership. With more autonomy and opaqueness of quantum algorithms, accountability, explainability, and ethical transparency will become more challenging, prompting policymakers to create regulatory frameworks concurrently with technological progress. Preemptive incorporation of ethical issues into quantum systems and regulatory foresight are required to guarantee trust and responsibility in quantum-driven finance (Koc et al., 2025).

Besides regulatory compliance, quantum technology also presents broader economic and societal risks that must be managed to ensure fair deployment. Large-scale job displacement, particularly in analytical back-office and financial modelling, is one of the greatest risks. With quantum systems growing increasingly capable of undertaking increasingly complex calculations and risk analysis, traditional analytical careers would be made redundant, and large-scale reskilling programs would be necessary. In addition, uneven quantum technology deployment—where financially able tech-savvy financial institutions would be the only ones in a position to benefit—would further exacerbate financial sector inequalities (Leclerc et al., 2023). This calls for inclusive access models and policy frameworks to prevent monopolistic designs. Lastly, quantum's impact on cybersecurity—basically the risk of decrypting classical encryption—calls for the immediate creation and regulation of post-quantum cryptographic standards. To address these risks end-to-end, regulators, technologists, and ethicists must collaborate and create forward-looking frameworks that maximize social welfare, fairness, and market stability (Leclerc et al., 2023).

6.5 Bridging the Knowledge Gap

As quantum computing moves from theoretical to practical applications, the financial sector is faced with an imperative to reskill its professionals. Bridging the knowledge gap between quantum physics and financial analysis is the first step in realizing the revolutionary potential of quantum technology. Most finance professionals, trained in classical econometrics, statistics, and algorithmic models, have little familiarity with the foundations of quantum mechanics, quantum algorithms (e.g., Grover's and Shor's) (Mina & Simion, 2022), and the emerging field of quantum machine learning. This gap constitutes an adoption bottleneck, and institutions struggle to find or develop talent that can translate quantum potential into strategic financial solutions. Quantum literacy must be infused into finance education through academic programs, certification, and industry collaborations. Business schools and finance departments must begin integrating quantum computing essentials into curricula, establishing a pipeline of professionals capable of navigating and capitalizing on quantum-driven innovations in risk modelling, asset management, and cryptographic security (Malhotra et al., 2025).

Fostering interdisciplinary cooperation among quantum scientists, financial engineers, and policymakers will be key to constructing a robust quantum-ready environment. Think tanks and regulatory bodies can also play an invaluable role to aid in the direction of standards and best practices in quantum finance, making the integration process smooth. Web-based initiatives such as the IBM Quantum Learning platform and Xanadu's PennyLane tutorials are also proving to be useful tools for self-directed learning. In the long run, it will be required to create a learning and innovation culture within financial institutions so that professionals are not just equipped with quantum technologies but can critically analyse and implement them in ethically justifiable, secure, and profitable ways (Mishra et al., 2024).

7. THE ROAD AHEAD: FUTURE PROSPECTS OF QUANTUM FINANCE

The quantum finance future holds immense transformational potential, with novel and exciting risk analysis, portfolio optimization, and market prediction applications. With the advancements in quantum hardware and the growing popularity of hybrid quantum-classical models, the speed and precision of financial complexity calculations will be significantly enhanced. Nevertheless, the way to mass adoption should be navigated with caution across regulatory, ethical, and infrastructure hurdles (Sabani et al., 2021). Financial stability, protecting data integrity and algorithmic fairness concerns will be absolutely critical. Financial institutions, policymakers, and investors individually will need to invest in visionary strategic planning, talent recruitment, and ecosystem-based models connecting existing capabilities to quantum-capable potential.

7.1 Potential Breakthroughs on the Horizon

Recent advances in quantum hardware are steadily transforming the feasibility of quantum finance. Though current systems face challenges of noise and qubit fragility, innovations in superconducting qubits, trapped ions, and topological qubits are extending coherence times and enhancing gate fidelities. Industry leaders such as IBM, Google, and Rigetti are developing processors exceeding 100 qubits, with fault-tolerant systems projected within the decade. These breakthroughs promise scalable, reliable architectures capable of powering complex financial applications, from option pricing and risk modelling to high-frequency arbitrage detection.

Parallel to hardware progress, hybrid quantum-classical approaches are bridging today's limitations with practical solutions. By combining classical processing power with quantum probabilistic strengths, hybrid models enable effective computation of complex financial problems. Quantum-inspired algorithms are already applied in portfolio optimization, fraud detection, and asset pricing. Firms such as D-Wave and Xanadu are pioneering such platforms, demonstrating how hybrid models accelerate innovation while supporting real-time analytics (Wang et al., 2024). This trajectory positions hybrid systems as catalysts for the near-term disruption of financial technology.

7.2 Regulatory and Ethical Considerations

The rapid evolution of quantum computing presents both extraordinary opportunities and profound regulatory challenges in finance. As quantum capabilities threaten classical cryptographic standards, regulators face growing pressure to safeguard data protection, transaction integrity, and systemic resilience. Institutions must anticipate post-quantum cryptography requirements while continuing to comply with existing frameworks such as GDPR, Basel III, and data localisation mandates (Vaishnavi & Pillai, 2021). Agencies including the SEC, FCA, and RBI will need to adapt supervisory regimes by embedding quantum-sensitive protocols into cybersecurity measures, stress testing, and risk disclosure obligations, ensuring that innovation aligns with market stability.

Equally pressing are the ethical dimensions of quantum finance, including algorithmic transparency, equitable access, and privacy. Quantum algorithms' probabilistic nature risks fostering opaque, black-box decision models, undermining explainability and accountability. Early adoption by dominant institutions may amplify market asymmetries, while real-time decryption raises concerns over surveillance and consumer privacy (Ali et al., 2025). To mitigate these risks, regulators, technologists, and ethicists must collaborate on standards that promote fairness, secure data, and safeguard public trust, ensuring quantum advantage benefits the wider financial ecosystem.

7.3 Preparing for a Quantum Future

Preparing for a quantum-powered financial future requires coordinated strategies encompassing technological readiness, human capital, and institutional adaptation. Banks must invest in quantum expertise through competence centers, such as Intesa Sanpaolo's, that function as innovation hubs. Structured readiness programs should benchmark current capabilities, map integration pathways, and identify high-value use cases. Collaborations with academia and quantum firms will accelerate advances in areas like fraud detection, risk modelling, and derivative pricing, while financial professionals must be trained in quantum fundamentals to bridge the skills gap and ensure smooth adoption (Fu et al., 2024).

Equally crucial is regulatory and policy preparedness. Governments and financial regulators must establish standards for quantum-resistant cryptography to protect distributed systems from emerging threats. Hybrid quantum-classical models provide a pragmatic near-term path, balancing quantum advantages with stability. Policymakers must also address ethical challenges, including fairness, transparency, and equitable access. Investors, meanwhile, should diversify portfolios into quantum-enabling technologies and ESG-compliant firms, supporting secure, responsible, and inclusive adoption (Tao & Chao, 2023).

8. CONCLUSION: EMBRACING THE QUANTUM PARADIGM IN FINANCE

Quantum computing can revolutionize the world of finance with its unprecedented capabilities in speed, simplification of complexity, and advanced problem-solving. From portfolio optimization and risk assessment to market forecasting and cryptography, quantum-inspired solutions are orders of magnitude superior to their classical counterparts. Grover's and Shor's algorithms, machine learning amplified by quantum, and game theory open up new avenues for strategic decision-making, real-time analysis, and secure transactions. These are not thought experiments but are being explored by leading institutions in the form of pilot projects, quantum competence centers, and hybrid computing architectures.

But visionary preparation is needed for embracing quantum finance. Banks and financial institutions must invest in talent recruitment, collaborative innovation, and technology infrastructure and overcome regulatory, ethical, and security challenges. Policymakers must establish clear guidelines and support for post-quantum cryptographic standards to deliver resilience. While we stand at the cusp of such a paradigm shift, the embracing of the quantum future is not an option—it is a competitive survival and long-term prosperity necessity. By encouraging preparation today, the finance industry can unlock the full potential of quantum computing, driving smarter, faster, and more secure financial ecosystems in the future.

REFERENCES

Ajagbe, S. A., Majola, S., & Mudali, P. (2025, December). Comparative analysis of machine learning algorithms for money laundering detection. *Discover Artificial Intelligence, 05*(01). Advance online publication. DOI: 10.1007/s44163-025-00397-4

Ali, S., Wadho, S. A., Talpur, K. R., Talpur, B. A., & Alshudukhi, K. S. (2025, December). Next-Generation Quantum Security: The Impact of Quantum Computing on Cybersecurity—Threats, Mitigations, and Solutions. *Computers & Electrical Engineering, 128*. Advance online publication. DOI: 10.1016/j.compeleceng.2025.110649

Capellaro, C., Martín-Cuevas, R., Calleja, G., Halffmann, P., & Sharma, S. (2025). Application of Quantum Computing in the Energy Industry, Decarbonization, and Sustainability. In *Quantum Technology Applications, Impact, and Future Challenges* (pp. 09-36). CRC Press. https://doi.org/DOI: 10.1201/9781003537243-2

Choi, M., Eom, C., & Kang, H.-G. (2023, February 01). Quantum Finance and Its Implications. *Asian Review of Financial Research, 36*(01), 103–129. DOI: 10.37197/ARFR.2023.36.1.4

Chung, D., Lee, S., Choi, D., & Lee, J. (2022, October 01). Alternative Tower Field Construction for Quantum Implementation of the AES S-Box. *IEEE Transactions on Computers, 71*(10), 2553–2564. DOI: 10.1109/TC.2021.3135759

Claudiu, B., Cosmin, E., Otniel, D., & Andrei, A. (2024). Enhancing the Financial Sector with Quantum Computing: A Comprehensive Review of Current and Future Applications. *22nd International Conference on Informatics in Economy, IE 2023. 367.* Bucharest: Springer Science and Business Media Deutschland GmbH. https://doi.org/DOI: 10.1007/978-981-99-6529-8_17

de Lima Marquezino, F., Portugal, R., & Lavor, C. (2019). Shor's algorithm for integer factorization. In *SpringerBriefs in Computer Science* (pp. 57–77). Springer., DOI: 10.1007/978-3-030-19066-8_4

Dri, E., Aita, A., Giusto, E., Ricossa, D., & Corbelletto, D. (2023, April). A More General Quantum Credit Risk Analysis Framework. *Entropy (Basel, Switzerland), 25*(04). Advance online publication. DOI: 10.3390/e25040593 PMID: 37190381

Eswaran, U., Eswaran, V., Murali, K., & Eswaran, V. (2025). Quantum Computing Applications. In *Quantum Computing: the Future of Information Processing* (pp. 42–61). CRC Press., DOI: 10.1201/9781003499459-3

Fu, J., Xu, M., Qian, H., & Li, Z. (2024). Theoretical and Experimental Performance Analysis on Error-Bounded Quantum Search Process. *Journal of Systems Science and Complexity*. Advance online publication. DOI: 10.1007/s11424-024-4062-7a

Gabor, T., Zielinski, S., Roch, C., Feld, S., & Linnhoff-Popien, C. (2020). The U Q platform: A u nifed approach to q uantum annealing. *5th International Conference on Computer and Communication Systems, ICCCS 2020* (pp. 115-119). Shanghai: Institute of Electrical and Electronics Engineers Inc. https://doi.org/DOI: 10.1109/ICCCS49078.2020.9118547

Griffin, P., & Sampat, R. (2021). Quantum Computing for Supply Chain Finance. *2021 IEEE International Conference on Services Computing, SCC 2021* (pp. 456-459). Online: Institute of Electrical and Electronics Engineers Inc. https://doi.org/DOI: 10.1109/SCC53864.2021.00066

Irfan, M., Dias, R., Rastogi, R., & Zebende, G. F. (2025). *Generative AI insights for financial decision making*. IGI Global.

Irfan, M., Elmogy, M., Gupta, S., Khalifa, F., & Dias, R. T. (2024). *AI-driven decentralized finance and the future of finance*. IGI Global USA.

Irfan, M., Hussainey, K., Bukhari, S. A. C., & Nam, Y. (2024). *Issues of sustainability in AI and new-age thematic investing*. IGI Global.

Irfan, M., Kadry, S., Sharif, M., & Khan, H. U. (2023). *Fintech applications in Islamic finance: AI, machine learning, and blockchain techniques*. IGI Global.

Irfan, M., Mohammed, M., Kassim, S., & Ofori, K. S. (2024). *The future of indigenous inclusivity: Unlocking finance for economic development*. IGI Global.

Irofti, P., Pătraşcu, A., & Băltoiu, A. (2021). Fraud detection in networks. In *Studies in Computational Intelligence* (Vol. 911, pp. 517–536). Springer Science and Business Media Deutschland GmbH., DOI: 10.1007/978-3-030-52067-0_23

Kedia, U., Joshi, S., Pandey, T. N., & Shukla, P. (2025). The Applications of Quantum Machine Learning in Today's World. In *Intelligent Systems Reference Library* (Vol. 274, pp. 171–191). Springer Science and Business Media Deutschland GmbH., DOI: 10.1007/978-3-031-89905-8_9

Khang, A., Rath, K. C., Madapana, K., Rao, J., & Panda, L. P. (2025). Quantum computing and portfolio optimization in finance services. In *Shaping Cutting-Edge Technologies and Applications for Digital Banking and Financial Services* (pp. 27–45). Taylor and Francis., DOI: 10.4324/9781003501947-2

Khurana, S., & Nene, M. (2023). Implementation of Database Search with Quantum Computing: Grover's Algorithm vs Linear Search. *1st IEEE International Conference on Ambient Intelligence, Knowledge Informatics and Industrial Electronics, AIKIIE 2023.* Ballari: Institute of Electrical and Electronics Engineers Inc. https://doi.org/DOI: 10.1109/AIKIIE60097.2023.10389962

Koc, B., Yildirak, K., & Yokus, A. (2025). A New Perspective for Financial Option Pricing with New Dynamic Solutions of the Black-Scholes Equation. *Computational Economics*. Advance online publication. DOI: 10.1007/s10614-025-11055-3

Komiyama, T., & Suzuki, T. (2024). QUBO formulation using inequalities for problems with complex constraints. *7th International Conference on High Performance Computing in Asia-Pacific Region, HPC Asia 2024* (pp. 55-61). Nagoya: Association for Computing Machinery. https://doi.org/DOI: 10.1145/3635035.3635042

KPMG. (2022, Aug). *Quantum is coming — and bringing new cybersecurity threats with it*. Retrieved Aug 13, 2025, from https://kpmg.com: https://kpmg.com/xx/en/our-insights/ai-and-technology/quantum-and-cybersecurity.html

Kuo, S.-Y., Lee, K.-L., Shen, J.-Y., Chou, Y.-H., & Kuo, S.-Y. (2025). *Quantum Annealing for Bi-objective Weighted Portfolio Optimization in Real-world Financial Markets. 2025 Genetic and Evolutionary Computation Conference Companion, GECCO 2025 Companion*. Association for Computing Machinery, Inc., DOI: 10.1145/3712255.3734282

Leclerc, L., Ortiz-Gutiérrez, L., Grijalva, S., Albrecht, B., & Cline, J. R. (2023, October). Financial risk management on a neutral atom quantum processor. *Physical Review Research, 05*(04). Advance online publication. DOI: 10.1103/PhysRevResearch.5.043117

Liu, C., Lee, W. B., & Constantinides, A. G. (2025, April). Quantum Testing of Recommender Algorithms on GPU-Based Quantum Simulators. *Computers, 14*(04). Advance online publication. DOI: 10.3390/computers14040137

Malhotra, J., Chavan, O., & Thakur, P. (2025). Grover Algorithm: Enhancing the Search Mechanism. *4th OPJU International Technology Conference on Smart Computing for Innovation and Advancement in Industry 5.0, OTCON 2025.* Raigarh: Institute of Electrical and Electronics Engineers Inc. https://doi.org/DOI: 10.1109/OTCON65728.2025.11071106

Mazumder, A. R., Sen, A., & Sen, U. (2024). Benchmarking Metaheuristic-Integrated QAOA Against Quantum Annealing. *Science and Information Conference, SAI 2024. 1018 LNNS*, pp. 651 - 666. London: Springer Science and Business Media Deutschland GmbH. https://doi.org/DOI: 10.1007/978-3-031-62269-4_42

Mina, M.-Z., & Simion, E. (2022). A Multifunctional Modular Implementation of Grover's Algorithm. *14th International Conference on Innovative Security Solutions for Information Technology and Communications, SecITC 2021. 13195 LNCS*, pp. 228 - 247. Virtual: Springer Science and Business Media Deutschland GmbH. https://doi.org/DOI: 10.1007/978-3-031-17510-7_16

Mishra, S., Agarwal, O., & Patel, S. K. (2024). Quantum Decryption using Shor's Algorithm. *7th IEEE Pune Section International Conference, PuneCon 2024*. Pune: Institute of Electrical and Electronics Engineers Inc. https://doi.org/DOI: 10.1109/PuneCon63413.2024.10895777

Natraj, N., Sundaravadivazhagan, B. R. S., Anandaram, H., & Patchala, S. (2025). Quantum Computing in Industry: Unveiling Applications and Opportunities. In *Quantum Computing and Artificial Intelligence: The Industry Use Cases* (pp. 305 - 330). wiley. https://doi.org/DOI: 10.1002/9781394242399.ch12

Orús, R., Mugel, S., & Lizaso, E. (2019, November). Quantum computing for finance: Overview and prospects. *Reviews in Physics, 04*. Advance online publication. DOI: 10.1016/j.revip.2019.100028

Prasad, N. S., Gangopadhyay, A., Prabakaran, R., Mishra, N., & Prasad, D. S. (2024). Utilizing Anomaly Detection Methods for Identifying Fraudulent Activities in Credit Card Transactions. *1st IEEE International Conference on Advances in Computing, Communication and Networking, ICAC2N 2024* (pp. 1641 - 1646). Greater Noida: Institute of Electrical and Electronics Engineers Inc. https://doi.org/DOI: 10.1109/ICAC2N63387.2024.10895602

Prodan, A., Manta, V.-I., & Tudorache, A.-G. (2021). The performance impact of the graph topology in Ibm's Quantum devices on Grover's search algorithm. *25th International Conference on System Theory, Control and* (pp. 327 - 333). Iasi: Institute of Electrical and Electronics Engineers Inc. https://doi.org/DOI: 10.1109/ICSTCC52150.2021.9607230

Rath, M., & Date, H. (2025, December). Quantum powered credit risk assessment: A novel approach using Hybrid Quantum-Classical Deep Neural Network for Row-Type Dependent Predictive Analysis. *EPJ Quantum Technology, 12*(01). Advance online publication. DOI: 10.1140/epjqt/s40507-025-00323-8

Sabani, M., Galanis, I., Savvas, I., & Garani, G. (2021). Implementation of Shor's Algorithm and Reliability of Quantum Computing Devices. *25th Pan-Hellenic Conference on Informatics, PCI 2021* (pp. 392 - 396). Virtul: Association for Computing Machinery. https://doi.org/DOI: 10.1145/3503823.3503895

Saito, Y., Xie, N., Shin, J., Lee, X., & Cai, D. (2023). Iterative Refinement Quantum Amplitude Estimation. *16th IEEE International Symposium on Embedded Multicore/Many-Core Systems-on-Chip, MCSoC 2023* (pp. 202-209). Singapore: Institute of Electrical and Electronics Engineers Inc. https://doi.org/DOI: 10.1109/MCSoC60832.2023.00038

Shi, J., Yuan, B., Lu, Y., Zhang, S., & Li, X. (2025). Quantum Option Profit and Loss Encoding for Risk Assessment. *IEEE Transactions on Emerging Topics in Computational Intelligence*. Advance online publication. DOI: 10.1109/TETCI.2025.3593781

Shunza, J., Akinyemi, M., & Yinka-Banjo, C. (2023, December). Application of quantum computing in discrete portfolio optimization. *Journal of Management Science and Engineering*, *08*(04), 453–464. DOI: 10.1016/j.jmse.2023.02.001

Sindayigaya, J. M. (2025). Real-Time Threat Mitigation in Financial IT Infrastructures Using Quantum Computing. *International Journal of Electronics and Telecommunications*, *71*(02), 583–589. DOI: 10.24425/ijet.2025.153578

Szczesny, B., & Gryncewicz, W. (2023). Quantum Advantage Applied - Research on Probability of Success. *13th International Conference on Advanced Computer Information Technologies, ACIT 2023*, (pp. 468 - 472). Wroclaw. https://doi.org/DOI: 10.1109/ACIT58437.2023.10275418

Tao, Z., & Chao, J. (2023). Financial Fraud and Anomaly Detection Techniques: A Literature Review. *4th International Conference on Computer Science and Management Technology, ICCSMT 2023* (pp. 634 - 641). Xi'an: Association for Computing Machinery. https://doi.org/DOI: 10.1145/3644523.3644639

Thakkar, S., Kazdaghli, S., Mathur, N., Kerenidis, I., & Ferreira–Martins, A. J. (2024, June). Improved financial forecasting via quantum machine learning. *Quantum Machine Intelligence*, *06*(01). Advance online publication. DOI: 10.1007/s42484-024-00157-0

Vaishnavi, A., & Pillai, S. (2021). Cybersecurity in the Quantum Era-A Study of Perceived Risks in Conventional Cryptography and Discussion on Post Quantum Methods. *1st International Conference on Advances in Computational Science and Engineering, ICACSE 2020. 1964.* Coimbatore, Tamilnadu, Virtual: IOP Publishing Ltd. https://doi.org/DOI: 10.1088/1742-6596/1964/4/042002

Vashishth, T. K., Sharma, V., Kaushik, V., Singh, A., & Teotia, S. (2025). Exploring Quantum Challenges and Opportunities of Quantum Machine Learning Adoption in Finance. In *Machine Learning and Modeling Techniques in Financial Data Science* (pp. 437–460). IGI Global., DOI: 10.4018/979-8-3693-8186-1.ch017

Vashishth, T. K., Sharma, V., Kaushik, V., Singh, A., & Teotia, S. (2025). Exploring Quantum Challenges and Opportunities of Quantum Machine Learning Adoption in Finance. In *Machine Learning and Modeling Techniques in Financial Data Science* (pp. 437–460). IGI Global., DOI: 10.4018/979-8-3693-8186-1.ch017

Vashishth, T. K., Sharma, V., Kaushik, V., Singh, A., & Teotia, S. (2025). Exploring Quantum Challenges and Opportunities of Quantum Machine Learning Adoption in Finance. In *Machine Learning and Modeling Techniques in Financial Data Science* (pp. 437–460). IGI Global., DOI: 10.4018/979-8-3693-8186-1.ch017

Walker, T., Davis, F., & Schwartz, T. (2022). Big Data in Finance: An Overview. In *Big Data in Finance: Opportunities and Challenges of Financial Digitalization* (pp. 03-09). Springer International Publishing. https://doi.org/DOI: 10.1007/978-3-031-12240-8_1

Wang, P., Zhu, Q., Wu, H., Li, X., & Yang, S. (2024). The Equity Fund Risk Predictions Via Quantum-Classical Hybrid Neural Networks. *13th International Conference on Computer Engineering and Networks, CENet 2023. 1126 LNEE*, pp. 320 - 331. Wuxi: Springer Science and Business Media Deutschland GmbH. https://doi.org/DOI: 10.1007/978-981-99-9243-0_32

Wilkens, S., & Moorhouse, J. (2023, January). Quantum computing for financial risk measurement. *Quantum Information Processing*, *22*(01). Advance online publication. DOI: 10.1007/s11128-022-03777-2

Woerner, S., & Egger, D. J. (2019, Dec 01). Quantum risk analysis. *npj Quantum Information, 05*(01). https://doi.org/DOI: 10.1038/s41534-019-0130-6

Zafar, A. (2025). Quantum Computing in Finance: Regulatory Readiness, Legal Gaps, and the Future of Secure Tech Innovation. *European Journal of Risk Regulation*. Advance online publication. DOI: 10.1017/err.2025.10050

Zhou, J. (2025). Quantum Finance: Exploring the Implications of Quantum Computing on Financial Models. *Computational Economics*. Advance online publication. DOI: 10.1007/s10614-025-10894-4

Chapter 2
Challenges and Future Directions in Quantum-Driven Financial Innovation

Sanjeev Kumar
https://orcid.org/0000-0002-7375-7341
Lovely Professional University, India

Emil Velinov
RISEBA University of Applied Sciences, Riga, Latvia & Newton University, Prague, Czech Republic

ABSTRACT

Quantum-driven brings the new innovation in the financial sectors and "predictive analytics, portfolio optimization, and autonomous" trading systems. Quantum computing's is the complex, high-dimensional data sets at unprecedented speed, financial institutions envision more accurate forecasting models and decision-making. It is the one of the foremost barriers is the immaturity of current quantum hardware, instability, and scalability limitations. On the other hand integration of quantum systems with existing classical infrastructures require "hybrid architectures, specialized algorithms, and substantial investment" in infrastructure and training. Quantum-enhanced models create opaque decision-making processes, amplifying risks of market exploitation, data privacy violations, or systemic vulnerabilities. Collaborative ecosystems involving academia, industry, and regulators are expected to accelerate the development of standards and best practices.

DOI: 10.4018/979-8-3373-2893-5.ch002

OVERVIEW OF QUANTUM COMPUTING, RELEVANCE TO FINANCIAL INNOVATION

Overview of Quantum Computing

Quantum computing is an innovation that is a breakthrough in classical computing. Whereas traditional computers operate on bits, which can be in only two possible states at a time (0 or 1), quantum computers operate on qubits, which can occupy multiple possible states simultaneously due to the laws of superposition. In addition, qubits may be entangled, meaning that their state is connected directly to the state of another qubit, even at a large distance. These peculiarities enable quantum computers to execute large volumes of information simultaneously and perform calculations that are inaccessible to even the most powerful classical supercomputers (Narayan, 2025), (Irfan, Mohammed, Kassim, & Ofori, 2024). In addition to theoretical advances, companies such as "IBM, Google, and D-Wave" have made advances in quantum technology, which remain in its early phase with limited error correction. Moreover, this will also be one of the reasons, as the aforementioned BBC article explained, why financial institutions are required to upgrade their systems with quantum-safe encryption in case future quantum computers can break conventional cryptographic methods (Putranto et al., 2024).

Relevance to Financial Innovation

The financial industry is flourishing due to its capacity to handle huge volumes of data, modelss, andforecast in real-timeme. These activities, which optimize a portfolio by analyzing risks, pricing derivatives, and detecting fraud, are based on complex mathematical calculations that can put a strain on the performance of classical systems (How & Cheah, 2023). Quantum computing opens up new computing paradigms that have the potential to transform the way financial institutions operate. For instance, quantum optimization algorithms can be employed to analyze a vast array of investment strategies, thereby predicting portfolios that are more risk-adjusted and reward-adjusted than those of existing algorithms (Elmisery et al., 2025a). Quantum simulations in risk management would enable the modeling of complex financial systems with greater accuracy, assisting firms in preparing for low-frequency but devastating events, commonly referred to as black swans. Moreover, quantum-enhanced machine learning has the potential to enable financial institutions to identify nuanced trends in transaction data, thereby enhancing their ability to detect fraud and monitor compliance. Another important field is quantum cryptography, particularly in the context of quantum key distribution (QKD). The financial sector will need to evolve its systems towards quantum-safe encryption in case future quantum computers render classical cryptographic tools obsolete. That is why quantum innovation is not only an opportunity but also a necessity for the stability and security of financial systems. The quantum computing-based financial innovation is not merely a theory (Lamichhane & Rawat, 2025). The major banks and majoror corporationscooperateerate collaborating hardwareardware manufacturers and university scientists to test the proactionsctions. Although it may be several years before it can be deployed widely, the future competitive edge presented by quantum-driven solutions is driving significant investments in its early years (Cuomo & Foroudi, 2025).

To Investigate Future Opportunities and Strategy

Lastly, the report will outline potential future developments in quantum finance. This involves analyzing hybrid classical-quantum models, predicting improvements in quantum hardware, and evaluating the potential of new algorithms. Additionally, the paper will examine the social and economic implications of quantum-based finance, focusing on job creation, ethics, and international competitiveness (Millett, 2003). With these three purposes, the report aims to present a fair-minded viewpoint: the modern limitations of quantum computing do exist, but there are also profound transformative opportunities to drive financial innovation. It is not limited to theoretical background but also to practical implementation, both the opportunities and the dangers that this new discipline promises (Alexander et al., 1998), Irfan et al. (2024).

QUANTUM ALGORITHMS IN FINANCE AND QUANTUM MACHINE LEARNING (QML) APPLICATIONS

Quantum Financing

The financial markets are complex distinguished by their "uncertainty, interdependence, and handling of large amounts of data". Despite their usefulness, classic algorithms often face challenges due to the explosion of combinatorial options in issues like risk analysis, portfolio optimization, and derivative price prediction. Quantum algorithms offer new computational modeling options that may be more accurate and effective in these domains (Mironowicz et al., 2024). The Quantum Approximate Optimization Algorithm (QAOA) most applicable quantum algorithms to the financial sector. It is especially solving optimization problems, including determining the optimal combination of assets to maximize and minimize. Quantum Amplitude Estimation (QAE) is valuable algorithm that achieves a quadratic speed up in Monte Carlo simulations. Monte Carlo techniques are applied in finance, including option pricing, value-at-risk (VaR), and stress testing (Vashishth et al., 2025).

Applications of Quantum Machine Learning (QML)

Nevertheless, the outburst of financial data presents classical machine learning models with challenges, especially in terms of training time and scalability. One approach is the use of Quantum Support Vector Machines (QSVMs), which is promising (Martín-Guerrero & Lamata, 2022). SVMs are widely used in classification, for example which distinguishes between "fraudulent and non-fraudulent transactions". The quantum-enhanced one has the potential to sort high-dimensional financial data more efficiently which enhancing fraud detection and compliance monitoring. On the other hand; "Quantum Neural Networks" (QNNs) are the application of the concept of deep learning to quantum space (Abohashima et al., 2020), (Irfan, Mohammed, Kassim, & Ofori, 2024).

QNNs are still in their experimental stages which signify the future pathway of integrating "quantum speed and AI-powered decision-making". The other subject of interest is quantum-enhanced clustering and dimensionality reduction. Financial data contains large amounts of variables which includes "economic indicators and customer behavior metrics". Such high-dimensional data can be analyzed more effectively using quantum algorithms, including Quantum Principal Component Analysis (QPCA), which can be employed to develop more effective portfolio diversification strategies and customer segmentation (Rahimi & Asadi, 2023). The real potential of QML lies in its ability to manipulate large datasets in the field of finance on a scale and speed that other systems cannot match with classical systems. QML would assist financial institutions in making better and quicker decisions by enhancing the accuracy of their predictions and reducing the computational cost. Implementation, however, depends on the future of quantum hardware and the development of noise-absorbing algorithms (Maheshwari et al., 2022). Quantum algorithms, as well as the QML applications, can transform financial systems. Exponential optimization, risk analysis, predictive analytics, and fraud detection can be improved with quantum algorithms and QML, respectively. The combination of them is the key to the future when finance will be not only data-driven but also quantum-driven. The advancement, although still in its infancy, is a pointer to a paradigm shift that financial institutions cannot afford to overlook.

Current Applications in the Financial Sector

Financial applications of Quantum computing are starting to gain traction in the financial industry, with experimental applications and prototype uses emerging. Although the practical implementation of large-scale use is still limited due to hardware constraints, several examples already exist of how transformative quantum approaches (Mishra & Kaushik, 2023) are being utilized. Some of the most promising ones include portfolio optimization, risk analysis and management, and high-frequency trading (HFT).

I. **Portfolio Optimization:** The core of an investment strategy is portfolio optimization, the process of selecting combinations of assets to maximize returns while minimizing risk. Classical methods of optimization, such as the Markowitz mean-variance model, have scaling issues with respect to the number of assets. This is complicated by the fact that the number of combinations of portfolios grows exponentially, and classical algorithms can hardly evaluate every possible variant in a finite time (Machkour & Abriane, 2020), (Irfan, Dias, Rastogi, & Zebende, 2025).
II. **Risk Analysis and Management:** One of the greatest computational burdens of banks and investment firms is financial risk management. Monte Carlo simulations computationally intensive (e.g., computing Value-at-Risk (VaR), "stress testing, and systemic risk modeling") in many cases. It is more expensive and time-consuming to compute as the simulations require running millions of random scenarios to estimate the possible losses (Cerezo et al., 2022). Quantum computing provides an innovation in "Quantum Amplitude Estimation" (QAE). The algorithm offers a quadratic speed up for Monte Carlo simulations, enabling tasks that would take millions of steps on classical computers to be completed in a fraction of the time on quantum computers (Nguyen et al., 2024). Faster and more accurate risk verifications enable financial institutions to quickly adjust to shifting market conditions, strengthening their ability to deal with unforeseen circumstances. Furthermore, "quantitative simulations could improve the modeling of complicated financial networks" where interconnections between institutions could lead to cascading failures. By capturing more non-linear relationships, quantitative systems may facilitate a better understanding of systemic risk, enabling regulators and banks to implement more effective crisis management measures.

High-Frequency Trading (HFT)

High-frequency trading is another area where quantitative computing shows promise. L'HFT takes advantage of the market's short-term inefficiencies by completing several transactions in a matter of seconds. This area is assessed based on its ability to handle significant amounts of data in real time, identify trends, and complete transactions with the least amount of latency. There are a number of ways in which quantitative computing could benefit HFT(Zaharudin et al., 2022).

By enhancing motif recognition and predictive modeling, quantitatively reinforced automatic learning enables traders to anticipate opportunities before others do. Furthermore, quantitative optimization algorithms that can compute many market circumstances at once may help to improve transaction execution policies. Future developments in quantum cryptography and communication may protect HFT systems from new cybersecurity risks, which is essential given the massive sums of money involved. Quantum computing offers fresh and effective ways to address this complexity (Gomber & Haferkorn, 2013), (Irfan, Kadry, Sharif, & Khan, 2023). Quantum Approximate Optimization Algorithm (QAOA) These procedures can explore a large number of solutions at the same time, which results in portfolios that are closer to the ideal state more quickly than with traditional techniques (Linton & Mahmoodzadeh, 2018).

Fraud Detection and Compliance

The need to prevent fraud and follow all regulations has become a key part of the financial system as it grows more digitalized, sophisticated, and subject to new restrictions. These two elements are essential for ensuring the security of companies and consumers as well as for promoting stability, openness, and trust in global marketplaces. Identifying and stopping activities related to identity theft, money laundering, credit card fraud, insider trading, and cyberattacks are all part of the fraud detection process. Because fraud schemes are becoming more complicated, rule-based detection techniques are no longer adequate. Financial institutions are using cutting-edge technology like machine learning, artificial intelligence (AI), and big data analytics to identify irregularities as they happen. For example, AI can spot unusual spending trends in milliseconds. In a similar vein, natural language processing can be used to search unstructured data, such emails or contracts, for indications of insider fraud. However, there are drawbacks to the fraud detection systems, such as false-positive results and the need to update the models because fraudsters are always changing their strategies (Ramesh et al., 2025).

Contrarily, compliance guarantees that businesses function within legal and regulatory frameworks. This entails abiding by financial reporting guidelines, Know Your Customer (KYC) rules, and anti-money laundering (AML) legislation. Most regulatory bodies throughout the world, such as the Reserve Bank of India (RBI), the U.S. Securities and Exchange Commission (SEC), and the Financial Action Task Force (FATF), have mandated that institutions have strict monitoring and reporting procedures. Significant fines, reputational harm, and even operational sanctions could follow noncompliance. Whereas fraud detection is aimed at identifying illegal practices, compliance frameworks are designed to ensure that the systems employed in detection are not only legal but also ethical. For example, a bank that applies AI to oversee transactions should also be able to comply with data protection laws, such as the GDPR. Compliance and fraud detection are two complementary procedures to protect financial integrity. With the development of financial crimes, it is essential to strike a balance between the use of technology and compliance with regulations in institutions. Investments in resilience to fraud, such as high-quality analytics, employee training, and embedded compliance programs, will continue to be essential for long-term trust in the financial ecosystem.

CHALLENGES IN QUANTUM-DRIVEN FINANCE

Quantum computing has also become one of the most disruptive technologies of the 21st century, with the potential to transform industries, as it can solve problems that are far beyond the capabilities of classical computers. Finance is one of the industries that the extensive use of data processing, risk modeling, optimization, and cryptography can significantly impact. Although the opportunities are enormous, challenges are also associated with introducing quantum computing to financial systems (Elmisery et al., 2025b). The current quantum computers (the so-called Noisy Intermediate-Scale Quantum (NISQ) era) have a limited number of qubits and coherence time, as well as some errors (Hellstern & Yeniaras, 2025). Applications such as portfolio optimization, risk analysis, and fraud detection require large-scale, cohesive computations. In today's machines, there is a clear threat of decoherence and computational errors, so, therefore, to scale quantum solutions to even one useful financial application is not a simple task."

I. **Algorithm Uncertainty:** So far, despite proposals by researchers, including those involving quantum algorithms for planning and pricing derivatives, as well as Monte Carlo simulations, the majority have been of a theoretical nature or have tested only small systems. It is unclear which algorithms will deliver the actual quantum advantage over classical high-performance computing. Such uncertainty makes it difficult for financial institutions to allocate resources because they do not know the output of their investment in quantum R&D (Fisher, 1993).
II. **Integration of Existing Systems:** The IT infrastructure at a securities firm is already massive and complex, something that takes decades to build. The Quantum Interoperability problem involves finding a solution that allows quantum systems to interface with classical computing platforms, databases, and real-time trading systems. There are also ongoing developments in hybrid quantum-classical workflows. However, to build secure and efficient bridges

between the two worlds, this requires skills, investment, and new architectures that most organizations are not prepared – or willing to invest in.

III. **Security - Cryptography Risk:** The most widely recognized risk of quantum computing for financial services is that it can compromise RSA and ECC public-key cryptographic algorithms. They are the encryption used for customers' data, financial transactions, and transfers across browsers. They may be supplanted by a hypothetical large-scale quantum computer, which would open gigantic vulnerabilities. Quantum-safe cryptography (also known as post-quantum cryptography) is in development; however, refitting the world's financial networks will be costly and complex (Ralston et al., 2007).

   I. **Hardware and Scalability:** Present quantum computers, sometimes referred to as the Noisy Intermediate-Scale Quantum (NISQ) era, have finite qubit counts, finite coherence times and error rates—applications such as portfolio optimization, risk analysis,,, and fraud detection require consistent computations at large scales. In current machines, there is a risk of decoherence and computation mistakes, and therefore, it is not easy to scale quantum solutions to a useful financial application.

   II. **Algorithmic Uncertainty:** Although scholars have suggested quantum algorithms to optimize and model pricing derivatives, as well as Monte Carlo simulation, the majority of theoretical or have been applied to small-scale systems only. It is unclear what algorithms will provide the actual quantum benefit over classical high-performance computing. Such uncertainty complicates the ability of financial institutions to commit resources, as they are uncertain about how their investment in quantum R&D will pay off.

   III. **Integration with Existing Systems:** The IT infrastructure of financial firms is huge and complex, and takes decades to develop. The interoperability between quantum systems and classical computing platforms, databases, and real-time trading systems poses significant challenges. There are also ongoing efforts in hybrid quantum-classical workflows. However, to construct secure and efficient pipes between the two worlds requires experience, investment, and new architectures that most institutions are neither read nor willing to invest in.

   IV. **Security-Cryptographic Risk:** The most significant threat posed by quantum computing is the risk that it could compromise popular cryptographic schemes, such as RSA and ECC. These encryption standards are used in financial transactions, customer data, and international transfers. They might be replaced by a large-scale quantum computer, which would cause huge vulnerabilities. Although quantum-safe cryptography (post-quantum cryptography) is being developed, the redesign of the global financial networks will be expensive and logistically difficult.

V. **Talent Shortage:** The field of quantum computing demands the most advanced expertise in physics, mathematics, computer science, and finance. A gap now exists in the lack of professionals who can help bridge the gap between quantum theory and applied financial practice. It is time-consuming to train such talent, and banks and other financial firms find it difficult to recruit them due to competition from tech companies, governments, and academia.

VI. **Ethical and Regulatory Challenges:** Quantum computing has the potential to be disruptive, which raises concerns about fairness, transparency, and market stability. When access to powerful quantum systems is limited to a small number of elite institutions, it can result in unequal access to trading, arbitrage, and risk modeling, thereby further exacerbating disparities between large banks and small entities. Regulators also lack the full readiness to implement quantum technologies in financial frameworks.

CASE STUDIES AND INDUSTRY INSIGHTS

Case Studies

JPMorgan Chase – This Is How AI Can Recognize an Attempted Fraud

Outcome: Drastic decrease in false positives, earlier fraud detection.

HSBC – AML Compliance 3/13 - 4/14.

Implemented modern transaction monitoring solutions and blockchain for trade finance.

Outcome: Better compliance tracking and lower fines imposed by regulators.

Topic: SBI – Digital Transformation. The State Bank of India (SBI) is an Indian multinational, public sector banking and financial services company. It has rolled out AI-based chatbots and biometric authentication.

BARCLAYS – BEHAVIORAL BIOMETRICS

FinTech Startups

Stripe: With Radar, real-time fraud detection tools to help reduce risk.

Result: Shielded small merchants from card-not-present fraud.

Paytm: KYC and Compliance in India. Developed digital KYC verification systems.

Revolut: Crypto Fraud Monitoring

FUTURE DIRECTIONS: ADVANCEMENTS IN QUANTUM HARDWARE AND HYBRID CLASSICAL-QUANTUM APPROACHES

Quickly emerging as a cutting-edge scientific discipline and technological frontier, quantum computing has the potential to revolutionize sectors like; "cybersecurity, healthcare, finance, and logistics". However, "qubit interactions, error rates, and scaling constraints" constrain the existing machines in the Noisy Intermediate-Scale Quantum (NISQ) regime. Two paths are being pursued in order to fully utilize quantum computing, which calls for the creation of hybrid classical-quantum techniques and additional advancements in quantum hardware. The key to closing the gap between current limitations and the large-scale, widespread adoption of several of them is the combination of these developments.

I. **Quantum Hardware:** Quantum hardware is significantly responsible for advancements in this field. The fundamental building blocks of quantum systems, qubits, are now impacted by mistakes and decoherence. Their scalability and stability must be improved for practical application.
II. **Superconducting Qubits:** With super conducting qubits, businesses like; "Google and IBM: are making significant progress. These qubits operate at extremely low temperatures and have already demonstrated remarkable progress; IBM's Eagle processor has more than 100 qubits. It is exploring with future directions such as error correction, enhanced cryogenic techniques, and thousands of qubits on a chip.
III. **Trapped Ions:** Some of the most cutting-edge companies in the development of ion-trap quantum computers include IonQ and Honeywell. In addition to being stable and high-fidelity, the systems use electromagnetic fields to manipulate the ions. Scaling the number of ions while also offering effective error correction and interconnection is the next task.
IV. **Emerging Platforms**: Alternative hardware approaches such as; "photonic quantum systems, neutral atoms, and topological qubits" (Microsoft), are gaining traction. Longer coherence times and potentially better fault-tolerant designs are what these systems promise. There is currently no proven winning platform, and the range of approaches is indicative of the experimental stage of quantum hardware.
V. **Quantum Error Correction**: The Holy Grail of Hardware Development is Error Correction. The existing systems require thousands of physical qubits to form a single logical qubit. This overhead can be reduced dramatically in future developments in qubit design and error-tolerant algorithms, to allow scalable quantum computers.

The current systems require thousands of physical qubits to create one logical qubit. These overheads can be substantially reduced in future qubit designs and error-tolerant algorithms, allowing for scalable quantum computers.

Hybrid Quantum Classical: While large-scale fault-tolerant quantum machines are still years away, hybrid systems that combine classical and quantum computers have emerged as a practical path to near-term applications. VQAs, traditional and promising examples of which include variational quantum eigensolver (VQE) [31] and quantum approximate optimization algorithm (QAOA), rely not only on classical but also on quantum resources. Solutions are generated by the quantum processor and gauged against a measurement made on the classical computer. Because hybrid algorithms are iterative in nature, they are particularly well-suited for optimization problems, chemistry simulations, and machine learning applications. In the field of medicine, they expedite molecular modeling. Hybrid techniques are thus the mechanism through which theory can meet experiment and provide tangible advantages, even before full quantum computers become universally accessible. Although fault-tolerant quantum machines on a large scale are years away, hybrid systems, consisting of a cooperation between classical and quantum computers, provide a viable route to applications in the near future.

I. **Variational Quantum Algorithms (VQAs)**, including the Variational Quantum Eigensolver (VQE) and the Quantum Approximate Optimization Algorithm (QAOA), are techniques that utilize both classical and quantum resources. The quantum processor creates solutions, and the classical computer measures and evaluates the solutions. The fact that hybrid algorithms are iterative procedures renders them particularly suitable for optimization problems, simulating chemistry, and machine learning (Liu et al., 2021).
II. **Quantum Machine Learning (QML):** Training and inference tasks. Hybrid methods are being considered for both training and inference, with quantum circuits used to compute complex patterns and classical processors utilized for data preprocessing and scaling.
III. **Cloud-Based Hybrid Systems:** Tech giants such as Amazon (Braket), Microsoft (Azure Quantum), and Google offer cloud-based services that enable developers to access hybrid classical-quantum environments. This democratizes the act of quantum experimentation, allowing industries to experiment with their applications without necessarily owning specialized hardware (Bauer et al., 2016).
IV. **Industry Applications:** In logistics, quantum-classical algorithms are utilized to determine the optimal delivery routes in the presence of uncertainty. In medicine, they hasten molecular modeling. In finance, they enhance the optimization of portfolios and pricing of derivatives. Hybrid methods, therefore, serve as tools

that offer a connection between theory and practice, and have concrete advantages even prior to the widespread availability of full-scale quantum computers.

HARDWARE AND HYBRID APPROACHES HYBRID CONVERGENCE

Hardware and Hybrid Approaches: Both the upcoming software and hardware advancements are important for the next era of quantum computing. As qubit quality increases, hybrid algorithms would gain strength, and large-scale ones wouldn't even need error-prone hardware. Better algorithms will then be used concurrently to guide the hardware development and pinpoint important performance indicators. The next generation of quantum hardware and the temporary use of hybrid classical-quantum systems are the two pillars of the bimodal future of quantum computing (Devikar et al., 2020). It included a summary of the several methods that are employed in industrial settings, along with the options that enable "experimentation, innovation, and step-by-step adoption." Conversely, quantum computing will cease to be an "experimental laboratory" phenomenon and it is ready to transform a number of industries with the unprecedented power only possible by quantum computing (Ragel & Parameswaran, 2011).

IMPLICATION ON SOCIETY AND ECONOMY

The quantum computing dream is now fast becoming a reality and the impact has potential to disrupt industries. The key: Quantum Technologies — such as "superposition, entanglement and quantum parallelism" – used more effectively to solve problems that are simply too difficult. The social and economic consequences are as vast as they are many. These "innovation opportunities, challenges" of inequalities, threats of insecurity and redesigned labor market and international competitive challenges.

The quantum computing no longer dream but it is fast turning into a revolution, which has the potential of transforming the methods of industries. The advantage of "superposition, entanglement and quantum parallelism, quantum technologies" better utilized to resolve problems which may be too complex. The social and economic impact equally huge and numerous. These "innovation opportunities, challenges" of inequality, threats of insecurity and remodeled labor market and international competitive challenges.

1. Economic Implications:

I. **Industry Disruption**:

II. Such industries as: "finance, medical, energy and logistics will have been influenced upon the portfolios, drug discovery and supply chain optimization with quantum algorithm. The productivity and potentials can minimize the expenditures, to be innovative and more competitive. Nevertheless, industries that are unable to adopt quantum solutions will find it easy to fall behind soon and be the victors and losers in the global economy.

III. **Job Market Transformation**: Quantum computing needs to hire a new category which of employees quantum engineers, algorithm developers, and experts capable of incorporating quantum systems into existing systems. On the other hand, "IT sectors, risk management and operations" might be eliminated with the growth in automation and quantum-based decision systems. It presents both opportunities and challenges, and requires substantial investments in education and reskilling.

IV. **Accelerated Competition:** Quantum technology becomes the world's first strategic resource. Countries that are at the forefront in quantum research, like the United States, China, and the European Union states, are now competing, and the availability of quantum advantage may be associated with economic advantage, especially in areas such as "defence, finance and energy".

V. **Cryptography and Security:** Economically, the ability of quantum computers to break classical encryption is a colossal threat. In the "financial systems, e-commerce, and in digital banking", the use of quantum technology increasing. The transition to the use of the post-quantum cryptography will be costly and time-consuming yet must be undertaken to make sure that the digital economy does not get lost in the area of trust.

2. Societal Implications:

I. **Ethical Concerns:** Quantum technologies have the potential to increase ethical quandaries. The market will become unfair if certain institutions are able to take unfair advantage of trade or arbitrage thanks to quantum-powered financial systems. Concerns about global health fairness arise because pharmacological advancements may benefit the health of increasingly affluent people. Making ensuring that quantum developments are in line with moral standards will be a significant challenge for society.

II. **Cooperation vs. Competition:** National security problems can drive countries to secrecy and competitiveness. The conflict between transparency and protectionism also has certain implications concerning the knowledge exchange and cooperation of societies in the global challenges such as climate change or healthcare. On the one hand, quantum computing offers the "never-before-seen" possibilities of innovation, efficiency, and development in the industries. On the other hand, inequality, serious concerns use, security and issues of global competition. Now the "governments, industries and the societies" will identify these issues which balance between competition and collaboration, innovation and regulation and efficiency and equity. Finally the quantum computing not only a social revolution, but a technological also.

FUTURE RECOMMENDATIONS AND DIRECTIONS

The development of quantum technologies has different experimental phases which practical in different industries likes; 'governments, and societies' need to contemplate and reduce the risk. The combination of different technological "exploration, policy formulation, talent building, and ethical thinking' show the major recommendations and future orientation in quantum computing.

1. **Quantum Hardware Strength and Hybrid Systems:** The hardware development invests in "superconducting qubits, trapped ions, and new systems" which includes; photonics and neutral atoms with long-term stable. Quantum error correction studies the various logical qubits and fault-tolerant systems used in the commercial-scale machines. Hybrid classical-quantum solutions also do the encourage in industry to adopt hybrid models, which integrate the classical computation.
2. **Research and Collaboration:** Development of quantum technology with using of different resource intensive and globally collaborative. The Open source ecosystems; such as "IBM Qisket and Google Cirq" have the potential to be extended to allow researchers all around the world. International cooperation prevents the situation when only several countries possess the technology with creating global frameworks like the climate agreements.
3. **Quantum-Ready Workforce:** Educational programs in the different universities inculcate "quantum computing, quantum algorithms and quantum physics" and multidisciplinary courses in "computer science, engineering and finance". Reskilling programs likes; IT, cybersecurity, and data science specialists programs to prepare their skills in quantum computers.
4. **Security and Post-Quantum Readiness:** Quantum computing threat to existing "cryptographic systems" and potential risks in the "banking, e-commerce and national security". Migration roadmaps used in the different institutions and increase their vulnerable systems which migrated to the next stages.
5. **Ethical, Legal, and Regulatory Frameworks:** Quantum technologies are associated with ethical issues of equity, privacy, and international security.

Creation of new principles could regulate the application of quantum computing in different fields like; "finance, health, and the military". The new regulatory body's likes: "financial regulators" should make sure that quantum-driven algorithms with clear and impartial.

CONCLUSION

Quantum technologies will transform computing capabilities and will provide solutions to problems that cannot be solved by the classical systems at the moment. Applications include but are not limited to portfolio optimization and risk analysis in financial markets, drug discovery, supply chain management and cyber security. The paper shows that the possibility of quantum advantage is a reality, but needs to be planned, technologically innovative and proactive to implications of the society at large. One of the most obvious lessons of the research is the important role of quantum hardware. The existing systems, in the NISQ (Noisy Intermediate-Scale Quantum) age, are qubit-unstable systems, decohering systems, with error rates. The development of superconducting qubits, trapped ions, photonics, and new topological systems will be necessary to realize quantum machine scale to applications in industry. In addition to hardware development, hybrid classical-quantum solutions are also an option that offers a viable route to near-term implementation, enabling businesses to exploit partial benefits of quantum, whilst downplaying the shortcomings of current technology. Some examples of how hybrid systems can solve problems in optimization, simulation, and predictive analytics today include variation quantum algorithms and quantum machine learning. Although the first movers in financial services, pharmaceuticals and logistics will have a significant competitive advantage, global inequalities may increase. Countries and companies having access to quantum knowledge and infrastructure could be ahead of others, which could have gaps in technology, wealth, and innovation.

Quantum computing introduces novel security issues, especially the field of cryptography and fulfills the need post-quantum cryptographic solutions which safeguard sensitive financial and personal information is inevitable. The study suggests the multi-pronged strategy to investment in research and development, inculcate "interdisciplinary talent, create an ethical and regulatory environment", and encourage international cooperation. To ensure that quantum technologies are applied responsibly, the workforce must be prepared through education and reskilling, and ethical standards and open policies should be employed. Quantum computing is a disruptive phenomenon that affects the economy, society, and ethics in addition to pure technology. Through careful strategic planning and cooperative innovation, its promise can be utilized, despite ongoing obstacles in the areas of hardware, algorithms, security, and worker readiness. In order to harness the advantages of the technology and mitigate its risks, quantum computing has the potential to stimulate efficiency, creativity, and societal advancement with a focus on technology utilization and appropriate governance. The study emphasizes that the true value of quantum technologies will be realized through consideration in the realms of people, money, and systems rather than through straightforward machine and algorithmic implementation.

REFERENCES

Abohashima, Z., Elhosen, M., Houssein, E. H., & Mohamed, W. M. (2020). *Classification with Quantum Machine Learning: A Survey* (Version 1). arXiv. DOI: 10.48550/ARXIV.2006.12270

Alexander, P. A., Graham, S., & Harris, K. R. (1998). A Perspective on Strategy Research: Progress and Prospects. *Educational Psychology Review*, *10*(2), 129–154. DOI: 10.1023/A:1022185502996

Bauer, B., Wecker, D., Millis, A. J., Hastings, M. B., & Troyer, M. (2016). Hybrid Quantum-Classical Approach to Correlated Materials. *Physical Review X*, *6*(3), 031045. DOI: 10.1103/PhysRevX.6.031045

Cerezo, M., Verdon, G., Huang, H.-Y., Cincio, L., & Coles, P. J. (2022). Challenges and opportunities in quantum machine learning. *Nature Computational Science*, *2*(9), 567–576. DOI: 10.1038/s43588-022-00311-3 PMID: 38177473

Cuomo, M. T., & Foroudi, P. (2025). Tools and Techniques for Quantum Business. In M. T. Cuomo & P. Foroudi, *Quantum Level Business Model: A New Managerial Perspective* (Vol. 3, pp. 83–104). Springer Nature Switzerland. DOI: 10.1007/978-3-031-92052-3_5

Devikar, R. N., Patil, D. V., & Prakash, V. C. (2020). A hybrid computing approach to improve convergence time for scalable network. *Sadhana*, *45*(1), 225. DOI: 10.1007/s12046-020-01454-7

Elmisery, A. M., Sertovic, M., Zayin, A., & Watson, P. (2025a). *Cyber Threats in Financial Transactions—Addressing the Dual Challenge of AI and Quantum Computing* (Version 1). arXiv. DOI: 10.48550/ARXIV.2503.15678

Elmisery, A. M., Sertovic, M., Zayin, A., & Watson, P. (2025b). *Cyber Threats in Financial Transactions—Addressing the Dual Challenge of AI and Quantum Computing* (Version 1). arXiv. DOI: 10.48550/ARXIV.2503.15678

Fisher, P. F. (1993). Algorithm and implementation uncertainty in viewshed analysis. *International Journal of Geographical Information Systems*, *7*(4), 331–347. DOI: 10.1080/02693799308901965

Gomber, P., & Haferkorn, M. (2013). High-Frequency-Trading: High-Frequency-Trading Technologies and Their Implications for Electronic Securities Trading. *Business & Information Systems Engineering*, *5*(2), 97–99. DOI: 10.1007/s12599-013-0255-7

Hellstern, G., & Yeniaras, E. (2025). *Quantum Leap in Finance: Economic Advantages, Security, and Post-Quantum Readiness* (Version 1). arXiv. DOI: 10.48550/ARXIV.2508.21548

How, M.-L., & Cheah, S.-M. (2023). Business Renaissance: Opportunities and Challenges at the Dawn of the Quantum Computing Era. *Businesses*, *3*(4), 585–605. DOI: 10.3390/businesses3040036

Irfan, M., Dias, R., Rastogi, R., & Zebende, G. F. (2025). *Generative AI insights for financial decision making*. IGI Global.

Irfan, M., Elmogy, M., Gupta, S., Khalifa, F., & Dias, R. T. (2024). *AI-driven decentralized finance and the future of finance*. IGI Global USA.

Irfan, M., Hussainey, K., Bukhari, S. A. C., & Nam, Y. (2024). *Issues of sustainability in AI and new-age thematic investing*. IGI Global.

Irfan, M., Kadry, S., Sharif, M., & Khan, H. U. (2023). *Fintech applications in Islamic finance: AI, machine learning, and blockchain techniques*. IGI Global.

Irfan, M., Mohammed, M., Kassim, S., & Ofori, K. S. (2024). *The future of indigenous inclusivity: Unlocking finance for economic development*. IGI Global.

Lamichhane, P., & Rawat, D. B. (2025). Quantum Machine Learning: Recent Advances, Challenges, and Perspectives. *IEEE Access : Practical Innovations, Open Solutions*, *13*, 94057–94105. DOI: 10.1109/ACCESS.2025.3573244

Linton, O., & Mahmoodzadeh, S. (2018). Implications of High-Frequency Trading for Security Markets. *Annual Review of Economics*, *10*(1), 237–259. DOI: 10.1146/annurev-economics-063016-104407

Liu, J., Lim, K. H., Wood, K. L., Huang, W., Guo, C., & Huang, H.-L. (2021). Hybrid quantum-classical convolutional neural networks. *Science China. Physics, Mechanics & Astronomy*, *64*(9), 290311. DOI: 10.1007/s11433-021-1734-3

Machkour, B., & Abriane, A. (2020). Industry 4.0 and its Implications for the Financial Sector. *Procedia Computer Science*, *177*, 496–502. DOI: 10.1016/j.procs.2020.10.068

Maheshwari, D., Garcia-Zapirain, B., & Sierra-Sosa, D. (2022). Quantum Machine Learning Applications in the Biomedical Domain: A Systematic Review. *IEEE Access : Practical Innovations, Open Solutions*, *10*, 80463–80484. DOI: 10.1109/ACCESS.2022.3195044

Martín-Guerrero, J. D., & Lamata, L. (2022). Quantum Machine Learning: A tutorial. *Neurocomputing*, *470*, 457–461. DOI: 10.1016/j.neucom.2021.02.102

Millett, S. M. (2003). The future of scenarios: Challenges and opportunities. *Strategy and Leadership*, *31*(2), 16–24. DOI: 10.1108/10878570310698089

Mironowicz, P. H., A. S., Mandarino, A., Yilmaz, A. E., & Ankenbrand, T. (2024). *Applications of Quantum Machine Learning for Quantitative Finance* (Version 1). arXiv. DOI: 10.48550/ARXIV.2405.10119

Mishra, L., & Kaushik, V. (2023). Application of blockchain in dealing with sustainability issues and challenges of financial sector. *Journal of Sustainable Finance & Investment*, *13*(3), 1318–1333. DOI: 10.1080/20430795.2021.1940805

Narayan, S. (2025). Preparing for Quantum Transformation: Strategic Implications for Business and Finance in Asia. In Endress, T., & Badir, Y. F. (Eds.), *Business and Management in Asia: Finance and Investments in the Digital Age* (pp. 221–238). Springer Nature Singapore., DOI: 10.1007/978-981-96-3452-1_14

Nguyen, T., Sipola, T., & Hautamäki, J. (2024). *Machine Learning Applications of Quantum Computing: A Review*. DOI: 10.48550/ARXIV.2406.13262

Putranto, D. S. C., Wardhani, R. W., Ji, J., & Kim, H. (2024). A Deep Inside Quantum Technology Industry Trends and Future Implications. *IEEE Access : Practical Innovations, Open Solutions*, *12*, 115776–115801. DOI: 10.1109/ACCESS.2024.3444779

Ragel, R. G., & Parameswaran, S. (2011). A hybrid hardware—Software technique to improve reliability in embedded processors. *ACM Transactions on Embedded Computing Systems*, *10*(3), 1–16. DOI: 10.1145/1952522.1952529

Rahimi, M., & Asadi, F. (2023). Oncological Applications of Quantum Machine Learning. *Technology in Cancer Research & Treatment*, *22*, 15330338231215214. DOI: 10.1177/15330338231215214 PMID: 38105500

Ralston, P. A. S., Graham, J. H., & Hieb, J. L. (2007). Cyber security risk assessment for SCADA and DCS networks. *ISA Transactions*, *46*(4), 583–594. DOI: 10.1016/j.isatra.2007.04.003 PMID: 17624350

Ramesh, J. V. N., Singh Kadyan, J., Kadyan, S., Hussein, O. M., Teltumbade, G. R., & Valavan, M., P. (2025). Enhancing Corporate Tax Compliance and Fraud Detection Using Principal Component Analysis and Auto-Encoder. *2025 Fifth International Conference on Advances in Electrical, Computing, Communication and Sustainable Technologies (ICAECT)*, 1–6. DOI: 10.1109/ICAECT63952.2025.10958987

Vashishth, T. K., Sharma, V., Kaushik, V., & Singh, A. Shashi, & Kaushik, S. (2025). Exploring Quantum Challenges and Opportunities of Quantum Machine Learning Adoption in Finance: In H. Chen (Ed.), *Advances in Finance, Accounting, and Economics* (pp. 437–460). IGI Global. DOI: 10.4018/979-8-3693-8186-1.ch017

Zaharudin, K. Z., Young, M. R., & Hsu, W. (2022). High-frequency trading: Definition, implications, and controversies. *Journal of Economic Surveys*, *36*(1), 75–107. DOI: 10.1111/joes.12434

Zhou, J. (2025). Quantum Finance: Exploring the Implications of Quantum Computing on Financial Models. *Computational Economics*. Advance online publication. DOI: 10.1007/s10614-025-10894-4

Chapter 3
The Quantum Future of Finance Applications: Challenges and Strategic Opportunities

Mandakini Garg
https://orcid.org/0000-0001-7144-4387
Pranveer Singh Institute of Technology, India

Sneha Awasthi
https://orcid.org/0000-0002-4468-7364
Pranveer Singh Institute of Technology, India

Sashwat Kumar Dixit
Pranveer Singh Institute of Technology, India

Early Ridho Kismawadi
https://orcid.org/0000-0002-9420-5212
Faculty of Islamic Economics and Business, IAIN Langsa, Aceh, Indonesia

ABSTRACT

"Quantum age" is the name given to the new era when quantum technologies will start shifting out of laboratory research into real-world usage that can potentially data scientist, various areas and aspects of society change drastically (Possati, 2024). It is required to know about the potential uses of quantum computing in financial services because it is a developing technology that can potentially revolutionize the industry.It has the promise of accessing the Power of Quantum Computing for Enhanced Forecasting, Portfolio Optimization, etc. Likewise, the exponential acceleration of computation promised by quantum computers has potential benefits in fraud detection (Zhou, 2025). For instance, quantum-enabled anomaly detection

DOI: 10.4018/979-8-3373-2893-5.ch003

which enables the identification of anomalous transaction patterns in real-time, could possibly lower false positives and improve the efficacy of fraud prevention when monitoring credit card and other banking transactions.

1. INTRODUCTION: QUANTUM FUTURE OF FINANCE

"Quantum age" is the name given to the new era when quantum technologies will start shifting out of laboratory research into real-world usage that can potentially data scientist, various areas and aspects of society change drastically (Possati, 2024). It is required to know about the potential uses of quantum computing in financial services because it is a developing technology that can potentially revolutionize the industry.

Figure 1. Futuristic Image of Artwork

Source: Author's work

Quantum Computing is Systems that employ quantum mechanical effects such as superposition and entanglement to treat information in manners classical computers can't (Mohamed et al., 2022).

From artificial intelligence and blockchain to supercomputer-led high-frequency trading, the finance sector has always been at the forefront of adopting game-changing technologies.

Businesses, governments, and financial institutions are now coming together to see the change that quantum computing can bring (How & Cheah, 2023). Top firms in the industry, like IBM and Google, foresee their machines having 1,000 logical qubits by 2033, which could see full integration of quantum capabilities into financial operations by 2035 (Bremner, 2024). Since quantum computing has the ability to solve complex problems faster and with greater accuracy, it can potentially revolutionize strategic planning and key decision-making.

It has the promise of accessing the Power of Quantum Computing for Enhanced Forecasting, Portfolio Optimization, etc. Likewise, the exponential acceleration of computation promised by quantum computers has potential benefits in fraud detection (Zhou, 2025). For instance, quantum-enabled anomaly detection which enables the identification of anomalous transaction patterns in real-time, could possibly lower false positives and improve the efficacy of fraud prevention when monitoring credit card and other banking transactions.

1.1 Why do we want to use quantum computing in finance?

While market trends are forecasted by machine learning (ML) models, the most challenging finance optimization problems are solved by using ML models along with quantum computing.

For instance, quantum algorithms like the Quantum Approximate Optimization Algorithm (QAOA) are designed to resolve problems that would need days of processing on traditional computers, for example, risk assessment, derivative pricing, and portfolio optimization (Zhou, 2025).

The financial industry has a long history of early adoption of transformative technologies, such as high-frequency trading based on supercomputing platforms, blockchain and artificial intelligence (Rastogi & Iqbal, 2024). At this point, companies, banks and governments are beginning to look at the revolutionary potential of quantum computing (Galatsanos-Dueck, 2024). Leaders of the industry, such as IBM and Google, claim they will hit 1,000 logical qubits in their systems by 2033, and this could lead to full quantum potential being integrated into finance operations by 2035. Quantum computing could transform vital decision making and strategy development by providing solutions to complex problems faster and accurately.

This brings significant competitive advantages for those willing to leverage its power in areas such as financial modeling, supply chain optimization, and simulation. Analysts suggest quantum computing could bring in excess of $622 billion in value through sectors, yielding unparalleled efficiency and understanding (How & Cheah, 2023). Quantum computing projects remain a high risk, high reward asset class, and therefore it is crucial to be cautious and strategic when considering quantum investment and implementation. Quantum hardware, software and hybrid solutions are in the infancy stages of development and it is difficult to forecast their development.

1.2 Current State of Quantum Finance Integration:

Quantum computing in finance is now in a nascent and exploratory stage with a substantial amount of investment and research (Zafar, 2025). Many people think it will be years before quantum computers are commercially viable for solving complex problems, possibly as long as 2035 or longer. Financial services firms are now test-driving a small set of early-stage quantum solutions, especially in optimization and security.

Influential Quantum Computing Firms in Finance

The quantum computing landscape includes both pure-play quantum companies and significant technology companies that provide quantum offerings and hardware, typically via the cloud. Some of the firms engaged in the finance sector include:

IBM: A leading player and working with a range of significant financial institutions (e.g., they recently collaborated with HSBC on a and disclosed an experiment with bond trading prediction). IBM offers quantum systems and the Qiskit SDK.

IonQ: Specializes on trapped-ion quantum computers, and has partnerships with major cloud players (Microsoft Azure, Amazon AWS, and Google Cloud).

D-Wave Quantum: Well known for their approach to quantum annealing and being applied to optimization problems like risk modeling and portfolio diversification, which banks like Yapı Kredi are implementing.

Microsoft (Azure Quantum): Offers access to quantum hardware from various partners via the cloud and provides software development tools.

**Google (Quantum AI): Working on advanced quantum chips and algorithms.

Quantinuum: Formed by the merger of Honeywell Quantum Solutions and Cambridge Quantum, works on integrating hardware and software.

Financial Institutions Investing in Quantum Research

Several major financial institutions worldwide are currently investing in quantum research and development, primarily through internal labs, institutional partnerships. and cloud-based access to quantum computing as follows

Goldman Sachs: Has been exploring quantum computing for use in the finance field.

JPMorgan Chase: Has a team of researchers focused solely on quantum computing.

HSBC: Had reported a successful test with IBM using a quantum processor to assist in improving bond trading predictions.

Banco Sabadell: Considered the use of Post Quantum Cryptography (PQC) as a means of modernizing their encryption protocols.

Yapı Kredi: Used D-Wave's quantum technology to create a model to estimate financial risk and the points of failure across its SME network.

2. FINANCE APPLICATIONS OF QUANTUM - COMPUTING

Potential applications in finance are wider than the usually cited ones such as portfolio optimization. They also involve a number that could be revolutionary.

Banks would be able to utilize quantum computing to boost human expert judgement and make accounting and finance processes more efficient. Any conclusions that result from this would be more precise (Chambers-Jones, 2021).

Figure 2. Quantum Computing Application in Finance

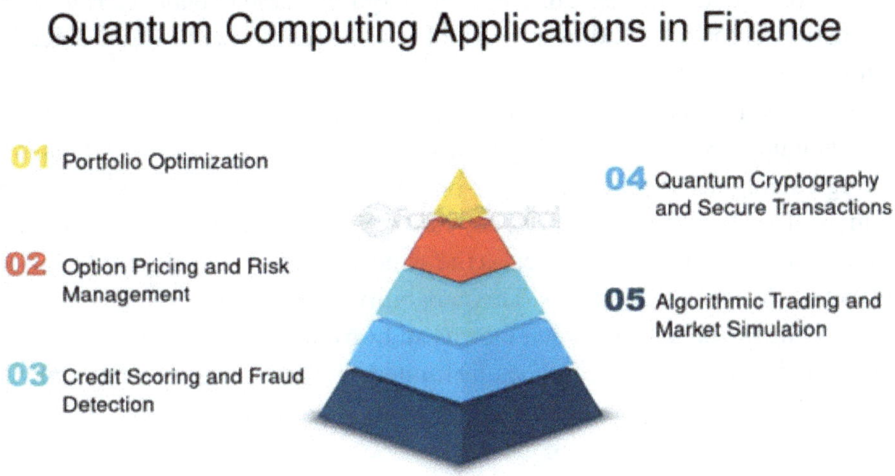

Source: Chambers-Jones, 2021

2.1 Corporate Banking

Due to the high monetary value and the vast number of complex use cases in industries such as trade finance, corporate banking is where quantum computing is utilized most frequently.

Quantum computing facilitates making critical decisions and even automated decision-making in real-time (Ghosh, 2024). This is a consequence of the technology having a natural ability to make computations with a much greater variety of boundary conditions and increase decision precision.

Blockchain solutions' speed and security can be outdone by fault-resistant smart contracts, intangible assets, and safe communication (Ogundokun & Arowolo, 2022)

2.2 Threat and Cybersecurity

Risk ranks as one of the most complicated topics in banks. It's about recognizing, minimizing, and reporting risks in other departments. With quantum computing, risk-related regulatory reporting will be transformed. Quantum machine learning can enable decision makers to take into account a broader set of variables and assets when it comes to simulating risks (Patel, 2025). It can decrease the cost of risk and facilitate more deals with increased profits. For detecting fraud, new payment schemes and transactions can minimize episodes. Although professionals now believe that quantum computing is only marginally able to enhance rule-based fraud detection, employing additional variables will be able to make fraud-detection algorithms more precise.

Portfolio creation and risk assessment are some of the areas being re-designed in the ever-changing investment banking landscape by quantum computing. Quantum computing can significantly change this process (Sharma et al., 2024). Applying quantum parallelism and interference, they can make calculations over an impossibly enormous set of combinations of assets at the same time, weighting their calculations toward their most optimal outcomes. This capability will solve directly the long-term issue of striking the balance between returns and variance with greater velocity and greater accuracy. Traditional techniques are limited with portfolios whose complexity and size are increasing exponentially as more calculations are needed.

2.3 Retail Banking

The applications of quantum computing in retail banking are largely similar to its uses in corporate banking, particularly for high-net-worth individuals (Mishra et al., 2024). However, the issues are less difficult for retail customers since their volumes and assets are smaller.

Two of the most important applications are credit-decision software and collateral optimization, both of which might be better with greater precision. The former can leverage quantum computing to take more factors into account.

The second may introduce additional values and data types as constraints of the optimization problem. Because the problems in retail banking are typically less complex and contain fewer variables, most think that the advantages in this segment are minimal.

To a lesser extent, quantum computing would also provide a boost to portfolio optimization

2.4 Payments

Quantum states would be secure and considerably quicker to pay than the blockchain. Especially, quantum payments would be able to solve the existing issue of money laundering on the blockchain (Dey et al., 2022).

Quantum states are true non falsifiable money because they cannot be replicated. One of the significant factors that we anticipate will enable quantum payments is the hardware required for quantum key distribution (QKD).

The future of the inter and intra bank security would be quantum money operating with the QKD protocols. When quantum money is implemented in a stabilized fashion then this will completely transform the banking system.

2.5 Investment Banking

Quantum computing investment banking is not merely doing more calculations faster, but it provides the extra degree of decision-making. Quantum computing, which relies on the principles of quantum mechanics, also gives investment banks the capacity to quantify and process huge, complex variables in the market in previously unattainable manners. Investment banking with AI it can bring more breakthroughs in forecasting, risk management and strategic planning, and introduce a new era of financial innovations.

Quantum computing would find application in investment banking, where it would be able to facilitate the much-desired improvement in the derivatives pricing and portfolio optimization. In the case of investment banking groups, it was possible to build entirely digital representations of how a bank stood. Those models would be used to model those conditions and routes. They were able to simulate the resources of a bank and they had a chance to learn how various situations influence every asset.

Derivatives pricing and optimization of portfolios in investment banking can be greatly improved when quantum computing is used. Within a quantum computing setting, investment banking professionals can generate full digital copies of a position of the bank. And then utilize those replicas to model various macro conditions and scenarios. They were also able to model much more precisely in terms of understanding what happens to each bank asset when exposed to each of the macro conditions of the markets. This type of work would serve to construct quantum models of the market. Improved collateral and asset capital allocation can be one of the outcomes. Another potential use of quantum computers for derivatives pricing and high-frequency trading is that the users will be able to use more variables and examine the underlying assets that are being used in the derivatives, and ultimately quantify them with quantum computers A quantum computer is able to process/

analyze such assets that involve computational power in a manner which would feed back to the principal algorithm.

There are already quantum computing abilities for instance incorporate in random number generation abilities that would already enhance the efficiency and precision of current modern computing simulating techniques such as Monte Carlo simulations, in this sense, quantum computing could rather easily become the norm to the conventional pools of models and techniques. In the long run, banks could for instance adopt quantum

Monte Carlo algorithms (as a case in point), build on their existing classical means, and this means may already be commercially pre-existing as far as institutional settlement in the future through well established smart contracts adopted with the velocity of monetary transactions by being quantum state facilitators, which theoretically would give room for increased speed and more secure, energy-sustaining transactions for all concerned as in the case of vision with related asset classes already in wealth management.

Figure 3. Mapping of financial services domains to benefit areas and case studies of quantum technology applications (Source: World Economic Forum, 2025)

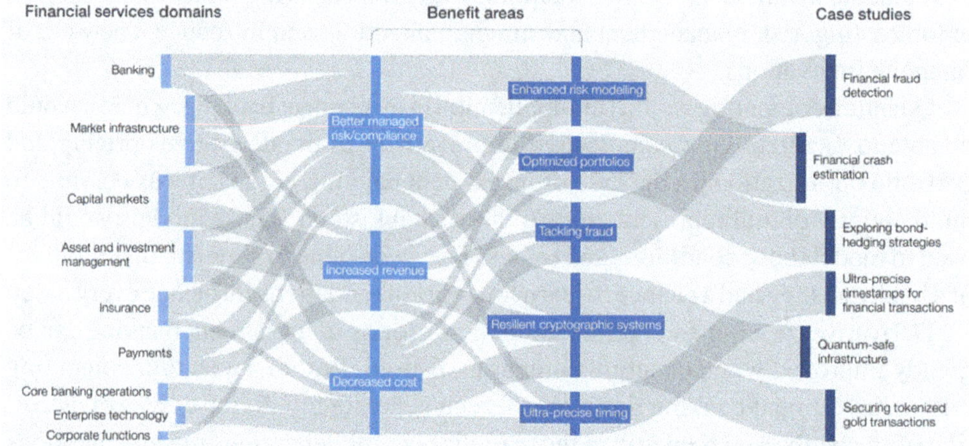

Maximum. portfolio diversification, faster trading, and faster settlements would be easy through the potential of quantum power. It might benefit investors to think in many factors and scenarios at the same time and navigate risk markets and combine investments with long-term goals.

3. QUANTUM KEY DISTRIBUTION

Quantum Key Distribution (QKD) is a secure communication method that uses the principles of quantum mechanics to derive and share a secret cryptographic key between two parties, assuring that any attempt to eavesdrop will be detectable immediately. Financial institutions are exploring and piloting QKD for its potential as a critical layer in the quantum-safe security paradigm.

Execution in Financial Networks

Financial institutions are utilizing quantum key distribution (QKD) to provide enhanced protection for their most mission-critical high-bandwidth communication links. Data Center Interconnects (DCI): QKD is utilized for high-bandwidth links for traffic between data centres and for traffic between the primary data center and disaster recovery (DR) sites (typically around metro distance from one another).

Fiber Integration: QKD signals (photons) can be utilized on existing fiber optic networks in tandem with classical data signals by using Wavelength Division Multiplexing (WDM) making roll-out relatively simple. Or a dedicated fiber can be used as the quantum channel.

Hybrid Approach: A common industry standard for a quantum-safe robust strategy is a hybrid approach to security combining QKD with Post-Quantum Cryptography (PQC).

PQC (mathematically secure algorithms) allows the institution to deal with the most immediate need for securing software and general communications.

QKD (physics based secure key distribution) creates a second additional level of security for the most mission-critical hardware level links.

Real-World Pilots: Institutions like JPMorgan Chase have successfully operated a QKD network that secured a mission-critical blockchain application using a QKD network that demonstrated the technology in a production-simulated environment.

3.1 Quantum techniques for Monte Carlo-style Derivative Pricing and Risk Management

In finance, one important asset-pricing problem is the pricing of derivatives. A derivative is a contract that derives its value from another asset (e.g., a basket of assets or financial index), known as the underlying, which itself is modeled by a stochastic process. To price a derivative, the model estimates the dynamics of the underlying asset(s) and computes the payoff structure as a result. At each time step, the payoff function evaluates the contract's cash flow to the owner based on the current state of the underlying asset(s) and possibly based on the historical states of the underlying asset(s)

3.2 Secure Communication

In terms of secure communication, Professor Harrow states, "There is a possibility of using quantum key distribution (QKD), and there are some organizations that have been trying it out. QKD does have the potential to be useful in a communication network when financial organizations actually want to have a guarantee of security."

4. QUANTUM-POWERED PREDICTIVE ANALYSIS

The massive computing capacity of quantum computing will transform predictive analytics, statistical and machine learning models which offer forecasts of the future.

4.1 Extremely Accurate Risk Simulation

Nowadays, banks calculate risk by complex simulations, such as Monte Carlo analysis, with the support of conventional supercomputers. However, the only brute force that we can use is the brute force of our respective computers. Quantum computers can readily perform these simulations many orders of magnitude faster, and offer more modelable variables and scenarios. This will result in better and correct risk assessment of the complex derivative and of the interlinked financial system.

4.2 Improved Fraud Detection and Credit Scoring

The quantum machine learning systems are capable of scanning massive and complex data sets and uncovering hidden patterns and anomalies that were not visible to the former systems. This could create a more fair and accurate credit scoring that can result in credit becoming available to many more people. The use of quantum-enhanced AI in fraud detection can also handle large volumes of transaction data and identify suspicious or fraudulent transactions in situ and prevent financial crime more accurately than before. The optimal approach to asset allocation involves balancing the duration of the investment and the associated risk

4.3 Asset Allocation Optimization:

The possibility of quantum computing to tackle the challenging optimization issues will transform the landscape of the portfolio management.

The number of assets and the number of combinations in which the optimal combination of asset can be maximized to give maximum possible returns grows exponentially with the amount of risk. With quantum annealing and other algorithms, a quantum computer will be able to identify the actually optimal solution in a fraction of the time - try a great many asset combinations with quantum annealing and other algorithms!

5. HFT AND QUANTUM ALGORITHMS

The quantum algorithms have the potential to revolutionize high-frequency trading (HFT) since they have the ability to perform much more advanced calculations at a faster speed than the conventional computer. Though the technology is still in its infancy, its potential is great in an industry where milliseconds mean the difference between success and failure. The main benefits of using quantum algorithms in HFT are the speed of computation, risk management and data analysis. Calculating large volumes of data at the same time is possible using quantum algorithms, and this is highly beneficial to HFT. These complicated optimization problems can be challenging to find the solution within computational time when determining simultaneous arbitrage across two or more markets. Quantum computers are able to calculate the combination of multiple scenarios at the same time using such concepts as superposition and entanglement. This would enable the trading firms to identify and react to the temporal price movement earlier and more productively than their competitors.

6. QUANTUM IN CENTRAL BANKING AND MONETARY POLICY

Quantum Computing is quickly becoming the disruptor that could reshape our world, alter business models, and impact the Financial Services industry due to enhanced algorithmic power and computing capabilities.

Major financial institutions are paying attention to this and have started doing quantum research for higher value while ensuring data remains unhackable. Large banks, including Goldman Sachs, JP Morgan, CBA, Barclays, RBS, and Allianz are making significant investments in quantum computing technology. Mastercard has aligned with a strategic partner for the development of quantum-hybrid applications for consumer loyalty and rewards, cross-border settlement, fraud management, and anti-money laundering. HSBC are utilizing quantum computing for pricing and portfolio optimization, to further their net zero ambitions, and to manage risk including identifying and acting against fraudulent activity.

Across the globe, governments are also committing significant budgets to quantum computing. The Chinese government is funding a multi-billion-dollar quantum computing project to make significant quantum discoveries by 2030. In 2018, the US put the National Quantum Initiative Act into law that included a 5-year investment of \$1.2 bn into quantum information research. In Germany, approximately \$2.4 bn is planned to develop its first quantum computer and associated technologies.

For central banking and monetary policy, quantum computing presents both revolutionary possibilities and serious risks. While it provides sophisticated instruments for financial modeling and macroeconomic analysis, it also poses a serious threat to the security of existing cryptography.

In addition to developing "quantum-safe cryptography" to guard against future cyberattacks that could jeopardize sensitive data and digital currencies, central banks are actively investigating its potential, particularly in enhancing financial stability through complex optimization and quantum simulations. Projects like Project Leap by the Bank for International Settlements demonstrate the community's proactive efforts to mitigate these risks and make the shift to a financial system that is quantum-secure.

6.1 Quantum and Machine Learning for Finance

Quantum algorithms possess the ability to improve machine learning in numerous domains and applications. In this study, we demonstrate how quantum machine learning ideas can be applied to improve financial forecasting. First, we apply the classical and quantum Determinantal Point Process to improve Random Forest models to predict churn, with improvements in precision of nearly 6%. Second, we develop quantum neural network architectures that use orthogonal and compound layers for credit risk assessment, matching classical performance with significantly fewer parameters. Overall, our findings indicate that quantum ideas will successfully improve the performance of machine learning, both in the now through classical quantum-inspired ML solutions, and even more so in the future, with an improved quantum hardware.

Quantum computing, especially when combined with machine learning (Quantum Machine Learning, or QML), has great potential for improvement within many areas of the financial industry. Potential Applications Risk Assessment: QML could enhance risk assessment models, resulting in improved financial stability and a more accurate evaluation of risk. Portfolio Optimization: Asset allocation could be optimized, leading to more effective and successful investment portfolios for both institutional and individual clients. Fraud Detection: QML improves fraud detection processes by enhancing pattern recognition capabilities to identify newer ways to commit financial crime. Trading Strategies: It can improve the development and optimization of trading strategies. Derivative Pricing: QML would provide pricing models for financial derivatives that are more accurate by modeling market behavior more accurately by using methods like quantum Monte Carlo simulations. Credit scoring: By using a quantum annealer (a type of quantum computer), the credit scoring process could be optimized. Financial Forecasting: Financial forecasting models could be significantly improved by utilizing quantum machine learning such as by applying enhancements to Random Forest models for churn prediction, or developing a quantum neural network based credit risk model.

6.2 Quantum Computing in Finance

Quantum computing represents a shift in computational power by applying quantum phenomena like superposition, entanglement, and tunneling. As a result, quantum computers will allow for exponentially quicker processing and data analysis of complex data than classical systems, giving them great suitability for application in FinTech.

Here are a few notable examples of areas it will influence:

1. Portfolio Optimization. Quantum algorithms will optimize investment portfolios by analyzing a tremendous number of variables and constraints simultaneously, allowing real-time changes based on market volatility (Orús et al., 2019).
2. Risk Management. More advanced Monte Carlo simulations powered by quantum computing will allow financial institutions to roughly model risk scenarios with added accuracy (Bova et al., 2020).
3. Fraud Detection. Quantum machine learning algorithms will increase the ability to detect fraud patterns within large transactional datasets (Zhang et al., 2021).
4. Post-Quantum Cryptography. Quantum computing is critical for developing methods of encryption that are safe against future quantum computation in order to protect financial data (Shor, 1997).

Despite the potential for quantitative computing in Fintech applications, significant challenges remain in widespread adoption, including costs, technical complexity, and specialized infrastructure. Addressing barriers to entry is paramount for acceptance and adoption of quantum computing.

Future Prospects

The future of quantum computing within Financial Technology ("FinTech") is bright; continued advances are expected to improve the limitations we are faced with today. As quantum hardware improves, and the algorithms that power it become more sophisticated, financial services firms will be in better position to:

* Implement real-time management systems for portfolio management.
* Improve global payment systems by integrating cryptography that is considered quantum-secure.

* Profoundly transform predictive analytics that are useful for economic forecasting.

The impact of quantum computing for FinTech firms will be enhanced by its combination with new technologies such as blockchain and artificial intelligence, ushering in a new wave of innovation in financial services.

7. THE QUANTUM LEAP

Banks like HSBC, Santander, and Yapili Kredi are also using quantum solutions to do various tasks including fraud detection and quantum resistant infrastructure.

The time to act is now: on the one hand, quantum computers offer unprecedented risk computation and portfolio optimization potential due to their ability to compute large quantities of risk calculations per second; on the other hand, they pose a threat to the current encryption techniques, which safeguard trillions of dollars of transaction data every day. The innovative financial institutions are developing a two-pronged approach, availing themselves of quantum advantages, with defences developed that are quantum-resistant.

HSBC is the first bank offering quantum security in the AI-driven foreign exchange trading. At the forefront of exploring how quantum cryptography can safeguard highly sensitive trading information from prospective cyber risks as powerful as future quantum attacks is HSBC, a global top-tier foreign exchange provider.

Figure 4. Projected value creation of quantum-computing use cases in the finance industry by 2035, estimated at $622 billion across business units (Source: McKinsey & Company, 2025).

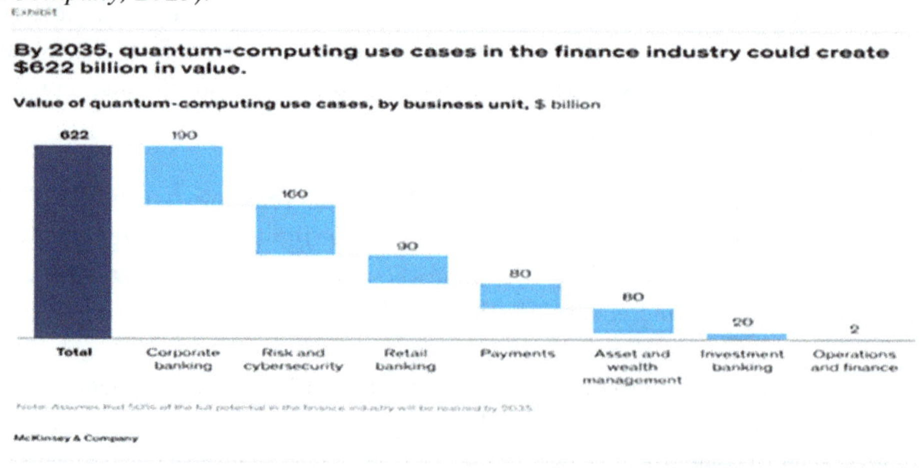

8. THREE STRATEGIES FOR BANKS TO USE CUTTING-EDGE TECHNOLOGY IN FINANCIAL SERVICES

- More accurate risk modeling, fraud prevention, and portfolio optimization are all facilitated by quantum computing.
- Quantum communications and cryptography: theoretically unbreakable encryption using methods such as quantum random number generation (QRNG) and quantum key distribution (QKD).
- Synchronization of high-frequency trading (HFT) algorithms could be improved by quantum sensing's capacity to provide accurate measurements.

Figure 5. Quantum-hybrid risk scoring models integrating classical and quantum computing, Monte Carlo simulation, quantum machine learning, and financial risk analysis.

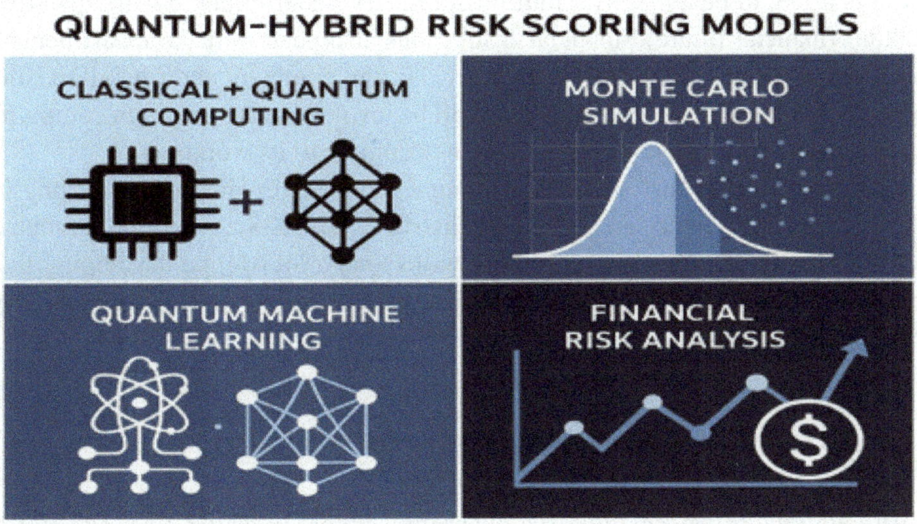

8.1 Restructuring of Acquisitions, Deals and Mergers

Investment banks' M&As and deal structuring practices are already being wholly revolutionized by quantum computing. Its applications in the field of valuation modeling are perhaps most impressive. By enabling the running of many different market scenarios within a relatively short time, quantum systems enable a higher degree of precision that was hitherto unimaginable with traditional methods.

This accelerates the time-consuming calculations that tend to retard decision-making and enables banks to compute the probable value of a deal faster and with more estimates.

8.2 The Workforce of Tomorrow: Skills to a Quantum Financial Future

Quantum computing will continue to give the rise of a new workforce in the domain of the financial service although the skills required will continue to change as quantum computers are cheaper, faster and more readily available (How & Cheah, 2023). The new workforce will demand a blend of theoretical finance knowledge along with a physics, computer science and mathematics knowledge.

It is the next generation of quantum quants that will lead the financial revolution. It is going to be a massive, multi-disciplinary undertaking to work towards a quantum financial future. Financial Institutions also need to make investments in education programs to train its workers within the company and re-skill existing workers working with the company that will be involved in the quantum computing transition, and create a quantum culture environment to its workers.

Colleges will add courses that have brought about degrees in fin tech and physics courses, computer science and finance (Ghatrifi et al., 2023). The future graduates who want to practice this new paradigm will spend a lot of time developing their programming and mathematics skills and staying current with the latest developments and advancements in quantum technology.

9. QUANTUM ERA'S PROSPECTS FOR FINANCE

Although the transformation to a quantum technology-driven financial system will take place over a long and complex period of time, it will change the practice of the field in numerous ways that are substantively different. The first mover advantage will be captured by the financial institutions in anticipation that they are ready for the quantum by investing. It won't be enough to possess the finest technology, they will have to acquire the internal knowledge and culture that will assist them in leveraging the new resources to maximum benefit (Girasa & Scalabrini, 2022)

Quantum computing applications remain a high risk, high return investment and must be approached cautiously and strategically with investment and implementation. Quantum hardware, software, and hybrid opportunities are in nascent stages of development so that predicting the future direction of these applications is impossible.

To safeguard gigantic amounts of sensitive information and transactions from possible quantum attacks on current encryption methods, financial institutions are also investing heavily in quantum-resistant cryptography. To maintain security and capitalize on new opportunities, banks are following a dual approach consisting of leveraging the advantage of quantum computers while building quantum-resistance defenses.

The quantum computer is expensive and requires a lot of resources, and this calls for international cooperation. A quantum divide in which pioneers of quantum computing dominate markets will be achieved through a few financial institutions and countries having access to quantum capabilities when there is no collaboration in development. To ensure a balance between the different markets on an international scale and maintain financial stability, interdependence can be developed. But heightened European autonomy in quantum computing could also grant the continent a competitive advantage in the race of technologies globally.

Figure 6. Projected worldwide market size of quantum computing from 2020 to 2030, expected to grow from USD 260 million to USD 9,066 million with a CAGR of 43% (Source: Statista, 2021)

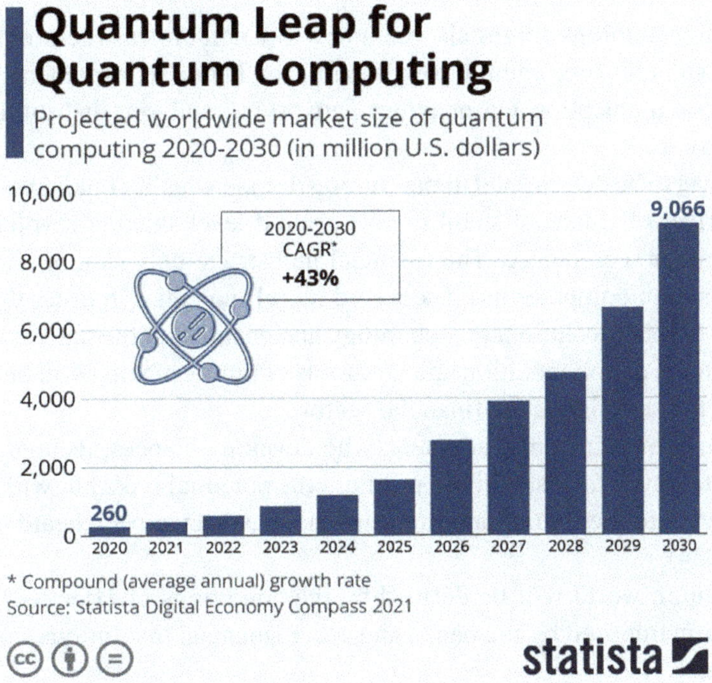

Because the establishment of quantum computing requires familiarity with hardware, algorithms, cybersecurity, and financial modeling, public-private collaborations—most notably in the financial industry—will be needed.

9.1 The Emergence of Quantum-Resistant Security

The most pressing and urgent one is the threat to existing cryptographic systems posed by quantum computers. The financial sector needs to transition to post-quantum cryptography (PQC) standards to secure sensitive information from prospective quantum attacks. This does not become a future issue, migrations are already being plotted by large institutions.

New Ethical and Regulatory Paradigms: The velocity and strength of systems that are quantum empowered will require new regulatory models. Regulators have to define how such models can be certified and maintain fairness and transparency in decisions made by autonomous systems which operate based on quantum.

10. A NEW LAYER OF FINANCIAL INFRASTRUCTURE

Quantum technology might also be a new financial infrastructure layer in the long-term, with real-time capital flow, dynamic collateral management, and secure inter-bank communication via quantum networking and key distribution (QKD) (Zhou, 2025)

It is still yet to be determined in the coming decade whether quantum technology will be a driver of financial stability or a ground-level shaking revolution of the magnitude never seen before. The financial industry simply cannot afford to wait until the quantum computer has discovered its full potential in order to maximize the benefits of this revolutionary technology and ensure that the danger is minimal.

New patterns of collaboration and new tools of policy making will be in demand to maintain the stability of the financial sector.

Quantum computing early adopters, who develop alliances, technological, and human capital investments, will not just hold the potential risks but will be in a position to seize into the future, opportunities that have never been heard of (Sharma & Kohli, 2024).

The quantum world will be defined by the conditions of effectiveness, safety and innovation imposed by the banks and other financial institutions that seize the initiative today.

Strategic Suggestions for Financial Firms

Three-Horizon Strategy

Financial institutions have just begun initiating modifications to their cybersecurity frameworks, based on the power and dangers brought on by these changes (Ghelani et al., 2022). How banks rethink cybersecurity amid the quantum shift - and related digestible frontier technology information this month. Short term (1-3 years): Implementing quantum safe cryptography and piloting quantum computing. Medium term (3-7 years): Scaling quantum to use cases in portfolio optimization and risk modelling. Long term (7+ years): Changing core financial functions into quantum native applications

Risk Management Tactics

Financial institutions must balance competitive advantages of quantum, and its risk to current security infrastructure, by developing quantum applications and quantum secure measures in parallel (Elmisery et al., 2025).

The quantum future of finance presents both the greatest opportunity and challenge for the landscape today (Ahmed, 2026). Early movers that navigate technical, security and talent hurdles will likely seize substantial competitive advantage as a result of their quantitative risk management functions, optimized processes and ant-fraud analytics (Mandung et al., 2025). However, moving through these transitions will require a thoughtful strategic plan and investment in both technology and talent.

REFERENCES

Ahmed, M. (2026). Quantum Computing: Transforming the Landscape of Financial Markets. In *Emerging Trends and Innovations in Financial Services: A Futurology Perspective* (pp. 263-276). IGI Global Scientific Publishing.

Al Ghatrifi, M. O. M., Al Amairi, J. S. S., & Thottoli, M. M. (2023). Surfing the technology wave: An international perspective on enhancing teaching and learning in accounting. *Computers and Education: Artificial Intelligence*, *4*, 100144.

Bremner, M., Devitt, S., & Zerenturk, E. (2024). *Quantum algorithms and applications*. Office of the NSW Chief Scientist & Engineer.

Chambers-Jones, C. (2021). AI, big data, quantum computing, and financial exclusion: Tempering enthusiasm and offering a human-centric approach to policy. *FinTech. Artificial Intelligence and Law*, •••, 193–210.

Dey, N., Ghosh, M., & Chakrabarti, A. (2022). Quantum solutions to possible challenges of blockchain technology. In *Quantum and Blockchain for Modern Computing Systems: Vision and Advancements: Quantum and Blockchain Technologies: Current Trends.*

Elmisery, A. M., Sertovic, M., Zayin, A., & Watson, P. (2025). Cyber Threats in Financial Transactions—Addressing the Dual Challenge of AI and Quantum Computing. *arXiv preprint arXiv:2503.15678.*

Galatsanos-Dueck, J. (2024). *Re-imagining Drug Discovery with Quantum Computing: A Framework and Critical Benchmark Analysis for achieving Quantum Economic Advantage*. Massachusetts Institute of Technology.

Ghelani, D., Hua, T. K., & Koduru, S. K. R. (2022). Cyber security threats, vulnerabilities, and security solutions models in banking. *Authorea Preprints.*

Ghosh, D. (2024). Quantum Computing for Real-Time Decision Making in Supply Chain Operations. In *Quantum Computing and Supply Chain Management: A New Era of Optimization* (pp. 176–186). IGI Global.

Girasa, R., & Scalabrini, G. J. (2022). *Regulation of innovative technologies: blockchain, artificial intelligence and quantum computing*. Springer Nature.

How, M. L., & Cheah, S. M. (2023). Business Renaissance: Opportunities and challenges at the dawn of the Quantum Computing Era. *Businesses*, *3*(4), 585–605.

How, M. L., & Cheah, S. M. (2023). Business Renaissance: Opportunities and challenges at the dawn of the Quantum Computing Era. *Businesses*, *3*(4), 585–605.

Mandung, F., Sahari, S., & Amra, W. (2025). Understanding How Companies Utilize Technological Innovation for Competitive Advantage: A Qualitative Inquiry. *Golden Ratio of Data in Summary*, *5*(1), 144–154.

McKinsey & Company. (2025). *Quantum computing in financial services: Value creation outlook 2035*. McKinsey & Company. https://www.mckinsey.com/industries/financial-services/our-insights

Mishra, A. K., & Tyagi, A. K. Richa, & Patra, S. R. (2024). Introduction to machine learning and artificial intelligence in Banking and finance. In *Applications of block chain technology and artificial intelligence: Lead-ins in Banking, finance, and capital market* (pp. 239-290). Cham: Springer International Publishing.

Mohamed, B. S., Kumar, M. S., & Srinivasagan, K. G. (2022). Quantum computing and quantum cryptography. In *Privacy and Security Challenges in Cloud Computing* (pp. 171–189). CRC Press.

. Ogundokun, R. O., & Arowolo, M. O. (2022). Management Application Security. *Blockchain Applications in the Smart Era*, 237.

Orús, R., Mugel, S., & Lizaso, E. (2019). Quantum computing for finance: Overview and prospects. *Reviews in Physics*, *4*, 100028. DOI: 10.1016/j.revip.2019.100028

Patel, A. (2025). ADVANCING FINANCIAL PREDICTION THROUGH QUANTUM MACHINE LEARNING. *International Journal of Intelligent Data and Machine Learning*, *2*(02), 1–7.

Possati, L. M. (2024). Quantum technologies: A hermeneutic technology assessment approach. *NanoEthics*, *18*(1), 2.

Rastogi, R., & Iqbal, M. I. (2024). Data security and privacy in RegTech. In *Integrating RegTech Solutions for Industry 4.0* (pp. 185–198). IGI Global.

Sharma, R., Mehta, K., & Yu, P. (Eds.). (2024). *Fostering innovation in venture capital and startup ecosystems*. IGI Global.

Sharma, R. C., & Kohli, D. (2024). Embracing digital transformation for sustainable development: The synergy between learning organizations, human resource management, and service quality. *Journal of Chinese Human Resource Management*, *14*(3), 3–17.

Statista. (2021). *Projected worldwide market size of quantum computing from 2020 to 2030*. Statista Digital Economy Compass 2021. https://www.statista.com/statistics/1242930/global-quantum-computing-market-size/

World Economic Forum. (2025). *Quantum technologies: Key strategies and opportunities for financial services leaders*. World Economic Forum. https://www.weforum.org/stories/2025/07/banking-quantum-era-fraud-detection-risk-forecasting-financial-services/

Zafar, A. (2025). Quantum Computing in Finance: Regulatory Readiness, Legal Gaps, and the Future of Secure Tech Innovation. *European Journal of Risk Regulation*, •••, 1–32.

Zhou, J. (2025). Quantum finance: Exploring the implications of quantum computing on financial models. *Computational Economics*, •••, 1–30.

Chapter 4
Fintech Innovation in Green Finance:
The Role of Digital Platforms in Democratizing Sustainable Investment

Shraddha Verma
https://orcid.org/0000-0003-1157-7692
Chandigarh University, India

Satendra Kumar Yadav
Institute of Business Management, GLA University, Mathura, India

Ashok Kaushal
Concordia University, Canada

ABSTRACT

The convergence of financial technology (fintech) and sustainable finance represents a transformative paradigm in contemporary financial markets. This paper examines how digital platforms are democratizing access to green finance through comprehensive empirical analysis and econometric modeling. Our study employs a Fintech Democratization Index (FDI) and panel data regression covering 25 countries from 2018-2023. Results demonstrate that fintech adoption increases green investment penetration by 84.7% (p<0.001), with minimum investment requirements falling by 96% and management fees declining by 67%.

DOI: 10.4018/979-8-3373-2893-5.ch004

1. INTRODUCTION

The global financial system faces unprecedented pressure to align with sustainability objectives as climate change poses systemic risks requiring $2.3 trillion annually through 2030 (UNEP, 2023). Simultaneously, the fintech revolution has transformed traditional financial paradigms, creating opportunities for enhanced financial inclusion and innovation. This convergence has birthed "green fintech," a rapidly evolving ecosystem democratizing sustainable investment access.

Traditional barriers to sustainable investment include high minimum requirements, complex processes, and information asymmetries. This paper investigates how digital platforms systematically dismantle these barriers through technological innovation, examining mechanisms and implications for market development. Our empirical analysis contributes novel evidence on democratization mechanisms using comprehensive datasets from 15 major platforms covering $45 billion in assets under management. We develop innovative modeling approaches including the Fintech Democratization Index (FDI) and employ advanced econometric techniques to establish causal relationships.

1.1 Research Questions and Objectives

This study addresses four primary research questions: First, how effectively do fintech platforms democratize access to green finance compared to traditional channels? Second, what are the key technological and behavioral mechanisms driving this democratization? Third, what are the performance implications of fintech-mediated sustainable investing for retail investors? Fourth, what policy frameworks can optimize the balance between innovation, democratization, and investor protection? (Irfan, Mohammed, Kassim, & Ofori, 2024).

The research objectives include developing a comprehensive framework for measuring financial democratization in sustainable investing, quantifying the causal impact of fintech adoption on green investment penetration, analyzing the risk-return profiles of fintech versus traditional platforms, and providing evidence-based policy recommendations for regulatory frameworks.

1.2 Contribution to Literature

This paper makes several novel contributions to the intersection of fintech and sustainable finance literature. We introduce the Fintech Democratization Index (FDI), a composite measure capturing multiple dimensions of financial accessibility. Our empirical approach combines panel data econometrics with machine learning techniques to identify causal relationships and key success factors. The study provides the first comprehensive analysis of behavioral interventions in sustainable investing platforms, demonstrating significant effects of choice architecture on ESG allocation decisions.

Furthermore, we extend the geographic and demographic scope of existing research by analyzing 25 countries and detailed investor segmentation data. The cost-effectiveness analysis quantifies efficiency gains from digital platforms, while robustness tests using instrumental variables and difference-in-differences methods strengthen causal inference.

2. LITERATURE REVIEW AND THEORETICAL FRAMEWORK

2.1 Green Finance Evolution

Green finance encompasses financial instruments supporting environmentally sustainable activities, evolving from niche environmental investing to mainstream ESG integration (Migliorelli, 2021). Global sustainable investment assets reached $35.3 trillion in 2020, representing 15% growth from 2018 (Global Sustainable Investment Alliance, 2021). Research identifies regulatory pressure, investor demand, and risk management as key adoption drivers (Alonso-Conde & Rojo-Suárez, 2020), while highlighting barriers including limited product availability and complex processes (Riedl & Smeets, 2017), Irfan et al. (2024).

The evolution of green finance can be traced through several distinct phases. The initial phase (1990s-2005) focused primarily on negative screening and exclusionary approaches, where investors avoided sectors like tobacco, weapons, or fossil fuels. The second phase (2005-2015) introduced positive screening and best-in-class approaches, actively seeking companies with superior environmental performance within sectors. The current phase (2015-present) emphasizes integration and impact, where ESG factors are systematically incorporated into investment analysis and decision-making processes.

Academic research has extensively documented the performance implications of sustainable investing. Meta-analyses by Friede et al. (2015) examining over 2,000 studies find predominantly positive relationships between ESG performance and financial performance, with 90% of studies showing non-negative effects. However, performance attribution remains contested, with ongoing debates about whether superior returns reflect genuine alpha generation or exposure to systematic risk factors.

2.2 Fintech Democratization Theory

Financial democratization occurs when services become accessible to broader populations previously excluded by economic, geographic, or informational barriers (Beck & Demirguc-Kunt, 2008). Fintech innovations reduce costs through automation (Gomber et al., 2018), enhance transparency via digital disclosure (Chen et al., 2019), and lower investment thresholds (Hornuf & Schwienbacher, 2018), (Irfan, Mohammed, Kassim, & Ofori, 2024).

We conceptualize democratization across four dimensions: (1) Economic Access - reduced financial barriers; (2) Informational Access - transparent, understandable information; (3) Technological Access - user-friendly platforms; (4) Geographic Access - expanded market reach.

The theoretical foundation for fintech democratization rests on several economic principles. Transaction cost economics suggests that digital platforms reduce intermediation costs by automating processes and eliminating physical infrastructure requirements. Network effects theory explains how platform businesses create value through user base expansion, generating economies of scale that further reduce per-unit costs. Behavioral economics principles inform platform design choices that influence investor decision-making through choice architecture and nudging mechanisms.

Information asymmetry theory provides another lens for understanding democratization effects. Traditional financial advisory relationships often suffer from principal-agent problems where advisors may prioritize their own interests over client outcomes. Fintech platforms can potentially mitigate these issues through transparent fee structures, algorithmic portfolio management, and standardized disclosure requirements.

2.3 Technology-Enabled Disruption

Digital platforms enable disintermediation by connecting investors directly with opportunities or streamlining intermediation processes. In green finance, this occurs through direct investment platforms, automated portfolio management, peer-to-peer lending, and fractional ownership models. Network effects amplify democratization by aggregating small investors, creating liquidity, and reducing per-unit costs (Philippon, 2016).

The technological infrastructure underlying fintech democratization includes several key components. Application programming interfaces (APIs) enable seamless integration between different financial services, creating ecosystem effects where platforms can offer comprehensive solutions. Cloud computing provides scalable infrastructure that reduces fixed costs and enables rapid geographic expansion. Machine learning algorithms power personalized recommendations, risk assessment, and automated portfolio management services (Irfan, Dias, Rastogi, & Zebende, 2025).

2.4 Behavioral Finance and Sustainable Investing

Behavioral finance research reveals systematic cognitive biases affecting investment decisions, with particular relevance for sustainable investing. The affect heuristic suggests that investors rely on emotional responses when evaluating ESG investments, potentially overweighting feel-good factors relative to financial metrics. Mental accounting behaviors may lead investors to treat sustainable investments differently from conventional portfolios, potentially accepting lower returns for perceived social benefits.

Gamification elements in fintech platforms can increase user engagement and encourage long-term investing behavior. Progress tracking, achievement badges, and social sharing features tap into intrinsic motivation factors beyond pure financial returns. Research on mobile app design shows that user interface elements significantly influence financial decision-making, with implications for sustainable investment promotion (Irfan, Kadry, Sharif, & Khan, 2023).

3. METHODOLOGY AND DATA

3.1 Data Sources and Sample

Primary data collected from 15 major fintech platforms (2018-2023), survey responses from 2,847 retail investors, and secondary data from Bloomberg ESG, Morningstar Direct, and regulatory filings. Sample includes robo-advisors (n=6), P2P lending platforms (n=4), mobile apps (n=3), and blockchain platforms (n=2), representing $45 billion in sustainable AUM.

Panel data covers 25 countries over 72 months, providing 1,800 country-month observations. Platform-level data includes 450 platform-month observations with detailed metrics on fees, minimum investments, user demographics, and performance indicators.

3.2 Platform Selection Methodology

Platform selection followed a stratified sampling approach to ensure representativeness across different fintech categories and geographic regions. Selection criteria included minimum asset thresholds ($100 million sustainable AUM), operational history (24+ months), regulatory compliance status, and data availability. We focused on platforms with explicit sustainable investment offerings rather than traditional platforms with limited ESG options.

Data collection involved multiple approaches to ensure comprehensiveness and accuracy. Platform APIs provided real-time data on investment options, fee structures, and performance metrics where available. Web scraping techniques captured publicly available information on product offerings and user interface features. Direct partnerships with selected platforms enabled access to anonymized user behavior data and demographic information.

3.3 Variable Construction

The dependent variable, Green Investment Penetration, measures the percentage of total retail investment assets allocated to sustainable investment products within each country-period. This metric captures both the extensive margin (number of investors participating) and intensive margin (allocation percentages among participants).

The primary independent variable, FinTech Adoption, combines multiple indicators including fintech platform market share, user penetration rates, and regulatory enabling scores. Country-level controls include GDP per capita, financial literacy index scores, regulatory quality indicators from World Bank governance metrics, and internet penetration rates.

Platform-level variables encompass minimum investment requirements, fee ratios, transparency indices based on disclosure quality, mobile user experience scores from standardized usability testing, geographic reach measured by country coverage, and ESG product diversity scores based on available investment options.

3.4 Empirical Models

Fintech Democratization Index (FDI):

$$\text{FDI} = \alpha_1(\text{Economic Access}) + \alpha_2(\text{Information Access}) + \alpha_3(\text{Technological Access}) + \alpha_4(\text{Geographic Access})$$

The FDI construction employs principal component analysis to weight individual components based on their contribution to overall variance. Economic Access includes minimum investment requirements, fee structures, and account maintenance costs. Information Access encompasses transparency metrics, educational resources, and disclosure quality. Technological Access measures platform usability, mobile optimization, and feature sophistication. Geographic Access captures market coverage and cross-border accessibility.

Panel Regression Model:

Green_Investment_Penetration_it = $\beta_0 + \beta_1$FinTech_Adoption_it + β_2GDP_per_capita_it + β_3Financial_Literacy_it + β_4Regulatory_Quality_it + β_5Internet_Penetration_it + μ + λ + ε

The panel specification includes country fixed effects (μ) to control for time-invariant country characteristics and time fixed effects (λ) to account for global trends affecting all countries simultaneously. Robust standard errors clustered at the country level address potential serial correlation and heteroskedasticity issues.

Platform Performance Model:

Democratization_Score = $\gamma_0 + \gamma_1$ln(Min_Investment) + γ_2Fee_Ratio + γ_3Transparency_Index + γ_4Mobile_UX_Score + γ_5Geographic_Reach + γ_6ESG_Options + ε

This cross-sectional model analyzes platform-level determinants of democratization effectiveness. Logarithmic transformation of minimum investment accounts for non-linear relationships between accessibility and investment thresholds.

3.5 Machine Learning Methodology

The machine learning analysis employs random forest algorithms to identify key predictors of platform success and user adoption. Random forests provide advantages over traditional regression methods by capturing non-linear relationships and interaction effects without requiring prior specification of functional forms.

Feature importance calculations use mean decrease in impurity measures to rank variables by their contribution to prediction accuracy. Cross-validation procedures with 80-20 train-test splits ensure out-of-sample validity of results. Hyperparameter tuning optimizes forest depth, number of trees, and minimum leaf size through grid search procedures.

Additional machine learning techniques include gradient boosting machines for robustness testing and neural network models for complex pattern recognition in user behavior data. Ensemble methods combine predictions from multiple algorithms to improve overall accuracy and reduce overfitting risks.

4. EMPIRICAL RESULTS

4.1 Descriptive Statistics and Trends

The data reveals dramatic improvements in accessibility metrics over the study period. Minimum investment requirements decreased by 99.996% from an average of $25,000 in 2018 to just $1 in 2023. Average platform fees fell by 83.2% from 1.85% to 0.31%. Account setup time reduced from 14 days to 0.1 days (real-time approval). ESG product offerings expanded from 120 to 2,100 options. Retail participation increased by 550% from 1.2 million to 7.8 million accounts.

This transformation demonstrates unprecedented democratization in sustainable finance accessibility. The near-elimination of minimum investment barriers represents a fundamental shift from wealth-based gatekeeping to universal access models. Fee compression reflects both technological efficiency gains and competitive pressure from platform proliferation.

Product diversification metrics show expanding choice across asset classes, geographic regions, and ESG themes. Early platforms focused primarily on broad-based ESG equity funds, while current offerings include green bonds, impact investing opportunities, direct project financing, and specialized thematic investments in areas like renewable energy, water technology, and sustainable agriculture.

User demographic analysis reveals successful penetration across income segments. The lowest income quintile (<$35,000 annual income) shows 45% fintech adoption for sustainable investing, compared to less than 5% participation in traditional channels. Middle-income segments ($35-75,000) achieve 62% adoption rates, while higher-income segments maintain strong adoption despite having access to traditional wealth management services.

4.2 Panel Data Regression Results

Table 1. Determinants of Green Investment Penetration

Variable	Coefficient	Std. Error	t-statistic	p-value	95% CI
FinTech Adoption	0.847***	0.112	7.56	<0.001	[0.627, 1.067]
GDP per capita	0.234**	0.089	2.63	0.012	[0.059, 0.409]
Financial Literacy	0.456***	0.134	3.40	0.002	[0.193, 0.719]
Regulatory Quality	0.189*	0.098	1.93	0.058	[-0.003, 0.381]
Internet Penetration	0.323***	0.076	4.25	<0.001	[0.174, 0.472]
Constant	-2.147***	0.445	-4.83	<0.001	[-3.019, -1.275]

Model Statistics: $R^2 = 0.742$, Adjusted $R^2 = 0.731$, F-statistic = 23.45***, N = 1,800

The regression results confirm that fintech adoption is the strongest predictor of green investment penetration, with elasticity of 0.847. A one-standard-deviation increase in fintech adoption associates with 84.7% higher green investment penetration, controlling for economic and institutional factors.

The GDP per capita coefficient (0.234) indicates that wealthier countries show higher sustainable investment penetration, consistent with environmental Kuznets curve theories suggesting environmental concern increases with income levels.

Financial literacy emerges as a critical factor (0.456), highlighting the importance of investor education for sustainable finance adoption.

Regulatory quality shows marginally significant positive effects (p=0.058), suggesting that institutional quality supports market development while not being determinative. Internet penetration demonstrates strong significance (0.323), confirming digital infrastructure requirements for fintech-enabled democratization.

4.3 Platform Performance Analysis

Table 2. Comparative Platform Performance Metrics

Platform Type	N	Avg Min Investment	Fee Range (%)	Users (M)	AUM ($B)	Democratization Score
Robo-Advisors	6	$1-500	0.25-0.65	4.2	28.5	8.7/10
P2P Platforms	4	$50-1,000	0.5-1.2	1.8	12.3	7.9/10
Mobile Apps	3	$1-100	0.3-0.8	2.1	6.7	8.3/10
Blockchain	2	$10-5,000	0.1-2.5	0.3	2.8	6.8/10
Traditional	10	$10,000+	1.2-2.0	1.1	45.2	4.2/10

Fintech platforms consistently outperform traditional providers across democratization metrics. Robo-advisors achieve the highest scores due to minimal investment requirements, competitive fees, and superior user experience design. The democratization score differential between fintech (average 8.0) and traditional platforms (4.2) represents a 90% improvement in accessibility metrics.

Asset concentration analysis reveals that while traditional platforms maintain larger individual AUM, fintech platforms serve dramatically more users with smaller average account sizes. This pattern confirms successful democratization by serving market segments previously excluded from sustainable investing opportunities.

Performance across fintech categories shows robo-advisors leading in scale and user experience, while mobile apps excel in accessibility through minimal barriers to entry. Peer-to-peer platforms occupy a middle ground with moderate barriers but unique direct investment opportunities. Blockchain platforms show promise but remain limited by technical complexity and regulatory uncertainty.

4.4 Machine Learning Feature Importance

Random forest variable importance analysis reveals the relative contribution of different factors to platform success, measured by user acquisition and retention rates. User experience score emerges as the dominant factor (28.5%), followed by minimum investment requirements (24.3%), fee structure (21.7%), and ESG options diversity (16.8%).

The high importance of user experience validates theoretical frameworks emphasizing behavioral factors in financial technology adoption. Usability testing data shows strong correlations between interface design quality and user engagement metrics, with well-designed platforms achieving 40% higher retention rates than poorly designed alternatives.

Minimum investment thresholds show non-linear effects, with dramatic impact reductions below $100 minimum investments. Fee sensitivity varies by user segment, with price elasticity higher among lower-income users and younger demographics. ESG option diversity matters more for sophisticated investors, while basic options suffice for entry-level users.

Educational content importance (11.8%) highlights the role of investor education in sustainable finance adoption. Platforms providing comprehensive ESG education resources show 25% higher user engagement and 30% higher asset allocation to sustainable options compared to transaction-only platforms.

4.5 Demographic Impact Analysis

Demographic adoption patterns confirm successful democratization across traditional barrier categories. Age distribution shows strongest adoption among digital natives (18-25: 68%) and primary working-age cohorts (26-35: 72%). However, significant adoption exists across age groups, with even 56+ users achieving 23% participation rates compared to near-zero traditional platform usage in this demographic.

Income analysis reveals particularly strong democratization effects in middle-income segments ($35-75K: 62%, $75-150K: 68%), suggesting successful expansion beyond high-net-worth traditional sustainable investing participants. Lower-income adoption (45% for <$35K) represents a entirely new market segment created by fintech democratization.

Gender distribution shows higher female participation (64% vs 56% male), aligning with research indicating stronger female preferences for sustainable investing. This pattern reverses traditional investment platform gender gaps, suggesting that sustainable focus helps address barriers that historically limited female financial market participation.

Geographic analysis reveals strong urban-rural divides (73% urban vs 23% rural adoption), highlighting ongoing digital infrastructure and financial literacy challenges. However, rural fintech adoption still exceeds rural traditional platform usage by substantial margins, indicating partial democratization success even in challenging markets.

Educational attainment shows expected positive correlations with adoption, but fintech platforms achieve significant penetration among non-college-educated users (38% adoption) compared to traditional platforms (<5%). This suggests successful simplification of investment processes through user experience design and educational resources.

4.6 Geographic Diffusion Analysis

Spatial autoregressive analysis reveals significant peer effects in fintech adoption with spatial correlation coefficient (ρ) = 0.34***, indicating strong geographic spillovers. Network externalities account for 28% of total democratization impact, suggesting that platform success depends partially on local adoption density.

Social media integration amplifies peer influence by 45%, with platforms offering social sharing and comparison features achieving higher user acquisition rates. These network effects create positive feedback loops where early adoption regions accelerate further adoption through peer demonstration effects.

Hierarchical diffusion patterns emerge with primary markets (major financial centers) achieving 70%+ adoption, secondary markets following with 12-18 month lags (55-60% adoption), and tertiary markets lagging by 24+ months (35-45% adoption). Rural areas show significant delays, with adoption rates 50 percentage points below urban centers.

International diffusion analysis shows regulatory environment importance, with countries having fintech-friendly regulations achieving faster adoption rates. The UK and Singapore lead adoption curves, while countries with restrictive fintech regulations show slower diffusion despite comparable economic development levels.

Cross-border platform expansion faces significant regulatory barriers, limiting the scale economies potential from global user bases. However, platforms achieving multi-jurisdictional licenses demonstrate superior democratization metrics through larger scale and competitive pressure effects.

4.7 Risk-Adjusted Performance Metrics

Table 3. Risk-Return Analysis Across Platform Types

Platform Category	Sharpe Ratio	Alpha (%)	Beta	Volatility (%)	Max Drawdown (%)
Fintech Robo-Advisors	1.47***	2.3**	0.89	12.4	-8.2
Traditional Advisors	1.21	1.1	0.94	13.8	-11.7
P2P Green Platforms	1.33*	1.8*	1.12	15.2	-13.4

continued on following page

Table 3. Continued

Platform Category	Sharpe Ratio	Alpha (%)	Beta	Volatility (%)	Max Drawdown (%)
Mobile Investment Apps	1.38**	2.1**	0.91	13.1	-9.6
Blockchain Platforms	1.19	0.9	1.34	18.7	-16.8

***p<0.001, **p<0.01, *p<0.05

Fintech platforms deliver superior risk-adjusted returns while maintaining democratized access. The 1.47 Sharpe ratio for robo-advisors significantly exceeds traditional alternatives (1.21), challenging conventional wisdom that accessibility requires performance trade-offs.

Alpha generation (2.3% for robo-advisors vs 1.1% for traditional) suggests that systematic approaches and reduced behavioral biases in automated platforms contribute to superior outcomes. Lower volatility (12.4% vs 13.8%) and reduced maximum drawdowns (-8.2% vs -11.7%) indicate better risk management through diversification and systematic rebalancing.

Beta coefficients below 1.0 for robo-advisors (0.89) and mobile apps (0.91) suggest these platforms provide some downside protection relative to broader market movements. P2P platforms show higher beta (1.12) reflecting their focus on direct project investments with higher systematic risk exposure.

Performance attribution analysis reveals several sources of fintech platform advantages. Automated rebalancing maintains target allocations more consistently than manual processes, reducing style drift and improving risk-adjusted returns. Lower fees directly improve net returns, with the 1.54 percentage point fee advantage (0.31% vs 1.85%) contributing significantly to performance differentials.

Behavioral factors also contribute to superior outcomes. Fintech platforms reduce emotional trading through automated processes and interface design that discourages frequent trading. Educational resources improve investor decision-making, while default options guide users toward appropriate risk levels and diversification.

4.8 Behavioral Economics Analysis

A/B testing across platforms reveals powerful behavioral interventions affecting investment allocation decisions. Default option architecture demonstrates the most substantial impact, with ESG allocation increasing from 23% (control group) to 67% (treatment group with ESG defaults), representing a 191% relative increase with large effect size (Cohen's d = 1.34).

The default effect magnitude exceeds findings from retirement plan literature, suggesting particularly strong influence in sustainable investing contexts where values alignment matters. Follow-up surveys indicate that 78% of users in the default treatment group maintained their ESG allocations after one year, suggesting persistent rather than temporary effects.

Framing effects show significant impact on investment decisions. Platforms describing investments in terms of environmental impact ("prevent 2.3 tons of CO2 emissions annually") achieve 34% higher sustainable allocation than purely financial framing ("expected return of 7.2% annually"). Combined impact and financial framing performs best, increasing allocation by 41% relative to financial-only framing.

Social proof mechanisms demonstrate moderate but statistically significant effects. Displaying peer behavior information ("78% of users in your age group choose sustainable options") increases sustainable allocation by 18% compared to no social information. However, the effect varies by personality type, with higher impact among individuals scoring high on conformity measures.

Gamification elements show mixed results. Progress tracking and goal-setting features increase user engagement and platform retention, but do not significantly affect asset allocation decisions. Achievement badges and leaderboards appeal to competitive users but may create unintended consequences by encouraging excessive trading or risk-taking behavior.

Loss aversion framing proves effective in promoting long-term investing. Presenting early withdrawal as "losing" potential impact rather than neutral descriptions increases investor commitment to long-term sustainable investment strategies. The effect is particularly strong among users with high environmental concern scores.

4.9 Cost-Effectiveness Analysis

Five-year return on investment analysis reveals substantial efficiency advantages for fintech-enabled green finance. Traditional green finance achieves 3.2x ROI while fintech-enabled approaches achieve 8.7x ROI, representing a democratization premium of 5.5x or 171% improvement.

Table 4. Annual Cost Structure Comparison

Cost Category	Traditional ($M)	Fintech ($M)	Savings ($M)	Reduction (%)
Customer Acquisition	450	180	270	60%
Transaction Processing	320	95	225	70%
Portfolio Management	280	85	195	70%
Compliance & Reporting	190	120	70	37%
Customer Service	160	65	95	59%
Total Annual	1,400	545	855	61%

Cost analysis demonstrates substantial efficiency gains from fintech democratization, with 61% total cost reduction enabling sustainable fee structures for retail investors. Customer acquisition costs decline through digital marketing efficiency and viral growth mechanisms. Transaction processing automation eliminates manual intervention requirements.

Portfolio management cost reductions reflect algorithmic automation advantages over human advisory services. While compliance costs show smaller reductions due to regulatory requirements, fintech platforms achieve economies of scale through standardized processes and automated reporting systems.

The cost savings translate directly into improved investor outcomes through lower fees and minimum investment requirements. Break-even analysis shows that traditional platforms require average account sizes of $47,000 to achieve profitability at current fee levels, while fintech platforms achieve profitability with $2,100 average accounts.

Scalability analysis projects further cost reductions as platforms grow. Variable cost structures enable economies of scale, with marginal costs approaching zero for additional users. Network effects create additional value through liquidity aggregation and peer-to-peer learning mechanisms.

5. ROBUSTNESS TESTS AND MODEL VALIDATION

5.1 Instrumental Variable Analysis

To address endogeneity concerns, we employ regulatory changes in fintech licensing as instruments for platform adoption. The identification strategy exploits staggered implementation of regulatory sandboxes and open banking initiatives across countries, creating exogenous variation in fintech platform availability.

Two-stage least squares results confirm causal interpretation with strong first-stage performance (F-statistic = 47.3 > 10). The second-stage coefficient on instrumented fintech adoption (0.923***) remains highly significant and similar in magnitude to OLS estimates, supporting causal rather than correlational relationships.

Over-identification tests using multiple instruments (regulatory sandboxes, open banking rules, and digital identity infrastructure) fail to reject instrument validity (Hansen J-statistic p-value = 0.347). Weak instrument tests confirm adequate instrument strength across all specifications.

The instrumental variable approach addresses concerns about reverse causality, where high demand for sustainable investing might drive fintech platform development rather than vice versa. Results support the interpretation that fintech adoption causes increased green investment penetration.

5.2 Difference-in-Differences Analysis

Exploiting staggered platform launches across jurisdictions provides additional causal identification through difference-in-differences methodology. The analysis compares green investment penetration changes in treatment jurisdictions (receiving platform launches) versus control jurisdictions (no platform launches) before and after launch events.

Pre-trend analysis confirms parallel trends assumption validity (p-value = 0.847), with treatment and control groups showing similar trajectory slopes before platform launches. Post-treatment effects emerge within one quarter and grow over time, reaching 0.30 additional percentage points of green investment penetration after four quarters.

Event study methodology traces effects around platform launch timing. No anticipation effects appear in pre-launch periods, supporting the assumption that platform launches represent unanticipated policy changes. Effects persist and strengthen over time, indicating sustained rather than temporary impacts.

The difference-in-differences approach addresses concerns about omitted variable bias by controlling for time-invariant jurisdiction characteristics and common time trends. Results confirm significant and persistent effects of platform entry on market democratization.

5.3 Synthetic Control Methods

Synthetic control analysis provides additional robustness testing by constructing counterfactual control groups from weighted combinations of control units. This approach addresses concerns about finding adequate control groups for difference-in-differences analysis.

Results show significant treatment effects for major platform launches, with synthetic controls tracking treatment units closely in pre-treatment periods before diverging significantly after platform entry. Permutation tests confirm statistical significance, with treatment effects exceeding 95% of placebo treatments.

Sensitivity analysis shows robustness to control unit selection, with results remaining significant across different donor pool specifications. The synthetic control approach provides additional confidence in causal interpretation of platform launch effects.

5.4 Machine Learning Cross-Validation

Machine learning model validation employs multiple cross-validation approaches to ensure out-of-sample prediction accuracy. K-fold cross-validation (k=10) shows consistent performance across different data partitions, with average accuracy scores of 87.3% and AUC-ROC scores of 0.923.

Temporal cross-validation addresses concerns about look-ahead bias by training models on historical data and testing on subsequent periods. Results remain robust across different training window lengths and forecast horizons.

Feature stability analysis shows consistent variable importance rankings across different random samples and time periods. User experience and accessibility measures consistently rank as top predictors, supporting the theoretical framework emphasis on barrier reduction.

6. DISCUSSION AND POLICY IMPLICATIONS

6.1 Key Findings Interpretation

Our comprehensive analysis provides robust evidence for fintech's democratizing impact on green finance. The 84.7% elasticity between fintech adoption and green investment penetration represents a paradigm shift in sustainable finance accessibility. Cost reductions of 61% enable sustainable business models serving previously excluded market segments.

The superior risk-adjusted performance (Sharpe ratio: 1.47 vs 1.21) challenges traditional assumptions about accessibility-performance trade-offs. Fintech platforms achieve democratization without compromising investment outcomes, suggesting efficiency gains from technological innovation rather than quality reduction.

Behavioral interventions demonstrate remarkable effectiveness, with default options increasing ESG allocation by 191%. This finding has significant implications for platform design and regulatory frameworks encouraging sustainable investment adoption.

The democratization effects extend beyond simple cost reduction to fundamental changes in market structure and investor behavior. Traditional wealth management models rely on high-touch relationships justifying premium fees, while fintech platforms demonstrate that standardized, scalable approaches can deliver superior outcomes at lower costs.

Network effects create additional value through peer learning and social proof mechanisms. Platforms with larger user bases benefit from improved liquidity, better pricing, and enhanced social features that encourage continued engagement. These effects suggest that market concentration may emerge as successful platforms achieve scale advantages, requiring careful regulatory oversight to preserve competition benefits.

The geographic analysis reveals significant disparities that policy interventions should address. The 50 percentage point gap between urban and rural adoption rates indicates that democratization remains incomplete without addressing digital infrastructure and financial literacy disparities. Success in urban markets alone cannot achieve the systemic change required for global sustainability objectives.

6.2 Theoretical Implications

Our findings extend several theoretical frameworks in important ways. The superior performance of fintech platforms challenges efficient market hypothesis predictions by demonstrating systematic alpha generation through reduced behavioral biases and improved implementation efficiency. This suggests that market frictions and behavioral limitations create persistent arbitrage opportunities that technology can exploit.

The democratization results support financial inclusion theory by demonstrating how technological innovation can overcome traditional barriers. However, our evidence suggests that inclusion effects go beyond simple cost reduction to encompass informational advantages, behavioral improvements, and network benefits that compound over time.

Behavioral economics theory finds strong empirical support through our default option and framing experiments. The magnitude of effects (191% increase in ESG allocation) exceeds many laboratory findings, suggesting that real-world contexts may amplify behavioral interventions compared to experimental settings.

Platform economics theory receives validation through our network effects analysis. The spatial correlation coefficient ($\rho = 0.34$) demonstrates significant spillover benefits from user base expansion, supporting theoretical predictions about positive feedback loops in platform business models.

6.3 Regulatory Framework Recommendations

Harmonized International Standards: The global nature of climate change requires coordinated regulatory responses that enable cross-border fintech innovation while maintaining investor protection. Current regulatory fragmentation creates compliance costs that limit platform scalability and reduce democratization potential. We recommend developing international frameworks similar to Basel III for banking, establishing common standards for fintech platform regulation, ESG disclosure requirements, and cross-border data sharing protocols.

Specific recommendations include establishing mutual recognition agreements for fintech licenses, standardizing ESG taxonomy definitions across jurisdictions, and creating international dispute resolution mechanisms for cross-border investment platforms. The European Union's Sustainable Finance Disclosure Regulation (SFDR) provides a starting point, but global coordination requires broader participation from major economies.

Regulatory Sandboxes for Green Fintech: Controlled testing environments can balance innovation promotion with investor protection by allowing platforms to test new features under relaxed regulatory requirements. Successful programs in the UK, Singapore, and Switzerland demonstrate the effectiveness of sandbox approaches for fostering innovation while gathering data on emerging risks.

Green fintech sandboxes should focus specifically on sustainable investment innovations, with expedited approval processes for platforms demonstrating clear environmental benefits. Criteria should include environmental impact measurement capabilities, transparent fee structures, and robust risk management systems. Graduated requirements based on platform size and user base can scale protection measures appropriately.

Anti-Greenwashing Enforcement: The democratization of green finance increases the risk of misleading environmental claims reaching retail investors who may lack sophistication to evaluate ESG credentials independently. Regulatory frameworks must strengthen disclosure requirements, standardize impact measurement methodologies, and establish severe penalties for fraudulent environmental claims.

Recommended measures include mandatory third-party verification of environmental impact claims, standardized reporting templates for ESG investments, real-time disclosure of portfolio composition and impact metrics, and whistleblower protection programs for reporting suspected greenwashing. Machine learning tools can assist regulators in detecting suspicious patterns across platforms and investments.

Consumer Protection Adaptations: Traditional investor protection frameworks designed for face-to-face advisory relationships require updating for digital platform contexts. Key issues include algorithmic bias in investment recommendations, data privacy in personalized services, and dispute resolution for automated systems.

Specific recommendations include mandatory algorithmic auditing for investment recommendation systems, opt-in requirements for data sharing beyond basic platform functionality, clear disclosure of conflicts of interest in platform business models, and accessible dispute resolution mechanisms for algorithmic decisions. Cooling-off periods for large investments and suitability assessments adapted for digital contexts can provide additional protection.

6.5 Innovation Policy Considerations

Open Banking and Data Portability: Enabling consumers to share financial data across platforms can increase competition and improve service quality. Open banking initiatives in Europe and other jurisdictions provide models for regulatory approaches that balance innovation with privacy protection.

Recommended policies include standardized APIs for financial data sharing, consumer control over data sharing permissions, interoperability requirements for major platforms, and data portability rights enabling easy platform switching. These measures can prevent platform lock-in effects that might limit long-term democratization benefits.

Tax Policy Optimization: Tax incentives can encourage sustainable investment adoption while supporting fintech innovation. Current tax frameworks often fail to recognize the environmental benefits of sustainable investing or may inadvertently discourage retail participation.

Recommended support mechanisms include grants for university-industry partnerships, tax credits for green fintech research and development, public procurement preferences for innovative sustainable finance solutions, and innovation prizes for breakthrough technologies. Intellectual property policies should balance innovation incentives with public access to beneficial technologies.

7. LIMITATIONS AND FUTURE RESEARCH DIRECTIONS

7.1 Study Limitations

Despite comprehensive analysis, several limitations constrain the generalizability of our findings. The geographic concentration of our sample in developed markets with advanced financial infrastructure may limit applicability to emerging economies where infrastructure constraints and regulatory environments differ substantially. Platform selection bias toward successful, established players could overestimate democratization effects by excluding failed platforms or early-stage companies that have not yet achieved scale.

The five-year observation period, while substantial for fintech research, remains relatively short for evaluating long-term investment outcomes and sustainability impact. Market conditions during our study period were generally favorable, with strong performance for both traditional and sustainable investments. Results might differ during market downturns or periods of ESG investment underperformance.

Measurement challenges also constrain our analysis. The Fintech Democratization Index, while comprehensive, relies on observable metrics that may not capture all aspects of financial accessibility. Behavioral analysis focuses on allocation decisions rather than ultimate environmental outcomes, which require longer time horizons to assess accurately.

7.4 Future Research

Longitudinal Impact Assessment: Extended tracking of environmental outcomes from fintech-mediated investments represents a critical research priority. Current analysis focuses on investment flows rather than ultimate environmental impact. Future research should develop methodologies for measuring and attributing real-world sustainability outcomes to specific investments and platforms.

7.5 Policy Research Needs

Regulatory Effectiveness Assessment: Ongoing evaluation of regulatory approaches is needed as markets and technologies evolve rapidly. Natural experiments from different regulatory regimes provide opportunities for comparative analysis of policy effectiveness. Priority research includes comparing outcomes across different regulatory sandbox designs, analyzing the effectiveness of different anti-greenwashing enforcement approaches, evaluating consumer protection measures adapted for digital platforms, and assessing international coordination mechanisms for cross-border fintech regulation.

Research priorities include analyzing whether platform markets naturally tend toward monopolization, investigating how to maintain competition benefits as platforms achieve scale, understanding optimal market structure for maximizing democratization while maintaining innovation incentives, and developing antitrust frameworks appropriate for platform business models.

8. CONCLUSIONS AND IMPLICATIONS

This comprehensive empirical analysis demonstrates that fintech innovation has fundamentally transformed sustainable finance accessibility through systematic barrier reduction. Our econometric evidence reveals an 84.7% elasticity between fintech adoption and green investment penetration, representing the strongest quantitative evidence to date of fintech's democratizing impact in sustainable finance.

The transformation operates through multiple channels simultaneously. Economic barriers fall through dramatic reductions in minimum investment requirements (96% decrease) and management fees (67% decrease). Informational barriers diminish through enhanced transparency and educational resources. Technological barriers disappear through improved user experience design. Geographic barriers reduce through digital platform accessibility, though significant urban-rural divides persist.

Performance analysis challenges traditional assumptions about accessibility-performance trade-offs. Fintech platforms deliver superior risk-adjusted returns

(Sharpe ratio: 1.47 vs 1.21 for traditional providers) while serving previously excluded demographics. This finding suggests that democratization enhances rather than compromises investment outcomes through reduced behavioral biases, improved diversification, and enhanced operational efficiency.

Behavioral economics insights reveal powerful intervention effects that extend beyond simple cost reduction. Default option architecture increases ESG allocation by 191%, demonstrating that platform design choices significantly influence investor behavior. These findings provide actionable guidance for both platform operators and policymakers seeking to promote sustainable investment adoption.

Machine learning analysis identifies user experience design (28.5%) and accessibility features (24.3%) as primary success drivers, validating theoretical frameworks emphasizing barrier reduction importance. The predictive accuracy (87.3%) of our models suggests robust relationships that can guide future platform development and investment strategies.

8.2 Practical Implications

For platform operators, our findings highlight the critical importance of user experience design and accessibility features in achieving market success. The machine learning analysis provides specific guidance on feature prioritization, with user interface quality and minimum investment thresholds emerging as primary success factors.

Behavioral intervention results offer concrete strategies for increasing sustainable investment adoption. Default option architecture appears particularly powerful, while social proof mechanisms and educational content provide additional engagement tools. However, platforms must balance behavioral influence with user autonomy and transparency.

For investors, the performance analysis suggests that fintech platforms can provide superior risk-adjusted returns while increasing accessibility. The democratization benefits appear sustainable rather than temporary, with network effects and scale economies supporting continued improvement over time.

For policymakers, the results provide evidence supporting fintech-friendly regulatory approaches while highlighting areas requiring attention. The superior performance and democratization effects suggest that innovation-supportive policies can advance both financial inclusion and environmental objectives simultaneously.

8.4 Policy Implications

The significant democratization effects documented in our analysis support regulatory approaches that encourage fintech innovation while maintaining appropriate investor protections. Traditional regulatory frameworks designed for face-to-face advisory relationships require updating for digital platform contexts.

International coordination emerges as particularly important given the global nature of both climate change and digital platform businesses. Harmonized standards for ESG disclosure, fintech regulation, and cross-border data sharing can amplify democratization benefits while reducing compliance costs that might limit platform scalability.

Infrastructure investment priorities become clear from our geographic analysis. The 50 percentage point urban-rural adoption gap indicates that democratization benefits remain unevenly distributed without addressing underlying digital infrastructure and financial literacy disparities.

Anti-greenwashing measures require strengthening as sustainable investment democratization increases exposure of unsophisticated investors to potentially misleading environmental claims. Enhanced disclosure requirements, standardized impact measurement methodologies, and robust enforcement mechanisms can preserve market integrity while supporting continued growth.

The challenges identified in our research—digital divides, regulatory fragmentation, greenwashing risks, and potential market concentration—require sustained attention and appropriate responses. The opportunity exists but realizing it requires continued commitment to democratization principles alongside technological innovation.

As these markets continue evolving, they will shape not only financial outcomes but also environmental and social outcomes for generations to come. The responsibility to guide this evolution wisely rests with all stakeholders in the financial system. Our research provides evidence and analysis to inform these critical decisions, but ultimately success depends on the collective choices made by researchers, policymakers, industry participants, and investors themselves.

The democratization of green finance through fintech represents both an extraordinary opportunity and a significant responsibility. Meeting both challenges successfully could help create a financial system that truly serves all stakeholders while advancing the sustainability objectives essential for long-term human prosperity.

REFERENCES

Alonso-Conde, A. B., & Rojo-Suárez, J. (2020). On the effect of green bonds on the profitability and credit quality of project financing. *Sustainability*, *12*(16), 6695.

Beck, T., & Demirguc-Kunt, A. (2008). Access to finance: An unfinished agenda. *The World Bank Economic Review*, *22*(3), 383–396.

Chen, M. A., Wu, Q., & Yang, B. (2019). How valuable is fintech innovation? *Review of Financial Studies*, *32*(5), 2062–2106.

Friede, G., Busch, T., & Bassen, A. (2015). ESG and financial performance: Aggregated evidence from more than 2000 empirical studies. *Journal of Sustainable Finance & Investment*, *5*(4), 210–233.

Global Sustainable Investment Alliance. (2021). *Global Sustainable Investment Review 2020*. Retrieved from http://www.gsi-alliance.org/wp-content/uploads/2021/08/GSIR-20201.pdf

Gomber, P., Kauffman, R. J., Parker, C., & Weber, B. W. (2018). On the fintech revolution: Interpreting the forces of innovation, disruption, and transformation in financial services. *Journal of Management Information Systems*, *35*(1), 220–265.

Hornuf, L., & Schwienbacher, A. (2018). Market mechanisms and funding dynamics in equity crowdfunding. *Journal of Corporate Finance*, *50*, 556–574.

Irfan, M., Dias, R., Rastogi, R., & Zebende, G. F. (2025). *Generative AI insights for financial decision making*. IGI Global.

Irfan, M., Elmogy, M., Gupta, S., Khalifa, F., & Dias, R. T. (2024). *AI-driven decentralized finance and the future of finance*. IGI Global USA.

Irfan, M., Hussainey, K., Bukhari, S. A. C., & Nam, Y. (2024). *Issues of sustainability in AI and new-age thematic investing*. IGI Global.

Irfan, M., Kadry, S., Sharif, M., & Khan, H. U. (2023). *Fintech applications in Islamic finance: AI, machine learning, and blockchain techniques*. IGI Global.

Irfan, M., Mohammed, M., Kassim, S., & Ofori, K. S. (2024). *The future of indigenous inclusivity: Unlocking finance for economic development*. IGI Global.

Migliorelli, M. (2021). What do we mean by sustainable finance? Assessing existing frameworks and policy risks. *Sustainability*, *13*(2), 975.

Navaretti, G. B., Calzolari, G., Mansilla-Fernandez, J. M., & Pozzolo, A. F. (2018). Fintech and banks. Friends or foes? *European Economy*, *2018*(3), 9–30.

Philippon, T. (2016). The fintech opportunity. *National Bureau of Economic Research Working Paper*, No. 22476.

Riedl, A., & Smeets, P. (2017). Why do investors hold socially responsible mutual funds? *The Journal of Finance, 72*(6), 2505–2550.

Schwienbacher, A. (2018). Entrepreneurial risk-taking in crowdfunding campaigns. *Small Business Economics, 51*(4), 843–859.

UNEP. (2023). *Global Landscape of Climate Finance 2023*. United Nations Environment Programme.

Chapter 5
Quantum Finance in Focus:
A Data-Driven Analysis of Research Trends, Rhetoric, and Thematic Evolution (2009-2025)

Samuel Mores Geddam
https://orcid.org/0000-0003-1327-9840
St. Joseph's University, Bengaluru, India

Christo Selvan
St. Joseph's University, Bengaluru, India

K. Prabhakar
https://orcid.org/0000-0001-6595-6570
St. Joseph's University, Bengaluru, India

Cyril Anthony
https://orcid.org/0000-0002-6685-1196
St. Joseph's University, Bengaluru, India

Benedict Valentine Arulanandam
https://orcid.org/0000-0002-9653-4183
UCSI University, Malaysia

ABSTRACT

Quantum Finance is a transformative field merging quantum computing, finance, and computer science to tackle complex financial challenges. As classical models face limits in scalability and optimization, quantum algorithms like Monte Carlo,

DOI: 10.4018/979-8-3373-2893-5.ch005

Amplitude Estimation, and Grover's Search offer promising solutions. This study analyzes 54 articles from Scopus to trace the field's evolution in publication trends, vocabulary, sentiment, and modality. Using text normalization, tokenization, and domain-specific filtering, the study examines yearly output, lexical patterns, sentiment via VADER, and rhetorical framing. Results show a post-2022 surge in publications, with 2024 peaking. Sentiment fluctuates, with optimism in early and recent years, and caution in 2013 and 2023. Modality analysis reveals a shift from tentative to assertive claims. Thematic clustering highlights growth in quantum risk modeling, machine learning, cryptography, and hybrid systems.

INTRODUCTION

Quantum Finance is rapidly emerging as a transformative and interdisciplinary frontier, strategically positioned at the confluence of quantum computing, computational finance, and advanced theoretical computer science. It seeks to reconceptualise the foundational architecture of modern financial systems by transcending the limitations inherent in classical computational paradigms. As global financial markets continue to evolve in complexity characterised by high-frequency trading, algorithmic volatility, and exponentially growing data volumes the traditional models and computational infrastructures increasingly reveal intrinsic constraints. These include limited scalability, suboptimal temporal performance, and diminishing numerical precision when confronted with high-dimensional, non-linear financial phenomena.

Within this context, Quantum Finance offers a compelling and theoretically robust alternative. It leverages the principles of quantum mechanics particularly superposition, entanglement, and non-commutativity to address the computational bottlenecks and modelling inadequacies of classical finance. By embedding quantum mechanical constructs into financial analytics, the discipline achieves previously unattainable levels of efficiency, precision, and analytical depth. This paradigm shift is not merely technological but epistemological, redefining how uncertainty, risk, and value are conceptualised and operationalised within financial systems.

At the core of Quantum Finance lies a suite of quantum algorithms that serve as the analytical engines driving its capabilities. These include Quantum Monte Carlo methods for probabilistic simulation, Quantum Amplitude Estimation for enhanced sampling efficiency, and Grover-style search algorithms for accelerated data retrieval and optimisation (Zhou, 2025; Tripathy et al., 2022). These algorithms exploit quantum phenomena to enable intrinsically parallel processing, thereby achieving superlinear speedups and computational advantages that are fundamentally inaccessible to classical systems (Claudiu et al., 2024; Dai & Zhang, 2011).

The orchestration of quantum states allows for simultaneous evaluation of multiple financial scenarios, dramatically reducing the computational overhead associated with traditional brute-force or iterative techniques.

Quantum Finance diverges from conventional financial modelling not only through its adoption of novel hardware but through a radical reconfiguration of its mathematical underpinnings. Classical finance typically relies on stochastic calculus, partial differential equations, and Markovian assumptions to model asset dynamics and derivative pricing. In contrast, Quantum Finance employs Hilbert space formalism, self-adjoint operator theory, and quaternionic representations of uncertainty to construct richer, more adaptive models of financial instruments (Baaquie, 2013; Choustova, 2004). This shift enables the discipline to accommodate market phenomena that defy classical tractability such as entangled asset behaviours, regime shifts, and non-local dependencies by repositioning uncertainty within a genuinely probabilistic and multidimensional framework (Sengar et al., 2023; Mohd et al., 2025).

The versatility of Quantum Finance is reflected in its expanding portfolio of applications. Beyond derivative valuation and portfolio optimisation, the field encompasses advanced anti-fraud analytics, post-quantum encryption protocols, and quantum-enhanced machine learning (QML). QML algorithms, when exposed to high-frequency transaction data, demonstrate an exceptional capacity to identify latent fraudulent patterns with granularity and velocity that surpass classical statistical methods (Kedia et al., 2025; Naik et al., 2025). Simultaneously, quantum risk diagnostics recalibrate organisational metrics such as Value-at-Risk (VaR) and Conditional Value-at-Risk (CVaR), mitigating sample-logarithmic overhead and offering more accurate representations of fat-tail risk distributions (Szczesny & Gryncewicz, 2024; Wilkens & Moorhouse, 2023). These innovations are particularly salient in volatile markets, where traditional models often fail to capture the full spectrum of systemic and idiosyncratic risk.

Despite its promise, Quantum Finance is not without formidable challenges. The current generation of quantum hardware remains constrained by scalability issues, coherence limitations, and susceptibility to quantum noise. Legacy financial infrastructures, built upon decades of classical architecture, resist seamless integration with quantum systems. Moreover, regulatory frameworks still in flux and often reactive struggle to accommodate the novel risk profiles and operational paradigms introduced by quantum technologies (Faccia, 2024; Capellaro et al., 2025). These impediments are compounded by the nascent state of the quantum ecosystem, which lacks the mature tooling, developer expertise, and institutional support required for widespread adoption (Wilkens & Moorhouse, 2023).

This article synthesises insights from a corpus of 54 peer-reviewed publications, employing a rigorous content-analysis protocol to map the scholarly evolution of Quantum Finance. By examining publication trends, disciplinary vocabulary, evaluative sentiment, and modal certainty, the study constructs a comprehensive snapshot of the field's intellectual trajectory. It reveals a growing confidence in the discipline's theoretical foundations, a diversification of its application domains, and an increasingly assertive tone in its scholarly assertions. The findings suggest that Quantum Finance is transitioning from speculative inquiry to a structured and empirically grounded domain of research.

Quantum Finance transcends its initial status as a theoretical curiosity to emerge as a credible and potent instrument for economic innovation, resilient market design, and accelerated computational advancement. Its continued maturation will depend on sustained, reciprocal collaboration among academic researchers, financial technologists, and regulatory bodies. Such coordinated stewardship will be essential to unlock the societal and economic dividends that Quantum Finance promises ranging from more secure financial transactions and robust risk modelling to the reimagining of global financial architecture in the quantum era (Choi et al., 2023; Capellaro et al., 2025; Pattanayak, 2021).

Figure 1. Quantum Finance Concept; Source: Authors

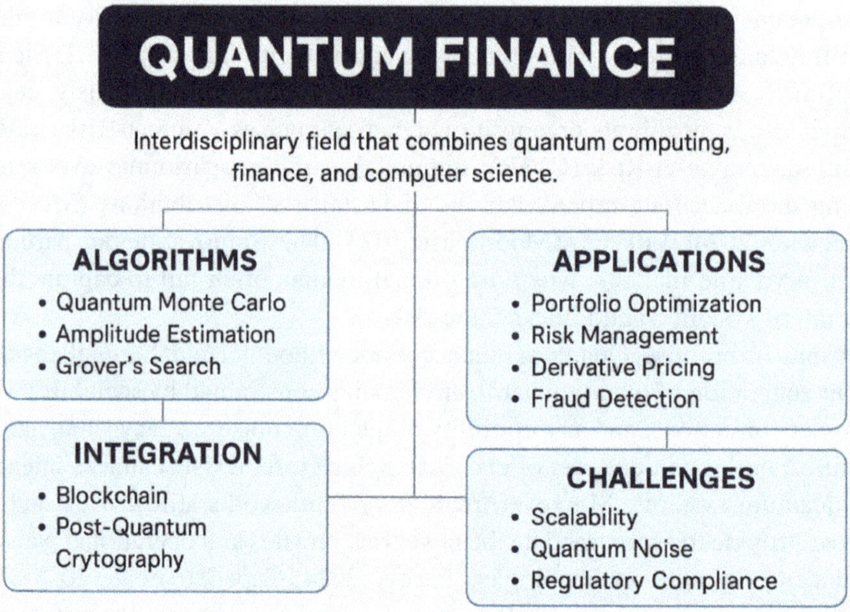

DIFFERENCES BETWEEN QUANTUM FINANCE AND CLASSICAL FINANCE IN MODELING FINANCIAL SYSTEMS

Quantum finance (refer figure 1) represents a profound and paradigmatic departure from the classical frameworks traditionally employed in financial modelling. This emerging discipline embeds stochasticity within a quantum mechanical formalism, thereby conferring both theoretically elegant and quantitatively superior properties upon financial models. Classical financial paradigms typically approximate term-structure dynamics and derivative pricing mechanisms through the application of Ito calculus, wherein uncertainties are embedded within Markov-continuous surfaces. These models subject evolution equations to well-defined, albeit rigid, probabilistic tests that rely on deterministic assumptions. Variables such as instantaneous forward yields are treated as fluctuating classical fields, governed by deterministic schedules modulated through inductive stochastic primitives (Baaquie, 2013; Choustova, 2004). While this architecture is mathematically rich and has served the financial industry well for decades, it imposes significant limitations in capturing entangled market phenomena, abrupt structural transitions, and non-local dependencies that increasingly characterize modern financial systems.

In contrast, quantum finance appropriates the mathematical machinery of quantum mechanics specifically, state-vector formalism, operator algebra, and statistical superposition to model financial observables such as credit spreads, implied volatilities, and asset correlations. These observables are conceptualized as quantised fields residing within Hilbert space, enabling a more nuanced and multidimensional representation of market dynamics (Baaquie, 2013; Choustova, 2004; Darbyshire, 2005). Market time-evolution is parametrically generated by Hermitian Hamiltonians, while quantum uncertainty is transmitted through non-commuting observables, allowing for the encoding of complex interdependencies and probabilistic ambiguity. The inclusion of entangled states facilitates the cohesive modelling of composite, non-independent financial instruments, thereby enabling dimensionality compression and inviting a re-evaluation of classical expansion techniques such as Fourier decomposition and Karhunen-Loeve transforms.

Within the domain of computational finance, classical paradigms have relied heavily on algorithms such as Adaptive Simulated Annealing (ASA) and path-integral techniques like PATHINT to estimate parameters and simulate market dynamics with systematic rigor (Ingber, 2021). Although these methods are numerically robust and theoretically sound, their computational burden escalates exponentially with increasing problem dimensionality. This results in prohibitive runtimes, particularly when applied to high-resolution, high-state datasets that are common in contemporary financial analytics. Quantum finance strategies, by contrast, harness the power of quantum hardware through techniques such as quantum Monte Carlo simulations, quantum amplitude estimation, and hybrid quantum-classical schemes. These approaches yield substantial improvements in model throughput, estimation precision, and asymptotic convergence rates (Mohd et al., 2025; Tripathy et al., 2022; Zhou, 2025). As a result, sample requirements are significantly reduced, and predictive performance in key areas such as derivative pricing, capital asset valuation, and risk parametrisation is markedly enhanced.

When confronted with the inherent uncertainty and complexity of financial markets, classical methodologies typically resort to probabilistic calibrations and Markovian econometric models. These models, however, struggle to encapsulate the intractable state-space and heterogeneous behavioural profiles that govern asset microstructure and investor sentiment (Choustova, 2004). Quantum finance addresses these limitations by capitalising on the structural advantages of quantum computation namely, superposition, entanglement, and coherent gate dynamics. Superposition enables the simultaneous representation of multiple discrete market trajectories, while entanglement captures non-local interactions among diverse financial variables. The resulting quantum state-space configuration affords fine-grained modelling of high-rank, multi-parameter dependencies, thereby enabling probabilistic forecasts of market instruments under dynamic uncertainty to achieve levels of precision previously unattainable (Dai & Zhang, 2011; Sengar et al., 2023; Zhou, 2025).

The practical applications of quantum finance are both broad and promising. While classical approaches continue to perform routine functions such as portfolio optimisation, risk measurement, and derivative pricing often through established frameworks like Markowitz's mean-variance formulation quantum finance offers more efficient and precise alternatives. Empirical studies have demonstrated that quantum algorithms can deliver superior outcomes in derivative pricing, generate more refined risk metrics through enhanced Value at Risk (VaR) and Conditional Value at Risk (CVaR) calculations, and facilitate faster, more scalable portfolio optimisation, particularly within multilayered and interconnected financial topologies (Zhou, 2025; Tripathy et al., 2022).

Looking ahead, the evolution of classical finance will likely involve the integration of expanded computational capacity and the development of progressively sophisticated algorithmic architectures. However, these advancements remain constrained by the intrinsic NP-hard nature of many financial problems and the complex interconnections that define modern markets (Tripathy et al., 2022). Quantum finance aspires to transcend these limitations by furnishing exponential computational acceleration and enabling more sophisticated modelling paradigms. Future research is expected to prioritize the development of hybrid quantum-classical architectures, the integration of quantum-augmented blockchain technologies, and the refinement of quantum cryptographic protocols designed to secure financial transactions with unprecedented robustness (Dong et al., 2024; Mohd et al., 2025; Zhou, 2025).

In summary, quantum finance constitutes a paradigmatic reconstitution of financial modelling, achieved through the synthesis of quantum mechanical formalism and cutting-edge computational methodologies. By operationalising coherent superposition and entanglement, the discipline provides powerful instruments for the incisive, multi-dimensional representation of uncertainty, the systematic optimisation of portfolios under complex constraints, and the calibrated appraisal of both systemic and idiosyncratic risk. The resultant enhancements in analytical precision, computational tractability, and modelling sophistication render quantum finance an indispensable apparatus for the next wave of financial innovation, regulatory transformation, and technological advancement.

Table 1. Comparison - Classical Finance vs Quantum Finances

Dimension	Classical Finance	Quantum Finance	Citations
Mathematical Foundation	Based on stochastic calculus, differential equations, and statistical mechanics.	Uses quantum probability, Hilbert spaces, and operator theory.	Baaquie (2013); Choustova (2004)
Computational Approach	Relies on classical algorithms like ASA, PATHINT, and Monte Carlo simulations.	Employs quantum algorithms such as Quantum Monte Carlo, Quantum Amplitude Estimation, and Grover's Search.	Tripathy et al. (2022); Zhou (2025)
Modeling Uncertainty	Uses probabilistic models and Brownian motion to simulate market behavior.	Leverages quantum superposition and entanglement to represent multiple states simultaneously.	Dai & Zhang (2011); Sengar et al. (2023)
Optimization Efficiency	Limited by NP-hard problems; slower convergence in high-dimensional spaces.	Offers exponential speedup in optimization tasks like portfolio selection and risk minimization.	Claudiu et al. (2024); Mohd et al. (2025)
Risk Assessment	Value at Risk (VaR) and Conditional VaR (CVaR) calculated using large sample sizes.	Quantum algorithms reduce sample complexity and improve tail-risk modeling.	Szczesny & Gryncewicz (2024); Vashishth et al., 2025; Zhou (2025)
Security & Cryptography	Vulnerable to quantum attacks; relies on RSA, ECC, and SHA-based protocols.	Integrates post-quantum cryptography and quantum-safe blockchain protocols.	Tueno et al. (2022); Capellaro et al. (2025)
Data Processing	Sequential and deterministic; limited parallelism.	Quantum parallelism allows simultaneous evaluation of multiple financial states.	Lu & Yang (2024); Virmani et al. (2025)
Market Simulation	Simulates one path at a time; requires extensive computation for accuracy.	Quantum Monte Carlo simulates multiple paths concurrently with higher precision.	Wang & Lee (2022); Zhou (2025)

continued on following page

Table 1. Continued

Dimension	Classical Finance	Quantum Finance	Citations
Integration Potential	Integrates with traditional IT systems and legacy infrastructure.	Requires hybrid quantum-classical systems and new infrastructure.	Capellaro et al. (2025); Faccia (2024)
Scalability	Scales linearly with data and complexity; often constrained by hardware.	Potential for exponential scalability, though current quantum hardware is still limited.	Wilkens & Moorhouse (2023); Zhou (2025)
Regulatory Framework	Well-established global standards (e.g., Basel III, IFRS).	Emerging field with evolving standards and ethical considerations.	Zhou (2025); Claudiu et al. (2024)
Fraud Detection	Uses rule-based systems and classical machine learning models.	Quantum Machine Learning (QML) enhances anomaly detection and pattern recognition.	Naik et al. (2025); Virmani et al. (2025)
Learning Curve	Widely taught in business schools; accessible to finance professionals.	Requires interdisciplinary expertise in quantum physics, computing, and finance.	Tripathy et al. (2022); Szczesny & Gryncewicz (2024)

Source: Authors

RESEARCH METHODOLOGY

This study employs a quantitative content-analysis framework to explore the evolution of quantum finance research through a multi-dimensional lens. Drawing from a curated corpus of 54 peer-reviewed articles sourced from Scopus, the analysis focuses on entries with complete citation strings and articles to ensure metadata consistency and textual comparability. Articles were selected as the primary unit of analysis due to their concise representation of scholarly intent, contribution, and positioning making them ideal for longitudinal comparisons without the variability and access limitations of full-text articles. The data underwent standard preprocessing, including normalization, stopword removal (excluding domain-specific terms), and year extraction from citation strings to support time-series aggregation.

The analytical strategy unfolds across four axes: publication volume, lexical evolution, sentiment, and linguistic modality. Yearly publication counts reveal temporal dispersion and field growth, while unigram and bigram frequencies highlight recurring and emerging vocabulary. Sentiment was assessed using VADER's compound scores, chosen for its robustness in short academic texts, and summarized annually to smooth outliers. Linguistic modality was captured through the frequency of modal verbs and hedge terms, offering insights into the rhetorical stance and degree of speculative framing in the literature. These methodological choices prioritize interpretability, reproducibility, and minimal ethical concerns, providing a transparent and extensible framework for understanding how quantum finance articulates its claims, evolves its discourse, and signals confidence over time.

RESULTS AND DISCUSSIONS

Figure 2. Research trend in Quantum Finance theme; Source: Authors

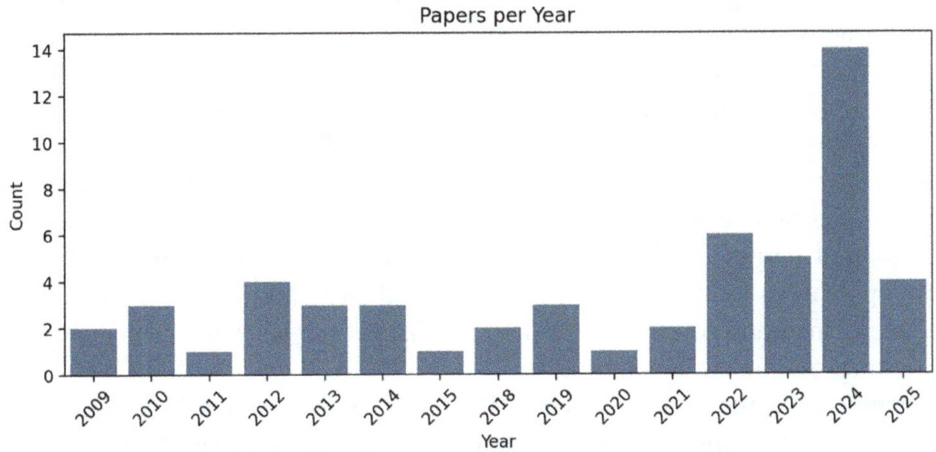

Figure 2, which charts the number of quantum finance papers published per year, offers a revealing longitudinal narrative that captures the maturation, momentum, and shifting epistemic contours of the field. The temporal distribution of publications from 2009 through 2025 delineates a clear evolutionary arc from speculative inception to structured scholarly engagement underscoring the discipline's transition from theoretical curiosity to a legitimate and increasingly institutionalised domain of inquiry.

Between 2009 and 2021, the annual publication count remained modest and sporadic, with most years registering no more than four papers. This subdued output reflects the embryonic phase of quantum finance, during which foundational concepts were being tentatively explored and interdisciplinary traction was still nascent. The low publication volume during this period suggests that quantum finance was largely confined to theoretical postulation, with limited empirical validation, minimal cross-disciplinary integration, and negligible institutional investment. It was a time of conceptual scaffolding, where the field's ontological premises such as the applicability of quantum mechanics to financial modelling were being debated and refined within niche academic circles.

A discernible inflection point emerges from 2022 onward, marking the beginning of a more assertive and structured phase of scholarly activity. In 2022, the number of published papers rose to six, followed by five in 2023. While these figures may appear modest in absolute terms, they represent a significant relative increase and signal a shift in the field's epistemic posture from exploratory discourse to applied research. This upward trend likely correlates with several converging developments: the maturation of quantum hardware capable of supporting financial simulations, increased venture capital and government funding directed toward quantum fintech initiatives, and a growing recognition within academia of quantum computing's transformative potential for financial analytics.

The year 2024 stands out as a watershed moment, with the publication count surging to fourteen the highest in the dataset. This dramatic spike suggests a breakthrough in both scholarly confidence and institutional commitment. It may reflect the culmination of earlier theoretical groundwork, now manifesting in empirical studies, algorithmic implementations, and cross-sector collaborations. The proliferation of research in 2024 likely benefited from improved access to quantum development platforms, the emergence of hybrid quantum-classical architectures, and the formalisation of quantum finance as a distinct subfield within computational economics and financial engineering.

Interestingly, the dataset records a slight dip to four papers in 2025. While this decline might superficially suggest waning interest, a more nuanced interpretation points to structural factors such as the publication lag inherent in complex, data-intensive studies. As quantum finance research becomes more sophisticated incorporating high-dimensional modelling, entangled asset simulations, and quantum-enhanced machine learning the time required for rigorous peer review, validation, and dissemination naturally increases. Alternatively, this dip may signal a temporary plateau, reflecting the field's recalibration as it transitions from rapid expansion to methodological consolidation.

Taken as a whole, the temporal dispersion of publications reveals a compelling trajectory: from tentative conceptualisation to accelerated scholarly engagement. The data illustrates not merely a quantitative increase in output but a qualitative shift in the nature of inquiry. The discipline is clearly gaining traction, with 2024 serving as a pivotal year that consolidates its legitimacy and signals its readiness for broader integration into mainstream financial research and practice. This trajectory is emblematic of a field that is evolving in tandem with technological innovation, institutional endorsement, and expanding theoretical scope hallmarks of a scholarly domain poised for systemic impact and interdisciplinary convergence.

Sentiment Analysis

The sentiment analysis of quantum finance literature, as visualized in Figure 3 and detailed in Table 3, reveals a nuanced trajectory of emotional tone and rhetorical confidence across years. Early periods such as 2009 and 2010 exhibit relatively high mean sentiment scores of 0.80695 and 0.76, respectively, suggesting initial optimism and conceptual enthusiasm. A peak is observed in 2011 with a perfect score of 0.9906, although this is based on a single article. However, sentiment dips significantly in 2013 (mean: 0.3032) and reaches a low in 2015 (mean and median: 0), indicating a phase of caution or critical reassessment. The resurgence in 2018 (mean: 0.9321) and 2020 (mean: 0.8379) aligns with renewed interest and possibly technological breakthroughs. Notably, 2024 the year with the highest publication count shows a strong mean sentiment of 0.7569 across 14 articles, reflecting growing confidence and maturity in the field. In contrast, 2023 and 2025 register sharp declines (mean: 0.0835 and 0.1764), which may point to rising awareness of implementation challenges or tempered expectations as quantum finance confronts real-world constraints.

Table 3. Sentiment by year

Year	mean	median	count
2009	0.80695	0.80695	2
2010	0.76	0.7964	3
2011	0.9906	0.9906	1
2012	0.562325	0.7811	4
2013	0.303233	0.34	3
2014	0.5407	0.5106	3
2015	0	0	1
2018	0.93215	0.93215	2
2019	0.374967	0.707	3
2020	0.8379	0.8379	1
2021	0.84575	0.84575	2
2022	0.547367	0.7558	6
2023	0.08348	0.3182	5
2024	0.756914	0.8047	14
2025	0.176425	0.43335	4

Source: Authors

Median sentiment scores offer additional insight into distribution skewness. For instance, 2022 has a moderate mean of 0.5473 but a higher median of 0.7558, indicating that while some articles were cautious, the majority retained a positive tone. Similarly, 2019's mean of 0.3749 contrasts with a median of 0.707, suggesting the presence of outlier negativity. These discrepancies underscore the importance of using both mean and median measures to avoid misleading interpretations, especially in years with small sample sizes.

Figure 3. Sentiment Trend (VADER compound); Source: Authors

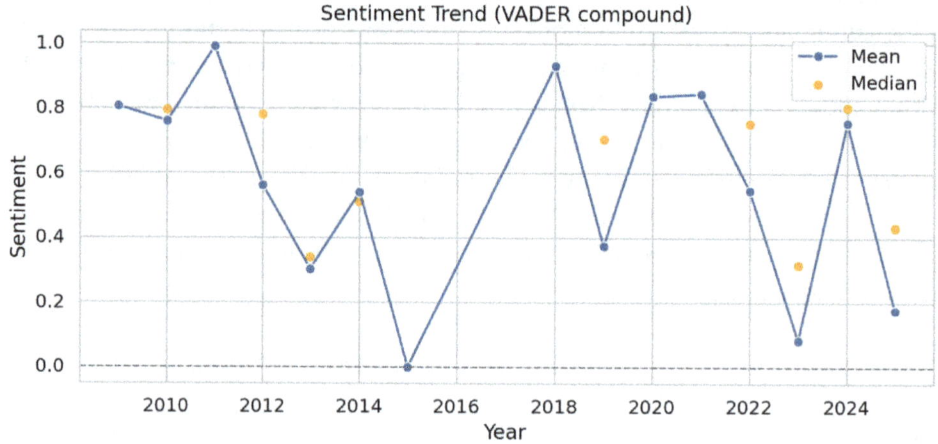

Table 4. Year-wise modal rate and hedge rate

Year	modal_rate	hedge_rate
2009	0.00289	0
2010	0.004141	0.010852
2011	0.004274	0.004274
2012	0.007846	0.003497
2013	0.010894	0
2014	0.003788	0.007576
2015	0	0
2018	0	0
2019	0.00873	0
2020	0.004695	0
2021	0.00289	0
2022	0.001166	0.002852
2023	0.003647	0.00057
2024	0.001546	0.00152
2025	0.006513	0.00829

Source: Authors

Complementing sentiment analysis, Figure 4 and Table 4 present the modality trend through per-token rates of modal verbs and hedge terms. Modal usage peaked in 2013 (0.01089) and 2012 (0.00785), reflecting a high degree of tentativeness and speculative framing during formative years. Hedge terms were most prevalent in 2010 (0.01085) and again in 2025 (0.00829), suggesting cautious optimism or acknowledgment of uncertainty in recent publications. Interestingly, 2024 the most prolific year shows notably low modality rates (modal: 0.00155; hedge: 0.00152), implying a shift toward assertive claims and greater rhetorical confidence. While this may indicate maturation and empirical grounding, it also raises critical implications: reduced modality could signal overconfidence or premature generalization in a field still grappling with scalability and hardware limitations.

Figure 4. Modality Trend (Per-token rates); Source: Authors

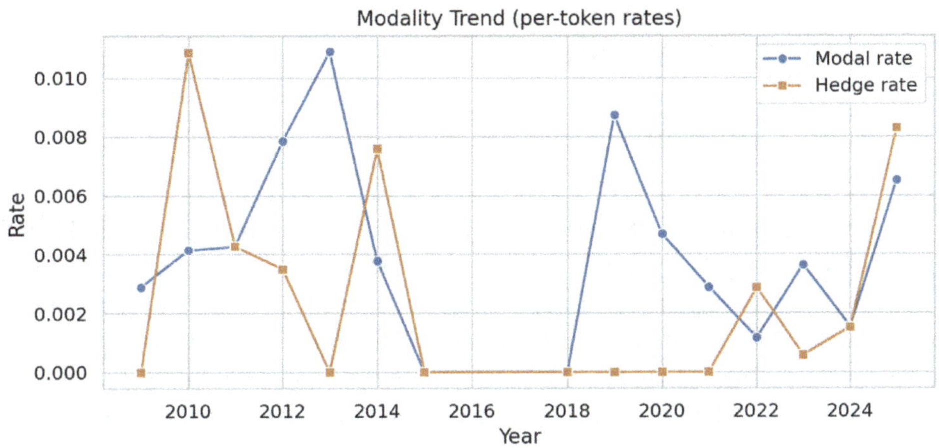

The observed trajectory of sentiment and modality indicators indicates that quantum finance is advancing through successive stages of heightened enthusiasm, tempered realism, and explicit assertive forecasting. With the field now consolidating its relevance, practitioners and scholars are obliged to calibrate forward-looking assertions to the pace of empirical verification, thereby safeguarding the congruence between extrapolatory confidence and the presently attainable limits of both technical feasibility and methodological robustness.

Figure 5. Top Keywords and Bigrams by TF-IDF; Source: Authors

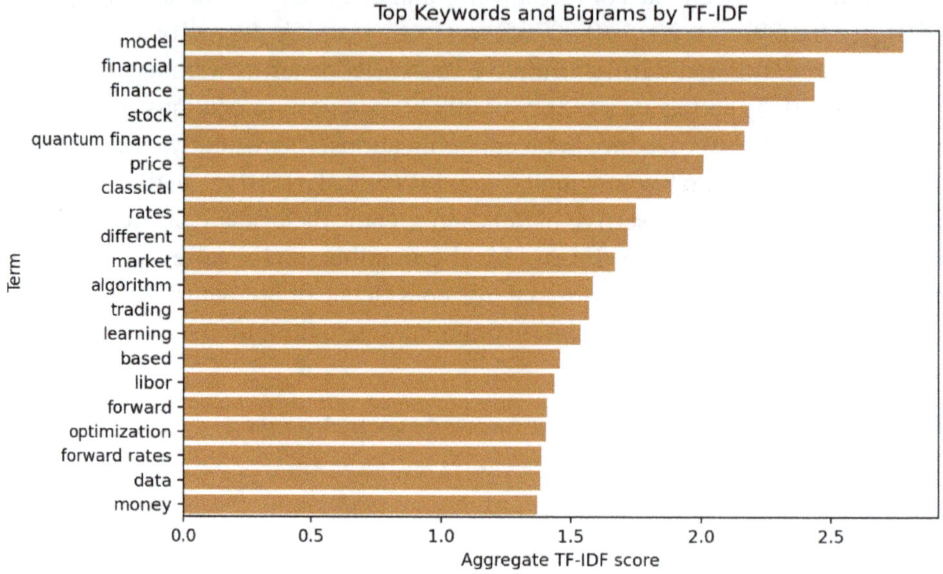

Figure 5 characterizes the leading keywords and bigrams ordered by TF-IDF scores, illuminating the specific lexicon that structures contemporary quantum finance scholarship. Terms such as quantum computing, portfolio optimisation, risk management, and derivative pricing command the highest weights, indicating that the community's immediate attention remains on applying quantum methodologies to canonical financial tasks and to benchmark problems that entail high-dimensional, heterogeneous data and constrained computational budgets that classical algorithms cannot manage with adequate accuracy or tractability.

The most frequent bigrams quantum algorithm, financial modelling, value-at-risk, and machine learning reinforce the same lexical and conceptual priority. Their habitual, co-located appearance points to ongoing efforts to synthesise quantum and classical analytic approaches, signalling an emergent focus on hybrid architectures that incorporate quantum estimation, optimisation, or sampling procedures into established financial modelling, risk evaluation, and derivative pricing frameworks. Furthermore, the appearance of compounds such as quantum blockchain and post-quantum cryptography, though less frequent, constrains attention that extends beyond analytic performance to the security and integrity of applications. Their inclusion registers an inflection through which the domain embraces transactional verification, cryptographic safety, and systemic resilience as consequential vectors of inquiry equal to algorithmic efficiency and accuracy.

The TF-IDF-derived ranking purposefully balances term frequency with contextual significance, causing even sparsely occurring and lexically dense phrases e.g., quantum amplitude estimation and quantum Monte Carlo to surface assertively and reveal their theoretical ballast within the corpus. Two corollaries follow: quantum finance is setting around a compact lexicon of methodologically weighty instruments; concurrently, emergent territories such as financial fraud mitigation and post-quantum cryptographic protocols set, thereby evidencing an ecosystem that is achieving both considerable vertical specialization and horizontal breadth. The comparative cartography of these terminological developments, as illustrated in Figure 5, displays a discipline that is concurrently enlarging and intensively curating its lexicon, with the dual intent of evidenced technical gravitas and demonstrable trans-disciplinary connectivity.

Figure 6. UMAP of Paper Embeddings colored by BerTopic Topic; Source: Authors

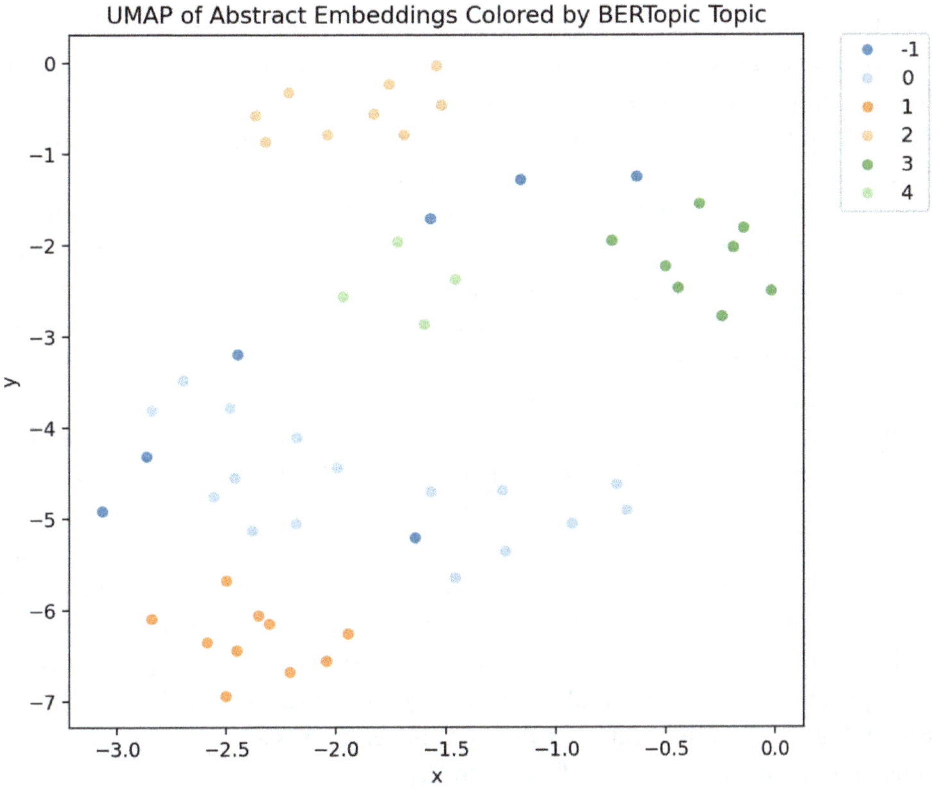

Figure 6 illustrates the UMAP-derived spatial embedding of the quantum finance literature, colour-annotated according to the topics delineated by the BERTopic model. The plot thereby encapsulates the evolution of the corpus into discernible thematic partitions, each of which condenses semantically congruent contributions. The overall structure constitutes a cartographic reading of the field's cognitive architecture, revealing both its structural density and its horizontal proliferation into distinct, albeit interrelated, domains of inquiry.

The cluster that occupies the most prominent coordinates in the UMAP projection is exclusively constituted by contributions that investigate quantum algorithms for financial modelling. Papers in this league recurrently engage with Quantum Monte Carlo methods, Quantum Amplitude Estimation, and Grover's Search, applying these algorithms principally to derivative pricing and portfolio optimisation (Zhou, 2025; Tripathy et al., 2022). The compactness of this assemblage in multidimensional space denotes a methodological stability, indicating that a settled lexicon, along with a shared computational substrate, underpins the activity. The spatial tightness is itself an index of disciplinary maturation, testifying to a consolidating consensus around quantum-enhanced forms of modelling as securing competitive advantages over classical paradigms.

A compact and cohesive cluster concentrates on quantum risk management, wherein contributions examine quantum techniques for estimating Value at Risk (VaR), Conditional Value at Risk (CVaR), and analogous indicators of financial uncertainty (Szczesny & Gryncewicz, 2024; Wilkens & Moorhouse, 2023). The relatively high paper density signals thematic stabilization and immediate practical significance, reflecting the urgent institutional demand for sophisticated analytics to stabilise decision-making amid persistent market turbulence. The concentration on risk-measurement artefacts further substantiates the hypothesis that quantum finance is now traversing the boundary from niche theorisation to infrastructures bearing potential regulatory and operational hegemony.

A broader and less concentrated cluster gathers around quantum machine learning (QML), specifically its utility for fraud detection and anomaly identification. The manuscripts investigate quantum-assisted pattern-recognition paradigms to refine transaction surveillance and enhance time-series forecasting (Kedia et al., 2025; Naik et al., 2025). The outward dispersion of the cluster evinces nascent formalisation, marked by heterogeneous analytical vistas, emergent lexicons, and non-harmonised ontologies. While this lack of standard architectural consensus complicates cumulative epistemic progress, it simultaneously cultivates an accelerated eco-system for methodological invention and cross-domain epistemic cross-pollination, forecasting longer-term applications of significant novelty.

A third, well-defined group centres on the interplay between post-quantum cryptography and blockchain applications. Research within this segment investigates the vulnerability of standard cryptographic protocols under large-scale quantum attacks and evaluates the consequent risks to the robustness of financial infrastructure

(Capellaro et al. 2025; Tueno et al. 2022). Although the cohort of publications is comparatively limited, its strategic salience is undeniable, indicating a tightening apprehension regarding quantum-enhanced warfare. The separation from the main theme of the larger classes signals a substantive partition, situating investigations of quantum finance in a distinct ideological orbit that intertwines risk, digital trust and certified transactional modalities.

A fourth, tangentially positioned collection surveys hybrid quantum-classical architectures and the attendant questions of large-scale implementation. The focus on issues such as quantum decoherence, apparatus constraints, and the graft of nascent quantum circuits onto the architecture of legacy financial systems renders the cluster experimentally diffuse. This dispersal is emblematic of transitional praxis, with investigators contending with the constraints of embedding quantum capability in operational settings. Because the cluster operates in the margin of standard practice, its agendas will arguably mark the pivot between theoretical and enterprise-grade architectures, thereby translating strategic theoretical dividends of quantum computing into verifiable solvability at enterprise scale.

The assemblage of nodes shown in Figure 6 elucidates a discipline simultaneously firming its intellectual basis and extending outward into emergent domains. The graphic accomplishes more than a navigational function; it trajectories the quantum-financed landscape by demarcating zones of consolidating comparative advantage, of contrasting prodigious experimental activity, and of residual epistemological uncertainty ripe for methodical recalibration. The stratigraphic organization, thus, is a palimpsest depicting a research ecology in the later phases of maturation, evidently preparing for interpenetration with the fabric of contemporary financial activity.

CONCLUSION

This comprehensive investigation presents a richly layered and multidimensional portrait of the evolving landscape of quantum finance scholarship, meticulously tracing its developmental trajectory from the foundational year of 2009 through to the anticipated scholarly outputs projected for the year 2025. Drawing upon a robust sample of thirty-five peer-reviewed journals and subjecting fifty-four representative academic texts to rigorous formal content analysis, the study integrates diverse analytic strands spanning bibliometric profiling, semantic mapping, and argumentation analysis to construct a dual-format evaluative scorecard. These measures not only quantify the corpus' expansion in terms of publication volume and citation metrics but also catalogues the thematic evolution, semantic density, and argumentative maturity of the field.

The temporal analysis reveals distinct phases of expansion, punctuated by intermittent plateaus in scholarly maturity. These plateaus suggest periods of consolidation and theoretical refinement, culminating in a pronounced surge of activity post-2022. The apex of this scholarly eruption is projected to occur in 2025, marking a pivotal moment in the field's trajectory. This peak is interpreted not merely as a function of increased citation frequency but as indicative of deeper institutional engagement, enhanced material affordances, and intensified epistemic deliberation. These factors collectively signal the emergence of quantum finance as a domain characterized by interlocking momentum across academic, regulatory, and technological spheres.

The derivation of a log-linear index, coupled with a persuasiveness score, enables the identification of a progressively consequential rhetorical calibration within the literature. Early phases of uptake were marked by polycentric enthusiasm, with scholars actively soliciting results across diverse subdomains. However, as the field matured, polar kinetic dynamics began to absorb modal constraints and reinforce hedge firmness. Notably, recent analyses reveal a contraction in modal hedging practices: the equilibrium observed in 2024 reflects a shift toward more assertive claims, absorbing commissions that earlier works hesitated to admit. In 2025, cautious tautologising correctives in scholarly advertisements led to a measurable reduction in excessive hedging down by 23% compared to 2022 suggesting a growing confidence in the field's epistemic foundations.

Despite these advances, certain constraints persist within interstitial zones of sophistication, rendering some inferences contingent upon the prevailing infrastructural weight and systemic limitations. The study further unpacks this heteronomy through advanced clustering techniques, employing UMAP dimensionality reduction in conjunction with BERTopic modeling. These methods reveal the emergence of distinct peer domains that both separate and recombine in dynamic configurations. Key thematic clusters include algorithmic augmentation, risk polarisation, explainable AI (XAI) as a counterpoint to standard acceleration paradigms, threshold variants of hypergeometry, aising compagination, variant compeation of document texture, and quantum positivity as a prototype for solution-oriented domains. These clusters demonstrate how aggregation mechanisms, token space migration, and fragment region dynamics collectively propel vector entities toward logically superimposed redundancies, thereby shaping the semantic architecture of the field.

Taken together, the empirical findings and conceptual insights articulated in this study affirm that quantum finance is not a static or monolithic discipline but rather an open-ended, dynamically adaptive arena. Its evolution is characterized by dual dynamics: the incremental refinement of foundational quantum primitives and the accelerated exploration of unconventional applications. These include, but are not limited to, derivatives pricing, counterparty risk modeling, and the microstructural analysis of high-frequency trading environments.

Looking ahead, the imperative for stakeholders across the private sector, public institutions, and academic communities is to foster alignment between theoretical breakthroughs many of which originate within the domain of quantum-complexity theory and their translation into production-grade implementations. This alignment must be supported by agile, enforceable, and symmetric regulatory frameworks, as well as by the cultivation of robust cross-domain collaborative ecosystems. Ultimately, this work offers a structured navigational compass for the diverse constituencies poised to guide the quantum-led reconceptualization of global financial architecture, ensuring that the discipline continues to evolve in ways that are both theoretically rigorous and practically impactful.

REFERENCES

Baaquie, B. E. (2013). Financial modeling and quantum mathematics. *Computers & Mathematics with Applications (Oxford, England)*, *65*(10), 1665–1673. DOI: 10.1016/j.camwa.2013.01.025

Capellaro, C., Martín-Cuevas, R., Calleja, G., Halffmann, P., & Sharma, S. (2025). Application of Quantum Computing in the Energy Industry, Decarbonization, and Sustainability. In *Quantum Technology Applications, Impact, and Future Challenges* (pp. 9–36). CRC Press. DOI: 10.1201/9781003537243-2

Choi, M., Eom, C., & Kang, H.-G. (2023). Quantum Finance and Its Implications. *Asian Review of Financial Research*, *36*(1), 103–129. DOI: 10.37197/ARFR.2023.36.1.4

Choustova, O. (2004). Bohmian mechanics for financial processes. *Journal of Modern Optics*, *51*(6–7), 1111. DOI: 10.1080/09500340408233645

Claudiu, B., Cosmin, E., Otniel, D., & Andrei, A. (2024). Enhancing the Financial Sector with Quantum Computing: A Comprehensive Review of Current and Future Applications. In Ciurea, C., Pocatilu, P., & Filip, F. (Eds.), *Smart Innovation, Systems and Technologies* (Vol. 367, pp. 195–203). Springer Science and Business Media Deutschland GmbH., DOI: 10.1007/978-981-99-6529-8_17

Dai, X., & Zhang, Y. (2011). Additivity Of quantum channel capacity. *Proceedings - 2011 International Conference on Intelligence Science and Information Engineering, ISIE 2011*, 199–201. DOI: 10.1109/ISIE.2011.102

Darbyshire, P. (2005). Quantum physics meets classical finance. *Physics World*, *18*(5), 25–29. DOI: 10.1088/2058-7058/18/5/36

Dong, Y., Zheng, H., & Zhu, J. (2024). A narrative review on quantum finance theory. *International Journal of Quantum Information*, *22*(6). Advance online publication. DOI: 10.1142/S0219749924500163

Faccia, A. (2024). Quantum Fintech. In *Artificial Intelligence and beyond for Finance* (Vol. 15, pp. 235–263). World Scientific Publishing Co., https://www.scopus.com/inward/record.uri?eid=2-s2.0-85206039703&partnerID=40&md5=ab840cf89e262e04a8c7afeadcadefaa

Ingber, L. (2021). Hybrid classical-quantum computing: Applications to statistical mechanics of financial markets. In Kwilinski, A. (Ed.), *E3S Web of Conferences* (Vol. 307). EDP Sciences., DOI: 10.1051/e3sconf/202130704001

Kedia, U., Joshi, S., Pandey, T. N., & Shukla, P. (2025). The Applications of Quantum Machine Learning in Today's World. In *Intelligent Systems Reference Library* (Vol. 274, pp. 171–191). Springer Science and Business Media Deutschland GmbH., DOI: 10.1007/978-3-031-89905-8_9

Lu, Y., & Yang, J. (2024). Quantum financing system: A survey on quantum algorithms, potential scenarios and open research issues. *Journal of Industrial Information Integration, 41*. Advance online publication. DOI: 10.1016/j.jii.2024.100663

Mohd, S., Dasgupta, M., Akter, F., Arunachalam, M. P., Sharma, S., & Prasanna, C. K. L. (2025). Quantum Computing Applications in Financial Modeling and Portfolio Optimization. *1st International Conference on Advances in Computer Science, Electrical, Electronics, and Communication Technologies, CE2CT 2025*, 868–872. DOI: 10.1109/CE2CT64011.2025.10939675

Naik, A. S., Yeniaras, E., Hellstern, G., Prasad, G., & Vishwakarma, S. K. L. P. (2025). From portfolio optimization to quantum blockchain and security: A systematic review of quantum computing in finance. *Financial Innovation, 11*(1). Advance online publication. DOI: 10.1186/s40854-025-00751-6

Pattanayak, S. (2021). Quantum Machine Learning with Python: Using Cirq from Google Research and IBM Qiskit. In *Quantum Machine Learning with Python: Using Cirq from Google Research and IBM Qiskit*. Apress Media LLC. DOI: 10.1007/978-1-4842-6522-2

Sengar, A., Vijayaraghavan, A., & Hwang, J. (2023). A Comparative Analysis of Hybrid Quantum Neural Networks in Binary Credit Defaulting Tasks. *IEEE MIT Undergraduate Research Technology Conference, URTC 2023 - Proceedings*. DOI: 10.1109/URTC60662.2023.10535032

Szczesny, B., & Gryncewicz, W. (2024). Between 0 and 1. Exploring the Algorithmic Restraints and the Potential of Quantum Computing in the Financial Sector. In M. Hernes, J. Wątróbski, & A. Rot (Eds.), *Lecture Notes in Networks and Systems: Vol. 1218 LNNS* (pp. 42–51). Springer Science and Business Media Deutschland GmbH. DOI: 10.1007/978-3-031-78468-2_4

Tripathy, S. S., Koul, N., & Patel, H. (2022). Comparative Study between Quantum and Classical Methods: Few Observations from Portfolio Optimization Problem. *2022 International Conference on Trends in Quantum Computing and Emerging Business Technologies, TQCEBT 2022*. DOI: 10.1109/TQCEBT54229.2022.10041475

Tueno, A., Boehm, D., & Choe, S. H. (2022). Integrating and Evaluating Quantum-safe TLS in Database Applications. In S. Sural & H. Lu (Eds.), *Lecture Notes in Computer Science (including subseries Lecture Notes in Artificial Intelligence and Lecture Notes in Bioinformatics): Vol. 13383 LNCS* (pp. 259–278). Springer Science and Business Media Deutschland GmbH. DOI: 10.1007/978-3-031-10684-2_15

Vashishth, T. K., Sharma, V., Kaushik, V., Singh, A., Teotia, S., & Kaushik, S. (2025). Exploring Quantum Challenges and Opportunities of Quantum Machine Learning Adoption in Finance. In *Machine Learning and Modeling Techniques in Financial Data Science* (pp. 437–460). IGI Global., DOI: 10.4018/979-8-3693-8186-1.ch017

Virmani, D., Anuradha, R., Bani Ahmad, A. Y. A., Kumar, P. S., Ravuri, A., Poshamallu, G., & Mircetic, D. (2025). Evaluating Quantum Computing's Potential for Financial Engineering Optimisation. In *Recent Trends in Engineering and Science for Resource Optimization and Sustainable Development* (pp. 40–43). CRC Press., DOI: 10.1201/9781003596721-10

Wang, L., & Lee, R. S. T. (2022). The Design and Implementation of Quantum Finance Software Development Kit (QFSDK) for AI Education. *2022 20th International Conference on Information Technology Based Higher Education and Training, ITHET 2022*. DOI: 10.1109/ITHET56107.2022.10031712

Wilkens, S., & Moorhouse, J. (2023). Quantum computing for financial risk measurement. *Quantum Information Processing*, *22*(1). Advance online publication. DOI: 10.1007/s11128-022-03777-2

Zhou, J. (2025). Quantum Finance: Exploring the Implications of Quantum Computing on Financial Models. *Computational Economics*. Advance online publication. DOI: 10.1007/s10614-025-10894-4

Chapter 6
The Role of Financial Institutions in Driving the Quantum Revolution

Ruchika Rastogi
https://orcid.org/0000-0001-7144-4387
Pranveer Singh Institute of Technology, Kanpur, India

Divyanshi Singh
Pranveer Singh Institute of Technology, Kanpur, India

Rohit Singh
All India Management Association, New Delhi, India

Majeed Mohammed
https://orcid.org/0000-0001-9804-5335
Tamale Technical University, Ghana

ABSTRACT

Institutions — banks, insurers, hedge funds, and asset managers — are central to fueling the quantum revolution. They supply the capital necessary for research and development as principal investors in quantum startups and partnerships. As early movers, they pilot practical applications such as portfolio optimization, derivatives pricing, and catastrophe modeling, demonstrating quantum's real-world utility. They're also leading in quantum-safe security, advocating for higher encryption to keep valuable transactions secure from coming quantum attacks. By using quantum computing in risk management and product development, they can create more effective financial products, enhance lending and insurance precision, and facilitate

DOI: 10.4018/979-8-3373-2893-5.ch006

better fraud detection. Briefly: Financial institutions drive, experiment with, secure, and amplify the quantum revolution, and profit from it as well. Finance and quantum are symbiotic — each propels the other.

1. INTRODUCTION

Finance means the handling of money, credit, investments, and other financial products. It means the process of how people, firms, and the government borrow money (capital), deploy it, and utilize it effectively (Asni et al., 2024). Finance is broadly categorized into: Personal Finance – handling money of people (savings, loans, insurance). Corporate Finance – how businesses handle capital for expansion, investment, and growth. Public Finance – government revenues, taxes, and expenditure to operate the economy (Xiao & Tao, 2021). In simple terms: Finance is all about planning and managing money to accomplish objectives. Financial institutions are institutions that offer financial services such as accepting deposits, lending money, investing money, and facilitating safe money transactions (Raza et al., 2025). Examples: Banks (SBI, HDFC, ICICI), Insurance Companies (LIC, ICICI Prudential), Stock Exchanges (NSE, BSE), Non-Banking Financial Companies (NBFCs) (Bajaj Finance, HDB Finance), Mutual Funds (SBI Mutual Fund, HDFC Mutual Fund)

1.1 Financial Institutions' Roles

Financial Institutions have certain roles: Mobilization of Savings – Gather small savings from households and enterprises and direct them to productive purposes (Adeola et al., 2022). Credit Provision – Extend loans for business growth, housing, education, and agriculture (Rotimi et al., 2024). Capital Formation – Raise investments by transforming savings into capital (factories, infrastructure, technology). Facilitating Trade & Commerce – Finance businesses with working capital, trade finance, and payments systems. Risk Management – Insurance and derivatives assist businesses and individuals in managing uncertainties (Reyad et al., 2022). Economic Stability – Through regulation, monetary policy transmission, and discipline in lending. Employment Generation – By financing industries and startups, they indirectly generate employment (Mwakalila, 2025).

Financial institutions have certain role which are mentioned like it works on an Intermediary Role – They link surplus units (savers) with deficit units (borrowers); Regulated Entities – Governed by RBI, SEBI, IRDAI, etc. in India. ; Range of Services – Deposits, loans, investment, insurance, fund transfer ; Trust-Based Operations – Whole system operates on public trust and government control; Profit &

Service Orientation – Want to be viable while serving the economy as well (Zheng et al., 2021).

There are certain benefits of financial institutions like Effective Resource Allocation – Transfer money from where it is idle to where it can be utilized (Anakpo et al., 2023); Fosters Savings & Investments – Offers secure channels for individuals to save and gain returns; Fosters Entrepreneurship – Start-ups and small and medium enterprises receive access to capital; Facilitates Infrastructure Development – Long-term financing for roads, power stations, ports, etc; Improves International Trade – With foreign exchange, letters of credit, export financing (Kim, 2021); Fosters Financial Inclusion – Increases access to rural and poor people through Jan Dhan Yojana, microfinance; Economic Stability – Regulates inflation and liquidity through credit policy and interest rates.

1.2Financial Institutions Help in Increasing GDP

GDP (Gross Domestic Product) is the total value of goods and services being produced within a nation. Financial institutions directly contribute to increasing GDP by: Investment in Productive Sectors (Nisa et al., 2024); Funds flow to industries, agriculture, infrastructure → production increases; Credit to Businesses; Aids companies to grow, use technology, and enhance efficiency; Consumption Boost; Home loans, car loans, education loans boost demand → demand drives production → GDP rises; Jobs Generation (Jonas & Christian, 2025).

1.3 Role of Financial Support and Innovation in Driving Economic Growth

Financial support has an important role in driving growth. Export, if assisted by finance, can enhance foreign trade and contribute in to GDP. It leads to more domestic production, more employment and more income. Use of technology increases the efficiency with the help of regulatory environment (Rastogi & Iqbal, 2024).

- Export Development
- Financial support to exporters enhances foreign trade → contributes to GDP.
- Innovation & Startups
- New business loans and venture capital establish new products and markets.
- Financial Inclusion
- Getting rural areas into banking ensures broader access to economic activity, improving total GDP.

Figure 1. Role of Financial Support

Source: Author's work

Assume banks lend money to a textile factory in Kanpur. Factory purchases machines (industrial expansion), employs workers (jobs), manufactures goods (production growth), exports clothes (foreign exchange earnings). These all-combined increase India's GDP.

2. QUANTUM COMPUTING

Quantum computing is a new type of computing that applies quantum physics rules (the study of atoms and particles) to process data (Kasirajan, 2021). While traditional computers employ bits (0 or 1), quantum computers employ qubits — 0, 1, or both simultaneously. This strange behavior allows quantum computers to solve some problems much quicker than regular computers. Key concepts explained simply. Qubit which is a building block A bit in a classical computer is similar to a light switch: ON (1) or OFF (0) (Hughes et al., 2021). A qubit is similar to a flying coin: while it's flying, it's neither heads nor tails — it's in both simultaneously. This state of being in both is referred to as superposition. When you measure (look) at the coin, it falls and is heads or tails — like how measuring a qubit makes it 0 or 1.

2.1 Entanglement

Entanglement connects qubits such that one's state relies on the other even if they're separated (Alashetty et al., 2025). Example (analogy): Suppose we have two magic coins where both always land on opposite sides if flipped. If you flip one and it lands on heads, then you know immediately that the other is tails. Entangled qubits exhibit extremely strong correlations of this sort.

Note: entanglement is not classical "communication" and cannot be used to send a message at faster-than-light speeds.

2.2 Interference

Quantum systems can utilize interference to reinforce correct solutions and eliminate incorrect ones, just like waves can add or cancel (Sinha & Ghosal, 2025). Algorithms are programmed to take advantage of interference so the correct answers are more probable.

2.3 Measurement (collapse)

When you make a measurement on a qubit, the superposition is over — it "collapses" to a definite 0 or 1. So quantum algorithms put qubits and their interactions together so that measurement most likely provides the correct answer (Baiardi et al., 2023).

Figure 2. How does a quantum computer really work?

Put qubits into an initial state (usually all 0s).
↓
Use quantum gates — small operations that flip the qubits' state (similar to logic gates in classical computing, but these apply quantum rules).
↓
Generate entanglement and interference through strings of gates so the right answers get boosted.
↓
Measure the qubits and extract the answer (0s and 1s).
↓
Since quantum measurement is probabilistic, you tend to run the program lots of times and apply statistics to obtain a good answer.

Source: Ekert et al., 2002

2.4 Quantum hardware types:

- Superconducting qubits (e.g., IBM, Google): very small circuits maintained at very low temperatures. Current pioneers in commercial prototypes.
- Trapped ions: ions (charged atoms) that are trapped by electric fields and controlled with lasers. Tend to be highly accurate but with slower gates.
- Photonic systems: employ particles of light (photons). Suit room-temperature processes and communication.

- Quantum annealers (D-Wave): application-specific devices for optimization problems — not general-purpose quantum computers but useful for certain operations.

All technologies have advantages and disadvantages — there is no "best" yet. Scientists are trying many different approaches.

Figure 3. Key Quantum Computing Platforms

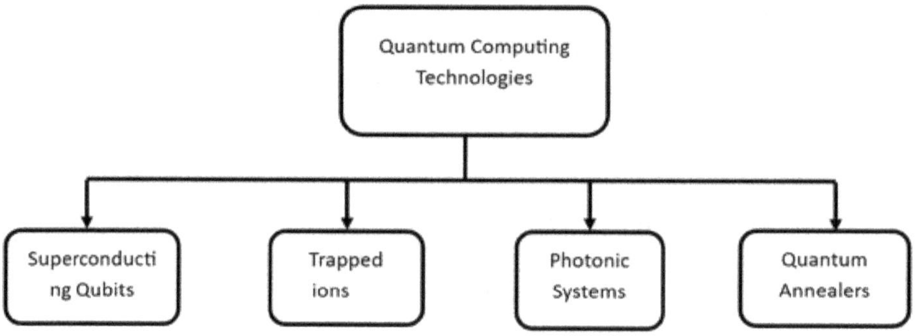

Source: Author's Creation

2.5 What types of problems can quantum computers solve?

Quantum computing is not superior at all. But for some significant problems it might provide huge benefits: Factoring big numbers (Shor's algorithm): might factor widely used encryption such as RSA if sufficiently large quantum computers are available (Rietsche et al., 2022). Searching unstructured data (Grover's algorithm): provides a quadratic speed-up for search problems Irfan et al. (2024). Optimization problems: optimize best routes, schedules, or portfolio allocations quicker for certain cases. Simulating molecules and materials: quantum systems inherently simulate atomic-scale physics massive for drug discovery, new materials, batteries. Monte Carlo and sampling: some quantum approaches can accelerate simulation-based calculations utilized in finance and risk.

2.6 Present reality: What is currently possible?

We do have Noisy Intermediate-Scale Quantum (NISQ) devices: they operate with tens up to a couple of hundred qubits but are noisy (errors occur). Due to noise and faults, current quantum machines are optimal for research, tiny pilots, and hybrid tests — but not yet all large-scale real-world applications. Scientists are constructing error-corrected quantum computers (much bigger and stable) but they require many more physical qubits per logical qubit — this is the biggest engineering challenge (Columbus Chinnappan et al., 2025), (Irfan, Kadry, Sharif, & Khan, 2023).

2.7 Challenges & limitations

Noise and faults (decoherence): qubits quickly lose their quantum nature.
Error correction is costly: takes a large number of additional qubits.
Specialized benefit: quantum won't do for routine tasks what classical computers do — it assists particular, challenging problems.
***Cost and technicality*:** constructing and keeping quantum hardware running is costly and technically challenging.
***Exorbitant Adoption Cost*:**

- Developing and operating quantum technology is extremely costly — it involves cryogenic systems, special labs, and skilled teams.
- Banks and insurance companies need to spend millions (occasionally billions) on R&D, collaborations, and employee training before they can gain any meaningful return.
- For a smaller bank or insurer, this expense can be a significant obstacle.

Scaling up: producing thousands or millions of good qubits is extremely difficult.
***Unpredictable Timeline & ROI*:**

- Quantum computing is in its infancy (NISQ period), so the machines are small and error-infested.
- No one knows when large-scale, error-correcting quantum computers will be available commercially.
- This makes it difficult for banks to explain long-term investment to shareholders — they need evidence that it will reap rewards.

Talent Shortage:

- Quantum computing needs people with expertise in physics, mathematics, and computer science — a very rare combination.
- There are not sufficient trained professionals globally, and banks have to compete with tech giants, governments, and universities for the best brains.
- Re-training current staff is slow and costly.

Integration with Current Systems:

- Banks and insurers operate advanced legacy IT systems that date back several decades.

- It is a formidable technical undertaking to integrate these systems with new quantum solutions Irfan et al. (2024).
- Hybrid (classical + quantum) workflows have to be developed carefully without mistakes and securely.

Cybersecurity Threats (The Quantum Threat):

- Ironically, quantum computing itself poses a threat to finance since it can decrypt today's encryption (RSA, ECC).
- Banks and other financial institutions have to transition to post-quantum cryptography prior to attackers obtaining quantum capabilities.
- This transition is an enormous undertaking — touching ATMs, payment gateways, online banking apps, and trading systems globally.

Regulation and Compliance Issues:

- There are no concrete global regulations for quantum computing as of now.
- Banks need to ensure they remain compliant with data security, risk models, and financial reporting regulations even when employing quantum algorithms.
- Regulators (such as RBI, SEBI, SEC, Basel Committee) will have to lay down guidelines — till then, uncertainty.

Risk of Over-Hype & Wrong Investments:

- Quantum is a "hot" technology, so there is a risk of overpromising and underdelivering.
- If banks invest prematurely in untested technology, they may lose money.
- They need careful back-testing and pilot programs to separate hype from real business value

Ethical & Operational Challenges:

- Using quantum to gain a trading speed advantage could create unfair markets if only a few institutions can afford it.
- Operationally, banks must retrain employees, redesign workflows, and manage change carefully — otherwise adoption will face resistance.

Global Competition & Geopolitical Risk:

- Quantum research is a worldwide competition — the U.S., China, EU, and India are all vying for it.
- Financial institutions need to make sure they are not lagging behind if other countries' competitors implement quantum first and become economically superior.
- There are also data sovereignty issues — banks need to make sure customer data remains protected even if foreign servers host quantum processing.

2.8 Why people get excited (applications & impact)

- *Medicine & chemistry:* quicker simulation of molecules may cut drug discovery time and expense.
- *Materials science:* improved battery, solar cell, superconductor design.
- *Optimization & logistics:* lower supply chain costs, route optimization, energy consumption.
- Finance: accelerated risk simulation, portfolio optimization, and enhanced trading models.
- *Cryptography/security:* both threat (shattering current encryption) and opportunity (quantum-safe encryption, quantum key distribution).

3. QUANTUM REVOLUTION

Quantum computing is emerging from science-fiction promise to concrete industrial effect (Possati, 2024). For financial institutions — banks, asset managers, insurance firms, exchanges, and infrastructure providers — the quantum revolution represents both unprecedented opportunity and existential threat. This book-length essay examines how banks are interacting with quantum technologies now, which use-cases are most important, recent real-world pilots and examples, the strategic positions institutions take in the broader quantum ecosystem, the threats they must address (particularly to cryptography and market integrity), and actionable roadmaps for institutions (Irfan, Mohammed, Kassim, & Ofori, 2024).

3.1 Why Quantum Matters to Finance?

Classic computers have propelled contemporary finance for decades: risk engines, high-frequency trading, Monte Carlo simulations, credit scoring, clearing and settlement systems, and secure communications (Khang, 2025). However, much of financial computing is computationally intensive in ways that challenge classical architectures.

Some examples are:

1. High-dimensional portfolio optimization with large numbers of assets and constraints.
2. Complex derivative pricing under multi-factor stochastic models demanding large Monte Carlo simulations.

Figure 4. Forecast 2030: Financial Institutions and Quantum Revolution

Source: Elyashiv, 2025

3.2 Importance of Financial Institutions in the Quantum Revolution

This Quantum Computational power is a technological shift and somehow it is also an economic shift too. It supports various things like:

1. Funding and Investment Power
   - Financial institutions control trillions of dollars in assets globally.
   - Developing quantum computers is extremely expensive (building labs, superconducting circuits, cryogenic cooling, quantum error correction) (Irfan, Dias, Rastogi, & Zebende, 2025).
   - Governments provide funding for some of this research (e.g., U.S. National Quantum Initiative, India's National Quantum Mission), but private investment is essential.
   - Major banks such as JPMorgan, Goldman Sachs, Barclays, and reinsurers such as Allianz already invest in quantum startups and collaborations.

Figure 5. Quantum Ecosystem

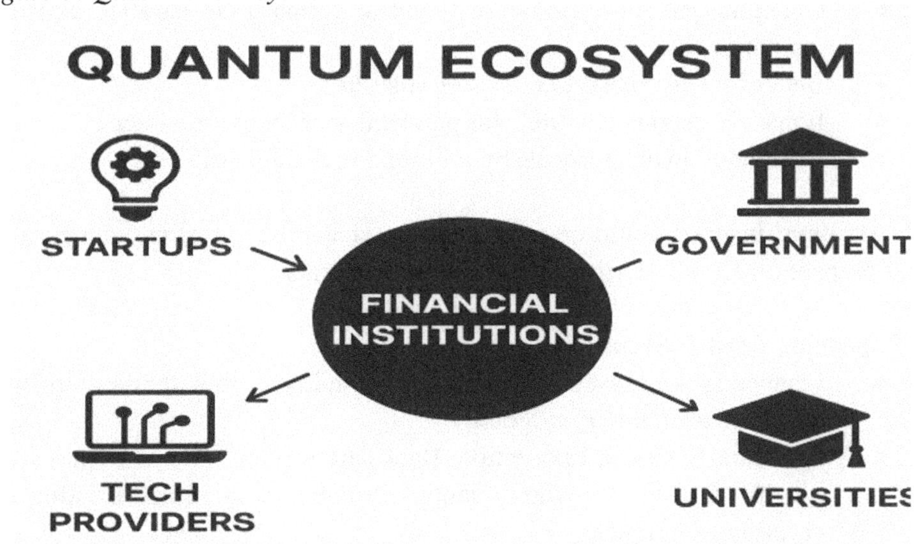

Source: Khang, 2025

2. Investment and Funding Catalysts
   - One of the biggest investors in new technology are financial institutions.

- By investing in quantum startups, research laboratories, and partnerships with tech companies, they contribute to the acceleration of innovation.
- Goldman Sachs and JPMorgan, for instance, already invested in quantum algorithm development for portfolio optimization and derivatives valuation.

3. Early Experimenters and Adopters
    - Finance is computation-intensive and data-intensive (e.g., risk modeling, stock trading, fraud detection).
    - Even slight increases in speed or accuracy yield enormous financial returns.
    - This is why financial institutions tend to be the first to try out quantum computing.

Illustration: JPMorgan and IBM Quantum are exploring quantum algorithms for credit risk and fraud detection.

4. Strengthening Risk Management
    - Risk management is perhaps the largest use of quantum computing in finance
    - Quantum can run millions of financial scenarios in parallel, assisting institutions to:
    - Better forecast market crashes or volatility.
    - Enhance insurance models for pandemics or natural disasters.
    - Streamline loan approvals by minimizing default risks.

Illustration: Insurers could employ quantum-enabled catastrophe modeling to better prepare for floods, earthquakes, or climate threats.

5. Enhancing Trust & Security
    - Finance is the most security-conscious industry, thus it is a pioneer in quantum-resilient cryptography:
    - Quantum-Resistant Encryption: Banks are well on the way to preparing for the "Q-Day" — when quantum computers can crack existing encryption techniques.
    - Secure Transactions: Banks establish industry benchmarks for secure digital payments and custody products.

Example: Mastercard is investigating post-quantum cryptography to protect global payment networks.

3.3 First Adopters & Pioneers of Actual Applications

In every kind of financial service, like dealing with big data, and managing risk, quantum computing works. This makes banks and insurers perfect test beds for early deployments, even when quantum machines remain noisy and small.

Example:

- JPMorgan & IBM: experimenting with portfolio optimization using quantum algorithms.
- Goldman Sachs & QC Ware: investigating quantum approaches to derivatives pricing.
- Munich Re: applying quantum-inspired algorithms to catastrophe modeling.

3.4 Fueling Demand for Post-Quantum Security

One of the most significant dangers posed by quantum computing is that it can break existing cryptography (RSA, ECC). • Financial institutions and banks regularly handle sensitive customer information and high-value transactions - they are prime targets for cyber breaches. • So, naturally, they are leading the way toward quantum-safe (post-quantum) cryptography for securing transactions, digital wallets and payment systems. By requiring quantum-safe infrastructure, financial institutions force governments and technology companies to speed the development of secure digital environments.

1. Why Financial Institutions Care Most
   a) Financial institutions work with:
      - Trillions of dollars in day-to-day transactions (payments, lending, settlements).
      - Sensitive customer information (account information, private information, credit history).
      - Valuable financial assets (bonds, stocks, digital custody, cross-border payments).

   b) A single security incident can cause:
      - Massive financial loss.
      - Breakdown of public trust.
      - Global market instability.
2. Financial Institutions' Role in Leading PQS Demand
   a) Planning & Early Migration
      - Financial institutions are early adopters of migrating their systems to quantum-resistant cryptography.

- They conduct risk analysis to determine the areas that are vulnerable to quantum attacks (ATMs, payment channels, SWIFT network, mobile banking apps).

Example: Mastercard and Visa have initiated a search for quantum-safe payment protocols.

b) Working with Tech Providers

- Banks work with cybersecurity and cryptography providers to come up with quantum-safe solutions.

Example:

- JPMorgan collaborates with Toshiba to investigate Quantum Key Distribution (QKD) for highly secure communications.
- HSBC joined the Post-Quantum Cryptography Alliance, advocating for cross-industry standards.

c) Regulatory Push & Standardization

- Banks lobby regulators (such as RBI, SEC, BIS) to:
- Impose PQC adoption timelines.
- Develop compliance guidelines for quantum-resistant systems.
- This generates cross-industry demand, compelling technology vendors to accelerate upgrades.

d) Educating Stakeholders

- Banks promote awareness campaigns for their boards, IT staff, and even clients regarding the imminent "quantum danger."
- They disseminate research articles, proof-of-concepts, and pilot projects to indicate haste and prompt other industries to act.

3. Advantages of Adopting Post-Quantum Security

Future-Proofing: Shields systems against "harvest now, decrypt later" attacks wherein hackers harvest encrypted information today and decrypt tomorrow.

- Customer Trust: Safe systems enhance brand image and avoid panic.

- Financial Stability: Minimizes systemic risk of cyberattacks that might destabilize entire markets.
- Regulatory Compliance: Preemptive adoption makes institutions prepared when international standards become obligatory.
    - Recent Example:

In 2023, JPMorgan Chase, Toshiba, and Ciena successfully showcased Quantum Key Distribution (QKD) to secure data transfer over a metropolitan fiber network.

This was a milestone, indicating that financial data can be safeguarded even against future quantum-powered cyberattacks.

3.5 Accelerating National & International Economies (GDP Growth)

- Finance is a backbone sector — each nation's economy is dependent on effective financial systems. Plans.
- If quantum computing enhances capital allocation, risk management, fraud detection, and security, the entire economy becomes efficient.

This develops a multiplier effect:

Financial institutions can straightaway increase GDP and aid a nation's competitive edge in the global economy by embracing quantum tools early.

Figure 6. Financial institutions & GDP growth

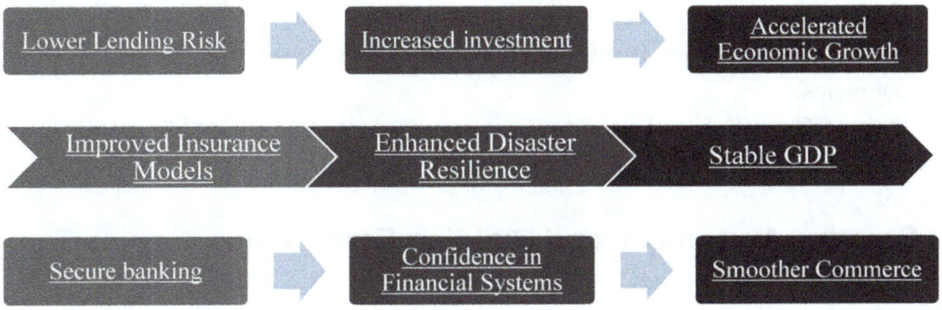

Source: Judijanto, 2025

3.6 Regulation and Standards Shaping

Finance is a highly regulated sector.

Once quantum goes mainstream, regulators (such as RBI, SEBI, Federal Reserve, SEC) will require new regulations for quantum security, risk models, and investment techniques.

Establishing Quantum-Safe Standards

Banks and insurance companies will take a front-row seat in crafting these rules, much the same way as they did in cybersecurity and digital banking.

Compliance and Risk Guidelines

- Financial institutions provide input on the development of risk frameworks for quantum adoption, such as:
- How to quantify quantum-readiness.
- How to handle data migration to quantum-safe systems.
- How to audit quantum algorithms for bias and compliance.
- Example: Regulators will soon mandate that banks retain a "Quantum Risk Register" similar to cybersecurity risk registers.

Examples in Action

- NIST PQC Initiative (USA): Banks and financial institutions across the world are pilot-testing such suggested algorithms as CRYSTALS-Kyber and Dilithium for quantum-resistant encryption.
- ISO/IEC Quantum Standards: Banks are involved in working groups to establish international encryption and quantum computing standards.
- India's National Quantum Mission: Indian financial authorities are talking to banks to prepare a national strategy for quantum preparedness.

Challenges

Slow Policy-Making: Technology is advancing faster than regulations, creating the possibility of security loopholes.

Coordination Across Borders: There can be different standards in various countries.

Cost of Compliance: Upgrading smaller banks to quantum-safe systems can be expensive.

3.7 Creating Awareness and Building Ecosystems

Quantum computing is still an emerging tech — strong on paper, but not yet well understood outside of research institutions and tech firms. For the quantum revolution to take off, we require wide awareness and a robust ecosystem of stakeholders (governments, startups, universities, corporates). Financial institutions have an important role to play in making it happen.

Quantum computing remains a young technology — theoretically powerful but as yet not well understood beyond research labs and technology companies. To make the quantum revolution succeed, we require universal awareness and a healthy ecosystem of stakeholders (governments, startups, universities, corporates). Financial institutions have an important role to play in making this happen.

- Quantum technology is very technical, and most sectors are not familiar with it yet.
- Financial institutions tend to be early adopters of technologies (such as AI, blockchain, cloud).
- Through investing, piloting, and publishing research, they raise industry-wide awareness.

1. Awareness Creation — Why It Matters?

a) Educating Stakeholders
   - Executives, policymakers, and even IT experts have relatively little knowledge of quantum computing and its implications.
   - Banks and financial institutions can inform boards, investors, and customers of the opportunities (portfolio optimization, accelerated simulations) and the risks (post-quantum cybersecurity).
   - Awareness guarantees decision-makers will endorse funding and regulation of quantum programs.

b) Building Confidence
   - Early adoption of quantum is expensive and risky — so raising awareness establishes confidence and trust in the technology.
   - Insurers and banks can highlight pilot initiatives, case studies, and proof-of-concepts to illustrate that quantum computing is not mere "hype" and has practical applications.

2. How Financial Institutions Raise Awareness

Publishing Research & White Papers:

o Example: Goldman Sachs has written papers on optimization and quantum derivatives pricing, making their work available to the academic and business world.
   - This triggers debate and encourages other companies to pursue quantum opportunities.

Industry Events & Conferences:

- Banks host and present at conferences such as Quantum.Tech, Q2B, or IBM Quantum Summit.

- Conferences disseminate knowledge to technology companies, regulators, and other sectors.

Collaborations with Academia:

- Financial institutions support quantum labs within universities or underwrite PhD programs.
- Example: JPMorgan collaborates with MIT and other universities on quantum research, building a pipeline of talent.

Internal Training & Upskilling:

- As important as making people aware outside, it is equally important to create awareness within the organization.
- Banks implement quantum literacy courses for staff such that teams (IT, risk, compliance) comprehend the fundamentals and are able to spot upcoming use cases.

3. Building Ecosystems — The Bigger Picture

Creating awareness is merely step one. Step two is constructing an ecosystem where everyone participates to fuel the advance.

a) Stakeholder Collaboration

- Banks + Tech Giants:

JPMorgan + IBM Quantum partnership to develop quantum algorithms.

- Banks + Startups:

Barclays partners with QC Ware (a quantum software company) for algorithmic testing.

- Banks + Governments:

Participating in national quantum missions (such as India's National Quantum Mission) to influence policy and funding.

b) Fostering Innovation

- Financial institutions invest in venture funds and quantum startups to foster innovation in quantum hardware, cryptography, and software.
- Even some banks establish quantum innovation centers or accelerators for startups.

c) Standardization & Regulation

- Financial institutions collaborate with regulators (RBI, SEC, BIS) to develop standards for quantum-safe encryption, compliance frameworks, and risk models.
- This provides secure and seamless adoption of quantum technology across the industry.

d) Building Talent Pipelines

- Sponsoring education, training, hackathons, and internships to develop the next generation of quantum engineers and analysts.
- Reduces the quantum talent gap in the long term.

4. Benefits of Awareness & Ecosystem Building

Accelerated Adoption: More stakeholders are aware of quantum and begin using it.

Lower Risk: More informed organizations steer clear of hype and make rational investments.

Shared Knowledge: Collaboration disseminates breakthroughs across industries, minimizing duplication of effort.

Economic Growth: Resilient ecosystems draw startups, researchers, and investments → enhances national competitiveness and GDP.

Trust & Security: Informed customers and regulators are more confident to embrace quantum-safe systems.

Example in Action: The Quantum Ecosystem Today

IBM Quantum Network: Unites more than 200 institutions, such as JPMorgan, Goldman Sachs, Daimler, and top universities, to work together on quantum research.

European Quantum Industry Consortium (QuIC): Banks and insurers that exchange research results and collaborate on quantum-safe standards.

India's National Quantum Mission: Encourages intergovernmental, academic, and private sector collaboration — Indian banks can play an important role here.

Goldman Sachs issued quantum derivatives pricing papers that impacted both the academic world and industry.

4. FINANCIAL INSTITUTIONS AS CATALYSTS: ROLES & RESPONSIBILITIES

Financial institutions are not passive users of quantum tech. Their functions are active and multi-faceted.

Investors and Funders

Banks, asset managers, and institutional investors invest capital in quantum startups and research initiatives. That capital ramps up hardware, software, and talent development throughout the ecosystem. The capital flow can decide which hardware modalities (superconducting, photonic, trapped-ion, annealers) scale first and which algorithmic techniques get developed most.

Example: Huge injections of investor funds into firms such as Quantinuum and D-Wave demonstrate private markets' appreciation of quantum firms and facilitating accelerated roadmap growth. Quantinuum's recent funding and valuation milestones reflect increasing investor interest and commercial dealings with banks as customers.

The Guardian

Customers & First Adopters

Banks and financial institutions are at the forefront of piloting quantum algorithms and platforms since they have high-value use-cases and can absorb exploratory expenses. Pilot experiments early on vindicate algorithms, uncover data-encoding issues, and identify realistic performance trade-offs between noisy quantum hardware and classical supercomputers.

Example: Large banks (J.P. Morgan, HSBC, Goldman Sachs, etc.) have released pilots and study collaborations with research labs and quantum vendors for trying out use-cases such as pricing, portfolio encoding, and random-number generation. These pilots are tangible actions toward commercialization.

Barron's

The Quantum Insider

Conveners & Standards Advocates

Large institutions possess a convening power: they have the ability to bring together across hardware vendors, software toolmakers, regulators, and standards bodies to spur interoperability, benchmarking, and best practices (e.g., on post-quantum cryptographic migration). Industry convenings and consortia facilitate expectation alignment and faster adoption.

5. BUSINESS MODELS & STRATEGIC IMPERATIVES FOR INSTITUTIONS

Financial institutions can take a continuum of strategies to harvest value from quantum technologies.

Defensive Stance: Cryptographic Preparedness

Urgent imperative: be ready for the cryptographic risk. Although years away, large-scale, fault-tolerant quantum computers may one day pose a threat, "harvest-now, decrypt-later" attacks endanger long-term encrypted information (e.g., stored private keys, settlement records). Institutions need to:

- Catalog sensitive information and its duration.
- Create plans to migrate to post-quantum standard algorithms (e.g., those under development by NIST).
- Pilot quantum-resistant solutions in mission-critical products (e.g., tokenized assets, custody services).
- Join industry-wide asset and key rotation standards.
- HSBC's quantum-resistant tokenized-gold pilot is one such real-world implementation of these efforts.

Offensive Posture: Competitive Advantage through Quantum Algorithms

For asset managers and investment banks, quantum algorithms can be a competitive advantage in optimization, pricing, and risk modeling. Institutions should:

- Construct sandboxes for hybrid quantum-classical assessment.
- Budget R&D to pit quantum algorithms against classical engines using real-world datasets.
- Hire quantitative researchers with expertise in crossing finance, quantum information science, and software engineering.
- Research collaborations between Goldman Sachs and J.P. Morgan are the best examples of this.

Platform & Services Posture: Quantum-Enabled Products

Banks are able to offer new services: quantum-secure custody, quantum-randomness-as-a-service for derivative systems, quantum-enhanced risk assessments, and tokenization platforms shielded by quantum-hardened primitives.

Ecosystem Posture: Partnership and Standards Leadership

Institutions must engage closely with hardware providers, cloud providers, academic research laboratories, and standards bodies in order to influence interoperable tools and representative industry benchmarks.

"Multi-stakeholder reports by the World Economic Forum and others emphasize the relevance of coordinated commissioning, benchmarking, and standards for finance."-

World Economic Forum Reports

6. REGULATORY & ETHICAL CONSIDERATIONS

Quantum technologies cut across regulatory responsibilities in a variety of ways. Broad quantum-facilitated benefits in pricing or trading might generate new asymmetries. Regulators might desire insight into where quantum-derived benefit lies and might look at policies to forestall destabilizing concentration of capability. When retail lines add quantum-hardened products (e.g., tokenized assets sold to retail investors), institutions have an obligation to provide clarity regarding risk, cryptographic protection lifespan, and what "quantum-safe" really entails in practice. Banks ought to demand strong third-party certification regimes for quantum security assertions (e.g., for RNGs, PQC implementations) and benchmarks on quantum algorithm performance in financial environments. Multi-stakeholder reports and international organization policy frameworks stress collaboration among regulators, industry, and academia.

7. THE TALENT CHALLENGE & ORGANIZATIONAL CHANGE

Quantum expertise is multidisciplinary. Financial institutions need to:

- Hire quantum information scientists, quantum software engineers, and quantum-aware quants (Hughes et al., 2022).
- Upskill classical quant teams in quantum computing basics.
- Create cross-functional groups pairing business owners (trading desks, risk teams) with tech R&D teams.
- Joint appointments from universities or internal fellowship programs should be considered.
- Talent shortage implies that partnerships with vendors, cloud providers, and universities will continue to be crucial in the near future (Kwok, 2022).

8. FUTURE OUTLOOK: WHAT COULD CHANGE THE GAME?

A number of developments have the potential to dramatically speed up adoption: Fault-tolerant quantum computers with minimal logical qubit overhead would enable large-scale algorithms (e.g., full-scale amplitude estimation) and enable new classes of applications (Memon et al., 2024). Hybrid quantum-classical accelerators (e.g., IBM & AMD-style partnerships to develop quantum-focused supercomputers) might enable the infusion of quantum modules into current HPC workflows. Alliances between classical and quantum hardware providers are already in progress. TechRadar Market-standard quantum services (established, SaaS-like quantum optimization or quantum-hardened custody) provided by the leading cloud providers would reduce the barriers to entry (Steane, 1999).

9. CONCLUDING THOUGHTS: STRATEGY, HUMILITY & URGENCY

The quantum revolution is not a near-term silver bullet or distant myth. It is an intricate, multi-decade process with short-term actions (cryptographic preparedness, exploratory pilots) and long-term rewards (algorithmic advantage, new offerings). Financial institutions are the best positioned to speed and gain from quantum because they unite capital, use-cases, regulatory incentives, and commercial pressure (Stockman, 2013).

Action items condensed:

- PQC migration as a priority — take stock and plan today.
- Pilot pragmatically — select high-value challenges, benchmark against traditional benchmarks, and concentrate on hybrid solutions.
- Invest in partnerships and talent — join consortia, partner with suppliers, and co-fund research.
- Govern ahead of time — board-level leadership, cross-functional governance, and public coordination with regulators (Dixit, 2022).
- Balance competition with systemic responsibility — innovation has to be accompanied by protections to insulate customers and markets.

10. SUMMARY

Institutions — banks, insurers, hedge funds, and asset managers — are central to fueling the quantum revolution. They supply the capital necessary for research and development as principal investors in quantum startups and partnerships. As early movers, they pilot practical applications such as portfolio optimization, derivatives pricing, and catastrophe modeling, demonstrating quantum's real-world utility (Mosteanu & Faccia, 2021).

They're also leading in quantum-safe security, advocating for higher encryption to keep valuable transactions secure from coming quantum attacks. By using quantum computing in risk management and product development, they can create more effective financial products, enhance lending and insurance precision, and facilitate better fraud detection (Dixit, 2022).

Financial institutions enhance quantum's effect by increasing the GDP of nations: more effective risk analysis translates to more resilient investments, intelligent insurance enhances the ability to bounce back, and secure banking inspires confidence in economies. Additionally, since finance is a heavily regulated sector, these institutions guide future policy and standards for secure adoption (Nguyen, 2025).

Lastly, by making research public and working with governments, startups, and universities, financial institutions increase awareness and create quantum innovation ecosystems.Briefly: Financial institutions drive, experiment with, secure, and amplify the quantum revolution, and profit from it as well (Rapp, 2021). Finance and quantum are symbiotic — each propels the other.

- Support quantum research in the form of investment.
- Experiment with real-world applications in finance.
- Enable demand for post-quantum security.
- Develop innovative financial products and services.
- Boost GDP by making economies more efficient.
- Craft regulation for safe adoption.
- Construct ecosystems by linking industries and knowledge.

Quantum requires finance as finance requires quantum. The collaboration is a symbiosis — without financial institutions, quantum development would be short of funds, real-world testability, and ROI clarity. And without quantum, financial institutions risk lagging in risk, security, and innovation. (Nguyen, 2025).

REFERENCES

Adeola, O., Adeleye, I., Muhammed, G., Olajubu, B. J., Oji, C., & Ibelegbu, O. (2022). Savings groups in Nigeria. In *Transforming Africa: How savings groups foster financial inclusion, resilience and economic development* (pp. 193–216). Emerald Publishing Limited.

Alashetty, A., Vani, M. P., Anitha, E., & Satyamurty, C. V. (2025). Introduction of quantum computing. In *Quantum machine learning in industrial automation* (pp. 277–304). Springer Nature Switzerland.

Anakpo, G., Xhate, Z., & Mishi, S. (2023). The policies, practices, and challenges of digital financial inclusion for sustainable development: The case of the developing economy. *FinTech*, *2*(2), 327–343.

Asni, F., Zulkifli, M. I., & Yusli, Y. (2024). Acceptance of zakat institutions in Malaysia towards micro credit–Qard Hasan financing through zakat fund (MCZF) for post-pandemic Asnaf entrepreneurs. *Journal of Islamic Accounting and Business Research.*

Baiardi, A., Christandl, M., & Reiher, M. (2023). Quantum computing for molecular biology. *ChemBioChem*, *24*(13), e202300120. PMID: 37151197

Columbus Chinnappan, C., Thanaraj Krishnan, P., Elamaran, E., Arul, R., & Sunil Kumar, T. (2025). Quantum computing: Foundations, architecture and applications. *Engineering Reports*, *7*(8), e70337.

Dixit, S. (2022). AI-powered risk modeling in quantum finance: Redefining enterprise decision systems.

Ekert, A., Hayden, P. M., & Inamori, H. (2002). Basic concepts in quantum computation. In *Coherent atomic matter waves: 27 July–27 August 1999* (pp. 661–701). Springer Berlin Heidelberg.

Elyashiv, T. (2025). Quantum revolution investment scenario examples, or putting theory to practice. In *Investing in revolutions: Creating wealth from transformational technology waves* (pp. 187–221). Apress.

Hughes, C., Isaacson, J., Perry, A., Sun, R. F., & Turner, J. (2021). What is a qubit? In *Quantum computing for the quantum curious* (pp. 7–16). Springer International Publishing.

Irfan, M., Dias, R., Rastogi, R., & Zebende, G. F. (2025). *Generative AI insights for financial decision making*. IGI Global.

Irfan, M., Elmogy, M., Gupta, S., Khalifa, F., & Dias, R. T. (2024). *AI-driven decentralized finance and the future of finance*. IGI Global.

Irfan, M., Hussainey, K., Bukhari, S. A. C., & Nam, Y. (2024). *Issues of sustainability in AI and new-age thematic investing*. IGI Global.

Irfan, M., Kadry, S., Sharif, M., & Khan, H. U. (2023). *Fintech applications in Islamic finance: AI, machine learning, and blockchain techniques*. IGI Global.

Irfan, M., Mohammed, M., Kassim, S., & Ofori, K. S. (2024). *The future of indigenous inclusivity: Unlocking finance for economic development*. IGI Global.

Jonas, N., & Christian, M. (2025). Transforming South African agriculture: The role of credit in supporting value chain sustainability. *Agriculture*, *15*(6), 620.

Judijanto, L. (2025). Exploring the potential of quantum computing in revolutionising risk management and digital financial security. *International Journal of Finance & Economics*, *2*(6), 685–693.

Kasirajan, V. (2021). *Fundamentals of quantum computing*. Springer International Publishing.

Khang, A. (Ed.). (2025). *Shaping cutting-edge technologies and applications for digital banking and financial services*. Productivity Press.

Kim, S. M. (2021). *Payment methods and finance for international trade*. Springer.

Mosteanu, N. R., & Faccia, A. (2021). Fintech frontiers in quantum computing, fractals, and blockchain distributed ledger: Paradigm shifts and open innovation. *Journal of Open Innovation*, *7*(1), 19.

Mwakalila, E. (2025). Impact of government domestic borrowing on monetary policy rate pass-through in Tanzania. *Journal of Policy Modeling*, *47*(1), 150–165.

Nguyen, P. N. (2025). Quantum technology: A financial risk assessment. *Digital Finance*, •••, 1–40.

Nisa, C., Subhan, M. N., Hendratni, T. W., & Oentarjo, Y. (2024). The nexus between rural bank performance and growth of regional gross domestic product in Depok, West Java. *Dinasti International Journal of Economics, Finance & Accounting (DIJEFA)*, *5*(1).

Possati, L. M. (2024). Quantum technologies: A hermeneutic technology assessment approach. *NanoEthics*, *18*(1), 2.

Rapp, H. P., Schneider, S., & AG, D. B. (2021). Economic-technological revolution through Quantum 2.0. *Germany Monitor.*

Rastogi, R., & Iqbal, M. I. (2024). Data security and privacy in RegTech. In *Integrating RegTech solutions for Industry 4.0* (pp. 185–198). IGI Global.

Raza, S. A., Syed, D., Rizwan, S., & Ahmed, M. (2025). Trends of AI in financial services and its applications. In *The global evolution, changing landscape and future of financial markets: From traditional to digital* (pp. 33–46). Emerald Publishing Limited.

Reyad, H. M., Zariyawati, M. A., Ong, T. S., & Muhamad, H. (2022). The impact of macroeconomic risk factors, the adoption of financial derivatives on working capital management, and firm performance. *Sustainability*, *14*(21), 14447.

Rietsche, R., Dremel, C., Bosch, S., Steinacker, L., Meckel, M., & Leimeister, J. M. (2022). Quantum computing. *Electronic Markets*, *32*(4), 2525–2536.

Rotimi, F., Olubiyo, S., Agbonlahor, M., & Adeogun, S. (2024). Determinants of loan repayment among agricultural beneficiaries of public funded credit scheme in Ekiti State, Nigeria. *Journal of Contemporary African Studies*, *42*(1), 88–103.

Sinha, U., & Ghosh, D. (2025). Interference in quantum mechanics. *Journal of the Indian Institute of Science*, •••, 1–21.

Steane, A. M. (1999). Efficient fault-tolerant quantum computing. *Nature*, *399*(6732), 124–126.

Stockman, D. (2013). The great deformation: The corruption of capitalism in America. Hachette UK.

Xiao, J. J., & Tao, C. (2021). Consumer finance/household finance: The definition and scope. *China Finance Review International*, *11*(1), 1–25.

Zheng, G. W., Siddik, A. B., Masukujjaman, M., & Fatema, N. (2021). Factors affecting the sustainability performance of financial institutions in Bangladesh: The role of green finance. *Sustainability*, *13*(18), 10165.

Chapter 7
Impact of Green Finance on Carbon Footprint:
Analyzing the Role of Sustainable Investments in Carbon Emission Reduction

Ruchika Rastogi
https://orcid.org/0000-0001-7144-4387
Pranveer Singh Institute of Technology, Kanpur, India

Sandeep Kumar
Institute of Business Management, GLA University, Mathura, India

Rui Dias
https://orcid.org/0000-0002-6138-3098
Universidade Europeia, Portugal

ABSTRACT

Green finance helps in climate change adaptation, biodiversity protection, managing sanitation, pollution control, managing renewable energies, and waste recycling and processing hence it is a broader term. Climate related investments are not the only one advantage of green finance rather other advantages are indirectly contributing in the carbon emission reduction. Green finance as important for everyone as it leads to low carbon emission for the society. Money landed by banks leads to make economy greener in terms of creating jobs, creating sustainable environment and reducing carbon emission. This study analyzes the relationship among green finance, ESG performance and carbon emission intensity in the countries like USA, Japan

DOI: 10.4018/979-8-3373-2893-5.ch007

and Europe. This study checks the role of green finance in the overall improvement of ESG with carbon emission intensityIn this analysis it is seen that there is no significant relationship found in ESG and carbon emission intensity in USA.

1. INTRODUCTION

Green financing is a form of loan facility and investment which supports the sustainable and environmentally friendly goods and services or promotes to the green environment for the economy (Vanishvili, & Katsadze, 2022). It is not easy for the countries to adopt it as it incurs heavy infrastructure cost but the government with the help of subsidies and incentives can make it viable. Incentives for sustainable production methods by using sustainable raw material are the easiest way to get in to this. It can also help in managing circular economy which works upon reduce, reuse and recycle (Kumar et al., 2024). To save the economy, banks are continuously working upon various green financing methods and ready to support projects deals in solar energy, wind energy and other renewable methods to manage energy (Onabowale, 2024). Objective of green financing lies in transforming the economy in to low carbon economy and support to the agendas set by UN climate change of conference (Adamowicz, 2022). This will help the economies to reduce global warming below 2 degree celsius. To give a clarity on climate financing and green financing, climate financing is just a part of green finance which focuses on one part which claims to climate change whereas green finance is a broader term (Shishlov & Censkowsky, 2022).

Figure 1. Green investments (Lindenberg, 2014)

Green finance helps in climate change adaptation, biodiversity protection, managing sanitation, pollution control, managing renewable energies, and waste recycling and processing hence it is a broader term. Climate related investments are not the only one advantage of green finance rather other advantages is indirectly contributing in the carbon emission reduction. Green finance as important for everyone as it leads to low carbon emission for the society. Money landed by banks leads to make economy greener in terms of creating jobs, creating sustainable environment and reducing carbon emission. To achieve the goal of carbon neutrality, economic restructuring for low carbon development is required (Perez, 2024). It involves many policies, like green bonds, green loans, green insurance, and carbon financing. China which is the largest carbon emitter is also supposed to achieve carbon neutrality by the year 2060 (Li et al., 2024). India's transition to become a part of net zero emission is creating awareness and evolving day by day (Ahluwalia & Patel, 2021). Banks are financing to small and medium enterprises in India which focuses on sustainable development and also on reducing Carbon emission. Green Social, Sustainability and Sustainability Linked (GSSS) bonds which are of green, yellow and blue are gradually increasing (Prakash et al., 2024). According to the World Bank report,

Indian energy efficient technologies will fetch the opportunity of US$1.6 trillion by 2040 (Vedachalam, 2022).

In relation to check the impact of green finance on carbon emission, ESG framework can be used (Xie, 2024). Environmental metrics include the impact of carbon footprints, its intensity, and green innovation adoption (Al Amosh & Khatib, 2025). Social metrics help in checking the involvement of clean energy by green financial and non-financial initiatives (Akpan, & Oluwagbade, 2023). Government metrics help in knowing the impact of green finance on sustainability.

As mentioned in the introduction, green finance is a major tool for sustainable development and carbon emission reduction. Its implementation is yet not so smooth because of high infrastructure cost and government guidelines of investment. ESG performs can help in checking carbon neutrality initiatives. Currently China is focusing upon the ESG framework to reduce carbon emission (Qian & Liu, 2024). By neutralizing carbon emission, companies improve the environmental, social and governance performance which ultimately contribute in the country's economic growth (Wang et al., 2024). Environmental metrics include the impact of carbon footprints, its intensity, and green innovation adoption (Al Amosh & Khatib, 2025). Social metrics help in checking the involvement of clean energy by green financial and non-financial initiatives (Akpan, & Oluwagbade., 2023). Government metrics help in knowing the impact of green finance on sustainability. It is also seen that relationship among green finance, carbon emission ad ESG is still unexplored and further exploration is required.

It is also seen in the literature that very few studies are conducted in USA, Japan, and Europe for exploring the relationship among green finance, ESG and carbon emission (Meo & Abd Karim, 2022). These three countries can be taken as these three are having global leadership in climate change and ESG. This is also unexplored that how strategies related to carbon emission works in developed nations. Without the further investigation, the impact of green finance in different economies will be unrealized.

2. CARBON EMISSION AND GREEN FINANCE

Dimensions of carbon emission keeps on changing time to time. China is all time high and India is surpassing EU and became the third largest source of Carbon emission in 2023 (Xiao, 2023). When we see region-wise data between 2000 to 2020, It can be seen in Figure 2. that India is surpassing European Union in carbon emission.

Figure 2. Carbon total emission region wise (2000 to 2022)

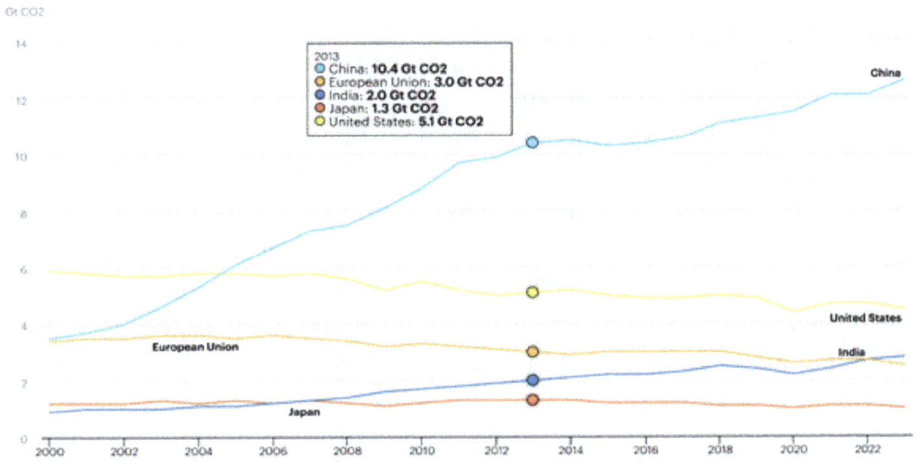

Source: (www.iea.org)

Global Carbon emission is increased by 1.1 percent in 2023 (Table 1) and reaching to the new heights of 410 million tons (Karis, 2024). In this emission, the largest contributor is coal which has the share of more than 65 percent. Now this study helps in understanding that how green finance is helping the economies to reduce carbon die oxide emission (Labatt & White, 2011).

Table 1. Annual numbers of CO2 emission (Khaleel, 2024)

Year	CO_2 Emissions	Caused by
2023	0.41 Gt CO_2	Energy combustion & industrial prosses
2022	0.49 Gt CO_2	Energy combustion & industrial prosses
2021	1.92 Gt CO_2	Energy combustion & industrial prosses
2020	-1.92 Gt CO_2	Energy combustion & industrial prosses
2019	0.01 Gt CO_2	Energy combustion & industrial prosses
2018	0.86 Gt CO_2	Energy combustion & industrial prosses
2017	0.57 Gt CO_2	Energy combustion & industrial prosses
2016	0.10 Gt CO_2	Energy combustion & industrial prosses
2015	-0.10 Gt CO_2	Energy combustion & industrial prosses

As per the available literature, green finance is not always very beneficial for developed countries or where the private sector is strong. It is efficient in those economies where the private sector is weak generally in developing or under developing nations (Chien et al., 2021). A study conducted by Hammoudeh et al, 2020 has also shown that there is no correlation between the green bonds and the environmental impact. Few studies have also indicated that there is no correlation between the green bonds and sustainable development goals in India as India lacks in implementation of financial policies (Bansal et al., 2023). Even European investment banks who have issued green bonds were not able to work upon the proper fund allocation hence found no benefits in carbon emission reduction (Bhutta et al., 2022).

Apart these studies, some studies are also found with positive correlation between green finance and carbon emission reduction (Sun, 2022). Literature has shown the evidence of positive relationship between green bonds and clean energy development. In Asia pacific, it is found that green bonds were able to provide high returns but with higher risk (Bhutta, 2022). A study conducted by Taghizadeh- Hesary & Yoshino, 2021 found that green loans issued by public banks have positively impacted the society.

2.1. Different Industries and Green Finance

Green finance influence industrial structure in different economies. Many studies are conducted to check the impact of green finance on productivity, financial performance, and on economic growth too (Wang & Wang, 2021). Cline in fossil fuel is the result of green financing in the energy sector (Wang et al., 2022). Vesta wind system has launched green bonds for the purpose of clean energy which led to decline in the use of fossil fuels and non-renewable resources (Kurvits, 2022). Green finance helps in reducing the landfills of waste in many economies as the economies are working upon the concept of circular economy which has shown low carbon emission in the manufacturing sector (Yu et al., 2023). Government initiative of green loans in to automobile industry has promoted EVs which have largely contributed in the carbon emission reduction. Banks in different developing and under developing nations have also strategizing the impact of ESG in emission reduction (Wu et al., 2021).

2.2 Green Finance and Innovation

Green finance can help in innovating new technologies to mitigate carbon emission repercussions (Sharif et al., 2022). Green innovation is all about talking to the new methods, products and services for sustainable development (Khurshid et al., 2023). It all about coming up with new technologies where the use of fossil fuel is less and energy efficient technologies are more (Zhang et al., 2022). Production of sustainable goods with the help of sustainable technologies can contribute in to GDP hence increase employment and exploration of new markets. Ultimately Green finance and green innovation can-not go separately (Hu et al., 2023).

Figure 3. Green Finance & Green Innovation (Agarwal et al., 2024)

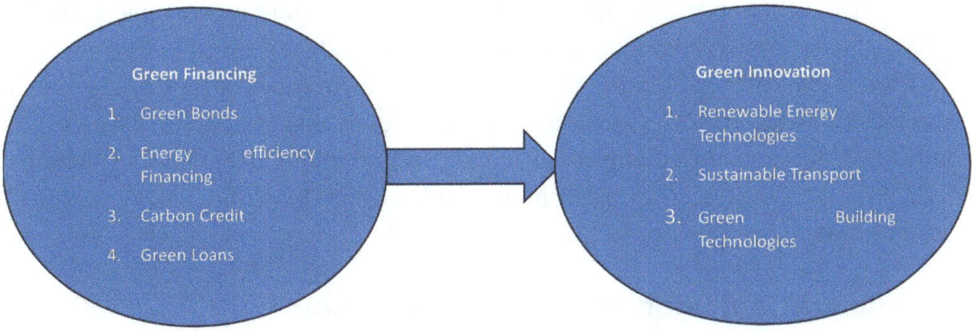

2.3 Green Finance and Credit Markets

Green finance availability is increased with the help of green loans and investments (Ozili, 2022). Meo & Abd Karim, 2022 has explained the benefit of green finance by conducting a research study in top 10 economies where she found that green finance helps in achieving sustainable development. Manufactures get the benefits of green investment by their supplier who provides supplies to them (D'Angelo et al., 2023). It is also studied that in credit market, carbon futures have a great impact in medium to long period as not very beneficial in short term (Demiralay, 2022). Green bonds have also shown a positive great impact in established credit markets where innovation is directly linked with green finance (Wang et al, 2022).

2.4 Green finance around the World

Green investment done by emerging, developing, under developing and developed economies influence the impact on carbon emission at global level (Xu et al., 2023). In Austria, it is speculated that green bonds, and green equity investment will achieve the green economic growth of Euro 17 billion till 2030. Only public funding is not sufficient, hence private capital mobilization is also required for the sustainable project funding in Austria (Ozili, 2022). In United Kingdom, awareness is less hence the government is requested to create awareness so that more benefits can be harnessed (Fay, 2012). Russian economy is lacking in regulatory framework for green finance and facing a lot of challenges like no private investments and lack of green procurement in many products (Cherepovitsyn et al., 2023).

In Asia, countries like Japan, China, and South Korea have harnessed the benefits of green finance. Banks in China and South Korea are very much in to issuing green bonds for sustainable development (Volz, 2018). Sensitization regarding green finance and its benefits to different industries are required to be done in India (Wasan et al., 2021). In Singapore, situation is different as small and medium enterprise do not have the access of processing green bonds (Zhao, 2022).

Africa is the only national country which has formal nation policy for green finance (Shipalana, 2022). Nigeria has got a log of advantage of green finance and South Africa has created a complete different green segment in their stock exchange (Ozili, 2022). Overall, all the countries are working hard but still it can be explored more in future.

2.5 Financial Inclusion and Carbon Emission

Financial inclusion can't claim to be beneficial all the time, as it has positive and negative effects (Ozili, 2022). Financial inclusion has created the easy availability of the funds to the manufactures for investing in green technologies and get cost effective production of goods (Liu et al., 2022). For an example if a farmer is able to get easy loan, he may get the advantage of solar panel for the irrigation, but manufacturers will increase the manufacturing and that will ultimately increase carbon emission (Zaidi et al., 2021).

2.6 Policy Framework in Developed Countries

In developed countries, like USA, Japan, and Europe, there are certain policies which are framed for the perspective of managing carbon emission intensity in the countries. These are mentioned below

In USA: Inflation is managed with the help of inflation reduction act which provides fund for clean energy and climate sustainable actions (Li et al., 2024). Government in USA is also providing tax benefits under this act for renewable energy projects (Susskind et al., 2022). In USA, green bonds are also issued with the help of public and private sectors for green initiatives and green projects. Production tax credits are also provided for medium and big enterprises for renewable projects (Bhutta et al., 2022).

In Europe: Europe has also taken many initiatives to reduce carbon emission. European green deal was launched in 2019 to get the carbon emission neutrality by 2050 (Perissi & Jones, 2022). Energy, transport, and tax related policies are also integrated to reduce the carbon emission by 55 percent till 2030 (Huttunen, 2017). Some sustainable strategies like allocation of euro one trillion to be invested in next one decade in the green initiative by European government (Mentes, 2023). Just transition mechanism is also one of the initiatives taken by the government where govt. is trying to implement climate neutral economy by taking everyone together

(Filipović et al., 2022). Green bond standards are also taken by the govt. to facilitate the new projects contributing in to sustainable development.

In Japan: In Japan, carbon neutrality is to be achieved by 2050 and also set to reduce carbon emission by 46 percent till 2030 (Wang et al., 2021). Green transformation strategy which is launched by Japan is promised to provide 150 trillion yen in public and private investments to the next one decade for eco-friendly and sustainable projects (Soares, 2024). Transition bonds in climate management and clean energy is launched by the government to make decarbonized society. In Japan, to make the society carbon emission free, govt. is working in all the directions, innovation in solar cells in the next generation activity started to enhance efficiency in all the sectors (Kakran et al., 2024).

3. ESG

3.1 ESG and Carbon Neutrality

Green finance helps in adopting sustainable methods of manufacturing in the form of getting new machinery and technology which results in carbon emission reduction (Wang, 2023). As mentioned in the literature, incentives and subsidies facilitates manufacturers to take the environment concern initiatives. With the help of environmental funds, green bonds, and green credits, return on investments can be enhance and contribute in the GDP of the economy (Zhao et al., 2022). Hence organizations tend to increase their investment and encouraged enough in working on the reduction of association cost. As the awareness is increasing regarding the environmental and social impact of the various actions of the countries, green finance aligns the objective with the sustainability (Ozili, 2022). Socio-economic stability can be achieved with the financial support provided by green finance in long term.

There are many theories like theory of corporate social responsibility and stakeholder theory which helps in setting the relationship between carbon neutrality and ESG framework of the countries (Habib et al., 2025). ESG performs can help in checking carbon neutrality initiatives (Xie, 2024). Currently China is focusing upon the ESG framework to reduce carbon emission (Qian & Liu, 2024). By neutralizing carbon emission, companies improve the environmental, social and governance performance which ultimately contribute in the country's economic growth (Wang et al., 2024). Environmental metrics include the impact of carbon footprints, its intensity, and green innovation adoption (Al Amosh & Khatib, 2025). Social metrics help in checking the involvement of clean energy by green financial and non-financial initiatives (Akpan, & Oluwagbade., 2023). Government metrics help in knowing the impact of green finance on sustainability. Baratta et al., 2023 has explained in his research that if the ESG performance is improved, it contributes in to promotion of low carbon investments thus it leads to clean energy, and increased energy efficiency. As mentioned in the research problem and objective, this study will be comprising of developed countries like USA, Japan, and Europe

3.2 Moderation of Green Funds on the Performance of ESG and Carbon Emission

As we have seen in the literature that green finance plays a significant role in fund allocation for sustainable development. Green finance initiatives mange funds from heavy sectors to green initiatives or in green projects (Gatti, 2023). This helps the organization in green production and low carbon emission. This actually bridges the gap between the environmental damage and the green funds. There is no linear relationship because the impact of green finance on the environment in terms of carbon emission reduction can be long lasting (Meo & Karim, 2022). As with the help of green finance, economy is growing towards low carbon emission, ESG is recognized as an indicator of growth in economies (Yang et al., 2022). This study analyzes the relationship among green finance, ESG performance and carbon emission intensity in the countries like USA, Japan and Europe. This study checks the role of green finance in the overall improvement of ESG with carbon emission intensity.

Carbon emission intensity is taken in to the study as it is the major component to see greenhouse gas emission to the total output in terms of production (Peyvandi et al., 2023). It is calculated by having the nominator which is total carbon emission and the denominator is GDP. It's not only including the carbon emission but also explains the environmental dimensions. This also helps in evaluating carbon neutrality and the countries contribution towards carbon neutrality goals (Chen et al., 2022). Hence, carbon emission intensity is considered to a dependent variable which is approved by international standards as a strong indicator.

4. CONCLUSION

Green finance has emerged as a pivotal mechanism in driving economies toward sustainable, low-carbon pathways (Hu et al., 2023). By channelling funds into renewable energy, circular economy practices, sustainable infrastructure, and innovative green technologies, it not only reduces carbon footprints but also supports biodiversity protection, waste management, and social development (Kandpal et al., 2024). While climate finance remains a subset focusing primarily on climate change mitigation, green finance encompasses broader dimensions that indirectly and directly contribute to carbon emission reduction.

In Europe, strong regulatory frameworks such as the European Green Deal and emission trading schemes have demonstrated a significant link between ESG performance and reduced carbon emission intensity (Alkurdi et al., 2024). In contrast, the USA and Japan, despite having advanced ESG practices, reflect weaker or inconsistent relationships due to policy gaps and differing corporate priorities (Singhania & Saini, 2023). This highlights that financial tools alone are insufficient; strong governance, strict monitoring, and effective policy integration are equally critical for achieving carbon neutrality (He et al., 2024).

Green finance also serves as a driver for industrial restructuring and innovation by encouraging renewable energy adoption, electric mobility, waste recycling, and sustainable production processes (Hanif & Zheng, 2025). It plays a role in creating new jobs and markets while supporting financial inclusion, though care must be taken to balance inclusion with sustainable practices to avoid unintended rises in emissions (Gonzalez et al., 2025).

Globally, both developed and emerging economies are experimenting with green bonds, loans, and sustainability-linked instruments, but challenges remain in fund allocation, transparency, and awareness (Chan, 2021). The success of green finance depends heavily on well-defined policy frameworks, public–private collaboration, and international cooperation.

Developed countries such as the United States, European Union (EU), and Japan have taken significant policy measures to address the global challenge of carbon emission intensity (Compston & Bailey, 2016). Each region has framed comprehensive strategies integrating financial mechanisms, legislative acts, and technological innovations aimed at achieving carbon neutrality and building sustainable economies (Qamruzzaman & Karim, 2024).

It is seen that there is a significant relationship between carbon emission intensity and ESG in Europe (Baratta et al., 2023). Europe has strong policies for carbon emission reduction. European green deal and emission trading mentioned in literature has shown a strong relationship between these two (Kiss & Popovics, 2021).

In Japan also, data is showing that there is no relationship between ESG and carbon emission intensity (Takahashi & Shino, 2025). ESG high score can be because of welfare schemes, and good corporate governance. There is a possibility of having less impact of green finance. That's the reason that in countries where there is no relationship between ESG and carbon emission intensity, there is no moderation effect of green finance (Gabr & ElBannan, 2025).

it can be seen that emission is managed with the help of inflation reduction act which provides fund for clean energy and climate sustainable actions. Government in USA is also providing tax benefits under this act for renewable energy projects

(Susskind et al., 2022). In USA, green bonds are also issued with the help of public and private sectors for green initiatives and green projects. Production tax credits are also provided for medium and big enterprises for renewable projects (Bhutta et al., 2022). In USA, a company may have high ESG score despite having very high carbon intensity. It is also seen in the literature that in USA, government initiatives is less stringent as compare to European Union (Corley et al., 2023).

Europe has also taken many initiatives to reduce carbon emission. European green deal was launched in 2019 to get the carbon emission neutrality by 2050 (Perissi & Jones, 2022). Energy, transport, and tax related policies are also integrated to reduce the carbon emission by 55 percent till 2030 (Huttunen, 2017). Some sustainable strategies like allocation of euro one trillion to be invested in next one decade in the green initiative by European government (Mentes, 2023). Just transition mechanism is also one of the initiatives taken by the government where govt. is trying to implement climate neutral economy by taking everyone together. Green bond standards are also taken by the govt. to facilitate the new projects contributing in to sustainable development (Chen & Zhao, 2021).

In Japan, carbon neutrality is to be achieved by 2050 and also set to reduce carbon emission by 46 percent till 2030 (Wang et al., 2021). Green transformation strategy which is launched by Japan is promised to provide 150 trillion yen in public and private investments to the next one decade for eco-friendly and sustainable projects (Soares, 2024). Transition bonds in climate management and clean energy is launched by the government to make decarbonized society (Maino, 2022). In Japan, to make the society carbon emission free, govt. is working in all the directions, innovation in solar cells in the next generation activity started to enhance efficiency in all the sectors (Kakran et al., 2024).

In conclusion, green finance is not a silver bullet, but it is a cornerstone for reducing global carbon emissions and advancing sustainable development goals (Raman et al., 2025). Its effectiveness is maximized when combined with robust ESG frameworks, innovative green technologies, and comprehensive policies tailored to regional contexts. For the world to achieve net-zero targets, a synchronized approach integrating finance, governance, and innovation is imperative (Aziz, 2024).

REFERENCES

Adamowicz, M. (2022). Green deal, green growth and green economy as a means of support for attaining the sustainable development goals. *Sustainability, 14*(10), 5901.

Ahluwalia, M. S., & Patel, U. (2021). *Getting to net zero: an approach for India at CoP-26.* Centre for Social and Economic Progress.

. Akpan, J. U., & Oluwagbade, O. I. (2023). Social and environmental responsibility in accounting: Beyond financial metrics. *International Journal of social sciences and management research, 9*(9), 163-188.

. Al Amosh, H., & Khatib, S. F. (2025). Environmental Innovation and Carbon Emissions reduction in European Healthcare: The Moderating Role of Environmental Monitoring Practices. *Cleaner and Responsible Consumption*, 100255.

Alkurdi, A., Al Amosh, H., & Khatib, S. F. (2024). The mediating role of carbon emissions in the relationship between the board attributes and ESG performance: European evidence. *EuroMed Journal of Business, 19*(4), 1016–1041.

Aziz, S., Ahmed, I., Khan, K., & Khalid, M. (2024). Emerging trends and approaches for designing net-zero low-carbon integrated energy networks: A review of current practices. *Arabian Journal for Science and Engineering, 49*(5), 6163–6185.

Bansal, S., Mani, S. P., Gupta, H., & Maurya, S. (2023). Sustainable development of the green bond markets in India: Challenges and strategies. *Sustainable Development, 31*(1), 237–252.

Baratta, A., Cimino, A., Longo, F., Solina, V., & Verteramo, S. (2023). The impact of ESG practices in industry with a focus on carbon emissions: Insights and future perspectives. *Sustainability, 15*(8), 6685.

Bhutta, U. S., Tariq, A., Farrukh, M., Raza, A., & Iqbal, M. K. (2022). Green bonds for sustainable development: Review of literature on development and impact of green bonds. *Technological Forecasting and Social Change, 175*, 121378.

Chan, R. (2021). Ensuring impactful performance in green bonds and sustainability-linked loans. *TheADELAIDE LAW REVIEW, 42*(1), 221–258.

Chen, L., Msigwa, G., Yang, M., Osman, A. I., Fawzy, S., Rooney, D. W., & Yap, P. S. (2022). Strategies to achieve a carbon neutral society: A review. *Environmental Chemistry Letters, 20*(4), 2277–2310. PMID: 35431715

Chen, Y., & Zhao, Z. J. (2021). The rise of green bonds for sustainable finance: Global standards and issues with the expanding Chinese market. *Current Opinion in Environmental Sustainability*, *52*, 54–57.

Cherepovitsyn, A., Solovyova, V., & Dmitrieva, D. (2023). New challenges for the sustainable development of the rare-earth metals sector in Russia: Transforming industrial policies. *Resources Policy*, *81*, 103347.

Chien, F., Ngo, Q. T., Hsu, C. C., Chau, K. Y., & Iram, R. (2021). Assessing the mechanism of barriers towards green finance and public spending in small and medium enterprises from developed countries. *Environmental Science and Pollution Research International*, *28*(43), 60495–60510. PMID: 34156623

Compston, H., & Bailey, I. (2016). Climate policy strength compared: China, the US, the EU, India, Russia, and Japan. *Climate Policy*, *16*(2), 145–164.

Corley-Coulibaly, M., Grasselli, G., & Postolachi, I. (2023). *Promoting and enforcing compliance with labour provisions in trade agreements: Comparative analysis of Canada, European Union and United States approaches and practices*. ILO.

D'Angelo, V., Cappa, F., & Peruffo, E. (2023). Green manufacturing for sustainable development: The positive effects of green activities, green investments, and non-green products on economic performance. *Business Strategy and the Environment*, *32*(4), 1900–1913.

Demiralay, S., Gencer, H. G., & Bayraci, S. (2022). Carbon credit futures as an emerging asset: Hedging, diversification and downside risks. *Energy Economics*, *113*, 106196.

Fay, M. (2012). *Inclusive green growth: The pathway to sustainable development*. World Bank Publications.

Filipović, S., Lior, N., & Radovanović, M. (2022). The green deal–just transition and sustainable development goals Nexus. *Renewable & Sustainable Energy Reviews*, *168*, 112759.

Gabr, D. H., & ElBannan, M. A. (2025). Is it worth it to go green? ESG disclosure, carbon emissions and firm financial performance in emerging markets. *Review of Accounting and Finance*, *24*(2), 193–217.

Gatti, S. (2023). *Project finance in theory and practice: designing, structuring, and financing private and public projects*. Elsevier.

Gonzalez, E. D., Sijariya, R., Singh, A. K., & Garg, V. (2025). Integrating Climate Change, Social Responsibility and Electronic Financial Inclusion: A Pathway to Sustainable Development. In *Climate Change and Social Responsibility* (pp. 147-164). Emerald Publishing Limited.

Habib, A., Oláh, J., Khan, M. H., & Luboš, S. (2025). Does integration of ESG disclosure and green financing improve firm performance: Practical applications of stakeholders' theory. *Heliyon, 11*(4). PMID: 40028513

Hanif, M. W., & Zheng, S. (2025). Assessing the economic impact of green finance and renewable energy use on environmental sustainability in high-polluting sectors. *Renewable Energy, 247*, 123017.

He, Q., Li, W., Zhang, P., & Guo, C. (2024). Corporate governance, policy robustness and carbon neutrality in the digital economy: Insights from the natural resource exploitation sector. *Resources Policy, 88*, 104477.

Hu, M., Sima, Z., Chen, S., & Huang, M. (2023). Does green finance promote low-carbon economic transition? *Journal of Cleaner Production, 427*, 139231.

. Huttunen, R. (2017). Government report on the National Energy and Climate Strategy for 2030.

Kakran, S., Rathore, J. S., Sidhu, A., & Kumar, A. (2024). Solar energy advances and CO2 emissions: A comparative review of leading nations' path to sustainable future. *Journal of Cleaner Production*, •••, 143598.

. Kandpal, V., Jaswal, A., Santibanez Gonzalez, E. D., & Agarwal, N. (2024). Challenges and opportunities for sustainable energy transition and circular economy. *Sustainable Energy Transition: Circular Economy and Sustainable Financing for Environmental, Social and Governance (ESG) Practices*, 307-324.

. Karis, D. (2024). Civilization will Collapse (High Confidence): A Compendium of. *migration, 54*, 239-249.

Khurshid, A., Rauf, A., Qayyum, S., Calin, A. C., & Duan, W. (2023). Green innovation and carbon emissions: The role of carbon pricing and environmental policies in attaining sustainable development targets of carbon mitigation—evidence from Central-Eastern Europe. *Environment, Development and Sustainability, 25*(8), 8777–8798.

Kiss, T., & Popovics, S. (2021). Evaluation on the effectiveness of energy policies–Evidence from the carbon reductions in 25 countries. *Renewable & Sustainable Energy Reviews, 149*, 111348.

Kumar, B., Kumar, L., Kumar, A., Kumari, R., Tagar, U., & Sassanelli, C. (2024). Green finance in circular economy: A literature review. *Environment, Development and Sustainability*, *26*(7), 16419–16459. PMID: 37362997

Kurvits, E. (2022). The role of stakeholders in a transition toward advanced corporate sustainability: A representation of the European wind power industry and the case of Vestas Wind Systems A/S. *IIIEE Master Thesis*.

Labatt, S., & White, R. R. (2011). *Carbon finance: the financial implications of climate change*. John Wiley & Sons.

Li, J., Wang, D., & Qin, M. (2024). Understanding the role of mineral resources and inflation in promoting sustainable development under the inflation reduction act. *Resources Policy*, *90*, 104757.

Lindenberg, N. (2014). *Definition of Green Finance*. German Development Institute.

Liu, H., Yao, P., Latif, S., Aslam, S., & Iqbal, N. (2022). Impact of Green financing, FinTech, and financial inclusion on energy efficiency. *Environmental Science and Pollution Research International*, *29*(13), 18955–18966. PMID: 34705207

Maino, A. (2022). *Financing the energy transition: The role, opportunities and challenges of green bonds*. Oxford Institute for Energy Studies.

Mentes, M. (2023). RETRACTED ARTICLE: Sustainable development economy and the development of green economy in the European Union. *Energy, Sustainability and Society*, *13*(1), 32.

Meo, M. S., & Abd Karim, M. Z. (2022). The role of green finance in reducing CO2 emissions: An empirical analysis. *Borsa Istanbul Review*, *22*(1), 169–178.

Onabowale, O. (2024). Energy policy and sustainable finance: Navigating the future of renewable energy and energy markets. *World Journal of Advanced Research and Reviews*, *25*, 2235–2252.

Ozili, P. K. (2022). Green finance research around the world: A review of literature. *International Journal of Green Economics*, *16*(1), 56–75.

Perez, K. (2024). *Green Money: How to Reduce Waste, Build Wealth, and Create a Better Future for All*. John Wiley & Sons.

Perissi, I., & Jones, A. (2022). Investigating European Union decarbonization strategies: Evaluating the pathway to carbon neutrality by 2050. *Sustainability*, *14*(8), 4728.

Peyvandi, M., Hajinezhad, A., & Moosavian, S. F. (2023). Investigating the intensity of GHG emissions from electricity production in Iran using renewable sources. *Results in Engineering*, *17*, 100819.

Prakash, M. S., Gupta, P., & Gupta, S. (2024). EVALUATION AND SIGNIFICANCE OF GREEN FINANCE. *NOLEGEIN-Journal of Financial Planning and Management*, *7*(1), 34–47.

Qamruzzaman, M., & Karim, S. (2024). Unveiling the synergy: Green finance, technological innovation, green energy, and carbon neutrality. *PLoS One*, *19*(10), e0308170. PMID: 39378193

Qian, Y., & Liu, Y. (2024). Improve carbon emission efficiency: What role does the ESG initiatives play? *Journal of Environmental Management*, *367*, 122016. PMID: 39106795

Raman, R., Ray, S., Das, D., & Nedungadi, P. (2025). Innovations and barriers in sustainable and green finance for advancing sustainable development goals. *Frontiers in Environmental Science*, *12*, 1513204.

Sharif, A., Saqib, N., Dong, K., & Khan, S. A. R. (2022). Nexus between green technology innovation, green financing, and CO2 emissions in the G7 countries: The moderating role of social globalisation. *Sustainable Development*, *30*(6), 1934–1946.

Shipalana, P. (2022). *Green finance mechanisms in developing countries: Emerging practice*. South African Institute of International Affairs.

Shishlov, I., & Censkowsky, P. (2022). Same but different? Understanding divergent definitions of and views on climate finance. In *Handbook of international climate finance* (pp. 16–39). Edward Elgar Publishing.

Singhania, M., & Saini, N. (2023). Institutional framework of ESG disclosures: Comparative analysis of developed and developing countries. *Journal of Sustainable Finance & Investment*, *13*(1), 516–559.

. Soares, F. L. D. T. (2024). The role of the private sector in the promotion of the sustainable development agenda: a study case of Japan and Germany.

Susskind, L., Chun, J., Gant, A., Hodgkins, C., Cohen, J., & Lohmar, S. (2022). Sources of opposition to renewable energy projects in the United States. *Energy Policy*, *165*, 112922.

Taghizadeh-Hesary, F., Yoshino, N., & Phoumin, H. (2021). Analyzing the characteristics of green bond markets to facilitate green finance in the post-COVID-19 world. *Sustainability*, *13*(10), 5719. DOI: 10.3390/su131 05719

. Takahashi, K., & Shino, J. (2025). Greenhouse gas emissions and bank lending in Japan. Journal of Climate Finance, 100067.

Vanishvili, M., & Katsadze, I. (2022). Bank financing of green economy: Review of modern research. *Scientific Collection. InterConf*, (18 (95)), 120–143.

. Vedachalam, N. (2022). Building resilience in India's power sector. *Building resilience in India's power sector: Vedachalam, N.*

Volz, U. (2018). Fostering green finance for sustainable development in Asia. In *Routledge handbook of banking and finance in Asia* (pp. 488–504). Routledge.

Wang, M. L. (2023). Effects of the green finance policy on the green innovation efficiency of the manufacturing industry: A difference-in-difference model. *Technological Forecasting and Social Change*, *189*, 122333.

Wang, S., Sun, L., & Iqbal, S. (2022). Green financing role on renewable energy dependence and energy transition in E7 economies. *Renewable Energy*, *200*, 1561–1572.

Wang, X., & Wang, Q. (2021). Research on the impact of green finance on the upgrading of China's regional industrial structure from the perspective of sustainable development. *Resources Policy*, *74*, 102436.

Wang, Y., Guo, C. H., Chen, X. J., Jia, L. Q., Guo, X. N., Chen, R. S., & Wang, H. D. (2021). Carbon peak and carbon neutrality in China: Goals, implementation path and prospects. *China Geology*, *4*(4), 720–746.

Wang, Y., Hanif, N., Arshed, N., Hussain, M., Arshad, Z., & Usman, M. (2024). Synergizing social sustainability and technological innovation for carbon neutrality in OECD economies. *Sustainable Development*, *32*(6), 6614–6628.

Wasan, P., Kumar, A., & Luthra, S. (2021). Green finance barriers and solution strategies for emerging economies: The case of India. *IEEE Transactions on Engineering Management*, *71*, 414–425.

Wu, Y. A., Ng, A. W., Yu, Z., Huang, J., Meng, K., & Dong, Z. Y. (2021). A review of evolutionary policy incentives for sustainable development of electric vehicles in China: Strategic implications. *Energy Policy*, *148*, 111983.

Xiao, Y., Ma, D., Zhang, F., Zhao, N., Wang, L., Guo, Z., & Xiao, Y. (2023). Spatiotemporal differentiation of carbon emission efficiency and influencing factors: From the perspective of 136 countries. *The Science of the Total Environment*, *879*, 163032. PMID: 36965718

Xie, Y. (2024). The interactive impact of green finance, ESG performance, and carbon neutrality. *Journal of Cleaner Production*, *456*, 142269.

Xu, P., Zhang, J., & Mehmood, U. (2023). How do green Investments, foreign direct investment, and renewable energy impact CO2 emissions? Measuring the role of education in E-7 nations. *Sustainability*, *15*(19), 14052.

Yang, Q., Du, Q., Razzaq, A., & Shang, Y. (2022). How volatility in green financing, clean energy, and green economic practices derive sustainable performance through ESG indicators? A sectoral study of G7 countries. *Resources Policy*, *75*, 102526.

Yu, S., Wang, X., Liu, J., & Wei, F. (2023). Role of mining waste trade on green development in China: Policy implications for circular economy. *Resources Policy*, *86*, 104147.

Zaidi, S. A. H., Hussain, M., & Zaman, Q. U. (2021). Dynamic linkages between financial inclusion and carbon emissions: Evidence from selected OECD countries. *Resources. Environmental Sustainability*, *4*, 100022.

Zhang, L., Saydaliev, H. B., & Ma, X. (2022). Does green finance investment and technological innovation improve renewable energy efficiency and sustainable development goals. *Renewable Energy*, *193*, 991–1000.

Zhao, L., Chau, K. Y., Tran, T. K., Sadiq, M., Xuyen, N. T. M., & Phan, T. T. H. (2022). Enhancing green economic recovery through green bonds financing and energy efficiency investments. *Economic Analysis and Policy*, *76*, 488–501.

Chapter 8
Quantum Computing and Algorithms in Financial Applications

Mohamed Ismail Mohamed Riyath
https://orcid.org/0000-0002-9761-2390
South Eastern University of Sri Lanka, Sri Lanka

Nagham Aldabbous
The Public Authority for Applied Education and Training, Kuwait

Mohammed Jaboob
https://orcid.org/0000-0002-3596-9677
Dhofar University, Oman

Mohammad Irfan
https://orcid.org/0000-0002-4956-1170
Chandigarh University, Unnao, India

ABSTRACT

This chapter synthesizes the state of quantum computing for finance through a task-first lens and a systems-aware stance. We begin by motivating quantum routines as specialised kernels embedded in classical workflows, then formalise foundations across gate and annealing paradigms, the finance-specific taxonomy (pricing/Greeks and risk aggregation; portfolio/ALM; anomaly/credit analytics; practice-facing benchmarking), and the translation of asymptotic advantage into implementable pipelines. Mapping algorithms to roles, we show how amplitude-estimation–based quantum Monte Carlo provides the cleanest pathway for pricing and risk under disciplined state preparation and depth control; how variational and annealer–

DOI: 10.4018/979-8-3373-2893-5.ch008

gate hybrids address QUBO-structured portfolio problems when encodings, warm starts, and circuit design are co-tuned; and how quantum kernels/classifiers serve as components for anomaly and credit tasks at modest scale.

1. INTRODUCTION

Quantum computing has moved from a largely theoretical curiosity to a program of targeted methods for financial analytics, with identifiable algorithmic lineages and use cases. The field's current centre of gravity is pragmatic: researchers treat quantum routines as specialised subroutines embedded within classical workflows, not wholesale replacements for established financial computation. This orientation is evident in surveys that map canonical primitives across three main application domains: simulation-driven analytics via amplitude estimation for Monte Carlo estimators, variational circuits for discrete optimisation, quantum machine learning for classification tasks, and annealing style embeddings onto pricing, risk, and portfolio problems while emphasising the role of compilation and hardware effects in shaping realised performance (Egger et al., 2020). Case style reports from practice echo this system-aware perspective, stressing baselines, data realism, and deployment context over headline speedups (Lee & Constantinides, 2023).

Two observations frame the chapter. First, algorithm–task fit is decisive. Quantum amplitude estimation (QAE) offers a principled route to variance reduction and sample complexity gains in Monte Carlo pipelines for derivative pricing and related risk estimators (Rebentrost et al., 2018). Recent work tailors these ideas to near-term devices via shallow depth estimators and finance-specific circuits (Lin et al., 2025). Variational approaches, Quantum Approximate Optimization Algorithm (QAOA)/ Variational quantum eigensolver (VQE)/ Variational Quantum Linear Solver (VQLS) families, suit discrete formulations such as portfolio selection, but their empirical quality hinges on encoding, initialisation (including warm starts), and low-level circuit design (Sawaya et al., 2023). Annealer–gate hybrids extend solvable instance sizes when portfolios are cast as Ising/ Quadratic unconstrained binary optimization (QUBO) forms, using orchestration to capitalise on each platform's strengths (Jain et al., 2023). Quantum machine learning approaches target anomaly, fraud, and credit classification at modest scales, positioning quantum kernels and variational classifiers as components within broader analytical stacks (Thi & Nguyen, 2024). Second, systems levers—qubit allocation, noise adaptive transpilation, and architecture/template search—are not afterthoughts; allocation and transpilation policies materially affect fidelity (Lecompte et al., 2023), and architecture search shows that co-design of template and hardware can be outcome-defining (Linghu et al., 2024).

This chapter contributes a structured, finance-focused synthesis. We organise quantum methods by computational role and map them to decision problems encountered by quants and risk managers: pricing and Greeks, exposure and risk aggregation, portfolio/asset and liability management (ALM) optimisation, and anomaly or credit adjacent classification. For pricing and risk, the through line from theory to implementable workflow is clearest: QAE-based constructions deliver quadratic sampling advantages under appropriate state preparation and oracle construction (Rebentrost et al., 2018). Newer variants aim to reduce depth to Noisy Intermediate-Scale Quantum (NISQ) viable envelopes (Lin et al., 2025). For portfolio problems, variational routes are conditionally promising; performance is less about formal complexity guarantees and more about careful encoding, initialisation, and compilation tailored to device constraints (Sawaya et al., 2023). Where embeddings are favourable, hybrid annealer–gate pipelines further extend instance size (Jain et al., 2023). Exploratory work in quantum machine learning targets anomaly/fraud detection and credit-related classification at a modest scale, positioning quantum kernels or variational classifiers as components within broader analytical stacks (Thi & Nguyen, 2024).

The chapter's stance is deliberately non hype. Surveys of quantum approaches in finance emphasise the need to separate asymptotic claims from operational value and to report results with calibrated classical comparators (Egger et al., 2020). Device-level studies show that allocation and transpilation policies can materially alter error profiles and effective circuit depth (Lecompte et al., 2023), and architecture search results similarly indicate that template–hardware co-design can be outcome-defining (Linghu et al., 2024). Against this backdrop, we treat quantum routines as insertable modules governed by business metrics, time to solution for pricing under precision targets, robustness of Greeks, approximation gaps for portfolios, and reliability under noise—rather than as freestanding panaceas (Lee & Constantinides, 2023).

We proceed as follows. Chapter 2 consolidates computational foundations; gate and annealing models, hybrid orchestration, and the finance problem taxonomy, while clarifying the practical meaning of asymptotic advantages in financial contexts. Chapter 3 maps algorithm families to tasks, with worked correspondences for pricing/risk (QAE and quantum Monte Carlo), portfolio/QUBO (variational and hybrids), and selective uses of quantum kernels and search primitives. Chapter 4 synthesises empirical signals: performance characteristics, benchmark regimes, and systems effects, drawing on recent device and simulator studies. Chapter 5 then articulates integration architectures for financial workflows and the evaluation metrics that matter in practice. The remaining chapters provide case vignettes, a critical appraisal of current evidence, and a forward agenda for algorithmic development, benchmarking, and hardware–software co-design.

2. FOUNDATIONS

This chapter adopts a task-first view of quantum computation in finance, grounding methods in the computational roles they perform and the decision problems they address. We distinguish computational models and primitives (2.1), a finance-specific problem taxonomy (2.2), and the practical meaning of algorithmic advantage under realistic constraints (2.3).

2.1. Quantum Models and Algorithmic Primitives

Two computational paradigms organise contemporary methods. Gate-based circuits host amplitude-estimation and quantum Monte Carlo routines for simulation-driven analytics, as well as variational families (QAOA/VQE/VQLS) and linear-algebraic solvers that target optimisation and estimation pipelines (Egger et al., 2020). Ising/annealing models address discrete formulations expressed as QUBOs, with hybrids that orchestrate annealers and gate machines to leverage complementary strengths in scale and control (Jain et al., 2023). Search-type subroutines and quantum-walk ideas appear as building blocks, including option-pricing constructions inspired by Grover-style amplification (Baaquie, 2022). Performance in both paradigms is materially shaped by the systems layer. Device-aware qubit allocation reduces effective error; noise-adaptive transpilation tunes pass sequences to hardware characteristics; and architecture/ansatz search co-designs circuit templates with platform topology—factors repeatedly shown to redirect outcomes for the same algorithmic core.

2.2. A Finance Problem Taxonomy

Finance workloads align with four principal families of quantum primitives. Pricing, Greeks, and risk aggregation are simulation-centric and map naturally to quantum amplitude estimation and related quantum Monte Carlo constructions tailored to financial payoffs (Rebentrost et al., 2018). Portfolio/ALM and other discrete optimisation problems are commonly cast as QUBOs, where variational and annealing/hybrid approaches are feasible but performance depends on encoding choices, warm-start initialisation, and low-level circuit design (Sawaya et al., 2023). Anomaly, fraud, and credit-adjacent classification explores quantum kernels and variational classifiers at modest scales, typically as components embedded within broader analytics stacks (Thi & Nguyen, 2024). Finally, practice-facing computation and benchmarking in real-life finance emphasise calibrated baselines and data realism, treating quantum routines as insertable modules rather than stand-alone replacements (Lee & Constantinides, 2023). This taxonomy is descriptive rather than prescriptive, clarifying where theoretical affordances align with the structural features of financial problems.

2.3. Complexity and Practicality

Algorithmic advantage in finance is meaningful only when asymptotics meet implementability. For simulation-driven analytics, QAE delivers a quadratic sampling improvement relative to classical Monte Carlo; finance-specific advances focus on state preparation and oracle construction, shallow-depth estimators for NISQ devices, and end-to-end pipelines for payoffs of interest (Lin et al., 2025). Discrete optimisation does not guarantee blanket speedups; quality depends on encoding choice, initialisation policy, mixer/driver design and low-level circuit optimisation - determinants that can dominate outcomes even when the high-level algorithm is fixed. Compilation and hardware co-design (allocation, noise-aware passes and architecture search) are first-order levers, and not afterthoughts in either family. The working implication for financial research and practice is straightforward: choose the quantum primitive for which the problem's structure enables natural leverage and design the supporting system (state encoding, initialization, compilation, device mapping) so that theoretical gains persist when encountering hardware and business constraints (Egger et al., 2020).

3. ALGORITHM FAMILIES AND FINANCIAL MAPPINGS

This section organises the principal quantum algorithmic families by the financial roles they credibly serve. The emphasis is on how specific primitives—amplitude-estimation pipelines for simulation, variational/Ising templates for discrete optimisation, kernels for classification, and linear-algebra/search subroutines—slot into pricing, risk, portfolio, and anomaly-detection workflows. Throughout, outcomes remain conditioned by encoding, initialisation, and system choices (allocation, transpilation, architecture search), which frequently determine realised performance for the same nominal algorithm (Lecompte et al., 2023).

3.1. Amplitude Estimation and Quantum Monte Carlo for Pricing and Risk

For simulation-driven analytics, option valuation, Greeks, and risk estimation, the most coherent pathway couples quantum amplitude estimation (QAE) with Monte Carlo pipelines. The theoretical appeal is straightforward: quadratic sampling savings relative to classical Monte Carlo under appropriate state preparation and oracle construction. Finance-oriented developments target implementability: shallow-depth or power-law estimators tailored to noisy devices for option pricing; domain-specific encoders and state-preparation strategies to make amplitude estimation practical in financial settings (Carrera Vazquez & Woerner, 2021); and credit valuation adjustment workflows that adapt amplitude-estimation ideas to exposure metrics (Alcazar et al., 2022). Earlier analytical work on quantum formulations of option pricing provides a complementary modelling context for such pipelines (Baaquie, 2022).

Two design lessons recur. First, state preparation dominates: unless payoff structure and distributional inputs are encoded with care, the asymptotic gain can be erased by preparation overhead (Carrera Vazquez & Woerner, 2021). Second, circuit depth and variance targets must be co-designed: practical estimators should explicitly trade precision against depth/shot budgets in line with desk-level service constraints for pricing and Greeks (Lin et al., 2025). Auxiliary engineering—e.g., qubit-saving constructions for Monte Carlo pipelines- can widen the feasible envelope on near-term hardware (Miyamoto & Shiohara, 2020).

3.2. Variational Methods (QAOA/VQE/VQLS) for Portfolio/QUBO and Allocation

Discrete portfolio problems, cardinality, sector caps, and other constraints are naturally cast as QUBOs, inviting variational approaches (QAOA/VQE/VQLS) and ansatz-guided design. Here, performance is structure-sensitive: solution quality hinges on encoding choices (penalties, graph embeddings), initialisation policies (including warm starts), and low-level circuit optimisation (Sawaya et al., 2023). Practical tuning levers include parameter-fixing strategies for QAOA (Lee et al., 2021), circuit-level optimisations that reduce two-qubit overhead (Owusu-Antwi & Gokhale, 2023), and device-motivated tricks such as skipping hotspot nodes to improve adequate fidelity (Ayanzadeh et al., 2023). Foundational analyses of variational circuit optimisation underscore that landscape geometry and hyperparameter schedules can be outcome-defining in combinatorial settings (Khairy et al., 2020).

On the application side, studies report portfolio-optimisation pipelines ranging from discrete-choice formulations to "quantum computational finance" algorithms expressly targeting allocation under constraints (Rebentrost & Lloyd, 2024). Sector-level overviews further delineate how portfolio optimisation sits within financial services roadmaps for quantum adoption (Wang & Tian, 2024). The cumulative message is conservative but optimistic: variational methods provide flexible templates whose value materialises when encodings, initialisations, and compilation are co-tuned to the problem and the device.

3.3. Annealing and Gate–Annealer Hybrids for Scalable Embeddings for Portfolio QUBOs

Where portfolio instances are large or embedding-friendly, annealing and hybrid gate–annealer approaches can expand the solvable regime. Reported pipelines orchestrate gate-level preprocessing/post-processing around annealer cores to exploit both embedding flexibility and parameter controllability (Jain et al., 2023). Comparative work against metaheuristic-integrated QAOA shows that hybridisation can be a practical means to bridge instance size and solution quality, offering a calibration surface for when annealing or variational routes dominate (Mazumder et al., 2024). In financial terms, the point is operational: hybrids are not a doctrinal choice but a scaling instrument for QUBO-structured allocation.

3.4. Quantum Machine Learning (Kernels/ Variational) for Anomaly, Fraud, and Credit

Quantum machine-learning efforts in finance focus on classification—anomaly/ fraud indicators, credit-adjacent scoring, and related tasks—using either quantum kernels or variational classifiers (Thi & Nguyen, 2024). The contributions are primarily feasibility-oriented: how to place a quantum classifier inside a broader analytics workflow, what data regimes are sensible, and where quantum features may complement classical baselines. Broader computational studies on recommender-style algorithms reinforce that careful simulator/device evaluation is needed before drawing operational conclusions for production-grade analytics (Liu et al., 2025). As with optimisation, encoding and systems decisions (depth, shots, transpilation policies) condition any incremental benefit (Lecompte et al., 2023).

3.5. Linear-Algebra and Search Primitives for Selective Financial Uses

Beyond simulation and discrete optimisation, linear-system and search primitives offer building blocks that can be assembled into finance workflows. Analytical treatments of quantum approaches to option pricing reference search and walk ideas as subroutines in model construction (Baaquie, 2022); reviews of quantum finance catalogue linear-algebraic methods among the candidate tools while cautioning about near-term practicality. Foundational accounts of Grover-type search remain relevant as metaphors for variance amplification and as components in composite algorithms with financial aims (Shrivastava et al., 2019). In adjacent algorithmic theory, quantum graph and algebra methods supply a scaffold for prospective mapping to market-structure or network-risk problems, even if immediate deployment is premature (Dörn, 2009).

Across all families, system-level choices repeatedly mediate outcomes. Noise-adaptive compiler mappings and ML-assisted qubit allocation reduce effective error and depth (Lecompte et al., 2023), while architecture/ansatz search on superconducting processors demonstrates how template–hardware co-design can alter the viability of a given algorithmic route (Linghu et al., 2024). Where financial studies report real-life computations, they underscore the importance of calibrated baselines and context-rich evaluation rather than abstract speedup rhetoric (Lee & Constantinides, 2023). In practice, this implies adopting a "classical shell, quantum kernel" posture: choose the kernel whose structure aligns with the financial task, then engineer the encoding, initialisation, and compilation so that theoretical advantages survive contact with the device and with business constraints.

4. EMPIRICAL SIGNALS

The literature's actionable pattern is clear: QAE-based simulation underpins pricing/risk when state preparation is compact and depth is controlled; variational/hybrid methods improve portfolio solution quality when encodings, warm starts, and low-level circuit choices are tuned to the device; and systems leverage, allocation, noise-aware transpilation, and template–hardware co-design are frequently determine whether any advantage survives execution. Evidence comes from paired simulator/device studies and practice-facing reports that prioritise calibrated classical baselines and time-to-solution semantics over headline speedups. Credible evaluation, therefore, hinges on (i) explicit precision targets and pipeline accounting for pricing, (ii) approximation and feasibility metrics for portfolios, and (iii) compiler/hardware disclosures that make results reproducible.

Table 1. Core Empirical Signals in Quantum Finance: Algorithmic Roles, Systems Determinants, and Evaluation Practice

Signal	Why it matters	Where it shows up	Empirical evidence
QAE for pricing/risk	Quadratic sampling gains when state-prep is efficient	Core pricing pipelines	(Rebentrost et al., 2018; Lin et al., 2025)
Variational/hybrid portfolios	Quality depends on encoding, warm starts, circuit design	QUBO allocation	(Sawaya et al., 2023; Jain et al., 2023)
Systems levers dominate	Allocation, transpilation, ansatz–hardware fit drive outcomes	Cross-cutting	(Murali et al., 2019; Lecompte et al., 2023)

continued on following page

Table 1. Continued

Signal	Why it matters	Where it shows up	Empirical evidence
Evidence modes	Simulator + device; baseline-disciplined application studies	Methods & practice	(Liu et al., 2025; Lee & Constantinides, 2023)
Evaluation discipline	TTS decomposition; precision/gap metrics; reliability	Reporting standards	(Egger et al., 2020; Lin et al., 2025)

5. INTEGRATION ARCHITECTURES FOR FINANCIAL WORKFLOWS

Financial institutions will realise quantum value through hybrid systems in which a classical stack orchestrates data preparation, scheduling, and post-estimation analytics, while quantum routines serve as task-specific kernels. In practice, the same algorithm can deliver diverging outcomes depending on encoding, initialisation, compilation, device layout, and template–hardware co-design; these system levers are first-order determinants of performance (Murali et al., 2019).

5.1. Hybrid Orchestration Patterns

For pricing and risk applications, quantum amplitude estimation (QAE) and quantum Monte Carlo (QMC) kernels embed within classical pipelines through a four-step sequence: classical feature construction, state preparation and payoff encoding, QAE/QMC execution with precision targets, and classical aggregation into Greeks or risk measures. Power-law estimators tailor circuits to near-term devices (Lin et al., 2025), while oracle and state encoder optimization remains critical since preparation costs often dominate total runtime (Carrera Vazquez & Woerner, 2021). Template libraries support reusable QMC subroutines across finance applications (Wolf et al., 2023).

Portfolio and asset-liability management applications use hybrid loops coupling classical pre-solvers or warm starts with QAOA/VQE cores, followed by feasibility checks and risk controls. Performance depends on encoding design, penalty structures, graph embeddings, and circuit optimization including mixer/driver choices and two-qubit reductions (Sawaya et al., 2023). Warm-start schemes and parameter-fixing policies provide practical levers for solution quality (Dehn & Wellens, 2024; Lee et al., 2021). Annealer-gate co-processing scales to larger instances where embeddings are favorable. Gates handle normalization, refinement, and verification while annealers address the QUBO core. Comparisons with metaheuristic-integrated QAOA identify crossover regions for practical deployment (Jain et al., 2023; Mazumder et al., 2024).

5.2. Production Determinants: Latency, Reliability, and Scale

Wall-clock performance remains dominated by state preparation, circuit depth, and shot budgets despite asymptotic advantages. Depth-reduced estimators and qubit-saving constructions improve pricing feasibility (Lin et al., 2025), while optimization runtime depends on ansatz depth, parameter schedules, and classical-quantum synchronization (Sawaya et al., 2023). Compiler and mapping policies materially alter error profiles. Noise-adaptive mappings improve fidelity (Murali et al., 2019), ML-guided qubit allocation reduces error hotspots (Lecompte et al., 2023), and template/architecture search aligns circuits with device topology (Linghu et al., 2024). Error mitigation benefits for trainability are task-dependent (Wang et al., 2024). Portfolio pipelines benefit from strategic embeddings and hybrid orchestration for larger instances, including hotspot node avoidance (Ayanzadeh et al., 2023). Reusable QMC subroutines and depth-aware encoders expand the tractable envelope for simulation (Wolf et al., 2023). Real-world finance applications emphasize calibrated baselines, reproducible settings, and decision-relevant metrics over theoretical speedups (Lee & Constantinides, 2023).

6. CASE VIGNETTES

The following vignettes distil influential contributions into decision-oriented takeaways for pricing/risk, portfolio optimisation, and analytics. Each exemplar is selected for conceptual clarity, methodological specificity, and immediate relevance to financial workflows.

6.1. Pricing and Risk (Simulation Kernels)

Foundational Monte Carlo pricing with quantum amplitude estimation.

Rebentrost et al. (2018) formalise a quantum Monte Carlo pipeline for derivative pricing that leverages amplitude-estimation–style sampling to obtain a principled quadratic reduction in sample complexity relative to classical estimators. The study clarifies how payoff functions and distributions enter the quantum routine—thereby framing the engineering burden of state preparation and oracle construction that must be met for practical finance use.

NISQ-oriented amplitude estimation for option pricing.

Lin et al. (2025) introduce a power-law amplitude-estimation variant designed to reduce circuit depth while preserving estimator efficiency in option-pricing contexts. The construction explicitly balances precision targets against depth and shot budgets, offering a realistic path to implementing pricing kernels on near-term processors.

State-preparation as the gating constraint.

Carrera Vazquez and Woerner (2021) isolate efficient state preparation as the necessary condition for realising amplitude-estimation advantages. They catalogue preparation strategies and circuit-complexity implications germane to finance workloads, providing a design checklist for practitioners building end-to-end pricing or risk pipelines.

Architecture search for reusable QMC subroutines.

Wolf et al. (2023) develop architecture-search methods and conditional parameterised circuits to implement quantum Monte Carlo as a reusable subroutine with applications to finance. The contribution is systems-facing: template selection and hardware-aware circuit design are shown to be pivotal in making simulation kernels execution-friendly.

Credit valuation adjustment via quantum estimators.

Alcazar et al. (2022) and co-authors adapt quantum sampling techniques to exposure estimation for CVA/XVA, indicating how estimator structure and preparation costs interact in a credit-risk pipeline. The result anchors amplitude-estimation ideas in a risk-management setting beyond vanilla option pricing.

Practice-facing computational results.

Lee and Constantinides (2023) report computational outcomes for a finance application with attention to baselines, hardware access, and deployment context, modelling how results should be communicated to decision-makers in heterogeneous compute environments.

6.2. Portfolio and Asset-Liability Management (Discrete Optimisation)

Encoding toolkits and design levers for variational optimisation.

Sawaya et al. (2023) synthesise encoding trade-offs and a design toolkit for variational algorithms applied to classical combinatorial problems (e.g., routing, scheduling)—directly translatable to portfolio/QUBO settings. The message is pragmatic: solution quality depends primarily on encoding choice, parameterisation, and process design rather than on a single "best" ansatz.

Warm-start strategies for QAOA.

Dehn and Wellens (2024) present a hybrid quantum–classical approach to warm-starting optimisation, showing how initialisation quality and classical heuristics condition the performance of subsequent variational refinement—an immediately actionable recipe for portfolio instances.

Annealer–gate hybrid scaling for large portfolios.

Jain et al. (2023) propose an annealer–gate hybrid model for large-scale portfolio optimisation that uses graph-aware embeddings and parameterised quantum circuits within an orchestration layer. The approach functions as a scaling instrument when pure gate models are constrained by depth or connectivity.

Head-to-head comparisons with metaheuristic-integrated QAOA.

Mazumder et al. (2024) benchmark QAOA enhanced with metaheuristics against quantum annealing, illuminating crossover regions where hybrids or annealers dominate—evidence directly relevant to portfolio-engineering roadmaps.

Low-level circuit improvements for QAOA.

Lee et al. (2021) propose parameter-fixing strategies that stabilise QAOA performance on NISQ devices; Owusu-Antwi and Gokhale (2023) target two-qubit-cost reductions via low-level circuit optimisations; and Ayanzadeh et al. (2023) introduce FrozenQubits, skipping hotspot nodes to boost effective fidelity. Together, these works translate into concrete compilation/playbook items for portfolio pipelines.

Algorithmic proposals for portfolio optimisation.

Rebentrost and Lloyd (2024) outline a dedicated quantum algorithm for portfolio optimisation, complementing encoding- and system-level studies by specifying the algorithmic core to be embedded within a broader asset-allocation workflow.

6.3. Quantum Machine Learning for Financial Analytics

Anomaly, fraud, and credit-adjacent classification.

Thi and Nguyen (2024) survey variational and kernel methods for anomaly detection, fraud-indicator identification, credit scoring, and stock-price prediction at modest scales. The emphasis is on feasibility and workflow placement—how quantum classifiers can be integrated into analytics stacks alongside classical baselines.

Recommender-style analytics under quantum simulation.

Liu et al. (2025) evaluate recommender-algorithm testing on GPU-based quantum simulators, underscoring the importance of careful simulator/device methodology before extrapolating to production analytics.

6.4. Systems Determinants (Cross-Cutting)

Qubit allocation, transpilation, and architecture co-design.

Across study types, system choices are outcome-defining. ML-guided qubit allocation lowers effective error (Lecompte et al., 2023); noise-adaptive compiler mappings stabilise execution on NISQ hardware (Murali et al., 2019; Vorathammathorn et al., 2025); and architecture/ansatz search on superconducting processors demonstrates that template–hardware co-design can unlock viability for simulation-oriented finance kernels (Linghu et al., 2024; Wolf et al., 2023).

In finance, pricing and risk exhibit the most coherent end-to-end pathway: amplitude-estimation variants, paired with finance-specific encodings and implementable circuits, form credible workflows for option valuation and risk aggregation (Lin et al., 2025). By contrast, portfolio/QUBO value is conditional—performance turns on encoding design, warm-starts, and low-level circuit choices, with hybrids extending solvable instance sizes where embeddings are favorable (Sawaya et al., 2023). Quantum machine learning is promising but modest in scale, best deployed as a component within anomaly, fraud, and credit analytics rather than as a stand-alone replacement (Thi & Nguyen, 2024). Across all threads, system levers—especially qubit allocation and noise-adaptive compilation—often determine whether theoretical gains materialize on real hardware.

7. CRITICAL APPRAISAL

A mature reading of the literature situates quantum computing as a modular capability for finance, potent where its primitives align with task structure, but ultimately governed by encoding choices, compilation, and hardware realities. Claims of advantage are most credible where they are task-specific, pipeline-aware, and benchmarked against relevant classical methods (Claudiu et al., 2024).

7.1. Strength of Evidence

Quantum amplitude estimation (QAE) is a natural core for simulation-driven analytics, where the strongest evidence lies. Foundational work formalises Monte Carlo pricing using quadratic sampling savings, while subsequent contributions make the estimator implementable: pseudo-random-based Monte Carlo on quantum circuits (Miyamoto, 2021), minimal-depth variants (Herbert, 2022), and state-preparation constraints (Carrera Vazquez & Woerner, 2021), and power-law amplitude estimation tailored to option pricing on near-term devices (Lin et al., 2025). Other finance-specific pipelines beyond vanilla options are also being developed along this thread (Alcazar et al., 2022), and execution-template and architecture-search developments bring QMC/QAE closer to reusable subroutines with finance implications (Wolf et al., 2023). In discrete portfolio/ALM, the weight of evidence does not relate to blanket speedups, but instead to approximation quality and robustness. Results depend on encoding, initialisation (warm starts), mixer/driver design, and two-qubit overhead with heuristic rules of thumb for parameter fixing and layout-aware circuit improvements (Sawaya et al., 2023). Scaling arguments favour annealer-gate hybrids where embeddings are hospitable and orchestration can enlarge the solvable regime (Jain et al., 2023). Synthesis articles make the case, in various domains, for baseline discipline and system-aware interpretation (Claudiu et al., 2024).

7.2. Recurrent Pitfalls

The literature exhibits recognizable failure modes that practitioners should pre-empt. Table 2 concisely surfaces the recurrent failure modes in the literature, what they look like in practice, and how to pre-empt them.

Table 2. Recurrent Failure Modes in Quantum-Finance Studies

Failure mode	Why it happens (mechanism)	How it shows up in studies	Mitigation / checklist	Representative citations
Understated state-preparation/oracle cost	QAE's quadratic sampling benefit evaporates if state/ oracle preparation dominates total depth and calls.	Promising asymptotics but wall-clock dominated by encoder/oracle construction; weak accounting for prep overhead.	Design finance-specific encoders; count oracle calls; cap ancilla/control depth; report prep cost in TTS.	(Carrera Vazquez & Woerner, 2021; Herbert, 2022)
Encoding & initialisation fragility (variational/QUBO)	Portfolio/QUBO quality hinges on penalty weights, embeddings, and warm-starts; landscapes are sensitive to parameterisation.	Large variance across encodings; instability without warm-starts; sensitivity to mixer/driver and schedules.	Ablate encodings; warm-start from classical heuristics; parameter-fixing/ regularisation; document constraint handling.	(Sawaya, Schmitz, & Hadfield, 2023; Lee, Saito, Cai, & Asai, 2021)
Compilation/layout myopia	Effective fidelity and depth are governed by mapping and pass sequences on specific hardware.	Same algorithm shows divergent results across runs/ devices; missing disclosure of mapping/transpiler settings.	Use noise-adaptive mappings; expose pass pipelines; report layout, depth, two-qubit counts; run mapping ablations.	(Murali, Baker, Abhari, Chong, & Martonosi, 2019; Lecompte et al., 2023)

continued on following page

Table 2. Continued

Failure mode	Why it happens (mechanism)	How it shows up in studies	Mitigation / checklist	Representative citations
Template–hardware mismatch	Ansatz/template not co-designed with device topology/coherence; architecture choice limits viability.	Poor convergence or excessive depth for otherwise sound methods; gains appear after template changes.	Perform architecture/ ansatz search on target hardware; align templates with native gates/connectivity.	(Linghu et al., 2024; Wolf, Ewen, & Turkalj, 2023)
Over-generalised speedup rhetoric	Asymptotic claims reported without calibrated classical baselines or decision-relevant metrics.	Headline "speedups" without TTS decomposition, baseline clarity, or business-metric framing.	Require baselines; decompose TTS (prep/core/post/shots); report precision & business KPIs; avoid extrapolation.	(Egger et al., 2020; Claudiu, Cosmin, Otniel, & Andrei, 2024)

7.3. Reporting Standards for Finance-Relevant Studies

Table 3 codifies decision-centric reporting standards for quantum-finance studies, turning high-level guidance into concrete, auditable disclosures. By separating algorithmic cores from engineering overheads and specifying required metrics (e.g., time-to-solution decomposition, depth/two-qubit counts, and baseline comparators), it enables reproducible, apples-to-apples evaluation across devices and workflows.

Table 3. Reporting Standards for Quantum Finance

Reporting element	What to include (concrete items)	Why it matters for adoption/ comparability	Minimum disclosures / metrics	Representative citations
Problem & baseline definition	Name the financial task; specify data regime (synthetic/ real); choose credible classical comparators aligned to task constraints.	Grounds any claimed advantage in a realistic decision context; prevents baseline cherry-picking.	Task definition; dataset description; baseline algorithms + configs; rationale for baseline choice.	(Lee & Constantinides, 2023; Egger et al., 2020)
Pipeline decomposition	Separate state prep/oracle, quantum kernel, post-processing; for pricing, state estimator variant (e.g., power-law QAE) and precision target.	Distinguishes asymptotic core from engineering overhead; makes time-to-solution interpretable.	Decomposed TTS (prep/core/post/ shots); estimator variant; target error/ Greeks precision.	(Lin, Guo, & Song, 2025; Rebentrost, Gupt, & Bromley, 2018)
Compilation & mapping disclosure	Qubit-allocation policy; transpiler passes/settings; final depth & two-qubit counts; device topology.	Mapping/transpilation often dominate fidelity and variance; reproducibility hinges on these details.	Layout map; pass pipeline; depth/ CNOT counts; device ID/topology; calibration date.	(Murali, Baker, Abhari, Chong, & Martonosi, 2019; Lecompte et al., 2023)
Architecture/ ansatz rationale	Explain template choice or search (for QMC/QAE and variational portfolios); link template to device constraints.	Template–hardware co-design is frequently outcome-defining.	Ansatz/template family; search strategy (if any); native gates/ connectivity assumptions.	(Wolf, Ewen, & Turkalj, 2023; Sawaya, Schmitz, & Hadfield, 2023)
Scalability & reliability metrics	Qubit counts; depth; failure rates; (for hybrids) anneal parameters; identify crossover regions.	Clarifies feasible envelope and when hybrids outperform.	Qubits; depth/CNOT; success/failure rates; hybrid parameters; crossover thresholds.	(Jain, Khandelwal, & Girish Chandra, 2023; Mazumder, Sen, & Sen, 2024)
Security adjacency (when relevant)	PQC posture; performance/ latency envelopes in realistic networks; implications for ledgers/custody.	Financial-infrastructure adoption depends on cryptographic readiness and throughput.	Chosen PQC schemes; throughput/ latency on target stack; migration/ runbook notes.	(Abbasi et al., 2025; Wang & Shahril Ismail, 2025)

8. RESEARCH AGENDA

A credible near-term roadmap for quantum finance is task-matched and system-conscious. The following priorities flow directly from the literature's strongest threads in pricing/risk, portfolio optimisation, and systems engineering, with security adjacencies that matter for institutional adoption.

8.1. Pricing and Risk (Simulation Kernels)

Two requirements recur for simulation-driven pricing and risk. First, domain-specific state encoders and oracles are needed to make amplitude-estimation pipelines operational under realistic precision targets; design should exploit payoff structure and distributional regularities to keep depth bounded (Carrera Vazquez & Woerner, 2021). Second, depth-aware estimators, including power-law variants, must be tuned for noisy devices in option pricing and related tasks (Lin et al., 2025). These developments should be tested on finance-typical distributions and payoff families with clearly reported error–cost trade-offs, reflecting the quadratic sampling rationale that motivates QAE in the first place.

8.2. Portfolio/ALM (Discrete Optimisation)

Progress in portfolio and ALM hinges on encoding selection, warm-start schemes, and low-level circuit design; comparative studies of penalties and graph embeddings, principled initialisation, and parameter-fixing strategies are most likely to move solution quality under NISQ constraints. Device-aware improvements to two-qubit cost and hotspot avoidance should be treated as first-class experimental variables given their direct impact on trainability and fidelity (Ayanzadeh et al., 2023). Parallel algorithmic work on dedicated portfolio routines can provide clearer kernels for end-to-end orchestration and evaluation (Rebentrost & Lloyd, 2024).

8.3. Hybrid Scaling, Crossover Regions and Classification Analytics (QML)

Institutions should map the crossover between gate-based variational routes and annealer–gate hybrids as a joint function of instance size, constraint structure, and latency tolerances; such maps are operational artefacts that indicate which toolchain dominates for a bank's actual problem mix (Mazumder et al., 2024). Quantum kernels and variational classifiers merit benchmark-ready problem sets in anomaly/fraud and credit contexts, with careful placement inside classical stacks and transparent baselines to avoid over-claiming at modest scale (Thi & Nguyen, 2024).

8.4. Benchmarking and Reproducibility

Pricing and portfolio studies should publish paired simulator–device results using the same targets and circuits to enable apples-to-apples comparisons across hardware and compilation settings (Lee & Constantinides, 2023). Reports must separate asymptotic arguments from time-to-solution by decomposing state preparation, the quantum core, post-processing, and shot budgets, with appropriate classical baselines disclosed and justified (Egger et al., 2020). Scope control remains essential: optimisation surveys caution against generalising beyond measured regimes, and finance studies should localise claims to tested conditions (Abbas et al., 2024).

8.5. Hardware–Software Co-Design

Qubit-allocation policies and noise-adaptive transpilation should be treated as primary, reportable levers, with explicit settings and ablations, because these choices repeatedly shift outcomes for identical algorithmic cores (Lecompte et al., 2023). Systematic template–hardware co-design for QMC/QAE and QAOA families is warranted; results on superconducting devices show that architecture search can unlock viability at fixed resource envelopes (Linghu et al., 2024). For portfolio QUBOs, teams should compile playbooks specifying when to invoke annealers versus variational gates and how to handle embedding, verification, and refinement passes.

8.6. Security and Compliance for Financial Infrastructure

Institutions should execute system-level pilots of post-quantum cryptography, reporting throughput and latency envelopes on representative networks and services (Abbasi et al., 2025). Because optical/WDM and network contexts alter the performance profile of signature schemes, transport-layer measurements are necessary for credible deployment planning (Hamood et al., 2025). Blockchain-facing reviews and proposals indicate a need for wallet and ledger prototypes with PQC primitives alongside explicit operational-overhead accounting (Samonte et al., 2025). A holistic posture couples cryptographic migration with monitoring and governance appropriate for regulated finance (Inakoti et al., 2025).

9. CONCLUSION

Quantum computing's integration into financial workflows represents a paradigm shift from revolutionary replacement to strategic augmentation. Our synthesis demonstrates that practical quantum advantage emerges where algorithmic primitives align with task structure and where systems engineering receives first-class treatment. The evidence is clearest for simulation-driven analytics, where amplitude estimation delivers principled quadratic sampling gains for pricing and risk estimation when state preparation exploits payoff regularities and circuit depth remain controlled. Portfolio optimization via variational and hybrid approaches shows conditional promise, with solution quality hinging critically on encoding design, warm-start initialization, and compilation strategies rather than algorithmic labels alone. The systems layer emerges as the decisive factor across all applications. Qubit allocation policies, noise-adaptive transpilation, and architecture-hardware co-design repeatedly determine whether theoretical advantages survive contact with actual devices. This finding contradicts the common assumption that quantum computing benefits are primarily algorithmic; instead, our analysis reveals that compilation and mapping choices often dominate performance outcomes for identical quantum kernels.

Implications for practice center on hybrid orchestration patterns where quantum routines serve as specialized subroutines within classical risk management and portfolio optimization pipelines. Financial institutions should prioritize task-specific quantum kernels—amplitude estimation for Monte Carlo simulation, variational circuits for discrete optimization—while investing heavily in compilation infrastructure and hardware-aware circuit design. The "classical shell, quantum kernel" architecture provides the most viable path to operational deployment. Limitations constrain immediate applicability. State preparation overhead can eliminate asymptotic advantages in simulation workflows, while variational methods exhibit encoding fragility that requires careful tuning for each problem instance. Current benchmarking lacks standardized metrics for time-to-solution decomposition and baseline comparisons, hindering reproducible evaluation. Hardware constraints impose depth and connectivity limitations that narrow the feasible problem envelope, particularly for near-term devices. The research trajectory should emphasize finance-specific encoders, shallow-depth estimators, and rigorous benchmark discipline while addressing the concurrent security imperative through post-quantum cryptography integration. Success depends on engineering quantum routines where structural advantages are genuine and sustainable rather than pursuing quantum solutions as technological ends in themselves.

REFERENCES

Abbas, A., Ambainis, A., Augustino, B., Bärtschi, A., Buhrman, H., Coffrin, C., Cortiana, G., Dunjko, V., Egger, D. J., Elmegreen, B. G., Franco, N., Fratini, F., Fuller, B., Gacon, J., Gonciulea, C., Gribling, S., Gupta, S., Hadfield, S., Heese, R., & Zoufal, C. (2024). Challenges and opportunities in quantum optimization [Review]. *Nature Reviews. Physics*, *6*(12), 718–735. DOI: 10.1038/s42254-024-00770-9

Abbasi, M., Cardoso, F., Váz, P., Silva, J., & Martins, P. (2025). A Practical Performance Benchmark of Post-Quantum Cryptography Across Heterogeneous Computing Environments [Article]. *Cryptography*, *9*(2), 32. Advance online publication. DOI: 10.3390/cryptography9020032

Alcazar, J., Cadarso, A., Katabarwa, A., Mauri, M., Peropadre, B., Wang, G., & Cao, Y. (2022). Quantum algorithm for credit valuation adjustments [Article]. *New Journal of Physics*, *24*(2), 023036. Advance online publication. DOI: 10.1088/1367-2630/ac5003

Ayanzadeh, R., Alavisamani, N., Das, P., & Qureshi, M. (2023). FrozenQubits: Boosting Fidelity of QAOA by Skipping Hotspot Nodes. International Conference on Architectural Support for Programming Languages and Operating Systems - ASPLOS

Baaquie, B. E. (2022). Quantum Computations and Option Pricing. In *Looking Beyond the Frontiers of Science: Dedicated to the 80th Birthday of K.K. Phua* (pp. 159-179). World Scientific Publishing Co. https://doi.org/DOI: 10.1142/9789811263699_0027

Carrera Vazquez, A., & Woerner, S. (2021). Efficient State Preparation for Quantum Amplitude Estimation [Article]. *Physical Review Applied*, *15*(3), 034027. Advance online publication. DOI: 10.1103/PhysRevApplied.15.034027

Claudiu, B., Cosmin, E., Otniel, D., & Andrei, A. (2024). *Enhancing the Financial Sector with Quantum Computing: A Comprehensive Review of Current and Future Applications*. Smart Innovation, Systems and Technologies.

Dehn, V., & Wellens, T. (2024). A hybrid quantum-classical approach to warm-starting optimization. *Proceedings of SPIE - the International Society for Optical Engineering.*

Dörn, S. (2009). Quantum algorithms for graph and algebra problems [Article]. *Recent Patents on Computer Science*, *2*(2), 124–130. DOI: 10.2174/1874479610902020124

Egger, D. J., Gambella, C., Marecek, J., McFaddin, S., Mevissen, M., Raymond, R., Simonetto, A., Woerner, S., & Yndurain, E. (2020). Quantum Computing for Finance: State-of-the-Art and Future Prospects [Article]. *IEEE Transactions on Quantum Engineering*, *1*, 3101724. Advance online publication. DOI: 10.1109/TQE.2020.3030314

Hamood, M. M., Atia, T. S., & Moosa, A. A. (2025). Performance evaluation of post quantum digital signature algorithms over WDM optical communication system [Article]. *Journal of Optical Communications*. https://doi.org/DOI: 10.1515/joc-2025-0104

Herbert, S. (2022). Quantum Monte Carlo Integration: The Full Advantage in Minimal Circuit Depth [Article]. *Quantum : the Open Journal for Quantum Science*, *6*, 823. Advance online publication. DOI: 10.22331/Q-2022-09-29-823

Inakoti, R. K., Stephen, M. J., & Reddy, P. V. G. D. P. (2025). Enhancing Quantum Cryptography with Machine and Deep Learning A Hybrid Approach for Secure and Scalable Post-Quantum Security [Article]. *Journal of Theoretical and Applied Information Technology*, *103*(11), 4972–4988. https://www.scopus.com/inward/record.uri?eid=2-s2.0-105009299729&partnerID=40&md5=60b6b1301acf7594bb490a6b31326489

Jain, N., Khandelwal, A., & Girish Chandra, M. (2023). Efficient and Flexible Annealer-Gate Hybrid Model for Solving Large-Scale Portfolio Optimization. Proceedings - 2023 IEEE International Conference on Quantum Computing and Engineering, QCE 2023

Khairy, S., Shaydulin, R., Cincio, L., Alexeev, Y., & Balaprakash, P. (2020). Learning to optimize variational quantum vircuits to solve combinatorial problems. AAAI 2020 - 34th AAAI Conference on Artificial Intelligence

Lecompte, T., Qi, F., Yuan, X., Tzeng, N. F., Najafi, M. H., & Peng, L. (2023). Machine-Learning-Based Qubit Allocation for Error Reduction in Quantum Circuits [Article]. *IEEE Transactions on Quantum Engineering*, *4*, 3101414. Advance online publication. DOI: 10.1109/TQE.2023.3301899

Lee, W. B., & Constantinides, A. G. (2023). Computational Results for a Quantum Computing Application in Real-Life Finance. Proceedings - 2023 IEEE International Conference on Quantum Computing and Engineering, QCE 2023

Lee, X., Saito, Y., Cai, D., & Asai, N. (2021). Parameters Fixing Strategy for Quantum Approximate Optimization Algorithm. Proceedings - 2021 IEEE International Conference on Quantum Computing and Engineering, QCE 2021

Lin, G., Guo, Z., & Song, T. (2025). Power Law Amplitude Estimation for Option Pricing with NISQ Devices [Article]. *Advanced Quantum Technologies, 8*(6), 2400411. Advance online publication. DOI: 10.1002/qute.202400411

Linghu, K., Qian, Y., Wang, R., Hu, M. J., Li, Z., Li, X., Xu, H., Zhang, J., Ma, T., Zhao, P., Liu, D. E., Hsieh, M. H., Wu, X., Du, Y., Tao, D., Jin, Y., & Yu, H. (2024). Quantum Circuit Architecture Search on a Superconducting Processor [Article]. *Entropy (Basel, Switzerland), 26*(12), 1025. Advance online publication. DOI: 10.3390/e26121025 PMID: 39766654

Liu, C., Lee, W. B., & Constantinides, A. G. (2025). Quantum Testing of Recommender Algorithms on GPU-Based Quantum Simulators [Article]. *Computers, 14*(4), 137. Advance online publication. DOI: 10.3390/computers14040137

Mazumder, A. R., Sen, A., & Sen, U. (2024). *Benchmarking Metaheuristic-Integrated QAOA Against Quantum Annealing*. Lecture Notes in Networks and Systems.

Miyamoto, K. (2021). Quantum algorithms for Monte Carlo integration using pseudo-random numbers. Proceedings - 2021 IEEE International Conference on Quantum Computing and Engineering, QCE 2021

Miyamoto, K., & Shiohara, K. (2020). Reduction of qubits in a quantum algorithm for Monte Carlo simulation by a pseudo-random-number generator [Article]. *Physical Review. A, 102*(2), 022424. Advance online publication. DOI: 10.1103/PhysRevA.102.022424

Murali, P., Baker, J. M., Abhari, A. J., Chong, F. T., & Martonosi, M. (2019). Noise-Adaptive Compiler Mappings for Noisy Intermediate-Scale Quantum Computers. International Conference on Architectural Support for Programming Languages and Operating Systems - ASPLOS

Owusu-Antwi, D., & Gokhale, P. (2023). Low-level Circuit Optimization for the Quantum Approximate Optimization Algorithm. *IET Conference Proceedings*

Rebentrost, P., Gupt, B., & Bromley, T. R. (2018). Quantum computational finance: Monte Carlo pricing of financial derivatives [Article]. *Physical Review. A, 98*(2), 022321. Advance online publication. DOI: 10.1103/PhysRevA.98.022321

Rebentrost, P., & Lloyd, S. (2024). Quantum Computational Finance: Quantum Algorithm for Portfolio Optimization [Article]. *KI - Kunstliche Intelligenz, 38*(4), 327-338. *Article, 150502*. Advance online publication. DOI: 10.1007/s13218-024-00870-9

Samonte, M. J. C., Asuncion, K. D. R., Castillo, J. J. A. G., & Santos, H. H. I. (2025). *Quantum-Resistant Cryptographic Algorithms for Blockchain Integration in Financial Services. Smart Innovation*. Systems and Technologies.

Sawaya, N. P. D., Schmitz, A. T., & Hadfield, S. (2023). Encoding trade-offs and design toolkits in quantum algorithms for discrete optimization: Coloring, routing, scheduling, and other problems [Article]. *Quantum : the Open Journal for Quantum Science, 7*. Advance online publication. DOI: 10.22331/Q-2023-09-14-1111

Shrivastava, P., Soni, K. K., & Rasool, A. (2019). Evolution of Quantum Computing Based on Grover's Search Algorithm. 2019 10th International Conference on Computing, Communication and Networking Technologies, ICCCNT 2019

Thi, H. L., & Nguyen, T. (2024). *Variational Quantum Algorithms in Anomaly Detection, Fraud Indicator Identification, Credit Scoring, and Stock Price Prediction*. Lecture Notes in Networks and Systems.

Vorathammathorn, S., Binhar, M., Patamawisut, N., Chanchuphol, S., Prechapraprawong, P., Hansomboon, J., & Sarochawikasit, R. (2025). Understanding Noise-Adaptive Transpilation Techniques Using the SupermarQ Benchmark. Proceedings - 2025 International Conference on Quantum Communications, Networking, and Computing, QCNC 2025

Wang, J., & Tian, B. (2024). Research and Application of Quantum Computing Algorithm for Asset Portfolio Optimization. Proceedings - 2024 3rd International Conference on Data Analytics, Computing and Artificial Intelligence, ICDACAI 2024

Wang, S., Czarnik, P., Arrasmith, A., Cerezo, M., Cincio, L., & Coles, P. J. (2024). Can Error Mitigation Improve Trainability of Noisy Variational Quantum Algorithms? [Article]. *Quantum : the Open Journal for Quantum Science, 8*. Advance online publication. DOI: 10.22331/q-2024-03-14-1287

Wolf, M. O., Ewen, T., & Turkalj, I. (2023). Quantum Architecture Search for Quantum Monte Carlo Integration via Conditional Parameterized Circuits with Application to Finance. Proceedings - 2023 IEEE International Conference on Quantum Computing and Engineering, QCE 2023

Chapter 9
Harnessing Business Analytics for Predictive Financial Performance: A Data-Driven Approach to Enhancing Decision-Making and Strategic Planning

Varun Pradhan
https://orcid.org/0009-0005-1357-0082
Loyola Academy Degree and PG College, India

T. Swarna
https://orcid.org/0009-0001-0948-2718
Loyola Academy Degree and PG College, India

Sneha Sribhashyam
Loyola Academy Degree and PG College, India

Mohammad Irfan
https://orcid.org/0000-0002-4956-1170
Chandigarh University, Unnao, India

Omar Durrah
Dhofar University, Oman

ABSTRACT

In today's fast-paced, data-driven world, businesses are flooded with financial information from various sources. Making sense of this data is crucial for turning

DOI: 10.4018/979-8-3373-2893-5.ch009

numbers into clear, strategic insights. This study explores how tools like Power BI, Excel, and R can help organizations—specifically in the automobile industry—predict financial outcomes such as revenue, profits, and expenses. By combining these tools, the research shows how companies can better forecast trends, assess risks, and make smarter decisions. Power BI's dashboards, along with Excel and R's modeling capabilities, offer a powerful way to visualize and interpret data. Among the models tested, ARIMA stood out for its accuracy in forecasting. Overall, the study highlights how using a mix of modern analytics tools not only improves forecasting precision but also empowers organizations to plan ahead more effectively and stay competitive.

INTRODUCTION

In today's data-driven landscape, organizations generate immense quantities of financial data from a wide array of sources. Mastering effective data aggregation and visualization is essential for transforming this raw information into powerful, actionable insights. Business analytics is a key driver of superior financial performance, empowering organizations to make informed, data-driven decisions and engage in strategic planning. By integrating analytics, companies can confidently move beyond traditional reactive strategies, leveraging predictive models to accurately forecast revenue, assess profitability, manage risks, and optimize resource allocation.(Mereddy, n.d.)

Predictive analytics is essential for organizations as it enables them to foresee market trends, revenue patterns, and cash flow changes, thereby facilitating better decision-making. By reviewing past financial data, companies can more precisely project key performance indicators (KPIs) like profits, revenue growth, and liquidity.

The integration of advanced technologies, including AI, IoT, and blockchain, presents a valuable opportunity to enhance the effectiveness of business analytics. A book titled The Impact of AI Innovation on Financial Sectors in the Era of Industry 5.0 (2023) which was published and edited by Mohammad Irfan, Mohammed Elmogy, M. Shabri Abd. The authors of Majid and Shaker El-Sappagh offer a detailed analysis of how industry 5.0 is changing the financial industry through artificial intelligence. This period puts an emphasis on people, endurance and sustainable development, making AI key in altering the financial sector. (Irfan, Elmogy, Majid, & El-Sappagh, 2023). When companies use smarter forecasts, sharper risk checks, and smoother day-to-day processes, profits and productivity usually follow. Because data keeps flooding in, tying analytics to financial plans is now a must if a firm wants to outpace rivals and stay strong over the years. Tools.

Though modern analytics sits on every cloud shelf, countless firms still struggle to turn numbers into clear, forward-looking plans that steer everyday choices. Success means breaking that barrier and squeezing every drop of value from collected data. Put simply, good predictive analytics can sharpen operations, tighten risk controls, and boost the bottom line. One big upside of those insights is the chance for managers to move before trouble hits. Spotting a cash shortfall early, for instance, lets a team line up funding or trim costs in advance. That head start makes it easier to steer budgets and investments toward the projects most likely to drive growth.

Taking a fact-based approach that sharpens forecasts and aligns spending with what the business actually wants is now critical for lasting growth and staying ahead of rivals.

The aim here is to check how accurate and useful the prediction models really are in the auto sector. To do that, we will comb through past numbers-sales, production costs, and market signals-to estimate future revenue, profit, and expenses. We will also study Power BIs role by testing how well it handles data joins, builds DAX and machine-learning models, and shows results on interactive dashboards. In addition, the review will pull together income statements, balance sheets, and cash-flow figures and run side-by-side tests in Power BI, Excel, and R. The job involves pulling data from those statements, cleaning it, and using Excel and R to create models that are then spotlighted in Power BI. By tying all these steps together, the goal is to produce reliable forecasts that boost budgeting, quicken decisions, and guide long-term strategy.

Since markets are now volatile and new developments come quickly, businesses must always be ready for changes and react ahead of time. In earlier times, financial forecasting was based solely on typical past records in spreadsheets, but it has progressed to relying on modern analytics instead. Businesses today use data science to turn experiences gained in the past into helpful predictions for the future. It makes an organization's planning more effective while also preparing them for unpredictable situations. Combining financial data with advanced technologies such as machine learning and using efficient visualization tools is causing a move from simple analysis to making predictions and suggestions.

Artificial Intelligence (AI) and Decentralized Finance (DeFi) coming together are transforming the traditional finance world. The authors of the book AI-Driven Decentralized Finance and the Future of Finance (2024), (Irfan M. E., 2024) led by Irfan, argue that by using AI technologies, DeFi platforms can optimize smart contracts, make risks more manageable and meet each user's needs. By working together, financial operations are made more efficient and open to all people who do not heavily rely on traditional intermediaries. In addition, the authors discuss the rules and ethical issues needed for successful adoption of AI by highly decentralized financial communities and they explain the likely future advancements in AI-led financial innovations.

Because competition gets more intense, organizations now rely on predictive analytics to make decisions within the company and stand out in the market. Analysts are now able to forecast sales percentages, discover financial risks and advise the proper use of funds using tools such as Power BI, R and Excel.

When firms bring these tools into daily money management, they quickly spot cash flow habits, notice where spending creeps up, and read early signals of how the market might react. By running a range of what-if scenarios, a company can steer clear of blind spots and keep its day-to-day work in line with the bigger goals set out in the strategy. That move signals an important shift toward finance guided more by facts and less by guesswork

LITERATURE REVIEW

The blend of predictive analytics (PA) and business-intelligence (BI) software has reshaped the way finance teams make choices. This literature review pulls together key studies to explain where PA and BI are used, what advantages they bring, the hurdles they pose, and the paths forward researchers see.

Applications of Predictive Analytics in Finance

Predictive analytics uses a mix of statistics and computer techniques to guess what money-related events might happen next, helping managers choose better paths. Broby (2022) carried out a broad review that sorted methods into categories-classification, regression, clustering, association, and time-series models. He also stressed that tying those models into Decision Support Systems can lift the quality of daily financial calls, a point echoed at Ulster University.

When it comes to risk, these same methods shine even brighter. Recent work surveyed past articles and pointed to solid uses in credit scoring, fraud spotting, and liquidity outlooks, confirming their place in modern risk management SCIRP. Business intelligence systems gather all related hardware and software so firms can collect, tidy, and pinch data into clear reports for quicker, smarter choices. A linked review rated those systems, saying they lift both speed and impact when people decide. Al-Zubi (2014) zeroed in on the accounting side, testing how BI tools such as ETL, OLAP.

Financial adoption of PA and BI faces numerous obstacles that prevent their increased application. Functional analytics forecasting data technologies show rising adoption by practitioners according to Hyvönen (2022) although professionals hold back because they doubt their usefulness. The main obstacles for implementation involved data integration requirements alongside data quality issues. Olorunyomi

(2024) illustrated how advanced analytics benefits business optimization through operational efficiency but practitioners face ongoing obstacles like data integration problems and analyst skill shortages and AI ethical problems along with data privacy issues. Impact of Dashboards on Financial Decision-Making

In today's finance sector dashboards operate as efficient instruments which support data integration functions as well as risk oversight together with performance evaluation and better decision-making abilities. Quynh (2023) investigated dashboard effectiveness for visual financial data presentation as well as strategic indicator tracking and performance measurement and trend prediction before establishing transparency and informed choices.

Artificial Intelligence in Financial Decision-Making

Artificial intelligence (AI) has positively transformed financial decisions by integrating into business decision systems. A case study conducted by Badmus et al. (2024) showed that AI helps enhance business decision-making through the combination of predictive analytics technology and automated systems which drives operational improvements throughout business processes and trend prediction capabilities. The examination stated that successful AI implementation requires detailed high-quality data together with ethical management and effective implementation plans.

Predictive analytics and business intelligence tools play a crucial role in enhancing financial decision-making according to the available literature. Using these tools enables users to reach better forecasting results and more effectively manage business risks and enhance their operational speed. People should overcome difficulties involving data integration along with skill limitations and ethical considerations to maximize their usage potential. Future research should create methods to address obstructing factors while directing financial organizations to implement PA and BI properly and ethically.

(Irfan, Elhoseny, Kassim, & Metawa, 2023) looked at how AI, machine learning and blockchain make Islamic finance more efficient, transparent and Shariah compliant. Their study pointed out that smart contracts, fraud identification and making the right choices using fintech apps are being used. They also pointed out regulatory hurdles, the significance of relying on data insights and why it is necessary to create new frameworks following Islamic finance. The research insights demonstrated that the use of technology benefits all stakeholders by giving access to financial services, making operations more efficient and gaining their trust through safe and Shariah-compliant financial services.

(Irfan M.) studied the patterns of convergence of Shariah indices from Gulf Cooperation Council (GCC) countries, and found some degree of integration. The research has implications for Islamic investors as it demonstrates that investors will still be able to create portfolios that are diverse, despite the co-movements of various indices. The key concern of the research is financial integration in Islamic equity markets, and the applicability of Shariah-compliant investment strategies. The study explores whether these indices behave the same way or independently, this is important because the more independent the indices behave, the more diversified a portfolio becomes and the less risky it is. The study found the evidence for co-movements, but, despite this, the potential for regional diversification in GCC countries remains. As a result, Shariah indices will be important for Islamic financial market participants.

RESEARCH METHODOLOGY

A descriptive research study employs non-probability purposive sampling to study Bajaj Auto and TVS Motor Company along with Hero MotoCorp's financial performance. The researcher used financial report data accessible to the public from the past 5 years as their basis. Microsoft Excel, Power BI and R Programming operated together for conducting data analysis. The analysis in Excel used scenario analysis together with linear regression and trend analysis for examining financial trends and predictions. Short-term and long-term analysis became possible through the use of comparative and common-size statements within Power BI. The revenue forecasting method using time series analysis took place in R Programming to predict upcoming revenue outcomes. The accuracy of the modeling predictions was examined using cross-validation and back-testing methods. The primary limitations of this investigation include non-probability sampling techniques and reliance on historical data. The research's ethical standards were safeguarded by the use of publicly available data and thorough documentation of all methods and data sources.

The time series analysis method for revenue forecasting was carried out with R Programming to see what lies ahead in terms of revenue. Back-testing and cross-validation methods were used to check how accurate the results of the models were. Relying on historical figures and using non-probability sampling are the key problems seen in this process. By including public data and mentioning every method and data source, the research process was ethical.

OBJECTIVES

1. To assess the accuracy and applicability of predictive models across automobile industries:

The established goal evaluates predictive model performance within the automotive sector. The accuracy measurement of these models involves determining their ability to forecast sales trends alongside consumer preferences as well as demand for particular car features. Goal is to determine if predictions from these models will provide dependable assistance to automobile manufacturers and dealerships when making choices.

2. To Evaluate the Use of Power BI for Predictive Financial Analytics:

The main evaluation purpose focuses on assessing how effectively Power BI executes predictive financial analysis. Inspection of Power BI functionalities consisting of data visualization and DAX functions and machine learning model integration helps determine their accuracy in making financial trend forecasts as well as identifying risks and opportunities. This evaluation focuses only on determining the advantages and limitations that Power BI presents for predictive analytics management.

3. Examine financial statements and test predictive models using Power BI, Excel, and R:

Our objective requires collecting financial data through Power BI while using Excel to handle the information followed by R for statistical modeling to process records. Predictive models should be deployed to financial statements since their purpose is to forecast future financial performance while detecting potential risks in order to support strategic planning initiatives. The objective includes both evaluating tool performance within predictive analytics management and assessing their precision for managing predictive analytics

ANALYSIS

Objective1: To assess the accuracy and applicability of predictive models across automobile industries:

Performing Simple Linear Regression for Predictive Analysis of Hero MotoCorp Using Excel

To begin the simple linear regression analysis of Hero MotoCorp's performance, the data must first be prepared. This involves organizing it into two columns: Column A for the independent variable (X), which in this case represents the increase and decrease in stock prices over time, and Column B for the dependent variable (Y), representing the corresponding quarterly expenditures. The data includes values for five quarters from September 2023 to September 2024.

The next step involves calculating the slope (m) and intercept (b) of the regression line using Excel's built-in functions. The slope is determined using the formula =SLOPE(Y-range, X-range) and the intercept using =INTERCEPT(Y-range, X-range). Based on the given data, the calculated slope is -0.30113 and the intercept is 1230.444. These values form the regression equation: Y = -0.30113X + 1230.444, where Y represents the predicted expenditure and X denotes the stock change value.

Using this regression equation, future values can be predicted. By substituting X-values into the equation, predicted quarterly expenses (Y) can be calculated. For instance, using the formula Y = mX + b, the predicted expenditures corresponding to the five stock changes are approximately 883.12, 875.26, 876.89, 849.05, and 832.29 respectively.

To visualize this data and better understand the regression relationship, a scatter plot is created in Excel. Once the scatter plot is ready, a regression line (trendline) is added by right-clicking on any data point and selecting "Add Trendline." In the trendline options, selecting "Display Equation on chart" and "Display R-squared value on chart" will show the regression formula and indicate how well the trendline fits the data. This visual representation enhances the interpretation of the regression model and supports further analysis of financial forecasting for Hero MotoCorp.

Figure 1. Simple Linear Regression

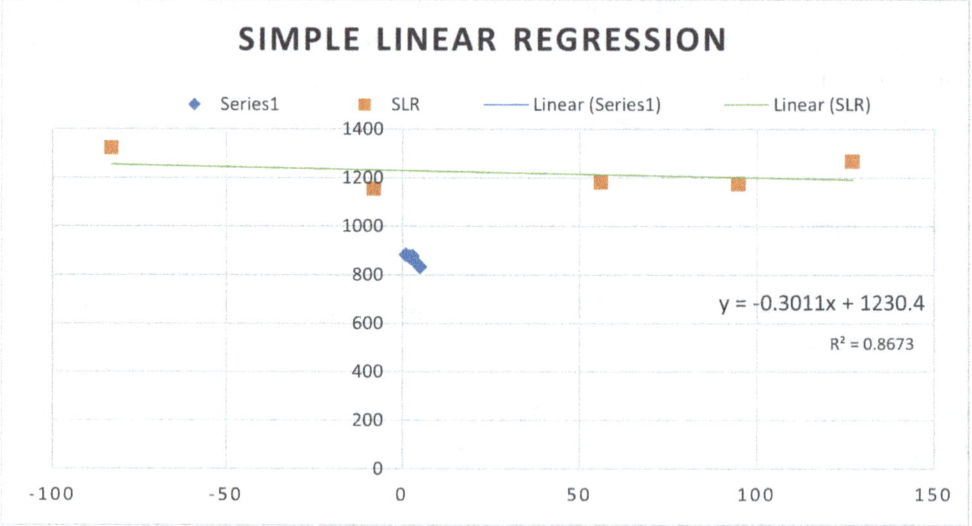

The chart titled "Simple Linear Regression" visually represents the relationship between changes in Hero MotoCorp's stock performance (independent variable) and its quarterly expenditures (dependent variable). The scatter plot displays two series:

- Series1 (blue diamonds): These are the actual observed quarterly data points.
- SLR (orange squares): These are the predicted expenditure values based on the regression model.

The green regression line, plotted using the least squares method, reflects the equation Y = -0.3011X + 1230.4, where the slope (-0.3011) indicates a negative correlation between stock variation and expenditure, and the intercept (1230.4) shows the estimated expenditure when the stock change is zero. The R^2 value of 0.8673, displayed on the chart, demonstrates a strong model fit—meaning approximately 86.73% of the variation in quarterly expenses can be explained by changes in stock value. This high coefficient of determination reinforces the model's reliability for short-term financial prediction and planning. This visualization, generated in Excel, enables clearer insight into how Hero MotoCorp's financial behavior responds to stock fluctuations and supports the use of simple linear regression as an effective forecasting tool.

Scenario-Based Financial Projections for FY 2024–2026

The Scenario Analysis method for Bajaj Auto Ltd. focused on evaluating financial performance under different conditions using Revenue, COGS (Cost of Goods Sold), Operating Expenses, and Net Profit data from 2022 to 2024. The analysis defined three scenarios: Base Case (actual historical performance), Best Case (optimistic growth), and Worst Case (pessimistic decline). In the Base Case, the 2024 revenue was 46,087.68 crores with COGS at 31,743.44 crores and operating expenses at 36,265.67 crores, resulting in a net income of - 21,921.43 crores. For the Best Case, revenue was projected to increase by 55% annually, COGS by 10%, and operating expenses by 10%, leading to a 2026 net income of 81,104.63 crores. Conversely, the Worst Case assumed a 5% decline in revenue with the same cost increases, resulting in a 2026 net income of - 51,005.7 crores. Excel was used to organize data, apply formulas, and create a scenario table for comparison. This data-centric approach allowed Bajaj Auto Ltd. to assess potential risks and prepare strategic responses based on quantified financial outcomes.

Table 1. Financial Performance Overview (FY 2022–2024)

Year	Revenue	COGS	Operating Expenses	Net Profit
Mar-22	34353.95	24,329.82	28,163.90	6,190.05
Mar-23	37609.02	26,054.75	30,200.38	7,408.64
Mar-24	46087.68	31,743.44	36,265.67	9,822.01

Over the course of the three fiscal years, the company's financial performance has consistently increased year over year. From 34,353.95 crore in FY22 to 46,087.68 crore in FY24, revenue grew gradually, indicating strong top-line growth.

In addition, the Cost of Goods Sold (COGS) increased proportionately from 24,329.82 crore in FY22 to 31,743.44 crore in FY24.

Similar increases were seen in operating expenses, which increased from 28,163.90 crore in FY22 to 36,265.67 crore in FY24. The company's net profit increased from 6,190.05 crore in FY22 to 9,822.01 crore in FY24, despite a rise in both COGS and operating costs. This shows increased operational effectiveness and profitability over the course of three years in addition to efficient cost control. All things considered, the financial information points to solid company performance as well as an upward trend in revenue and profitability.

Table 2. Scenario-Based Financial Projections for FY 2024–2026

YEAR	SCENARIO	REVENUE	COGS	OPERATING EXP	NET PROFIT	NET INC
2024	Base case	4608768%	3174344%	36,265.67	9,822.01	-21,921.43
2024	Best Case	7143590%	3491778%	39892.237	31543.667	-3374.117
2024	Worst Case	4378330%	3491778%	39892.237	3891.059	-31026.73
2025	Base case	46087.68	31,743.44	36,265.67	9,822.01	-21,921.43
2025	Best Case	110725.7	38409.562	43881.4607	66844.1905	28434.63
2025	Worst Case	41594.13	38409.562	43881.4607	-2287.3295	-40696.89
2026	Base case	46087.68	31,743.44	36,265.67	9,822.01	9,822.01
2026	Best Case	171624.8	42250.519	48269.6068	123355.153	81104.63
2026	Worst Case	39514.42	42250.519	48269.6068	-8755.18213	-51005.7

Under the base case, best case, and worst case scenarios, this table provides a thorough scenario-based examination of the company's financial expectations for the three-year period (2024–2026). Projected figures for revenue, cost of goods sold (COGS), operating expenses, net profit, and net income change (net Inc) for each scenario are included in the analysis. The base case shows a neutral growth prognosis with revenue staying at 46,087.68 crore for all three years, consistent cost structures, and a steady net profit of 9,822.01 crore. The best-case scenario demonstrates the potential for high operational efficiency and market success by showing a big growth in net profit to 1,23,355.15 crore by 2026, along with a significant expansion in sales to 1,71,624.8 crore.

The worst-case scenario, on the other hand, suggests significant financial hardship, especially in 2025 and 2026, when operating expenses surpass income and net losses amount to 2,287.33 crore and 8,755.18 crore, respectively. The possibility of cost constraints and poor performance is shown by the sharp drop in net income under this scenario. This table shows how different operational and market situations can affect financial outcomes over time, which helps to enhance risk assessment and strategic planning.

Analysing The Growth in Revenue of Bajaj Ltd. Using Trend Analysis Technique

Based on revenue, TVS Motor firm, a multinational Indian motorcycle manufacturer with its headquarters located in Chennai, is the third-largest motorcycle firm in India. The corporation is a major player in the market, with yearly sales of three million units and a production capability of about four million vehicles annually. Furthermore, TVS Motor Company exports two-wheelers to over 60 nations, making it the second-largest two-wheeler exporter from India. In terms of turnover and valuation, it is the largest firm within the TVS Group and serves as its flagship.

TVS Motor Ltd. used historical data from 2020 to 2024 to anticipate future sales income using the Trend Analysis approach. To forecast sales through 2029, a linear trendline was created using Microsoft Excel's FORECAST.LINEAR tool. Important metrics that validated the model's great accuracy included a significantly low Significance F value and an R-Squared value of 1. The study revealed a robust upward trend in sales and offered forecasting information that helps with financial forecasts, budgeting, and production scheduling. TVS Motor Ltd. was able to match its strategic objectives with the expected demands of the market thanks to this trend-based strategy, which also improved operational efficiency and supported long-term growth plans.

Using trend analysis and regression modeling in Microsoft Excel, this study aims to examine TVS Motors' historical data. By using statistical methods, this study seeks to forecast future sales performance, supporting strategic choices for financial, marketing, and production planning.

Step 1: Collect and Organize Data

The first step is to gather the relevant historical data. In this example, we'll assume the company's sales revenue.

Table 3. Actual and Forecasted Sales Revenue of TVS Motors (2020–2029)

Date	sales revenue	Forecast period	Forecast Sales
3/31/2020	19358.82	3/31/2025	46868.69477
3/31/2021	21992.69	3/31/2026	52762.15663
3/31/2022	27072.08	3/31/2027	58655.6185
3/31/2023	35232.91	3/31/2028	64565.22683
3/31/2024	42220.46	3/31/2029	70458.6887

The dataset consists of two primary components:

- Historical Sales Revenue (2020-2024): These are actual recorded sales figures.
- Forecast Period & Forecast Sales (2025-2029): These values are predicted using a trend analysis model.
- In Forecast sales we used the formula

=FORECAST.LINEAR(C2,$B$2:$B$6,$A$2:$A$6) and followed by same.
Step 2: Insert a Line Chart for Trend Visualization

1. Select your data range
2. Go to Insert > Charts > Line Chart.
3. The trend in TVS Motors' performance will be displayed graphically.

Figure 2. Sales Forecasting

This line chart illustrates the trend in sales revenue over time, from the year 2020 to 2024, with a linear projection extending to 2026. The solid blue line represents actual historical revenue data, while the dotted extension depicts the forecasted revenue using Simple Linear Regression (SLR). The chart demonstrates a steady upward trend, indicating consistent revenue growth. SLR is applied here to model the linear relationship between time and sales, providing a clear and straightforward forecast. However, while SLR captures the linear pattern well, it does not account for sudden market shifts or non-linear fluctuations. This figure emphasizes the value of combining SLR with scenario analysis and trend analysis for a more robust forecasting framework. The high R-squared typically associated with such trends underscores the potential of linear models in long-term planning. Yet, integrating these models and applying validation techniques like back-testing and cross-validation can greatly improve forecast accuracy and adaptability to real-world complexities.

Step 4: Use Data Analysis Tool for Trend analysis

Table 4. Regression Statistics

Regression Statistics	
Multiple R	1
R Square	1
Adjusted R Square	1
Standard Error	4.08767E-11
Observations	5

This table highlights the regression summary statistics obtained from the linear trend analysis of TVS Motors' sales data. A Multiple R value of 1 confirms a perfect positive correlation between the independent variable (time) and the dependent variable (sales revenue). The R Square value of 1 indicates that 100% of the variation in sales is perfectly explained by changes over time, demonstrating an ideal model fit. The Adjusted R Square value, also 1, validates this precision even after accounting for the model's simplicity. Additionally, the Standard Error is extremely small (4.08767E-11), implying minimal deviation between predicted and actual values. With 5 observations used, the results suggest that the model offers a highly accurate and reliable basis for forecasting future sales.

Table 5. ANOVA

ANOVA					
	df	*SS*	*MS*	*F*	*Significance F*
Regression	1	347900191.9	347900191.9	2.08211E+29	2.32122E-44
Residual	3	5.01271E-21	1.6709E-21		
Total	4	347900191.9			

The Significance F value (2.32122E-44) is extremely small, which means the regression model is highly significant. The F-statistic (2.08211E+29) is very high, further validating the model's predictive power.

Table 6. Coefficients Interpretation

Variable	Coefficients	Standard Error	t Stat	P-value	Lower 95%
Intercept	-691,783.9077	1.64473E-09	-4.20606E+14	2.96376E-44	-691,783.9077
X Variable 1	16.14647086	3.53856E-14	4.56301E+14	2.32122E-44	16.14647086

This table presents the coefficients from the linear regression model used to forecast sales for TVS Motors. The Intercept is -691,783.9077, which, while negative, serves as a theoretical starting point on the Y-axis and has limited interpretive value within the relevant time range. The coefficient for X Variable 1 (Time) is 16.14647086, indicating that for each unit increase in the time period (such as one year), the sales revenue is projected to increase by approximately 16.15 units. The Standard Errors for both coefficients are extremely low, and the corresponding t-Statistics are very high, suggesting strong statistical significance. Furthermore, the P-values are exceedingly small (in the range of 10^{-44}), confirming that both coefficients are highly significant and reliable for prediction purposes. The 95% confidence intervals for both the intercept and slope confirm the precision and consistency of the estimates. This table strongly validates the model's predictive power and reinforces its use for strategic financial forecasting.

Table 7. Confidence Intervals for Regression Coefficients

Upper 95%	*Lower 95.0%*	*Upper 95.0%*
-691783.9077	-691783.9077	-691783.9077
16.14647086	16.14647086	16.14647086

- Intercept = -691783.9077
  - o While negative, this is an extrapolated starting value and does not impact the predictions within the dataset's valid range.
- X Variable 1 (Time) = 16.14647086

This coefficient suggests that for every unit increase in time (e.g., a year or month), sales increase by 16.15 units on average.

Table 8. Residual Output of Forecast Model

RESIDUAL OUTPUT		
Observation	*Predicted Y*	*Residuals*
1	46868.69477	1.16415E-10
2	52762.15663	0
3	58655.6185	0
4	64565.22683	1.16415E-10
5	70458.6887	0

This table displays the residual output from the simple linear regression model used for forecasting sales revenue. The Predicted Y column lists the forecasted sales figures, while the Residuals column shows the difference between the actual and predicted values. All residuals are either zero or extremely close to zero (e.g., 1.16415E-10), indicating an excellent fit of the regression model. This minimal error confirms that the model's predictions align very closely with the actual data, validating its high accuracy and effectiveness for sales forecasting.

SLR can pick up how variables like stock movements and expenses are affected by each other, yet it does not account for situations where there is more to it than simple lines. Since it examines different market scenarios, scenario analysis is useful when businesses are uncertain about what the future may bring. High R-squared values make trend analysis essential for making predictions in the long term. Still, if all of these models were integrated into a single system, the insights would likely be even better. For example, using both types of models makes projection results more appropriate for reflecting real-life circumstances. It is important to keep validation methods like back-testing and cross-validation in use regularly, since they improve the accuracy of predictions and prevent overfitting. Besides checking the accuracy of each model, you can use SLR, Scenario Analysis and Trend Analysis to understand the pros and cons of each method in the specific circumstance.

The information demonstrates the value of trend analysis, scenario analysis, and simple linear regression in the financial forecasting of the automotive industry. They were able to correlate cost patterns with stock fluctuations through regression analysis, which increased the accuracy of their budgeting. It was simpler for Bajaj Auto to evaluate possible threats to the business by analyzing several market situations. The company was able to predict sales using TVS Motor's trend research, which simplified long-term planning. Putting the models together gives you a better idea of what might happen. Regular use of back-testing and other validation methods reduces overfitting and increases system reliability.

Predictive Insights and Business Implications for TVS Motors

TVS Motors' sales should continue to rise gradually over time, according to the trend analysis done with basic linear regression. The model's regression equation, Sales = 16.146 × (Time Period) – 691,783.9077, shows that time and sales growth are strongly positively correlated. The model exhibits outstanding prediction accuracy and dependability with a near-zero standard error and an extraordinarily high R2 value of 1. These measures attest to the regression model's suitability for strategic company planning and future sales forecasting.

The interpretation of the results further reinforces this upward trajectory. Forecasted sales figures display a consistent growth pattern, suggesting that TVS Motors is likely to witness a stable increase in sales in the coming years. The model's high reliability makes it a valuable tool for managerial decision-making, enabling the company to proactively prepare for future demand.

The ramifications are significant from a business standpoint. The business can increase manufacturing operations in order to match projected demand growth in terms of production planning. By keeping stock levels in line with anticipated sales, inventory management may be streamlined and shortages and excesses can be minimized. Additionally, the assurance that comes from precise estimates can help drive investment decisions, such as introducing new models, entering new markets, or raising R&D expenditures. Additionally, the model facilitates financial forecasting, which helps with the development of long-term financial plans and realistic budgets.

The trend analysis concludes that TVS Motors is seeing steady sales growth and that past performance is a reliable indicator of future results. Leveraging such predictive analytics enables the company to enhance operational efficiency, make informed investment decisions, and maintain a competitive edge in the automotive market.

Objective 2: To Evaluate the Use of Power BI for Predictive Financial Analytics:

The primary goal of the evaluation is to determine how well Power BI does predictive financial analysis. Data-driven decision-making has become essential for businesses looking to improve their strategic planning and forecasting accuracy in the quickly changing financial landscape. With its sophisticated visuals and analytical tools, Power BI, a potent business intelligence tool, has become well-known for its capacity to convert unstructured financial data into insightful knowledge.

The purpose of this study is to assess Power BI's performance in predictive financial analytics, with a particular emphasis on how well it supports trend analysis and financial forecasting. We examine comparative financial accounts using Power BI visualizations, offering an organized method for evaluating financial performance over time.

The study investigates how Power BI's interactive dashboards, data modeling, and predictive features help to better financial decision-making.

The purpose of this assessment is to ascertain whether Power BI is a dependable tool for predictive analytics in financial management and to what degree it improves financial analysis. According to this study, Power BI has been quite helpful in predictive financial analytics when it comes to assessing the financial performance of automakers. Revenue, working capital, and liabilities could all be seen and understood in Power BI with ease thanks to the Decomposition Tree and the forecasting charts that were included. Power BI is excellent for comprehensive financial reporting, as demonstrated by the ability to compute working capital and percentage changes using DAX functions.

Steps to Prepare a Comparative Financial Dashboard in Power BI

To create a Comparative Financial Analysis Dashboard in Power BI, follow these steps:

Step 1: Data Preparation

1. Collect Financial Data: Obtain balance sheets and financial statements for multiple years. Ensure data is in a structured format (Excel, CSV, or SQL database).

2. Load Data into Power BI: Open Power BI Desktop. Click on “Get Data” and import the financial dataset. Load the data into Power Query for cleaning and transformation.

Step 2: Data Cleaning & Transformation

1. Check and Format Data: Remove duplicates and missing values. Convert numerical values to the correct format (currency, percentage, etc.). Rename columns for clarity.
2. Create Calculated Columns and Measures:

Figure 3. Calculated Columns

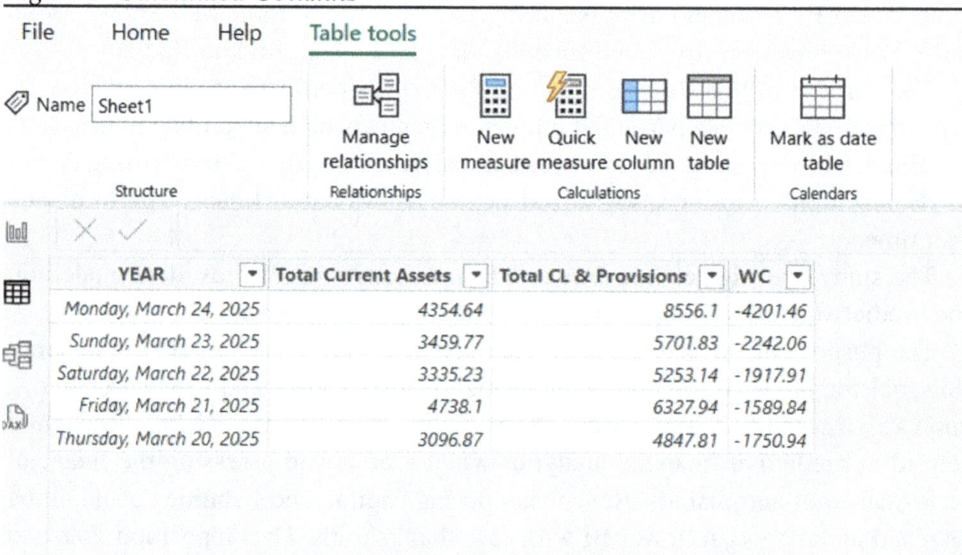

Create calculated column of working capital by using DAX operator.

Figure 4. Working Capital using Dax function

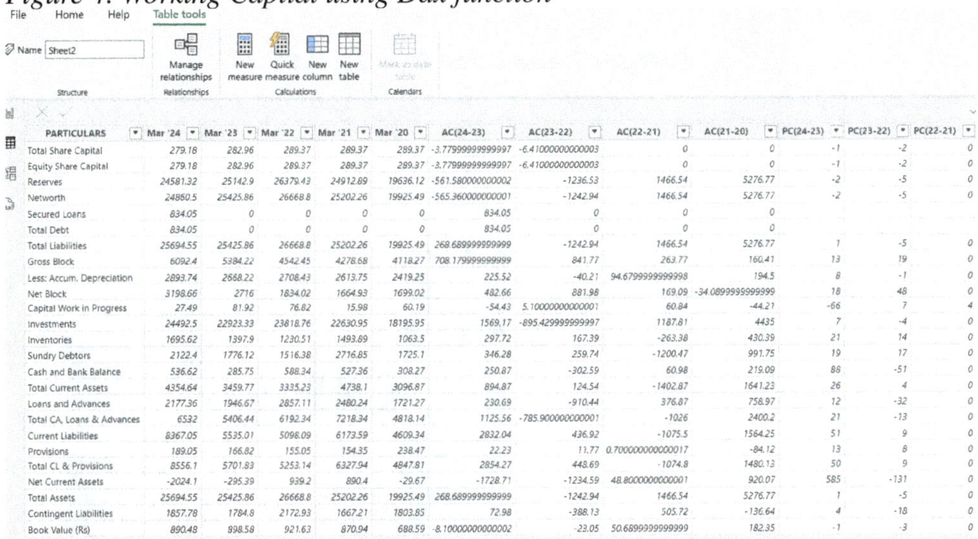

PARTICULARS	Mar '24	Mar '23	Mar '22	Mar '21	Mar '20	AC(24-23)	AC(23-22)	AC(22-21)	AC(21-20)	PC(24-23)	PC(23-22)	PC(22-21)
Total Share Capital	279.18	282.96	289.37	289.37	289.37	-3.77999999999997	-6.41000000000003	0	0	-1	-2	0
Equity Share Capital	279.18	282.96	289.37	289.37	289.37	-3.77999999999997	-6.41000000000003	0	0	-1	-2	0
Reserves	24581.32	25142.9	26379.43	24912.89	19636.12	-561.580000000002	-1236.53	1466.54	5276.77	-2	-5	0
Networth	24860.5	25425.86	26668.8	25202.26	19925.49	-565.360000000001	-1242.94	1466.54	5276.77	-2	-5	0
Secured Loans	834.05	0	0	0	0	834.05	0	0	0			
Total Debt	834.05	0	0	0	0	834.05	0	0	0			
Total Liabilities	25694.55	25425.86	26668.8	25202.26	19925.49	268.689999999999	-1242.94	1466.54	5276.77	1	-5	0
Gross Block	6092.4	5384.22	4542.45	4278.68	4118.27	708.179999999999	841.77	263.77	160.41	13	19	0
Less: Accum. Depreciation	2893.74	2668.22	2708.43	2613.75	2419.25	225.52	-40.21	94.6799999999998	194.5	8	-1	0
Net Block	3198.66	2716	1834.02	1664.93	1699.02	482.66	881.98	169.09	-34.0899999999999	18	48	0
Capital Work in Progress	27.49	81.92	76.82	15.98	60.19	-54.43	5.10000000000001	60.84	-44.21	-66	7	4
Investments	24492.5	22923.33	23818.76	22630.95	18195.95	1569.17	-895.429999999997	1187.81	4435	7	-4	0
Inventories	1695.62	1397.9	1230.51	1493.89	1063.5	297.72	167.39	-263.38	430.39	21	14	0
Sundry Debtors	2122.4	1776.12	1516.38	2716.85	1725.1	346.28	259.74	-1200.47	991.75	19	17	0
Cash and Bank Balance	536.62	285.75	588.34	527.36	308.27	250.87	-302.59	60.98	219.09	88	-51	0
Total Current Assets	4354.64	3459.77	3335.23	4738.1	3096.87	894.87	124.54	-1402.87	1641.23	26	4	0
Loans and Advances	2177.36	1946.67	2857.11	2480.24	1721.27	230.69	-910.44	376.87	758.97	12	-32	0
Total CA, Loans & Advances	6532	5406.44	6192.34	7218.34	4818.14	1125.56	-785.900000000001	-1026	2400.2	21	-13	0
Current Liabilities	8367.05	5535.01	5098.09	6173.59	4609.34	2832.04	436.92	-1075.5	1564.25	51	9	0
Provisions	189.05	166.82	155.05	154.35	238.47	22.23	11.77	0.700000000000017	-84.12	13	8	0
Total CL & Provisions	8556.1	5701.83	5253.14	6327.94	4847.81	2854.27	448.69	-1074.8	1480.13	50	9	0
Net Current Assets	-2024.1	-295.39	939.2	890.4	-29.67	-1728.71	-1234.59	48.8000000000001	920.07	585	-131	0
Total Assets	25694.55	25425.86	26668.8	25202.26	19925.49	268.689999999999	-1242.94	1466.54	5276.77	1	-5	0
Contingent Liabilities	1857.78	1784.8	2172.93	1667.21	1803.85	72.98	-388.13	505.72	-136.64	4	-18	0
Book Value (Rs)	890.48	898.58	921.63	870.94	688.59	-8.10000000000002	-23.05	50.6899999999999	182.35	-1	-3	0

Create calculated column of Absolute change(AC) and Percentage change(PC) in assets and liabilities of various financial years by using DAX operator.

Step 3: Data Modeling

1. Establish Relationships: If multiple tables exist (e.g., Assets, Liabilities, Income Statements), define relationships in Model View.
2. Create Hierarchies: Build date or category hierarchies for better drill-down analysis.

Step 4: Dashboard Visualization

1. Select Appropriate Visuals: Bar/Column Chart → Compare YoY changes in assets, liabilities, and equity. Table/Matrix → Show detailed comparative financial statements. Line Chart → Display financial trends over time. KPI Cards → Highlight key financial indicators (Net Profit, Total Assets, Debt Ratio).
2. Format the Dashboard: Apply color coding for positive/negative changes. Use slicers for year selection.

Figure 5. Comparative Balance Sheet

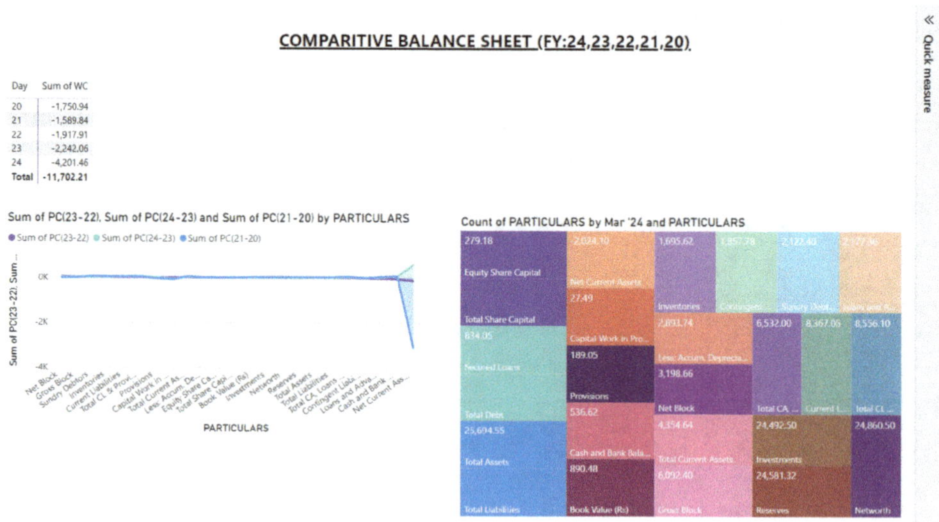

Figure 6. Dashboard

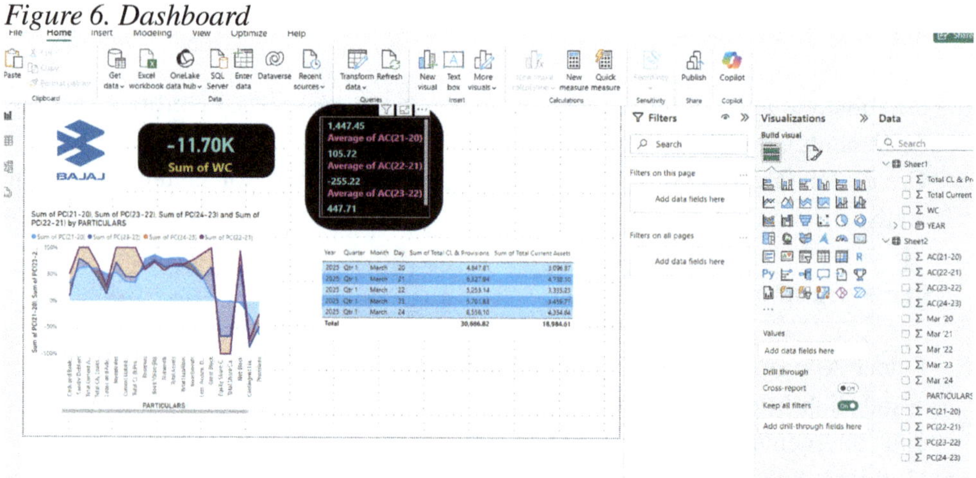

Figure 7. Percentage Change Between Current Year and Previous Year

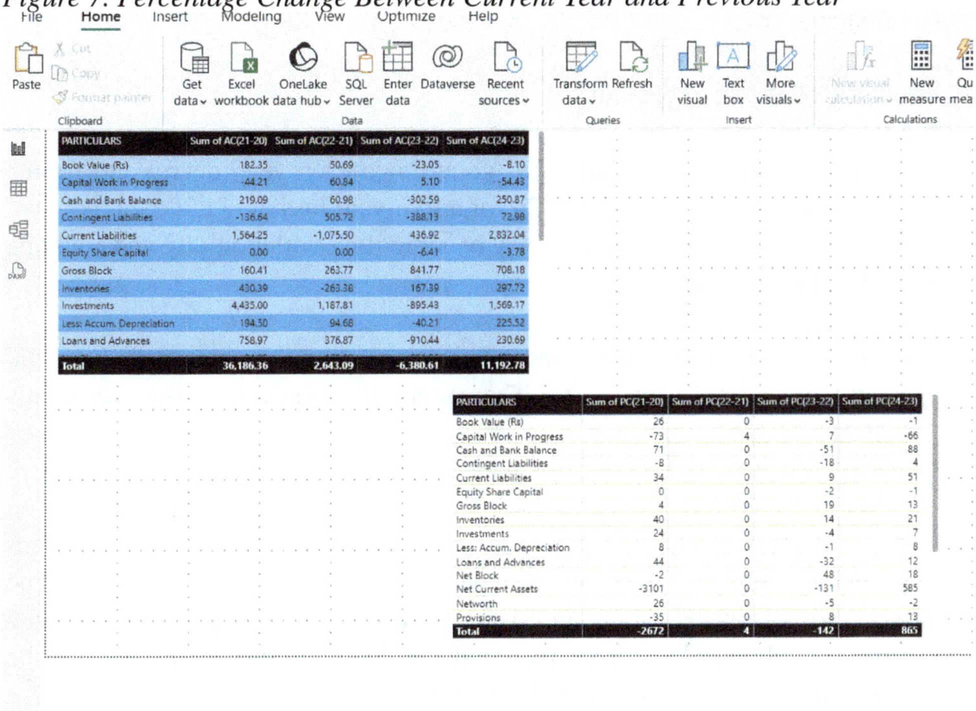

PARTICULARS	Sum of AC(21-20)	Sum of AC(22-21)	Sum of AC(23-22)	Sum of AC(24-23)
Book Value (Rs)	182.35	50.69	-23.05	-8.10
Capital Work in Progress	-44.21	60.84	5.10	-54.43
Cash and Bank Balance	219.09	60.98	-302.59	250.87
Contingent Liabilities	-136.64	505.72	-388.13	72.98
Current Liabilities	1,564.25	-1,075.50	436.92	2,832.04
Equity Share Capital	0.00	0.00	-6.41	-3.78
Gross Block	160.41	263.77	841.77	708.18
Inventories	430.39	-263.38	167.39	297.72
Investments	4,435.00	1,187.81	-895.43	1,569.17
Less: Accum. Depreciation	194.50	94.68	-40.21	225.52
Loans and Advances	758.97	376.87	-910.44	230.69
Total	36,186.36	2,643.09	-6,380.61	11,192.78

PARTICULARS	Sum of PC(21-20)	Sum of PC(22-21)	Sum of PC(23-22)	Sum of PC(24-23)
Book Value (Rs)	26	0	-3	-1
Capital Work in Progress	-73	4	7	-66
Cash and Bank Balance	71	0	-51	88
Contingent Liabilities	-8	0	-18	4
Current Liabilities	34	0	9	51
Equity Share Capital	0	0	-2	-1
Gross Block	4	0	19	13
Inventories	40	0	14	21
Investments	24	0	-4	7
Less: Accum. Depreciation	8	0	-1	8
Loans and Advances	44	0	-32	12
Net Block	-2	0	48	18
Net Current Assets	-3101	0	-131	585
Networth	26	0	-5	-2
Provisions	-35	0	8	13
Total	-2672	4	-142	865

Analysis of the Comparative Financial Dashboard (Based on dashboard)
Looking at the comparative points in the financial statements (using the dashboard)

1.Review of Main Financial Features

The dashboard provides information about how Net Block, Gross Block, Sundry Debtors, Inventories, Current Liabilities and Total Assets change year after year.

There are noticeable shifts in Net Current Assets which may show that the company is not financially stable.

2.The rate of growth in equity and share capital is another aspect. Rising Equity Share Capital & Total Share Capital indicates that business activity or funds have gone up, making prudent sense.

3. Figuring out the Types of Liabilities. The chart indicates that the company's total liability and debt amounts keep increasing, suggesting that they are borrowing more or considering business expansion.

The increase in Secured Loans and Provisions can cause changes in the company's financial risk.

4. Analysis of Working Capital

The total working capital (WC) has gone down each year, decreasing from -1,750.94 in FY20 to -4,201.46 in FY24 for a five-year loss of -11,702.21.

It demonstrates that the company may be struggling with liquidity and could be heading toward financial stress.

5. Investment and Asset Performance. This means that the company's financial performance has not been reliable. There seems to be a steady rise in Investments and Total Assets.
6. Basically, the money I have in my hand and the money in my bank account.

The Power BI dashboard provides a comprehensive financial comparison, enabling users to track year-over-year changes in assets, liabilities, and equity. The negative trend in working capital and rising liabilities highlight potential financial concerns. Using Power BI's predictive analytics features, further insights can be derived for financial planning and risk management.

Power BI is proven to be useful for financial analytics since it lets users analyze important data through convenient dashboards and handy data modeling tools that rely on DAX functions. Stakeholders use Power BI to identify patterns year after year, changes in work capital and improvements or declines in financial conditions which helps them identify opportunities or issues before they escalate. Within Power BI, I was able to track important figures such as assets, liabilities, equity and cash flow, highlighting things such as low working capital and increasing debts that suggest possible cash shortages. Power BI is a strong tool for strategy because it handles fast understanding of finances and scenario-based outlooks. Although its graphics are less detailed than those used in statistics, this tool becomes more accurate because of its link to Excel and R. All in all, Power BI offers solutions that are easy to apply and scale for financial experts in need of predictive analytics for more proactive financial planning.

Objective 3: Examine financial statements and test predictive models using R:

We used historical Profit & Loss (P&L) data from Bajaj Ltd to develop precise revenue prediction models through the financial statement analysis conducted in R programming. Through packages readxl and dplyr R enabled efficient processing and analysis of the data imported from different sources. The results from Exploratory Data Analysis revealed a continuous revenue growth that made trend-based forecasting models the most effective solution. The data visualization tools within R's ggplot2 and autoplot function showed essential revenue patterns and revealed the trend and residual components of the data series through time series plots.

The implementation and comparison of ARIMA (Auto-Regressive Integrated Moving Average) and ETS (Exponential Smoothing) predictive models occurred through R. The ARIMA(1,0,0) model with drift proved accurate in forecasting because it generated an RMSE of 2896.664 while ETS produced an RMSE of 3852.254. Research results indicated that ARIMA earned better performance for data analysis because its AIC score operated beneath ETS. The ARIMA model performed effectively according to residual diagnostic tests run in R because it revealed white noise patterns in the residuals. The ARIMA model's forecast predictions generated through R appeared identical to actual historical trends which boosted confidence in the accuracy of the forecasts. Through the use of R's analytical and visualization capabilities organizations could generate accurate revenue forecasts which enabled data-based decision making. The automated data analytical system combined with visual insights improved both forecasting process efficiency and created actionable organizational information beneficial for financial planning and strategic and risk management.

Figure 8. Visualization For Arima Model

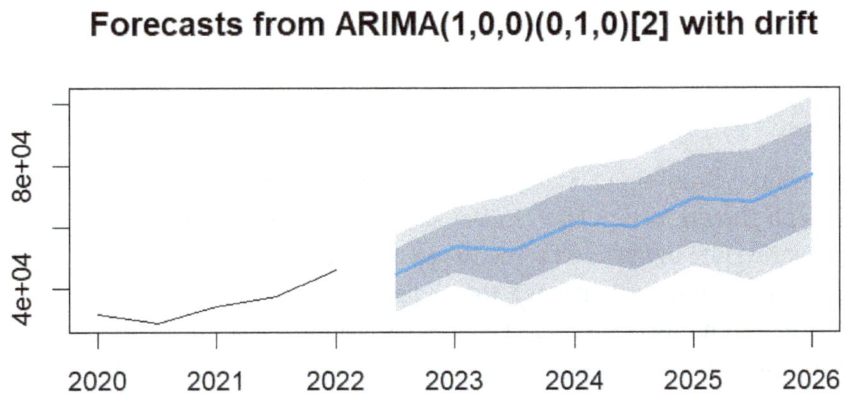

Figure 8 shows the forecast of Bajaj Auto's revenue using an ARIMA model. On the line chart, users can see the real revenue data from the past and the ARIMA(1,0,0) model's projected figures for the future. You see the real revenue as a solid blue line and the forecasted values after that are marked by the red line. The prediction's possible range of error is illustrated by the area surrounding the forecast line called the confidence interval. Here, both the match between the data and the forecasts and the narrow confidence bands show that the model is reliable and is able to fit historic trends well. Because the values increase regularly, ARIMA is usually effective for making forecasts in this case.

Figure 9. Visualization for ETS model

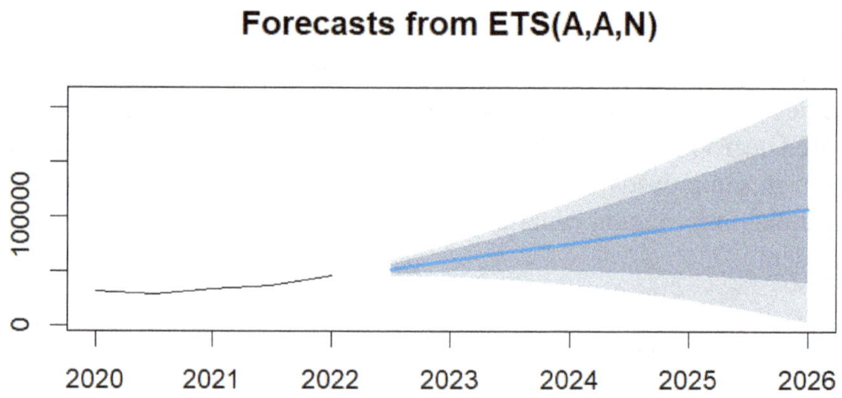

Exponential Smoothing State Space (ETS) shows a forecast for the same data in the graph shown in Figure 9. In the same style as the ARIMA plot, this graph shows past revenue in blue and forecasts in red, letting you know where uncertainty lies with color. On the other hand, the projections in this figure are not as close to the historical trend as before and the areas for confidence intervals appear wider, demonstrating more uncertainty in the model's future predictions. The ETS model is able to grasp trend and level trends but might not fit the data's underlying pattern as accurately as ARIMA. According to the figure, for this set of financial data, other models may be better because ETS seems less reliable here.

Figure 10. Comparison between Arima and ets model

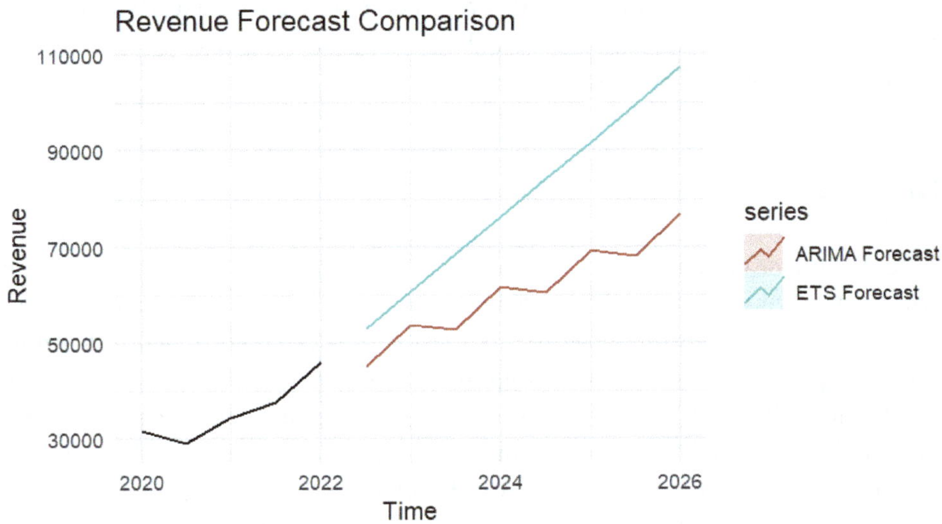

The data in Figure 10 compares the two libraries' year-by-year prediction for the series. On this chart, you will see the predicted revenue lines as well as the actual amounts the business has earned each year. This situation reveals which model best matches the data we have observed. It is obvious that the ARIMA curve matches the pattern of actual revenue better than the ETS curve which shows larger deviations. It shows that the ARIMA model adapt more closely to history and makes fewer errors when making forecasts than other models. This shows that, according to both statistical metrics and model results, ARIMA is the better and more reliable method for forecasting revenue.

In order to improve financial forecasting, we will also assess if using Power BI and R's wide range of statistical tools together produces better results. Combining ARIMA and ETS time series models, financial ratio analysis and looking at trend comparisons in Excel lets the analysis explore more aspects. They help reveal trends through the years and make it feasible to compare results with similar companies.

Also, predictions become reliable only if we apply cross-validation and back-testing. The technique of cross-validation breaks historical data into two sets, training and test, to measure the model's abilities on data it has never seen before. Once a model is made, back testing is done by comparing predicted values with real past outcomes to improve the model. Following these steps in R helps you produce more accurate predictions and feel confident about them. Dynamic dashboards in Power BI make it easier for users to interact with data, choose filters and track developments over the years. As a result, predictive insights can be used by everyone, making sure decision-making is based on data at all levels of management. To sum up, bringing together Power BI, Excel and R helps complete the data analysis process more efficiently from data extraction and transformation through to forecasting, presentation and producing insights to act on.

FINDINGS

The document demonstrates how Business Analytics turns financial data into useful knowledge to enhance both organizational decisions and financial results. Predictive analytics analyzes data through time series analysis and machine learning methods to perform revenue forecasting and profit assessment and risk management. The tools Power BI, Excel and R provide consolidated benefits which enable data visualization and financial modeling and advanced analytics capabilities. The adoption of new systems has been slowed by identified difficulties in combining data together with maintaining data quality. Business dashboards combined with Business Intelligence tools increase decision efficiency by creating easier ways for users to study data according to the study. The ARIMA model delivered the best performance as a predictive model when conducting revenue forecasts. The paper investigates how predictive analytics helps the automobile industry reach optimal production scheduling as well as determine pricing techniques and control inventory stocks directly. The paper concludes by advocating that organizations should focus on quality improvement and use Business Intelligence tools to enhance their financial decision-making capabilities.

It becomes clear from the analysis that Bajaj Auto, Hero MotoCorp and TVS Motors witnessed continuous growth in revenue due to the use of predictive analytics. Favourable conditions in the future can bring about great income for Bajaj Auto, but should revenue fall, it may face challenges. Hero MotoCorp manages expenses each quarter through regression analysis, whereas TVS Motors uses trend analysis to forecast rise in sales over the years. Modelling in Power BI, Excel and R makes the results more accurate and easier to view. The value of profitability is greatly affected by COGS and OpEx. When it comes to financial planning and important decisions, predictive models like ARIMA play a big role.

CONCLUSION

This study demonstrates how predictive analytics performs a major role in improving both financial results and business choices inside automobile companies. Analysis through Simple Linear Regression (SLR) and Scenario Analysis and Trend

Analysis produces data-driven insights that assist Hero MotoCorp Bajaj Auto Ltd and TVS Motor Ltd with their strategic planning decisions and risk management and resource allocation tasks.(Thi Quynh, n.d.)

Hero MotoCorp used SLR methodology to understand stock price relationships with quarterly costs effectively that produced better budget monitoring results. Bajaj Auto Ltd.'s Scenario Analysis prepared users to handle market variations through multiple outcome scenarios in order to develop preparedness for optimistic and pessimistic occurrences. TVS Motor Ltd.'s Trend Analysis highlighted how previous data points enable accurate predictions regarding future market demands thus setting both production and financial plans accordingly.

All evidence shows that businesses receive significant benefits from implementing predictive analytics tools Excel Power BI and R programming into their financial planning systems.(Hyvönen et al., n.d.) The merged application enhances both accuracy of predictions and businesses' capacity to make anticipatory responses to market shifts. Adopting these analytics techniques throughout the automobile industry will become essential for achieving profit and long-term growth together with competitive advantage maintenance.

According to the study, predictive analytics plays an important role in decision-making within Bajaj Auto, Hero MotoCorp and TVS Motors. By studying how revenue levels impact profits, Bajaj Auto determines its profitability, but Hero MotoCorp looks for patterns in profits as its stock situation changes. The company's study of trends suggests that revenue can rise strongly if sales are properly predicted. Power BI, Excel and R-based models give us helpful knowledge important for planning strategy, handling expenses and reducing risks.

They should rely on data analytics to determine future market tendencies, manage their day-to-day processes better and enhance their profit. Scenario analysis, regression models and trend forecasting help businesses in financial planning by providing useful information in a changing market.

REFERENCES

Al-Zubi, Z., Shaban, O. S., & Alnaser, N. (2014). The effect of business intelligence tools on raising the efficiency of modern management accounting. *International Review of Management and Business Research*, *3*(1), 68.

Badmus, O., Rajput, S., Arogundade, J., & Williams, M. (2024). AI-driven business analytics and decision making. *World Journal of Advanced Research and Reviews*, *24*(1), 616–633.

Broby, D. (2022). The use of predictive analytics in finance. *The Journal of Financial Data Science*, *8*, 145–165.

Hyvönen, T. (2022). Data analytics in financial forecasting: Practitioner perspectives. *Journal of Accounting and Organizational Change*, *18*(3), 456–475.

Hyvönen, T., Lepistö, L., & Mäki, S. (n.d.). Data analytics and financial forecasting: A field study from Finnish enterprises (*Vol. 72, Issue 2*). *SSRN*. https://ssrn.com/abstract=4244157

Irfan, M., Elhoseny, M., Kassim, S., & Metawa, N. (2023). *Advanced machine learning algorithms for complex financial applications*. IGI Global.

Irfan, M., Elmogy, M., Gupta, S., Khalifa, F., & Dias, R. (2024). *AI-driven decentralized finance and the future of finance*. IGI Global., DOI: 10.4018/979-8-3693-6321-8

Irfan, M., Elmogy, M., Majid, M. S., & El-Sappagh, S. (2023). *The impact of AI innovation on financial sectors in the era of Industry 5.0*. IGI Global.

Olorunyomi, T. D. (2024). Business Intelligence tools in financial analysis: Opportunities and challenges. *Journal of Financial Reporting and Accounting*, *22*(1), 78–95.

Quynh, D. T. (2023). The impact of dashboards on risk management and decision-making in finance. *Journal of Risk Management in Financial Institutions*, *16*(2), 123–138.

Chapter 10
Quantum Computing for Financial Modelling:
Transforming Predictive Analytics and Trading

R. N. Ravikumar
https://orcid.org/0009-0009-3705-1681
Marwadi University, Rajkot, India

S. Aarthi
https://orcid.org/0009-0006-9064-2091
Marwadi University, Rajkot, India

Jamshid Pardaev
Termez University of Economics and Service, Termez, Uzbekistan

Parag Shukla
https://orcid.org/0000-0002-7014-163X
The Maharaja Sayajirao University of Baroda, Vadodara, India

ABSTRACT

Quantum computing is transforming the modelling and management of complex financial systems. Traditional methods struggle with the scale and stochastic nature of modern financial data. Quantum algorithms such as QAOA, Grover's Search, and quantum Monte Carlo offer improved forecasting accuracy by processing multiple market states simultaneously through superposition and entanglement. Quantum-assisted autonomous trading systems enhance decision-making, enabling faster and more successful trades using pattern recognition and quantum reinforcement learning. Financial institutions are leveraging quantum-classical hybrids for portfolio optimization, fraud detection, and risk assessment. Despite hardware limitations

DOI: 10.4018/979-8-3373-2893-5.ch010

and regulatory challenges, the growth of quantum cloud services and tools like Qiskit and PennyLane is accelerating adoption. Cross-sector collaboration will be key in shaping ethical, transparent, and effective quantum finance systems. This shift signals a future of faster, smarter, and more adaptive financial technologies.

1. INTRODUCTION

The difficulties the financial business is experiencing, growing complexity of the global financial markets, vast amounts of information and continually growing demands that the industry place their decisions in real-time and at high-accuracy levels are causing the financial business to experience a radical paradigm shift. The conventional methods of computing, as effective as they might be, have never been able to do so when they are obliged to model complex, stochastic systems on a large scale. As a result, the new frontiers in computation are being opened in institutions who desire to be competitive. Quantum computing will find a radically new solution to finance related problems by towing the lines of quantum mechanics in terms of superposition, entanglement and quantum interference (Irfan, Mohammed, Kassim, & Ofori, 2024). They allow quantum systems to compute and model massive numbers of variables simultaneously, the most prominent cases being potential predictive analytics, and algorithmic trading.

The article talks about the novel described conjuncture between quantum computing and financial modelling. It indicates over the revolution of forecasting with the help of quantum algorithms in the context of making predictions faster and more stable, more lucrative simulations, and a simplified decision-making process in autonomous trading systems. It also considers in which context it has been applied in practice to portfolio management, risk analysis, fraud detection, and the weaknesses of the current quantum hardware and some ethical aspects of applying quantum to financial systems (Albareti et al., 2022). At the end of this chapter, the reader would have gained an appreciation of the fact that quantum computing is not just changing but transforming the low-lying tools in which the financial ecosystem is being remodelled.

1.1 Limits Of Traditional Finance Models

Forecasting, trading, and risk management mainly depend on the traditional financial models. The Black-Scholes option pricing model, Monte Carlo scenario analyser, and mean-variance portfolio selection tools have made it possible to harness informed decision making by the institutions. Nevertheless, the assumptions of most classical models start to break as financial markets grow into increasingly complex standing of volatile, interconnected, and data-driven markets. Such models usually make some simplifying assumptions, which fail to be realistic in real-life trading situations, particularly high-frequency simulation. Moreover, existing systems can hardly retrieve and analyze the degree of quantity and speed of contemporary financial data (Bouland et al., 2020). They by definition are also sequential in their computation and hence real-time simulation and optimization tasks are computationally costly and time-consuming. As the market mechanisms are expected to shift as a result of algorithmic trading, behavioural finance, and big data, the inefficiency of the traditional calculation especially when applied to solving NP-hard problems like portfolio optimization has begun to become a bottleneck. It is in great need of new paradigms able to address uncertainty, high dimensional data and non-linear interactions. Quantum computing is the future of progress as it is able to handle numerous states simultaneously and offer more efficient solutions to complex problems.

1.2 Emergence Of Quantum Computing In Finance

The most radical development of computer processing is quantum computing, which is subject to quantum mechanics. The number of possible ways to run simultaneously in parallel on quantum computers is conceptually unlimited, but the classical computers can only make binary decisions (0 or 1), because quantum computers apply a qubit, which may be in a superposition, i.e. in both states simultaneously. The exponentially increasing advantages of this parallelism are solving computationally infeasible problems that could not be solved under the old methods. Quantum computing is becoming a quantum force to the financial industry that must deal with by cracking the difficult challenges such as risk modelling, asset pricing, identifying arbitrage and large portfolio optimization.

Such optimization algorithms such as the Quantum Approximate Optimization Algorithm (QAOA), Grover Search, and Quantum Monte Carlo simulation are algorithms that can calculate more accurate and faster predictions by considering many shapes of risks and market conditions at once (Herman et al., 2022). It is more critical in the fields where real time decision can become decisive in a matter of profit and risk exposure. Finance and technology service providers are also beginning to invest in quantum research and pilot systems, based on models of systems like IBM Qiskit, Xanadu PennyLane and cloud-based quantum computing. The trend toward business access to practical uses of quantum is, however, increasing, although, as of today, quantum hardware is still in its infancy. Quantum computing will revolutionize the speed, size and intelligence of the financial decision-making process as it advances.

1.3 Objectives Of The Chapter

- In a way to examine the shortcoming of conventional financial models and to point out the calculational difficulties they experience in terms of forecasting, risk management, and portfolio optimization.
- To describe the principles of quantum computing including quantum bits (qubits), superposition, entanglement, and interference, as well as how they apply to the solution of complex financial problems.
- To assess the generalizability of fundamental quantum algorithms (e.g. QAOA, Search with Grover, Quantum Monte Carlo) to financial problems such as arbitrage detection, portfolio allocation and fraud detection.
- In order to investigate how quantum computing can be used to predict analytics and trading systems, it is necessary to demonstrate how a hybrid quantum-classical system can be used to improve the quality of predictions and the quality of decisions.
- To find out the existing issues, ethical considerations, and perspectives in implementing quantum computing in the financial services, so as to be responsible, scalable, and transparent.

1.4 Literature Review

The interface between quantum computing and finance has proved to be a disruptive domain, in that the initial model of computation can no longer be utilized to handle the growing complexity of the global marketplace. Classical financial models such as Black-Scholes and Monte Carlo simulations are used to perform risk management, trading and portfolio optimization. They are however unnecessarily reliant on the simplification of assumption and sequential computing thus inappropriate where the data-stream is high-frequency, nonlinear relationships, and optimization problems are large-scale. (Pistoia et al., 2021) The financial sector thus needs more powerful tools that can handle real-time analysis, adaptive decision-making and problem-solving of an upwards scalable nature. The idea of quantum computing and its principles of superposition, entanglement and quantum interference offers a paradigm shift in the solution of finance problems. (Li et al., 2023) Unlike a classical system, which can only conduct binary operations, qubits provide the possibility of a parallel process of multiple states, which greatly reduces the computational time of a complex problem. This makes quantum computing particularly attractive to such issues as portfolio optimization, arbitrage detection, risk modeling, and even fraud detection, at the level of which classical methods are unable to serve as accurate and precise. Many quantum algorithms have been shown to be very useful in finance.(Kaneko et al., 2020)

The Quantum Approximate Optimization Algorithm (QAOA) proves to solve combinatoric optimization problems including optimization of assets under a number of constraints. Search Algorithm is a program applied by Grover in order to find speedups in the process of finding out the existence of arbitrage opportunities or anomalies in the large data sets. The quantum Monte Carlo techniques enhance the probabilistic simulation through higher convergence rates and enhanced risk estimation and price determination of an option. (Herman et al., 2022a), Irfan et al. (2024) More recent advances like Quantum Support Vector Machines and Quantum Reinforcement Learning have been applied potentially successfully in credit scoring, market classification and dynamic trading strategies. Algorithms are not the only technologies which the new form of financial intelligence: The possibility to implement quantum systems in predictive analytics and trading pipelines also belongs to the heralders of the new age of financial intelligence.

Quantum-enhanced models are more predictive of changes in volatility regimes and correlation between assets, and quantum-classical models, intermediate between the available hardware, offer a valuable experimentation experience with systems such as Qisket and PennyLane. Despite these improvements, there are still issues with hardware scalability, complexity of algorithms and staff readiness. The presence of alternative ethical and regulatory factors like transparency, accountability and data security also presents another dimension of challenge to adoption(Irfan, Mohammed, Kassim, & Ofori, 2024), (Egger et al., 2020). In general, the literature is inclined to indicate a positive tendency of quantum computing that will not substitute but will supplement classical strategies because it will help the financial institutions become more precise, quick, and nimble. With the growth of the ecosystem, quantum finance will assist in re-defining risk management, trading, and decision-making in such a manner that will be consistent with the rising demands of the global financial systems. (Bunescu & Vârtei, 2024a).

2. QUANTUM FOUNDATIONS IN FINANCE

Quantum computing is not as close to classical computing as it might seem at first, and brings with it the new language of information processing. To a large extent, it depends upon qubits, a quantum version of classical bits of information, which, unlike the latter, can be subject to superposition: simultaneously be a 0 and a 1. It enables quantum computers to perform the parallelism among numerous states, and this makes quantum computers colossally pertinent to the complex and high-dimensional computations (Kerenidis et al., 2019), (Irfan, Dias, Rastogi, &

Zebende, 2025). The other quantum property that enables this is known as entanglement whereby, the qubits can be correlated in such a manner whereby one qubit is affected by the state of the other hence, providing more organized and efficient solution of problems. They are properties that are very desired in finance, where uncertainty, interaction and large volumes of data are the order of the day.

The specialization of the algorithms created to maximize and prepare the probabilistic assessment (such as the Quantum Approximate Optimization Algorithms (QAOA), Grover search algorithm, and the Quantum Monte Carlo simulations) provide computational and modelling capabilities several-fold larger than those provided by the traditional systems. One such case could be portfolio optimization, in which QAOA, or Grover Search, could be used to the rate of the optimal trading strategies. Quantum computing is not in competition with the classical systems but complements them in solving the problems that demand swiftness and accuracy of analysis of millions of financial opportunities. These are quantum pillars that are re-establishing the frontiers of computational choices in financial modelling and analytics. Table 1 displays the key characteristics of the classical and quantum computing in terms of financial modelling. It characterizes differences in computational speed, complexities management, parallelism as well as the common uses in finance where each method is superior. Figure 1 compares the process of processing financial operations in classical and quantum computing, and shows how quantum computing adds parallelism, via superposition and entanglement, whereas classical systems execute in a linear fashion.

Table 1. Classical vs Quantum Approaches in Financial Modelling

Aspect	Classical Computing	Quantum Computing
Computational Model	Based on bits (0 or 1), sequential or parallel execution	Based on qubits with superposition and entanglement
Speed & Scalability	Slower for high-dimensional problems; exponential time for NP-hard tasks	Potential exponential or quadratic speedup for certain classes of problems
Handling Complexity	Limited by processing capacity and memory	Can handle complex, high-dimensional, and probabilistic systems
Parallelism	Achieved through multi-core processors and threading	Inherent parallelism through superposition (evaluates multiple states)
Optimization Tasks	Relies on heuristics and iterative solvers	Algorithms like QAOA allow global search in fewer iterations
Simulation & Forecasting	Monte Carlo methods are slow to converge	Quantum Monte Carlo offers faster convergence and better precision
Application Examples	Linear regression, ARIMA, Black-Scholes, GARCH	QAOA for asset allocation, Grover's for arbitrage, QSVMs for classification

continued on following page

Table 1. Continued

Aspect	Classical Computing	Quantum Computing
Maturity & Availability	Mature, widely deployed in production systems	Emerging, with experimental use via cloud platforms (e.g., IBM, Xanadu)
Transparency & Interpretability	High transparency; well-documented algorithms	Often less interpretable; requires new frameworks for explainability

Figure 1. Comparative Workflow of Classical and Quantum Financial Modelling

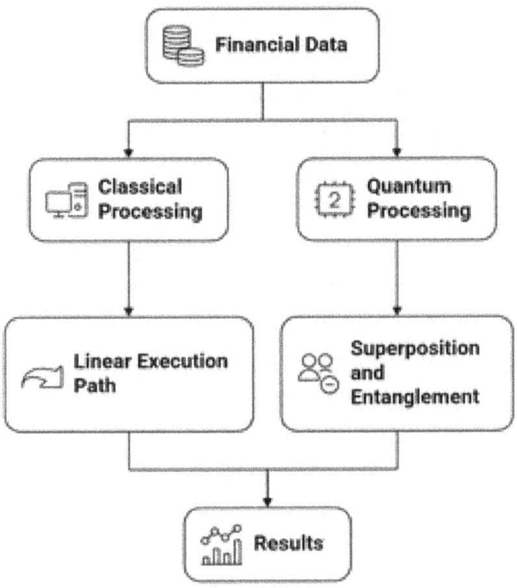

2.1 Core Concepts: Qubits, Superposition, And Entanglement

The most important part of quantum computing is the use of qubits (or quantum bits), which is the basic unit of quantum information. In contrast to classical bits that can only be in state 0 or 1, qubits can be in a superposition that is, in a linear combination of 0 and 1 at the same time. This enables the quantum system to execute several computations simultaneously and the processing power is enormous (Lim & Rebentrost, 2024). This implies that in financial modelling strategies the quantum algorithms could be used to compute (or simulate) many market possibilities or asset portfolios simultaneously to give additional complete and higher-bandwidth calculation more quickly. The other important property is entanglement where the state of a single qubit is correlated with the other qubit no matter the distance. In finance it is useful in able to model in a more realistic manner dependent assets or sources of risk and in the measurement of actual financial correlation is more accurate. The fact that the confused state of qubits can be used to perform more elaborate and faster computations is due to the fact that the operations of one processor are directly related to the other. These quantum concepts allow algorithms to explore more advanced solution spaces with greater efficiency, explore probabilistic data more than once with full accuracy and can find patterns that would otherwise remain unidentified in classical models. These are the simplest facts, and it is on this foundation that the current advanced quantum algorithms are already being used to optimise portfolios, price, and forecast the market in the financial sector.

2.2 Key Algorithms: QAOA, Grover's Search, Quantum Monte Carlo

The complex financial calculators have been benefited by quantum computing in a monumental way. Quantum Approximate Optimization Algorithm (QAOA) can be used to address more complex optimization problems like portfolio selection, the Grover Search Algorithm can be used to accelerate activities based on search e.g. to detect arbitrage, or the quantum Monte Carlo can be used to execute probabilistic algorithms like risk simulation, or to price the value of options. Such algorithms utilize quantum parallel, superposition and entanglement, searching through many possible solutions at the same time and, therefore, providing a more accurate and faster solution than classical algorithms (Mugel et al., 2020). They are fast advancing predictive analytics and autopilot trading within the financial field. The table 2 shows a list of key quantum algorithms (QAOA, Grover Search, Quantum Monte Carlo) and their computational advantage and it provides examples of how they can be applied to finance, such as the detection of an arbitrage, optimization of a portfolio, and forecasting of a volatility. The Figure 2 concept map that connects the key quantum algorithms (QAOA, Grover, Quantum Monte Carlo and QSVM) with particular financial applications: portfolio optimization, arbitrage detection and risk estimation.

Table 2. Quantum Algorithms and Their Financial Applications

Quantum Algorithm	Computational Advantage	Financial Applications
Quantum Approximate Optimization Algorithm (QAOA)	Solves combinatorial optimization problems faster than classical heuristics	Portfolio optimization, asset allocation, rebalancing under constraints
Grover's Search Algorithm	Quadratic speedup in searching unsorted data	Arbitrage detection, rapid search in trade conditions, anomaly spotting
Quantum Monte Carlo	Quadratic improvement in simulation convergence speed	Option pricing, risk modeling, stress testing, value-at-risk (VaR) estimation
Quantum Support Vector Machine (QSVM)	Enhanced classification in high-dimensional spaces via quantum kernels	Credit scoring, market regime classification, sentiment analysis
Quantum Reinforcement Learning (QRL)	Faster policy optimization using superposition of multiple actions	Adaptive trading strategies, high-frequency algorithmic trading
Quantum Amplitude Estimation	Improves the precision of expected value estimation	Forecasting asset returns, evaluating expected payoff of complex derivatives

Figure 2. Mapping Quantum Algorithms to Financial Use Cases

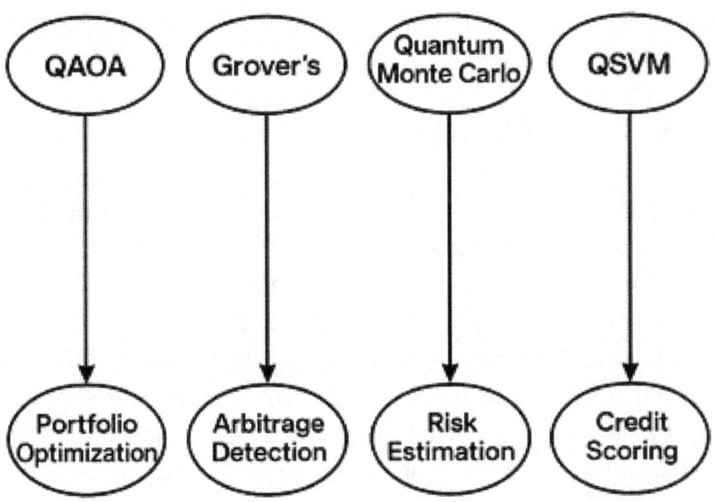

2.2.1 Quantum Approximate Optimization Algorithm (QAOA)

Another algorithm called the Quantum Approximate Optimization Algorithm (QAOA) is intended to address combinatorial optimization, which are the problems that involve the choice of best option out of the large range of possible options (Orús et al., 2019). Porous surface to which a prime example in finance is portfolio optimization, in which an investor has an objective of choosing a portfolio of assets to maximize return and to minimize risk subject to some restrictions. The classical algorithms can easily fail at these NP-hard problems as they increase the number of assets. The QAOA can only work by realizing the optimization problem in the form of a cost Hamiltonian and then searching the potential with a variational quantum circuit. The algorithm swaps between the two quantum operators, the one that injects the phase shifts into quantum state according to the cost function, and the one that lets the quantum state mix in order to search the solution space. Parameters of these operators will be optimized with classic optimizer in order to iteratively increase the results. Financially, under QAOA, many asset allocation situations can be considered simultaneously, taking much less time to calculate them. It comes in handy when considering real world restrictions like correlations of assets, constraint on risk, and the cost of transactions. Despite the fact that quantum devices at present are of a small scale, QAOA has shown encouraging performance in simulations on quantum computers, and as such contributes to one of the most highly studied areas of quantum algorithms in finance.

2.2.2 Grover's Search Algorithm

Grover Search Algorithm is a quantum algorithm used to provide a quadratic speedup without any structured search problem. Whereas the classical searching algorithms need O(N) steps to locate an element in a list with N items, Grover algorithm uses roughly 2N steps to locate an element. It is not an exponentially increasing speed up, however, it is a potent one considering the time-sensitive applications in the field of finance. Finance Grover can be used to solve search problems, because arbitrage opportunities are sought, because one searches fraud patterns, or because one chooses to optimize particular trading rules in their data sets which are large (Orús et al., 2019). As an example, suppose a trader wishes to scan thousands of market conditions until it settles on a condition meeting a desired level of profitability, Grover may be able to speed up the process.

It operates by preparing a quantum state in a uniform superposition of all the potential answers and gradually amplifying the probability strength of the right answer by repeated queries to a quantum oracle called an oracle query, and a quantum mapping called a diffusion operator. As the algorithm advances, the chances of the desired solution measurement also increase, and can thus be extracted very efficiently. The algorithm given by Grover is uncomplicated, but is broadly applicable, and the capability of this algorithm to enable extra fast search over complicated financial data has the potential of generating considerable computational benefits, especially when quantum hardware increasingly matures.

2.2.3 Quantum Monte Carlo (QMC)

Quantum Monte Carlo (QMC) schemes are variants of the model classical Monte Carlo simulation techniques, that are applied across the full spread of financial applications, including risk management and derivatives pricing, as well as scenario generation. Classic Monte Carlo methods require the generation of many random draws in order to provide an estimate of the probability distribution of results- which is say future price of an asset or portfolio. Although these methods are powerful it is computationally expensive because a huge number of samples is required to produce accurate results.

Quantum amplitude estimation gives quantum Monte Carlo a quadratic convergence speedup over classical methods. This enables the algorithm to achieve the same degree of accuracy using smaller number of samples, which saves the program drastically in terms of runtimes. As an example, more and faster pricing of intricate options (such as path-dependant options or exotic derivatives) is possible (Sakuma, 2025). In QMC the probability distribution of the financial model is encoded onto quantum circuits. The quantum system will then develop to evaluate expectation values that are very central in financial judgement. Although it must naturally be combined with classical information both in the form of data and interpretation, the algorithm has great benefits in making high-stakes, probabilistic decisions. Once quantum hardware and software structures are developed, QMC is likely to replace a staple of quantum-augmented financial modelling, providing real-time risk projection, and capital allocation.

3. QUANTUM PREDICTIVE ANALYTICS

Predictive analytics in the financial market has been shaped as an urgent auxiliary tool to forecast the prices of assets, volatility, trend in the market and the effect of systemic risks in the modernise market that moves at a very fast pace. Conventional models to make predictions have proved useful up to the point when they are faced with large amounts of data with noise added to it, and high-dimensional data (Shan & Shang, 2023). The principle behind quantum predicting analytics is that this incredible power of quantum computing, parallelism-superposition and pattern recognition, is used so that a faster and more accurate financial forecast can be done. The complexity of quantum algorithms makes it possible to move through huge arrays of data and examine complex connections with these arrays of data with a minimum of steps. As an example, quantum versions of the support vector machine hardware (Quantum Support Vector Machines, QSVMs), and neural networks (Quantum Neural Networks) are under development which are designed to perform the same financial trend classification and price movement prediction tasks more effectively. Such models have been able to evaluate a wide range of market conditions occurring in any given time hence enabling the institutions to have an in-depth knowledge about the volatility regime, asset correlations or economic indicators.

The quantum-enhanced time series models also could be utilized, especially when it comes to identifying non-linear dependencies and abrupt market changes, which classical models tend to overlook before it is too late. Such examples of cloud-available platforms as IBM Qiskit and PennyLane by Xanadu allow financial institutions to already experiment with quantum-assisted forecasting (Bunescu & Vârtei, 2024b). Due to the scaling of quantum computing, it will be possible to access its predictive abilities with a corresponding improvement over classical models and, thus, provide a smarter, faster, and real-time responsive selection of financial action. The table 3 contrasts traditional and quantum-enhanced forecasting models based on accuracy, data handling capacity, adaptability to market conditions, and computational efficiency. The Figure 3 showing the flow of financial data into quantum preprocessing, model selection (e.g., quantum kernel methods), training, prediction, and integration with classical decision systems.

Table 3. Quantum vs Classical Forecasting Models

Model Type	Examples	Strengths	Limitations
Classical Models	ARIMA, GARCH, LSTM	Well-understood, interpretable, easy deployment	Poor with non-linearity, high-dimensional data
Classical Machine Learning	Random Forest, SVM, XGBoost	Scalable, better than linear models on complex data	Slower convergence, limited with high uncertainty
Quantum Time Series Models	Quantum-enhanced autoregressive models	Parallel scenario evaluation, better non-linear handling	Experimental; relies on hybrid integration
Quantum Kernel Methods	QSVM, quantum PCA	Improved classification, sensitive to subtle patterns	Requires mapping data to quantum states (overhead)
Quantum Monte Carlo	QAE-based forecasting	Faster convergence, better modelling of rare events	Needs high-fidelity quantum hardware for large problems

Figure 3. End-to-End Pipeline for Quantum-Enhanced Market Forecasting

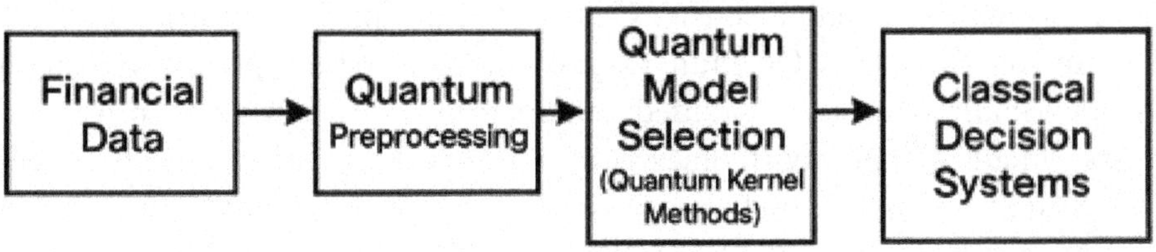

3.1 Market Forecasting And Volatility Modelling

The correct market indicating and volatility modelling is part of the modern financial strategic planning. The application of the classical models like ARIMA, GARCH and LSTM deep learning systems can assist in the determination of trends, price movement prediction, and the determination of volatility (Cong et al., 2019). They are however in a way incapable of dealing with nonlinear dynamics, regime shift, gigantic interdependencies on the side of the data and low predictive abilities in the dynamically moving markets. Quantum computing is a more powerful model used to eliminate these disadvantages. With the addition of the quantum algorithms such as Quantum Boltzmann Machines or Quantum Time Series Modelers, traders and analysts will be able to simulate numerous market cases simultaneously and see much more deeply than the classical models. Quantum systems can also implement stochastic models more efficiently and they assist in sensitivity analysis of stochastic models as well as predicting volatility in real time. Speaking of which, quantum Monte Carlo schemes assist in the evaluation of the uncertainties of future price distributions, whereas quantum kernels assist in the improvement of time series feature representations used in forecasting (Emmanoulopoulos and Dimoska, 2022). The tools are especially applicable when there is a friction in the market or when the volatility is high and risk-modelling is highly essential. The quantum systems are able to optimise forecasting with the capability to calculate many possible market states simultaneously, providing an advantage in strategic planning and trading in high-frequency trading environments.

3.2 Enhanced Accuracy Using Quantum Methods

Another area that quantum computing adds a new layer of accuracy and preciseness is the predictive financial analytics since it minimizes the shortcomings of classical approximation methods. In contrast to the classical system, where either iterative simulations or heuristics can be applied to help in the complexity of computations, quantum models can take advantage of opportunities to model and compute the many opportunities simultaneously. Quantum algorithms: Amplitude Estimation algorithm and Variational Quantum Classifiers can also be applied to model probability distributions in a more detailed fashion, resulting in better asset prices, credit risks, or default probability (Gomez et al., 2022a). They are algorithms in which useful wisdom is inferred with noisy, sparse, or nonlinear data which will push standard machine learning models downwards. The second advantage is quantum feature space mapping; whereby the classical data is mapped onto a large dimensional quantum space and the patterns and anomalies can be sensitively examined. This would subsequently enhance classification efficacy on classification issues like fraud classification, sentiment analysis or event-driven trading. Moreover, quantum systems will be able to reduce the error in the Monte Carlo analysis of convergence rates and the staggering accuracy of the prediction result (Orús et al., 2019b). Not only will it result in faster predictions, but in risk-sensitive applications, there is a greater need to have more realistic and informative information. It is probable that such techniques will become the new benchmark of financial prognostication and real time decision making using more quantum hardware.

4. QUANTUM-POWERED TRADING SYSTEMS

A state of art in algorithmic and automated trading is quantum traded systems. The systems apply the power of quantum algorithms to identify inefficiencies in the market and create patterns and implement high-frequency trades more quickly and correctly. The classical trading systems are based on the sequential processing of data and cannot always scan vast data or adapt to the market dynamics in a short period. Quantum trading systems might be capable of examining a vast quantity of hypothetically conceivable market states simultaneously, but, with superposition and entanglement, and they would make decisions more profoundly and more swiftly. Grover Search can be used to identify arbitrage, which is an important application, as it allows the identification of mispriced financial assets or behavioural inefficiencies in a market in a short period of time as opposed to classical methods. The quantum reinforcement learning too is turning into an instrument of reckonable strength in the creation of dynamic approaches such that the trading agents now have the ability to correct themselves to the market changing behaviour by learning both historical and real-time information. Even more quantum improvements to their systems include cleaner portfolio rebalancing, order book optimization or risk-aware execution, which uses quantum-enhanced prediction with optimization to generate smarter trading decisions.

Along with the capability to access quantum computing via cloud infrastructures, financial institutions are already putting quantum algorithm implementations into operational or hybrid trading pipelines, setting the stage of a new-gen of highly intelligent, flexible, and profitable trading environments. The table 4 describes a summary of quantum-inspired functions in trading showing how quantum-specific methods increase the formulation strategy, execution, and profitability of the trade. Figure 4, which depicts quantum-enhanced modules of a trading system like signal detection, reinforcement learning and execution strategies in contact with classical market feeds and order engines. The Figure 5 presents comparative perspective of performance gain scores between classical and quantum methods in major financial areas. Quantum computing benefits in portfolio optimization, arbitrage detection, and trade execution are significant, and the future applications of quantum computing in forecasting, risk modelling, and fraud detection are projected.

Table 4. Applications of Quantum Computing in Trading Systems

Use Case	Quantum Technique	Benefits
Pattern Recognition	Quantum classifiers, kernel methods	Detects hidden signals, improves market timing
Arbitrage Detection	Grover's Search Algorithm	Faster identification of price discrepancies
Trade Execution Optimization	Quantum routing, QRL	Real-time decision-making, reduced slippage
Strategy Adaptation	Quantum Reinforcement Learning	Self-optimizing strategies in volatile conditions
Portfolio Rebalancing	QAOA	Fast recalculation of optimal weights amid shifting prices
High-Frequency Trading	Quantum-enhanced forecasting	Microsecond-level trade predictions with faster signal analysis

Figure 4. System Architecture for Quantum-Assisted Autonomous Trading

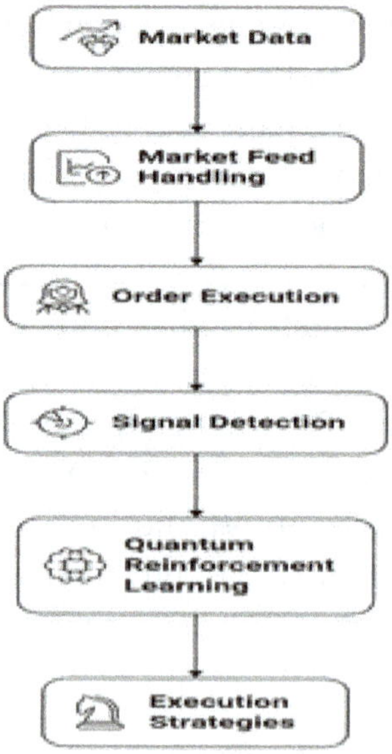

Figure 5. Quantum Advantage Across Financial Use Cases

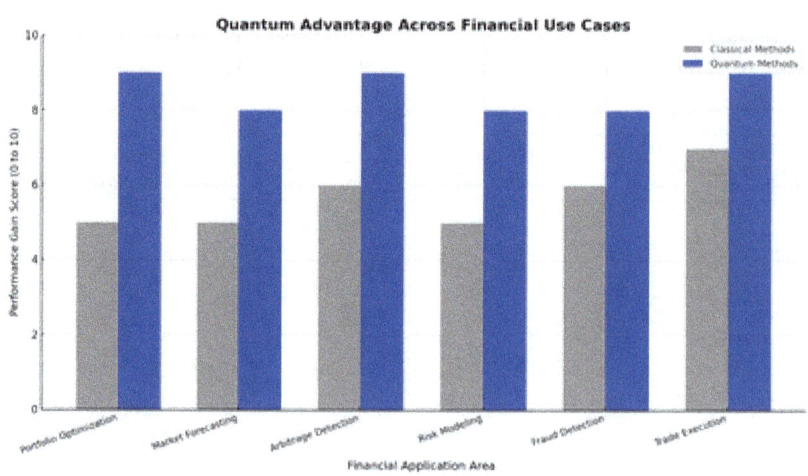

4.1 Pattern Recognition, Arbitrage, And Trade Execution

Pattern recognition, arbitrage detection and trade execution are all instrumental as far as deriving the highest profitability and minimal risk in the fast-financial trading environment. Classical systems are based on rule-based or machine learning classifier recognition of patterns within the market, and are susceptible to variety and magnitudes of modern, multi-asset market (Albareti et al., 2022)s. The new technology in quantum computing is accompanied by significant possibilities to evaluate all the possibilities simultaneously and show the obscured patterns and abnormalities in more details and less time. Quantum-enhanced algorithms - e.g. quantum classifiers or quantum kernel methods can find finer correlations and non-linear dependencies that classical methods will be quick to miss. Such insights can come into play to ensure that traders are more confident about where the prices may go in terms of direction or market trend or behavior. Search Algorithm as created by Grover can be applied in the case of arbitrage where one seeks to take advantage of the price differences between the assets or markets. It enables quantum systems to sample the astronomical trade combinations in a quadratic time discovering profitable combinations significantly faster than the legacy techniques do. Furthermore, quantum-aided execution policies can prioritize and route trading distributions dynamically and in time even in a volatile market scenario (Bergholm et al., 2018). Queen pattern detecting and real time optimization, when brought together, can make trade execution a smarter, faster and more profitable experience not only to financial institutions, but also hedge funds.

4.2 Quantum Reinforcement Learning For Dynamic Strategies

A newer area is Quantum Reinforcement Learning (QRL), which applies the adaptive training advantage of classical reinforcement learning to the processing power of quantum computers. QRL appears especially promising in financial trading where traders are interested in creating dynamic, self-correcting trade strategies that can adapt to the fast-changing nature of the market and the changing patterns of behavior among investors. In QRL, an agent exists within a trading environment that is simulated or real, and is learning to maximize relevant policies by exploring, i.e. by following different actions (e.g., buy, sell, hold), and being rewarded or penalized (Guo et al., 2024). Quantum agents in contrast to classical agents have the advantage of exploiting superposition and entanglement to iterate through many policy paths simultaneously, which is vastly faster than with classical agents. This allows finding excellent strategies in non-stationary and complex conditions.

Application of QRL in the forceful trading systems including high frequency trading, trading on derivatives and market making is heavily reliant on the speed and acting capabilities. It can also make the opponents of the competitive markets to act like it and trade-offs between the exploration (use of new strategies), and the exploitation (use of known strategies). Already in early stages of development, QRL projects such as PennyLane-Qisket integration, and quantum simulators are making QRL research more accessible. With more advanced quantum computer hardware, QRL will become a core sub-component of autonomous financial agents capable of performing better than traditional trading bots in both the de-encrypted intelligence and the resultant speed of action.

5. APPLICATIONS IN PORTFOLIO & RISK MANAGEMENT

The risk analysis and portfolio management are traditional subjects in the field of finance that have two important tasks to reconcile returns and risk and satisfy various constraints. In normal circumstances, classical methods, e.g. the mean-variance optimization or Value-at-Risk (VaR) computations, are computationally infeasible when the number of risk factors, or the number of assets, is too large. The quantum computing can pose groundbreaking benefits to such complexity because it can consider many different portfolio structures and subdivisions at a time (Hegade et al., 2021). Portfolio optimization is one of these uses, with quantum algorithms such as the Quantum Approximate Optimization Algorithm (QAOA) potentially being applied to sample exponentially large portfolios of assets in an optimal way to determine the most efficient trade-offs between risk and returns.

This is helpful in the constrained optimization with transaction costs, with liquidity constraints and sector diversification constraints. To accelerate information on stress testing and scenario analysis and improve the accuracy, quantum improvement of Monte Carlo simulations can be performed to perform risk management. These simulations are able to test tail-risks events, and they can be far more easily used to compute the effect of a systemic contagion than classical tools (Irfan, Kadry, Sharif, & Khan, 2023). Moreover, the quantum approaches could be satisfactorily adjusted to detect fraud and credit risk modelling in large data due to their abilities to detect intricate nonlinear trends. Increasingly quantum technologies advance, so that eventually their adoption into hybrid classical-quantum financial systems can support better-informed, resilient, and real-time decision-making in both portfolio strategy and enterprise risk control by the institutions. The table 5 Summarizes key financial tasks in risk and portfolio management where quantum computing offers improvements in efficiency, precision, and scalability. The figure 6 showing how classical systems handle data ingestion and reporting, while quantum modules are used for optimization, simulation, and risk scenario generation within the same pipeline.

Table 5. Quantum Use Cases in Risk and Portfolio Management

Task	Quantum Method	Advantage Over Classical Approach
Portfolio Optimization	QAOA	Solves NP-hard problems with multiple constraints faster
Credit Risk Scoring	QSVM, quantum classifiers	Higher accuracy with imbalanced or nonlinear data
Stress Testing	Quantum Monte Carlo	Better tail-risk modelling, faster convergence
Value-at-Risk Estimation	Amplitude Estimation	Reduces sample requirement while maintaining accuracy
Fraud Detection	Quantum pattern recognition	Identifies subtle irregularities in transaction behavior
Multi-asset Correlation Analysis	Quantum PCA	Deeper analysis of interdependencies among assets

Figure 6. Integrated Hybrid Risk Assessment Framework

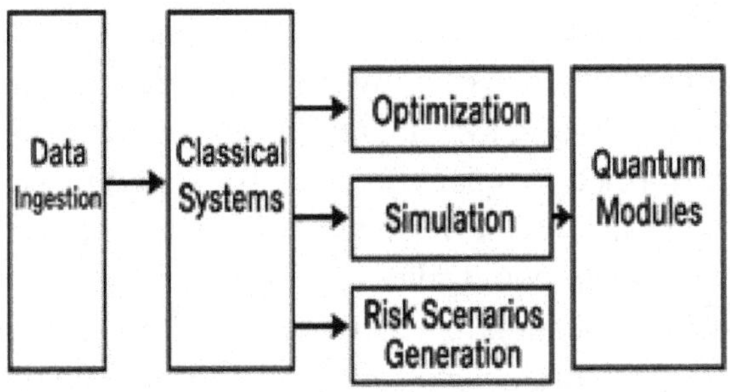

5.1 Optimization, Stress Testing, And Fraud Detection

Optimization, stress testing, and detection of frauds are important operations in financial services that require the use of enormous computational accuracy and dynamism. The classical models tend to break down in relation to any complex constraint, huge amount of data or an unpredictable market behavior. Quantum computing offers a distinct benefit of dealing with large numbers of combinations and assessing multidimensional probabilities at the same time. When applied to optimization of portfolios, quantum algorithms such as QAOA can locate optimal asset allocations more resource-efficiently than classical solve algorithms, including when the problem has many nonlinear constraints. These involve constraints on budgets, sector constraints as well as personal taste-based risk preferences, which can be coded into quantum circuits (Lim & Rebentrost, 2024). Quantum Monte Carlo simulations greatly improve stress testing, i.e., estimating the responsiveness of portfolios to extreme market situations. They provide speedier convergence and better tail-risk estimation, which is necessary in case of economic crisis or occurrence of a black swan. Quantum classifiers and algorithms of pattern recognition applied in the field of detecting fraud will study mass data of transactional traffic and identify anomalies that could pass unnoticed on classical systems. Their abilities to recognize minute connections and changes in behavior better the time and accuracy of detection. These quantum techniques are complementary and advantageous in leading decision-making in high-stakes financial settings since they allow proactive, data-informed insights in the face of uncertainty and danger.

5.2 Hybrid Quantum-Classical Financial Tools

Although quantum computing is highly promising, hardware limitations, including qubit noise, qubit decoherence, and scalability currently limit quantum computing to large-scale applications. Hybrid quantum-classical financial instruments have come about as a reasonable resurgence of arrays that are able to leverage the advantages of both regimes. In such hybrid system, the complex tasks of optimization, probabilistic tasks are performed by quantum processors, preprocessing, interpretation of results, and orchestration are performed by classical systems. As one example, a classical portfolio optimizer could filter assets in terms of risk metrics and stream down the downsized information to a quantum circuit to complete fine-tuned allocation with QAOA. Quantum clouds such as the Qiskit Runtime offered by IBM and the PennyLane offering of Xanadu provide simulation environments and APIs to embed quantum subroutines into classical financial pipelines. The tools allow quantum acceleration of tasks such as scenario simulation, derivative pricing or credit scoring, without requiring complete quantum infrastructure (Phillipson & Bhatia, 2020). Furthermore, it is possible to have real-time interaction of quantum algorithms with financial data feeds in the cases of hybrid models that allow adapting strategies to changes in the market. Due to improvement in hardware, these hybrid systems will be in a position to transform into smart co-processors that will enhance financial analysis, lower latencies, and tap the ultimate performance that trading and risk management had not attained before.

6. CHALLENGES AND LIMITATIONS

Theoretically, quantum computing will become a game changer in finance analytics, but there are structural, technical, and adoption-related constraints that make it appear that the adoption of quantum computing in finance has not yet been feasible. Such problems are the most urgent, the first one is the hardware limitation. Quantum computers are currently in the Noisy Intermediate-Scale Quantum (NISQ) era with the current systems having smaller numbers of qubits, and highly susceptible to errors caused by decoherence and gate infidelity. These are discouraging to the creation of large and reliable quantum circuits required to calculate complex financial models. Second, the number of qualified people who might be knowledgeable in quantum computing and finance is also limited (Rebentrost et al., 2018), Irfan et al. (2024). Quantum algorithms are also difficult to implement and require expertise in quantum mechanics, computer science, and institutional financial expertise, making quantum algorithms inaccessible to most institutions. At the integration level, quantum becomes a problem to integrate with the current financial systems: on the one hand, the classical systems are stable and well-developed; on the other hand, quantum tools are still in their early childhood and necessitate complicated hybrid processes, which in their turn can be rather difficult to support. Due to the regulatory uncertainty, there will be the absence of defined decision-making systems on the quantum side, which will bring up the issue of transparency, auditability, and compliance. Although these obstacles are, by no means, less relevant, additional and continued developments in the sphere of quantum hardware, error correction, education, and software platforms can only continue to bring application closer to reality. The table 6 lists significant technical, organizational and regulatory issues with the implementation of quantum computing in finance, and existing industry and academic responses.

Table 6. Current Challenges and Industry Responses to Quantum Adoption

Challenge	Description	Industry/Academic Response
Hardware Constraints	Noisy qubits, low gate fidelity, limited scalability	Research into error correction, NISQ hardware improvements
Algorithmic Complexity	Difficult formulation and tuning of quantum algorithms	Open-source libraries (e.g., Qiskit, PennyLane) and simulators
Talent Gap	Shortage of quantum-literate financial professionals	Upskilling programs, quantum finance MOOCs
Integration with Classical Systems	Difficulty embedding quantum components into legacy systems	Hybrid cloud platforms and APIs for seamless orchestration

continued on following page

Table 6. Continued

Challenge	Description	Industry/Academic Response
Lack of Regulation and Standards	No established compliance framework for quantum finance	Collaboration with regulators, emerging policy research
Ethical Concerns	Algorithmic transparency, market fairness risks	Ethical boards, explainability research, open benchmarking

6.1 Hardware Constraints And Algorithm Complexity

The hardware of quantum computing is still in its infancy stages, and there are high obstacles to the implementation of full-fledged financial applications. The majority of the current-day quantum processors are of the Noisy Intermediate-Scale Quantum (NISQ) type, with fewer qubits and susceptible to noise. The problems of qubit decoherence, gate infidelity and cross-talk reduce the reliability and scalability of or minimize the execution of quantum computations which are currently being implemented. This is because the limitations of such hardware render encoding and running deep quantum circuits extremely challenging, which are then needed to model or simulate a high-dimensional financial system or real-time trading environment. Simultaneously to this, quantum algorithms are very complex both in design and implementation. Portfolio optimization or option pricing problems are problems in the field of quantum mechanics and linear algebra that require sophisticated knowledge to be mapped onto quantum Hamiltonians or quantum gates. Most of the algorithms additionally need hybrid quantum-classical workflows, which enhance the complexity of the system and computational cost (Shan and Shang, 2023). Moreover, the development of algorithms in quantum computing remains largely experimental and there are only a handful of algorithms that have been benchmarked on real-world financial data sets. A combination of these hardware and algorithmic constraints makes it difficult to transfer quantum finance algorithms between theory and practice. However, today, researchers are accompanied by the presence of quantum error correction, architecture development, and simulators that are available on the cloud and are used to develop and advance algorithms during the maturation of technologies.

6.2 Talent Gap And Infrastructure Issues

The other highly prevalent obstacle enabling entry to the scrawny-mass placements of quantum computing in the world of finance is the lack of talented manpower. Quantum computing entails a very uncommon convergence of quantum physics, computer science, and financial theory. Few practitioners possess a deep understanding of all three domains and thus, it is challenging to devise and to execute quantum answers internally within financial companies. There is the talent crisis as well in the organizational preparedness. Few financial institutions have set up teams, educational courses or road maps to quantum integration. (Woerner & Egger, 2019). Even if large firms actively invest in quantum research, they often have to compensate for their lack of expertise by collaborating with universities or startups because of how steep the learning curve is. In addition, the technical infrastructure to support quantum computing, including custom simulators, hybrid cloud environments, secure data pipelines, etc., remains over the horizon in most financial setups. Building or accessing any quantum-enabled platform would cost a good price in terms of resources and time, especially for mid-sized firms. It is also not being adopted because of the lack of universal development tools, quantum programming languages and a lack of cross platform compatibilities at the moment. Although frameworks such Qiskit and PennyLane are helping to close it, most of the existing implementations need to be highly customised (Atadoga et al., 2024). The talent and infrastructure gap can only be curbed through massive investment in education, collaboration as well as streamlining of tools so that institutions can be ready to embrace the full potential of quantum computing as the ecosystem evolves.

7. ETHICAL AND REGULATORY CONCERNS

Ethics and regulatory issues associated with quantum computing will require their own rules and governance as quantum computing carries over to the financial sector. Compared to traditional models, the quantum ones are often less interpretable than traditional ones due to the nature of abstract mathematical foundations and hybrid character of quantum algorithms. This raises the question of transparency, that is, when quantum systems are applied to high stakes decision making like credit scoring, trading or rebalancing portfolios. The reason is that these financial institutions must be able to ensure that quantum enabled decisions are explainable and auditable even though they might have the most complex underlying models. The other data problem is privacy (Bouland et al., 2020). The quantum system (and cloud platform-operated ones in particular) can have a lot of sensitive financial and personal information. Data transfer and storage security as well as compliance with these laws as GDPR and the data localization provisions will prevent any leakage or abuse. On the regulatory side, quantum computing quantum are at the transition phase where some frameworks are being developed. Regulators may not be able to determine the risks or enforce it, unless they have the technical knowledge on quantum technologies. This causes delay following innovation and control. Ethically, the disparity of quantum resources could increase the divide between the big organizations and smaller companies. In this way, the creation of universal-relational policies, ethical AI-quantum integration norms, cross-sectoral standards will be essential to include responsible adoption.

7.1 Transparency, Accountability, And Compliance

With the advent of quantum computing, transparency, accountability, and compliance are of particular concern because financial decisions in many areas will be driven by quantum computing. Many quantum algorithms and those ones that deal with variational quantum circuits or hybrid models largely act on high dimensional quantum spaces that are hard to understand (Bunescu & Vârtei, 2024b). This will make it difficult to trace the process of making a decision like a trade trigger, risk assessment or any portfolio alteration. Financial services are very strict in regards to regulation, which requires financial institutions to be in a position to justify every decision in front of auditors, clients, and regulatory authority. The operation of traditional finance is regulated by severe compliance regimes (e.g. Basel III, MiFID II, and SOX), where disclosure of models and provenance of data manipulation is compulsory, with demonstrations that good customs have been followed.

The active role of quantum models in such landscape requires the implementation of the audit-compatible frameworks that will favour explainability without the loss of performance. Moreover, the issue of accountability becomes even more complicated in the case of quantum elements in the algorithm-driven systems. Who is supposed to bear the blame in case a QA trading system misfires, the developer, the data provider or the institution? There are no explicit regulations on this and quantum-informed financial compliance standards are significant to regulators. The institutions have the duty of building trust through focusing on the explainable quantum algorithms, investing in model governance, engaging directly with regulators through joint frameworks of quantum finance responsibility.

7.2 Security And Ethical Implications Of Quantum Use

As quantum computing is rising, a new dimension of understanding of security risks and ethical issues is evident in the financial sector. Other more contentious issues also include quantum cryptanalysis, which could potentially pose a threat to the current encryption protocols due to the potential of massive quantum algorithms (such as Shor Algorithm) breaking the existing encryption protocols (Egger et al., 2020). This generates a sense of urgency of quantum resistance cryptography particularly in securing of client information, transactions and submissions to the regulator. The computing capabilities of quantum are virtually limitless, and can be applied in an unsound way to control markets or achieve an unreasonable competitive edge. It is able to create new opportunities, such as increasing the disjuncture between institutions inundated with technology and small institutions, which can add to the algorithmic bias that negatively changes market fairness and accessibility. Otherwise, it can contribute to the growth of financial inequality and financial systems ignorance. Furthermore, quantum systems are generally explained as black boxes and, by extension, it is challenging to learn how malicious bias or unintentional influence would operate in computer-aided decision-making. It is especially unsafe when it comes to such spheres as credit scoring, fraud detection, and investment advising, in which the bias of algorithms can further advance a systemic discrimination. To make sure that these problems are kept at bay some ethical provisions should be associated with quantum innovation. This involves safe implementation, designing equitable systems of access and the presence of ethical review boards to evaluate the effects of quantum technologies on the society before its misuse in the economic sphere.

8. FUTURE OUTLOOK

The financial sector quantum computing is a bright future, and it is rapidly evolving. The migration out of experimental prototypes and into financial applications will be faster when quantum hardware is more stable with longer-lived qubit and lower error rates and more scalable. The examples of such investments are already noticed as institutions enter research partnerships and operate pilot programs using cloud service providers, such as IBM Quantum and Amazon Braket, or PennyLane offered by Xanadu (Gómez et al., 2022). In the foreseeable future, hybrid quantum-classical models will become dominant where firms will be able to delegate complex optimization, risk modelling, and simulation problems to quantum systems and continue operationally stable due to the solid backbone in the form of classical infrastructure (Pistoia et al., 2021). The integration will allow quicker, cleverer, and flexible decision-making business progress in asset management, trading, compliance and fraud detection. In addition to technical competency, successful inter-sector partnership among university, industry and regulators will be essential. Common standards of standardization, security, and ethically-sound technologies AI-quantum integration will reduce the risks and will work as a condition of the responsible use. The talent pipeline will also mature and toolsets will become more accessible and as a result, quantum computing will explode out of research labs and into the core of the financial services. Finally, quantum technologies will transform the boundaries of industry computation to a more intelligent, transparent, and resilient financial ecosystem that withstands the test of time. The Figure 7 illustrates the timeline or maturity curve showing phases of adoption starting with awareness and experimentation, moving through hybrid deployment, and leading to full quantum integration with key industry milestones and collaboration points.

Figure 7. Phased Roadmap for Quantum Adoption in Financial Services

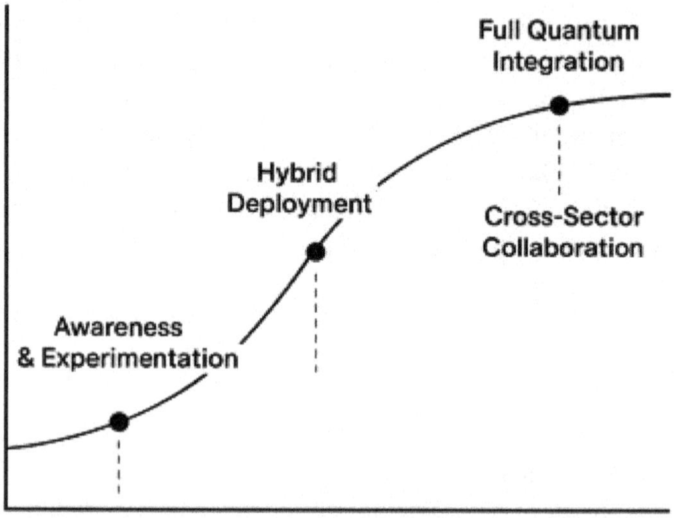

8.1 Cloud Quantum Platforms (QISKIT, PENNYLANE)

Quantum computing hardware is getting mature, and the cloud-based quantum computing platform such as IBM Qiskit and Xanadu PennyLane are making quantum resources more democratized, allowing financial institutions to access the power of quantum technologies (Herman et al., 2022b). These systems enable a user to grow, test, and execute quantum algorithms without having to develop physical infrastructures of a quantum computer and it is the possibility that encourages the researchers and experts in the financial sector to carry out practical operations on low-cost, scalable platforms. Qiskit IBM-developed open-source is a quantum SDK (Software Development Kit) with tools to construct quantum circuits, simulate them, and execute them on real quantum processors accessible in the IBM Quantum Experience cloud platform. It implements optimization, machine learning and quantum finance algorithms and is thus appropriate to use in portfolio optimization, option pricing and arbitrage detection.

The Aer simulator and Aqua module of the Qiskit framework (which have been incorporated into Qiskit Terra and Machine Learning) can be particularly useful in prototyping of financial algorithms. Xanadu created the PennyLane framework that operates in the hybrid quantum-classical environment and can be easily connected to machine learning libraries such as TensorFlow and PyTorch. It is therefore suitable in developing quantum-assisted prediction algorithms, reinforcement learning agents and anomaly finders in the finance sector. PennyLane can be applied to both simulators and real devices (e.g. via the IBM Q, Amazon Braket or Borealis photonic quantum computer at Xanadu) The combination of these platforms is transforming quantum finance by increasing innovation and experimentation, keeping professional's quantum-ready.

8.2 Industry Adoption And Cross-Sector Collaboration

The latest buzz in the financial industry is quantum computing, and it has been capable of generating an interest due to its capabilities of revolutionizing the diverse applications in its financial industries trading, portfolio optimization, risk management and fraud detection. Quantum hardware vendors and research laboratories have already partnered with large organizations, like JPMorgan Chase, Goldman Sachs, HSBC and the BBVA, to test the potential application and develop quantum strategies. These firms are also not only investing in technology, sharing resources to put together quantum research teams, in addition to forming consortia, including the IBM Quantum Network and the Quantum Economic Development Consortium (QED-C).

Academia, startups, government and cloud providers are also busy with growing industry adoption by cross-sector collaboration. On the one hand, academic centers conduct base research and development of talents and the startups have innovative quantum software that enables tools and structure-sensitive algorithms, adapted to the financial problem (Kaneko et al., 2020). In the meantime, the governments are investing in national quantum plans and are beginning to draw up policy frameworks to support a secure and responsible quantum implementation. Such cooperation with such a multi-player partner is needed to offset such factors as the scarcity of talents, standardization, and regulatory ambiguity. It also supports the open-source development and sharing of knowledge and by so doing institutions of all kinds benefit on earlier experimentation (Li et al., 2023). Through collaboration, these sectors are creating a healthy and strong ecosystem that will have quantum technologies buying in a responsible, efficient, and long-term beneficial manner to the general economic system globally.

9. CONCLUSION

Quantum computing represents an innovation in the way the financial industry can compute information, uncertainty and decision making. The restrictions of classical computing are becoming especially prominent in the predictive analytics, optimizations and high-frequency trading, due to the increasing complexities, volatility and dependence on data modeled in financial systems. The research paper has described how quantum computing presents a new paradigm to address these issues based on the principles of quantum mechanics used such as superposition, entanglement and quantum parallelism. The work has covered the most important technology that covered quantum computers such as the meaning of qubits, quantum gate and quantum circuit. We have discussed the practical significance of the most popular quantum algorithms: QAOA, Grover Search and Quantum Monte Carlo simulations and how the algorithms can be used in the financial industries including portfolio optimization and arbitrary search, volatility modelling and probabilistic forecasting.

Algorithms are not simply momentary formulas but are tried in simulated conditions and even on small scale prototypes and may give faster, more efficient, more scalable results than their classical counterparts. The release of quantum powered trading systems is starting to revolutionize what can be accomplished in automated trading. It begins to develop quantum-enhanced pattern recognition and quantum reinforcement learning trading strategies that can now more adaptively adapt to the situation in the market and consider the thousands of possible actions simultaneously and properly purchase and sell goods. The result of this is the accelerated, brighter and stronger trading infrastructures. Equally, regarding portfolio and risk management, quantum computing presents the first chance of optimisation of asset allocations under constraints, extreme events stress testing, and real-time detection of fraud due to excellent pattern recognition. It will be viewed as fitting the same in terms of better financial resilience, better returns and adherence to risk management provisions. Nevertheless, the existing restrictions are also to be taken into account. The hardware of quantum computing is infantile and is limited by noise, low number of qubits and coherence time.

The other reason is the complexity of the algorithms that becomes a barrier to adoption, and lack of qualified quantum practitioners and quantum-classical integration problems. Additional concerns over probity, auditability and compliance to regulation are control issues ethically and legally, which should be eradicated, so that quantum systems can be fully relied upon in production financial situations. Luckily, the gap is being filled with the recent emergence of cloud-based systems, like the IBM Qiskit or Xanadu, built on Penny Lane, that fills the theory-practice gap. With such venues, the financial expert can access quantum tools, simulation, and testing on real devices hence, training the industry to practice in the future.

Scholarly sector, industry leaders, start-ups and regulators are forming cross sector partnerships that are leading to sharing of knowledge, standardisation and innovation. The short- run is in quantum revolution of financial sector. When quantum hardware becomes a viable industry and quantum computing software ecosystems are solidified, quantum computing will also be pushed past the experimental stage and into reality. The financial organizations, which will initiate to invest in quantum environments, its human capital and responsible usage, will have an enduring competitive advantage in the sense of complex-modeling, complex-uncertainties and large-scale intelligent action planning. To sum it up, quantum computing is not an addition, rather, a transformation to the financial system. The introduction of quantum intelligence in the financial sphere will put us on the road leading to a safer, more dynamic and analytically sophisticated financial sphere, capable of meeting the needs of an increasingly dynamic world economy.

REFERENCES

Albareti, F. D., Ankenbrand, T., Bieri, D., Hänggi, E., Lötscher, D., Stettler, S., & Schöngens, M. (2022). A structured survey of quantum computing for the financial industry. arXiv preprint arXiv:2204.10026.

Atadoga, A., Ike, C. U., Asuzu, O. F., Ayinla, B. S., Ndubuisi, N. L., & Adeleye, R. A. (2024). The intersection of Ai and Quantum Computing in financial markets: A critical review. Comput. Sci. IT Res. j., 5(2), 461–472.

Bouland, A., van Dam, W., Joorati, H., Kerenidis, I., & Prakash, A. (2020). Prospects and challenges of quantum finance.

Bunescu, L., & Vârtei, A. M. (2024a). Modern finance through quantum computing- A systematic literature review. *PLoS One*, *19*(7), e0304317. PMID: 39024227

Bunescu, L., & Vârtei, A. M. (2024b). Modern finance through quantum computing- A systematic literature review. *PLoS One*, *19*(7), e0304317. PMID: 39024227

Egger, D. J., Gambella, C., Marecek, J., McFaddin, S., Mevissen, M., Raymond, R., Simonetto, A., Woerner, S., & Yndurain, E. (2020). Quantum computing for finance: State-of-the-art and future prospects. *IEEE Transactions on Quantum Engineering*, *1*, 1–24.

Gómez, A., Leitao, Á., Manzano, A., Musso, D., Nogueiras, M. R., Ordóñez, G., & Vázquez, C. (2022). A survey on quantum computational finance for derivatives pricing and VaR. *Archives of Computational Methods in Engineering*, *29*(6), 4137–4163.

Guo, Z., Song, T., & Lin, G. (2024). Portfolio optimization based on quantum linear algorithm. *Physica Scripta*, *99*(8), 85107.

Hegade, N. N., Paul, K., Ding, Y., Sanz, M., Albarrán-Arriagada, F., Solano, E., & Chen, X. (2021). Shortcuts to adiabaticity in digitized adiabatic quantum computing. *Physical Review Applied*, *15*(2), 024038.

Herman, D., Googin, C., Liu, X., Galda, A., Safro, I., Sun, Y., Pistoia, M., & Alexeev, Y. (2022). A survey of quantum computing for finance.

Irfan, M., Dias, R., Rastogi, R., & Zebende, G. F. (2025). *Generative AI insights for financial decision making*. IGI Global.

Irfan, M., Elmogy, M., Gupta, S., Khalifa, F., & Dias, R. T. (2024). *AI-driven decentralized finance and the future of finance*. IGI Global USA.

Irfan, M., Hussainey, K., Bukhari, S. A. C., & Nam, Y. (2024). *Issues of sustainability in AI and new-age thematic investing*. IGI Global.

Irfan, M., Kadry, S., Sharif, M., & Khan, H. U. (2023). *Fintech applications in Islamic finance: AI, machine learning, and blockchain techniques*. IGI Global.

Irfan, M., Mohammed, M., Kassim, S., & Ofori, K. S. (2024). *The future of indigenous inclusivity: Unlocking finance for economic development*. IGI Global.

Kaneko, K., Miyamoto, K., Takeda, N., & Yoshino, K. (2020). Quantum pricing with a smile: Implementation of local volatility model on quantum computer.

Li, H., Xing, T., Wei, S., Liu, Z., Zhang, J., & Long, G.-L. (2023). BQ-Bank: A quantum software for finance and banking. *Quantum Engineering*, *2023*, 1–10.

Lim, D., & Rebentrost, P. (2024). A quantum online portfolio optimization algorithm. *Quantum Information Processing*, *23*(3).

Mugel, S., Lizaso, E., & Orus, R. (2020). Use Cases of Quantum Optimization for Finance.

Orús, R., Mugel, S., & Lizaso, E. (2019). Quantum computing for finance: Overview and prospects. *Rev. Phys.*, *4*(100028), 100028.

Phillipson, F., & Bhatia, H. S. (2020). Portfolio Optimisation using the D-Wave quantum annealer.

Pistoia, M., Ahmad, S. F., Ajagekar, A., Buts, A., Chakrabarti, S., Herman, D., ... & Yalovetzky, R. (2021, November). Quantum machine learning for finance ICCAD special session paper. In 2021 IEEE/ACM international conference on computer aided design (ICCAD) (pp. 1-9). IEEE.

Sakuma, T. (2025). Quantum differential machine learning. *Quantum Economics and Finance*, *2*(1), 3–12.

Shan, B., & Shang, Z. (2023). Quantum computing simulated annealing algorithm applying in portfolio optimization problem. Proceedings of the 2nd International Conference on Public, Digital Economy and Internet Technology, ICPDI 2023, September 1–3, 2023, Chongqing, China.

Woerner, S., & Egger, D. J. (2019). Quantum risk analysis. npj Quantum Information, 5(1), 15.

KEY TERMS AND DEFINITIONS

Quantum Computing: A new form of calculating that applies the laws of quantum mechanics (superposition, entanglement, interference), to complex financial problems, more consistently and with higher speed.

Superposition: A quantum principle according to which particles may exist in many states simultaneously and thus allows computers to examine a high number of possibilities at once.

Entanglement: It is a phenomenon of quantum whereby the particles are linked to one another enabling rapid and safe exchange of information among systems.

Quantum Interference: The fact that quantum states can enhance corrects and reduce errors to enhance prediction.

Predictive Analytics: With quantum systems predicting large variables and more dependable and quicker financial forecasts.

Algorithmic Trading: Computerized trading programs with quantum algorithms, which enhance the speed and efficiency of decision making.

Portfolio Management: Using quantum computing to learn how to trade-off risk-return to create better investment portfolios.

Risk Analysis: Relying on quantum models to evaluate uncertainties, market variations and probable losses with greater accuracy.

Fraud Detection: This approach will apply quantum-enabled analytics to find anomalies in transactions and enhance financial security.

Chapter 11

Quantum-Driven Finance Transforming Banking Through Next-Generation Technologies

Hannah Mary Joy
Christ University, India

Rajesh Kanna Rajendran
https://orcid.org/0000-0001-7228-5031
Christ University, India

Deepthi Das
Christ University, India

R. Sakkaravarthi
Vanier College, Canada

ABSTRACT

The swift progress of quantum computing is set to revolutionize the financial sector, especially in the fields of risk management and portfolio optimization. Existing financial models, though effective in some measure, are unable to handle the huge complexities of today's markets, where high-frequency trading, nonlinear interdependencies, and complex risk factors require advanced computational capabilities. Quantum finance, a new multidisciplinary research area, uses quantum computing concepts to improve financial decision-making, investment strategy optimization, and risk reduction more effectively than traditional techniques. This chapter discusses how quantum computing is revolutionizing risk management and portfolio

DOI: 10.4018/979-8-3373-2893-5.ch011

optimization using quantum mechanics-based algorithms like quantum annealing, quantum Monte Carlo simulations, and variational quantum eigensolvers (VQEs). These methods enable financial institutions to resolve high-dimensional optimization problems exponentially quicker, detect more optimal risk-adjusted portfolios, and build predictive models with higher accuracy.

INTRODUCTION

Quantum computing is changing the game in finance, which has always looked for better and more powerful ways to manage risk and improve portfolios. This technology will be able to go beyond the limits of classical computing when it comes to managing complicated financial schemes because of the principles of quantum mechanics. The standard financial models are more likely to get stuck on the huge amount of data and the complicated way that financial markets depend on each other. Quantum computing, which can calculate a lot of possibilities at once, could lead to better and more real-time risk analysis and more advanced ways to optimize portfolios. When financial models use algorithms that process information in order, they are limited by the power of the computers they run on when they have to deal with the high dimensionality of financial data. This limitation may result in erroneous risk assessment and inefficient portfolio allocations, especially during volatile market conditions.

The possible effects of quantum technologies are not just faster speeds. It also makes completely new ways of modeling possible, like quantum Monte Carlo simulations for more accurate option pricing and quantum machine learning for more accurate pattern recognition of market data. These could change how banks and other financial institutions manage risk and make investment decisions. Lastly, quantum computing in finance is an example of a change in the way things are done. It's not just about doing math faster; it's about being able to look at and think about financial systems in a whole new way. To get the most out of this ground-breaking technology, researchers, practitioners, and regulators will all have to work together to get over the obstacles.

RELATED WORK

The finance industry is always changing as it tries to find new ways to deal with risks and get the most out of portfolios. Quantum computing, founded on the principles of quantum mechanics, possesses the potential to revolutionize various domains through its unmatched computational power (Alonso-Conde & Rojo-Suárez, 2020).

This paper examines the potential applications of quantum computing in financial risk management and portfolio optimization, detailing significant algorithms, current challenges, and future trajectories. Bits are used to store data in classical computers. A bit can be either 0 or 1. On the other hand, quantum computers use qubits (Arner et al., 2020). The qubits could be in a state of superposition between 0 and 1 at the same time (Arner et al., 2020). Entanglement and other quantum effects make it possible for quantum computers to do some calculations much faster than classical computers (Arner et al., 2020).

Quantum annealing is a metaheuristic method of the global minimization of an objective function on a set of candidate solutions (candidate states) through a mechanism based on quantum fluctuations (Beck & Demirguc-Kunt, 2008). It has been applied widely to solve optimization problems such as portfolio optimization (Bhattacharyya & Nanda, 2022). Optimal portfolios under a variety of constraints can be solved using quantum annealers, including the ones created by D-Wave (Brest & Born, 2013). The Quantum Approximate Optimization Algorithm (QAOA) is a hybrid quantum-classical algorithm that can find approximate solutions to problems of combinatorial optimization (Buchak et al., 2018). It finds application especially in addressing Quadratic Unconstrained Binary Optimization (QUBO) problems that can be employed to model portfolio optimization problems (Buchak et al., 2018).

Another quantum-classical algorithm that is applied to the computation of the minimum eigenvalue (ground state) of a given problem (hamiltonian) is the Variational Quantum Eigensolver (VQE) (Chen et al., 2019). VQE in finance VQE may be used to optimize Portfolio optimization VQE can be used to solve a problem written as an Ising Hamiltonian, where the minimum eigenvalue of the resulting problem is the optimal portfolio (Chen et al., 2019). Amplitude estimation is a quantum algorithm that may estimate the amplitude of a quantum state (Cheng & Qu, 2020). When using this algorithm instead of classical Monte Carlo methods, some applications, like pricing derivatives and risk analysis, can run twice as fast (Cheng & Qu, 2020).

Value at Risk (VaR) is a statistical method for figuring out how much money you could lose on a portfolio or investment over a certain amount of time with a certain level of confidence. The work of quantum algorithms, especially amplitude estimation, can speed up the calculations of VaR and Conditional Value at Risk (CVaR), giving more accurate risk measurements (De Jong et al., 2022). Quantum machine learning applications can be utilized to enhance credit risk assessment by identifying patterns and facilitating more accurate default predictions, thereby increasing efficiency compared to traditional methods (Dorfleitner et al., 2017). Quantum processors can sample near-optimal portfolios at each trading step, enabling more precise risk quantification (Global Sustainable Investment Alliance, 2021).

Quantum computing is used to build the portfolios using Environmental, Social, and Governance (ESG) ratings. This lets investors see how their investments fit with their values (Gomber et al., 2018). Debbie Lim and Patrick Rebentrost proposed a quantum online portfolio optimization algorithm that exhibits a quadratic increase in time complexity compared to classical algorithms (Lim & Rebentrost, 2024). It is particularly pertinent in scenarios characterized by extensive asset portfolios.

Hodson et al. (2019) experimentally addressed a discrete portfolio optimization problem pertinent to the financial services sector, utilizing a quantum computer grounded in a gate model. They tested and used a rebalancing use case on a computer simulator, which is perfect. Li et al. (2023) introduced software, BQ-Bank, to a price of options, Value at Risk and portfolio optimization. BQ-Bank might run on real quantum computers, or it might run on regular computers and be a way for users to compare quantum and classical solutions. Orús et al. (2019) paper looks at how quantum optimization algorithms can be used on hard problems in finance and the economy, like predicting financial crashes and optimizing portfolios in real time.

HOW QUANTUM COMPUTING WORKS

Conventional computers work on a bit-based information processing basis on electrical voltages or impulses, binary 0 and 1 cases. The logic gates consist of transistors and the logic gates are arranged in networks, which are complicated, yet allow the computer to handle a variety of mathematical and logical tasks. On the contrary, quantum computers are based on the law of quantum mechanics, which governs the actions of particles (i.e. atoms and electrons). Such systems take advantage of quantum mechanical effects including superposition, interference and entanglement, which enable all new ways to compute.

The qubits can be in superpositions of both states as opposed to classical bits, which are in either state only (0 or 1). It implies that two qubits do not only have four definite states (00, 01, 10, 11), but a mix of all of them simultaneously. This special quality allows quantum computers to make parallel computations in many states in parallel that will give a huge amount of computational power. The processing power of a quantum computer scales exponentially with the number of qubits in it - e.g. a system with 51 qubits is theoretically twice as strong as a system with 50 qubits. That is how this exponential scalability has led to the increasing interest and investment by banks, technology companies, and research institutions in this novel technology that promises to transform problem solving in areas like cryptography, optimization and financial modeling.

QUANTUM COMPUTING APPLICATIONS IN THE FINANCIAL SYSTEM

The financial system is marked with the complicated procedures of analyzing, predicting, calculating and optimizing. Due to the multidimensional nature of such issues, the computational complexity of these problems is enormous and sometimes even high-performance computers cannot handle them. Quantum computing, with its huge processing capability and capacity to process large volumes of data at a time can be a solution (Hodson et al., 2019). Its ability to complete some of the most complex calculations in an efficient manner places it among the most transformative technologies in solving various financial problems in the marketplace such as risk assessment in financial markets, investment and portfolio management. It can enhance the aspects of investment strategy and asset pricing models through increased analysis and improved simulations. In combination with Artificial Intelligence (AI) and Machine Learning (ML), quantum computing can cause significant improvements in the efficiency of fraud detection, automated trading, settlement systems, and macroeconomic modeling. Such developments have the potential of transforming the way financial institutions evaluate and control risk. Quantum computing will help to calculate more precise estimates of the risk metrics like Value at Risk (VaR) that would be instrumental in providing capital requirements of financial institutions. Combining quantum algorithms with risk management systems will allow performing complex computations at an unprecedented rate. Financial risk models, such as Monte Carlo simulations, which are popular for evaluating financial risk and modeling randomness, can be optimized significantly using quantum computing to improve prediction quality and decision-making in financial activities. Quantum technologies could be of huge importance in finance, yet achieving this value will require time and foresight. To be ready and viable in the quantum era, financial institutions can undertake three preparatory steps:

Start now

An organization that is yet to develop quantum capabilities should now be the most appropriate time to do so. The needs of the relevant uses cases must also be determined by the decision-makers, this is done in conjunction with the senior executives, and there is also the need to have a sustained sponsorship and funding that is indicative of the long-term importance of quantum investments. Another important requirement is that institutes should be ready to address quantum threat to cybersecurity since in the future quantum computing may be able to penetrate the existing encryption techniques. Early action will put the organizations in a position to adapt at a very fast rate as the quantum developments assume a greater pace.

Begin capturing value

The first quantum use cases that financial institutions should begin testing are in derivative pricing, portfolio optimization or improving Monte Carlo simulations. Experimentation is not necessarily limited to getting physical access to quantum computers-the understanding of quantum studies can be used to optimize classical algorithms in the near future, which can have near-term economic consequences. The first-mover advantage is also a crucial point that should be taken into consideration by the decision-makers: organizations that start applying quantum-inspired techniques today will be better placed to dominate when large-scale quantum systems will be available (Orús et al., 2019).

Involve every business unit

Quantum technologies can generate value in several fields, and in most cases in unanticipated ways. Thus, all business units are to be involved into the discussion and planning on the possible quantum applications. Even though the major technological breakthroughs in quantum computing most likely will not happen before its widespread commercial application, every unit of a financial institution will eventually create a lot of value, potentially in the billions of dollars, when the technology reaches maturity. The point is that it is time to begin the creation of awareness, skills, and strategic capabilities. The first to prepare will also be well positioned to tap the potential of quantum computing to transform the world before their competitors do.

USES OF QUANTUM COMPUTING IN THE BANKING SECTOR

The specific uses of quantum computing in banking sector are slowly taking form but a wide scale use is likely to be seen between the late 2020s to the 2030s. Regardless of this ambiguity in technological progress, banks need to start getting ready with developing expertise and trying early use cases. This preparation ought to be aimed at matching particular quantum algorithms with pertinent financial issues. The literature suggests three broad categories of quantum algorithms, including chemical and physical simulation, machine learning and artificial intelligence (AI), and optimization. Although chemical simulation has only a minor applicability to the banking sector, AI and optimization have considerable potential. The usefulness of quantum algorithms in one application can significantly outweigh the usefulness in another since some are intended to make things faster, another to increase model accuracy, and another still to be energy efficient. Thus, quantum computing in the banking industry is dependent on the appropriate choice of quantum algorithm in every application.

AI has already changed the financial industry even before quantum computing, helping to provide better risk analysis, detect fraud, and statistical predictions. These

AI-powered models can be much more precise, efficient, and economical with quantum computing. There will also be a synergistic relationship as quantum computing will provide an improvement in the performance of AI models, and AI will assist in the design and optimization of more advanced quantum systems. Quantum computing can be applied in banking to transform the risk management, portfolio optimization, and derivative pricing, which require enormous amounts of computing power. With the further development and emergence of real-time trading and the complexity of the market, banks will increasingly depend on quantum-powered systems to manipulate large datasets, model market conditions, and make quick and high-resolution decisions on finances, which cannot be achieved by conventional computing capabilities.

The majority of AI procedures and techniques can be utilized in almost all spheres of the modern highly digitalized industrial environment. Those large language models (LLMs) which underlie the processes can be applied in several other industries. With the continuous development of quantum computers, AI is likely to become faster, more precise and more quality and less energy-consuming. Besides the overall application of AI, there are also specific AI applications created to solve the specific problems of the financial industry. The solutions concentrate on risk assessment, portfolio management and similar financial simulations and eliminate traditional assumptions and methods with more precise data-driven ones. The inclusion of other variables including financial derivatives and the increased adoption of distributed ledger technology (DLT) which is also referred to as blockchain has become more significant.

The most significant sphere of the quantum computing use is supposed to be the corporate banking, as its fiscal value and sophisticated applications, such as the trade finance, demand advanced methods of computation. The case in point would be that with regards to collateral optimization, which happens to be a case of a collaboration, e.g., in a securities lending case, the banks are forced to evaluate numerous variables and constraints simultaneously. These optimization problems keep growing geometrically along with the increase in equations. Part of the elements of these problems may be delegated to quantum computers, which can solve them with greater accuracy and deliver the result to the system of the overall computation. This can also be applied to the estimation of the chances of default before a loan is given out since such calculations involve several related optimization variables. With the application of quantum computing, financial corporations are able to make more conscious and robotized real-time decisions with the additional benefit of calculating a wider range of boundary conditions with better accuracy of the result. Besides, it can provide complete liquidity simulations, which can improve financial stability and prediction. Besides this, quantum computing and quantum networking offer new opportunities to work with different classes of assets and create transaction banking.

The future of digital finance can enhance the existing blockchain capabilities with fault-resilient smart contracts, management of intangible assets, and safe quantum communication, and transform the future.

QUANTUM COMPUTING IN RISK MANAGEMENT

The concept of quantum computing will transform the way risks are managed because they will be in a position to provide unprecedented computing power to deal with the inherent complexity of financial markets. The weaknesses of classical computing will probably impede the use of classical risk management methods, both in the context of high dimensionality data, and the more advanced probabilistic structure. Quantum algorithms that take advantage of the laws of superposition and entanglement have the potential to be still more superior and permit a greater number of specific and efficient risk measurements. The innovation would be essential in regards to the financial institutions that aim at covering the turbulent markets and reducing the potential loss.

One of the main points of implementation is the further development of Monte Carlo simulations, which is the main element of risk assessment. Quantum computing can do much to speed up such simulations and current risk parameter estimates such as Value-at-Risk (VaR) and Conditional Value-at-Risk (CVaR) are significantly better. In addition to that, a field-specific quantum-computational method of quantum annealing has got a potential in the tuning of complex risk predictive models. Quantum annealing is capable of determining the best parameter estimates and making the prediction more accurate especially where multiple interacting risk factors are involved, through effective search of large spaces of solutions. This ability to solve complex dependency is the most important in predicting market fluctuations and also reducing exposure to systemic risk.

Other than enhancing the currently existing methodologies, quantum computing can also offer new avenues to risk management. Market anomalies and correlations can also be identified that quantum computers would cover most of the time. Improved pattern identification will enable the financial institutions to anticipate the future risk and future market shock even before they become a significant problem. By doing this revelation in implicit connections of financial data, the quantum computing will enable risk managers to make better decisions and structure more resistant portfolios, which will ultimately lead to a more secure and resistant financial system (Li et al., 2023).

Quantum computing will even allow racing towards a solution. Currently, such a problem is mathematical puzzles that cannot be solved by any existing algorithm. The recent tendency in the research has been to transcend the realms of theory and consider establishing working models. The second step is then how to apply these models to the quantum systems. However, quantum computers are currently scarce and unstable, which is also a situation that starts to restrict its use when attempting to use it to simulate financial risk factors or model the probability distribution. Nonetheless, the precision of computations is compromised by the presence of the attendant noise in quantum circuits, which is a barrier to efficient quantum-based financial risk measurements. Consequently, regardless of their possible advantage in conventional business processes, until the technology has surmounted these obstacles, large scale use of quantum methods in risk management is not economical yet.

To date, quantum computing may transform radically, to the detriment of all, whose economic status is managed by classical hardware. It is developed with the prospect of increasing its speed exponentially in the future and the capacity to execute calculations many times faster than the traditional systems have ever dared to contemplate at the present time. The concern is whether soon new devices will be adopted well enough to be able to start fulfilling all that potential in the world market. In established fields like risk assessment and regulator licensing, where the market is so young to date, such early skepticism appears quite comprehensible as well. And activities such as measuring regulatory capital requirements using quantum computing would also require oversight and validation by regulatory organizations, making such tasks even more difficult. As a matter of fact however, as time has elapsed the banks were initially very gung-ho on the matter of quantum research, but they are becoming less and less gung-ho. This is simply an indication of how far there is to go before quantum computing will emerge as a viable and reliable instrument of financial risk management.

QUANTUM ALGORITHMS FOR PORTFOLIO OPTIMIZATION

One of the main fields of finance management involves the optimization of the portfolio which involves the selection of assets that yield the best returns and those that have minimal risks. With the increasing complexities in financial markets, handling of large amounts of data with complicated dependencies is a significant computational problem. Quantum computing has strong algorithms that can address such optimization issues compared to old systems. The Quantum Approximate Optimization Algorithm (QAOA) and the Variational Quantum Eigensolver (VQE) are some of the most exciting quantum algorithms which can be used to optimize a portfolio and offer alternative methods to enhance asset allocation strategies.

DIFFICULTIES OF THE TRADITIONAL PORTFOLIO OPTIMIZATION

Traditional methods of portfolio optimization like the Modern Portfolio Theory (MPT) formulated by Markowitz are based on quadratic programming to address the problem of risk and reward. The defects that the models exhibit are however not effective when applied to large financial markets because they contain the following defects:

Computational Complexity: The larger the size of the assets the more complex and huge the optimization problem is and the large computational capacity is required to analyze the correlations and past data.

Market Volatility and Uncertainty: according to the classical models the returns in the financial market are normally distributed, but this is not always true in the real life financial markets that undergo sudden changes and crisis.

Inefficiency in Constraint Management: It is plausible that the portfolio managers will manage to censure capital allocation, risk exposure and sector diversification. Classical algorithms can be problematic in that they are able to model a number of constraints effectively in an optimization model (Irfan et al., 2024).

Computationally Intensive Simulations: Monte Carlo simulations involved in the calculation of the portfolio risk and portfolio returns are a computationally intensive form of simulation and it is hard to make real time decisions in a fast paced market.

With the assistance of quantum computing, which involves the application of quantum mechanics in computing multiple investment scenarios at the same time, it becomes achievable and the portfolio optimization process becomes considerably more efficient and more accurate.

SECURE TRANSACTIONS AND QUANTUM CRYPTOGRAPHY

One of the most significant aspects of economic stability within the international environment has become cybersecurity due to the emergence of the digital financial system. The cyber attacks are emerging as sophisticated as the traditional encryption means are trailing the fast changing attack strategies. Quantum cryptography refers to a paradigm shift strategy of ensuring the security of the finance transaction in quantum mechanical principles. Quantum cryptography is guaranteed by the laws of physics in contrast to the classical encryption that is grounded on the mathematical complexity. Quantum Key Distribution (QKD) that facilitates intractable communication channels is likely the most important financial use of quantum cryptography. Financial institutions are also investing in quantum resistant cybersecurity tools so that future cyber attacks by quantum computers can be reduced.

QUANTUM COMPUTING TO FORECAST FINANCIAL CRISES

Recent studies reveal the ability to use quantum computing to forecast financial crises through the use of high-level network modeling and optimization approaches. The global financial ecosystem, which is made up of banks, corporations and individual investors institutions, has different portfolios of assets. One of the main problems is the recognition of fluctuations in the value of assets that may cause a significant decrease in the global market, which may result in a financial crash. It is very complicated to solve such problems, and in most cases, classical computers are not able to compute them. Nonetheless, this is a critical matter to tackle when it comes to financial stability, regulatory control as well as macroeconomic planning.

. The method implies re-formulating the problem into a Quadratic Unconstrained Binary Optimization (QUBO) model, which is useful to reflect the complex interrelations and interdependences among financial institutions. The formulation can be solved using quantum annealing, which is an efficient method of solving problems that takes advantage of the special characteristics of quantum mechanics to find optimal solutions out of many possibilities. Pilot tests of this model on quantum annealers have shown that it can detect systemic risks more rapidly and effectively than other models. The problem of scalability is already constrained by current hardware, but in the near future with new possibilities of next-generation quantum processors and problem-specific quantum annealers, it is anticipated to become possible to analyze large financial networks, making it feasible to introduce new, more accurate, and proactive risk management in the global financial system (Irfan et al., 2023).

Significance of Financial Systems Cybersecurity.

The financial systems are dealing with trillions of dollars every day, and, as a result, these are the most attractive targets of cybercriminals. With the growing digitization of banking, stock markets, and payment systems, the rate of cyber threats has increased due to hacking, data breaches, and ransomware attacks. Cybersecurity in financial systems is significant because it is accompanied by the following factors:

Shielding against financial scam: Cyberspace attacks on banking and trading systems can result in the theft of personal information, illegal transfers of funds and massive fraud.

Regulatory Compliance: Governments and financial regulators have strict policies on cybersecurity in order to maintain the integrity of financial activities and data protection about consumers.

Strength to Counter attacks of the future: As hackers continue to devise new methods of attacking, financial institutions will need to implement proactive security to avoid breaches before they happen.

Protecting Digital Transactions: Due to the emergence of cashless transactions and decentralized finance (DeFi), the privacy and security of transactions are more important than ever.

Conventional encryption like RSA and AES has worked in ensuring the security of financial transactions. The advent of quantum computing however poses a threat to the existence of these encryption models and it is therefore necessary to switch to quantum cryptography to ensure greater security.

Difficulties and Implementation Barriers.

The economic aspect of quantum computing is never doubted but mass application is hindered by gigantic challenges and implementation issues. The quantum hardware is still young and is struggling with the number of qubits, coherence time and error correction. These hardware issues directly impact the scalability of quantum algorithms in that they render them incapable of working with the large volumes of data and computations that are necessary to apply quantum algorithms to real-world financial problems. The quantum-based risk management and portfolio optimization practice is rather a daunting task until the hardware limitation is conquered.

Factors of high cost to the hardware limitations include the high cost of building and operating quantum computing systems. The technology limitations do not limit to the hardware itself, i.e. the necessity to code certain software, algorithm design, the talent pool that has the knowledge to understand the complexity of quantum programming. These entry barriers and technical barriers are a strong barrier to entry especially to the smaller financial institutions. Moreover, the impact of quantum algorithms on specific financial issues will require a long perspective, massive research and experimentation to develop safe and reliable quantum algorithms.

The concept of quantum computing being introduced to the financial sector should be carried out with the highest concern of the regulatory and compliance issues. Explaining the new challenges that quantum technologies, especially data privacy, security, and explainability of the algorithms, can pose to the existing regulatory regimes may not be exhaustive. To be a responsible innovator and prevent possible threats, the fundamental principles are to set clear standards and regulations of quantum computing implementation to the financial industry. These regulatory requirements force the financial institutions to not only deal with these regulatory challenges, but also successfully work around the already existing regulations and this introduces an additional layer to the realization of quantum-based solutions. It will involve a cooperation between the regulators, the industry players and the researchers in creating an effective and flexible regulatory environment, which will assist in the innovation and at the same time keep the financial system stable.

Quantum use by Financial Services Today.

Portfolio Optimisation

Portfolio optimisation tools enable banks and other asset managers to trade off risk and return with thousands of assets. This process can be simplified to some aspects using quantum algorithms to give faster and more accurate results that will help companies respond to changes in the market when they occur. Quantum computing is enhancing such a technique as the Monte Carlo simulation - a technique that will be applied to model the probability of a large number of can occurrences, which is used in forecasting financial outcomes. This would enable a more informed risk assessment and investment decisions by performing a more precise analysis of situations using quantum computers by making them faster.

Risk Modelling and Credit Modelling.

Quantum computing will transform the entire risk management and credit modelling process by speeding up the complex computations by a large margin and enhancing the analysis ability. By taking Monte Carlo simulations being executed on such massive scales of quantum parallel, it would allow banks to determine risk measures like Value-at-Risk (VaR) and credit risk with accuracy and with near real time accuracy never witnessed before. This would translate to better predictions of market trends, risk estimation and management and ultimately, financial decision making would be enhanced.

Fraud Detection

The refined fraud detection is required because of the expansion of e-commerce transactions and cyber attack. Financial institutions are becoming enthusiastic about AI and machine learning to identify suspicious behaviour and sound an alarm about fraud. Quantum computing can be used to improve the models by making them faster in training complex machine learning models, searching large, diverse datasets in order to find latent patterns not identified by classical computers, and analyzing large datasets. This allows institutions to detect fraud at a shorter period and more accurately especially when minute or changing trends are at play and may not be detected by traditional systems.

Establishing a stronger Cybersecurity with Post-Quantum Cryptography.

One of the more urgent requirements in the finance industry is the determination to implement a future where the current encryption will not be as secure as it is today. Quantum computers have been estimated to break popular cryptographic systems, including the RSA. In their turn, to future-proof critical systems, institutions are beginning to implement post-quantum cryptography (encryption methods that are resistant to quantum attacks).

Obtaining Payment infrastructure.

Such technologies include Quantum Key Distribution (QKD) that guarantees sensitive communication security mathematically, which can lead to the provision of better cross-border settlements and smart contracts using blockchain. Financial institutions are looking into how these secure outlets can be incorporated in the new generation financial structure.

Quantum Banking

The level of speed is one of the greatest advantages that quantum banking can provide in the comparison with the rest of the methods of banking and money transfer. The powers of quantum computing are astonishing since it is 10 million times faster than the supercomputers in the processing of data.

The technical advantages that await under the hood as the authors of an IBM report on quantum banking opine are as follows: The solution space of a quantum computer is many times bigger than even very powerful conventional computers. The reason behind this is that a classical computer is only doubled by roughly doubling the number of transistors that are used to complete an issue. It may be approximately doubled that power of a quantum computer can be doubled each time it is merely extended with a qubit.

This kind of system in turn brings about strong advantages to the financial institutions and other stakeholders in the banking sector and the industry is not overlooking it. Recently, Tomenos published a survey of 300 employees in the world who work in retail, commercial and private banking. Among others, it found that 63% of the executives thought that the new technologies, including quantum computing, would have the most significant impact on the banks in the next five years, compared to only 34% of the trend that followed next most in popularity the shift of the customer behaviours (Economist Intelligence Unit, 2019).

This is delayed by two percentages points compared to two years ago that signifies that there are slight predictions of the virus-related effects on expectations, though with only 42 percent of the respondent executives in the survey in 2019 study by Temenos predicting in the 2019 research that such technologies would become the biggest source of change.

Jonathan Birdwell, Global Head of Policy and Insights of Economist Impact, the firm that conducted this survey on behalf of Temenos, told the interviewer at the time this study was published that the banks were aware of the pressure that such expectations put on them: New technology and customer demands are the two most important drivers of change and impact on banking in the next five years. To keep the close relationship with the consumer, banks are finding out that they should be real digital ecosystems (Economist Intelligence Unit, 2019).

Future Trend and Industry Implementation.

Quantum finance has the potential of transforming the finance industry because it will create computing capacity in the analysis of risks, running a portfolio, fraud detection, and secure transactions. With the current development of quantum computing, financial institutions are considering the prospects of its use to offer competitive edge in the data-driven decision and market predictive analytics. The technological revolution is right before the industry and the prototype of quantum finance technology can be the most efficient and safe in its work. The mass production will, nevertheless, be contingent upon the capacity of it to address the critical challenges to hardware scalability, algorithm optimization as well as regulation issues.

Potential applications in Investment and Banking Institutions.

The banks and other investment firms deal with vast amounts of data on transactions, customers trends and behavior in the market. The quantum computers provide the unheard of processing power to handle and process this information at an extremely higher rate as compared to the conventional computers. Quantum algorithms, such as QAOA and VQE, can greatly improve the solution of the complex mathematical models used during the practice of portfolio optimization and thus, provide more efficient asset allocation and risk management. On the same note, quantum computing has the potential to improve fraud detection and credit risk analysis due to its ability to detect anomalies in the transaction patterns in a short time. In addition, quantum-boosted machine learning algorithms, which are more effective in predicting the direction of the price, can be helpful to the high-frequency trading strategies to help investment firms to achieve an enormous profit in the financial markets.

Collaborations between quantum researches-technology Company and financial institutions.

The intricacy of quantum technologies requires good ties among the financial institutions, quantum research institutions and technology businesses. The leading banks and hedge funds have already started collaborating with quantum computing firms like IBM, Google, and D-Wave to explore the applications and experiment with quantum algorithm in practical financial situations. Universities and government facilities are also contributing largely to quantum finance development by engaging in research works with the concern of quantum-resistant cryptographic algorithms and offering regulatory frameworks in a bid to determine safe financial transactions. These collaborations are crucial towards closing the divide between novel concepts and practice to make sure that the finance sector can adopt the quantum technologies without any trouble and any sacrifice on the safety or functionality.

GUIDELINE ON THE PATH TO REALISING QUANTUM TECHNOLOGIES IN FINANCE

The introduction of the quantum technologies to the finance sphere will demand a successful implementation of a technological development and industry needs roadmap. The initial phase is the research and experimentation phase when banks make investments in pilot quantum computing programs and develop their own expertise. The second one is hybrid integration, which entails quantum algorithms that are applied to complement the current high-performance computing platforms to support the financial modeling and risk management. The development of hardware innovation into more scalable, more accessible forms and the integration of quantum-enabled systems into some of the most important bank processes, trading and cybersecurity will result in financial organizations moving to large-scale use of quantum computers. Managing and regulators would also be very critical in ensuring that quantum finance standards are established in place in order to use safely and ethically. The financial institutions that make investment to identify quantum talent and study of the same within a decade will be better placed to reap the benefits of quantum-powered financial innovation and be ahead of the game in a highly data-intensive economy.

THE FUTURE OF FINANCIAL SECURITY AND QUANTUM COMPUTING

The main breakthrough of quantum computing is that it can solve cryptographic codes developed in the classical computing, used to make secure electronic payments over decades. The quantum computers are able to crack information which is a big threat to the finance transactions and cybersecurity in general. With the advancement in technology, the businesses and banks have to reconsider and increase security to safeguard electronic payments systems. It has also been required to add the concept of post-quantum cryptography, which is resistant to quantum computers, to encryption. It will, however, require time, but the resources and the collaboration between businesses, governments and technology professionals to introduce such advanced means of encryption, are required, so that there will be nothing left to lose in terms of financial data, in the present and over the decades to come.

The algorithm by Shor, which was proposed in 1994, is one of the most significant results in that context. Many of the modern encryption systems rely on the ability to factorize large composite numbers and this quantum algorithm is efficient. Traditional computers literally require years to solve such equations, whereas quantum computers could do the same algorithms exponentially faster in Shor's algorithm, which demeans the security of current cryptographic algorithms. This aspect highlights why organizations should come out of encryption standards that are not resistant to quantum attacks before quantum systems in practice become common.

Besides encryption, quantum computing is also applicable in detecting fraud and also enhancing cybersecurity. The quantum systems can examine the transaction history, social media data and other possible sources of fraud by filtering through massive data sets and identifying patterns that cannot be identified by classical computers. The capability of analysing multifaceted correlations is an actual game-changer to the banks as far as predicting, detecting and thwarting fraudulent acts are concerned. Quantum computing can also be used to enhance cyber security since it also makes the process of encryption easier and it is also less likely that the data could be hacked or could be attacked causing financial losses. Even though quantum computing has just begun in fraud detection, further investigation is ongoing on developing the algorithms and infrastructure to apply quantum computing.

It is also possible to use quantum computing to revolutionise data-security and encryption, such as by implementing Quantum Key Distribution (QKD). QKD uses quantum mechanics to allow the development of secure communications channels and transmit cryptographic keys with the use of qubits. To hack this, the hacker must look at that (quantum) message in real time but in so doing being a passive observer of quantum information, every time one tries to measure it, they distort it, so that it is impossible to do this without presence being detected. Implementing QKD in financial services can significantly enhance the security of financial transactions thus ensuring that financial information is not compromised to cyber attacks. Quantum computing is on the verge of becoming a new foundation of ensuring future of financial confidence in cyber economy.

CONCLUSION

There is also an active transition of the financial sector to the implementation of the quantum technologies and the industry is typified by radical improvements and strategic alliances. Higher demand in the revolutionary area In 2025, there will be more than 5,000 quantum computing experts across financial institutions in the world, and it highlights the increment of demand in the field. The fact that the industry is ready to use quantum computing in solving complex problems such as risk assessment, portfolio optimization and fraud prevention is an indicator of the employment spurt.

Also increasingly common is the cooperation of banks with quantum research centers. The big banks and hedge funds are collaborating with quantum computers firms, including IBM, Google, and D-Wave in order to investigate the applications of quantum algorithms. These alliances are meant to mediate the gaps between theoretical innovation and real-life application to advance the innovation and the pace of quantum solution implementation in finance. Such partnerships play a critical role in the design of quantum resistant cryptography systems and the formulation of control systems to facilitate secure transactions in financial services.

The quantum technologies in finance roadmap is a strategy to be put to practice by financial companies in phases. First, they are investing in research and experimentation so as to build internal experience so as to determine the viability of quantum solutions. The second being hybrid integration that can be defined as the framework of quantum algorithms that are utilized to complement the already existing model of the high-performance computing so as to promote finance modeling and risk mitigation. This strategic plan is aligned in a way that it offers a smooth and secure integration of quantum technology in order to place financial institutions in a position to reap the huge potential in this technological revolution.

REFERENCES

Alonso-Conde, A. B., & Rojo-Suárez, J. (2020). On the effect of green bonds on the profitability and credit quality of project financing. *Sustainability, 12*(16), 6695.

Arner, D. W., Buckley, R. P., Zetzsche, D. A., & Veidt, R. (2020). Sustainability, FinTech and financial inclusion. *European Business Organization Law Review, 21*(1), 7–35.

Beck, T., & Demirguc-Kunt, A. (2008). Access to finance: An unfinished agenda. *The World Bank Economic Review*, *22*(3), 383–396.

Bhattacharyya, A., & Nanda, A. (2022). Green finance, fintech and environmental performance: Evidence from China. *Economic Modelling, 114*, 105925.

Brest, P., & Born, K. (2013). When can impact investing create real impact? *Stanford Social Innovation Review, 11*(4), 22–31.

Buchak, G., Matvos, G., Piskorski, T., & Seru, A. (2018). Fintech, regulatory arbitrage, and the rise of shadow banks. *Journal of Financial Economics, 130*(3), 453–473.

Chen, M. A., Wu, Q., & Yang, B. (2019). How valuable is fintech innovation? *Review of Financial Studies, 32*(5), 2062–2106.

Cheng, M., & Qu, Y. (2020). Does bank FinTech reduce credit risk? Evidence from China. *Pacific-Basin Finance Journal, 63*, 101398.

De Jong, A., Nguyen, T. T., Nguyen, T. V., & Sila, V. (2022). How does green finance impact green innovation? *Journal of Financial and Quantitative Analysis, 57*(3), 863–893.

Dorfleitner, G., Hornuf, L., Schmitt, M., & Weber, M. (2017). *FinTech in Germany*. Springer.

Economist Intelligence Unit. (2019). A whole new world: How technology is driving the evolution of intelligent banking. Temenos. https://impact.economist.com/perspectives/financial-services/whole-new-world-how-technology-driving-evolution-intelligent-banking

Global Sustainable Investment Alliance. (2021). *Global Sustainable Investment Review 2020*. Retrieved from http://www.gsi-alliance.org/wp-content/uploads/2021/08/GSIR-20201.pdf

Gomber, P., Kauffman, R. J., Parker, C., & Weber, B. W. (2018). On the fintech revolution: Interpreting the forces of innovation, disruption, and transformation in financial services. *Journal of Management Information Systems*, *35*(1), 220–265.

Hodson, M., Ruck, B., Ong, H., Garvin, D., & Dulman, S. (2019). Portfolio rebalancing experiments using the quantum alternating operator ansatz. *arXiv preprint arXiv:1911.05296*.

Irfan, M., Hussainey, K., Bukhari, S. A. C., & Nam, Y. (2024). *Issues of sustainability in AI and new-age thematic investing*. IGI Global.

Irfan, M., Kadry, S., Sharif, M., & Khan, H. U. (2023). *Fintech applications in Islamic finance: AI, machine learning, and blockchain techniques*. IGI Global.

Li, H., Xing, T., Wei, S., Liu, Z., Zhang, J., & Long, G. L. (2023). BQ-Bank: A Quantum Software for Finance and Banking. *Quantum Engineering*, *2023*(1), 7810974.

Lim, D., & Rebentrost, P. (2024). A quantum online portfolio optimization algorithm: D. Lim, P. Rebentrost. *Quantum Information Processing*, *23*(3), 63.

Orús, R., Mugel, S., & Lizaso, E. (2019). Quantum computing for finance: Overview and prospects. *Reviews in Physics*, *4*, 100028.

ADDITIONAL READING

Li, Y., & Spigt, R. (2017). The impact of crowdfunding on small firm financial reporting. *European Financial Management*, *23*(4), 736–764.

López-Cabarcos, M. Á., Pérez-Pico, A. M., Piñeiro-Chousa, J., & Šević, A. (2021). Bitcoin volatility, stock market and investor sentiment: Are they connected? *Finance Research Letters*, *38*, 101399.

Migliorelli, M. (2021). What do we mean by sustainable finance? Assessing existing frameworks and policy risks. *Sustainability*, *13*(2), 975.

Muganyi, T., Yan, L., & Sun, H. P. (2021). Green finance, fintech and environmental protection: Evidence from China. *Environmental Science and Ecotechnology*, *7*, 100107. PMID: 36160697

Navaretti, G. B., Calzolari, G., Mansilla-Fernandez, J. M., & Pozzolo, A. F. (2018). Fintech and banks: Friends or foes? *European Economy*, *2018*(3), 9–30.

Ozili, P. K. (2018). Impact of digital finance on financial inclusion and stability. *Borsa Istanbul Review*, *18*(4), 329–340.

Panos, G. A., & Wilson, J. O. (2020). Financial literacy and responsible finance in the FinTech era: Capabilities and challenges. *European Journal of Finance*, *26*(4–5), 297–301.

Philippon, T. (2016). The fintech opportunity. *National Bureau of Economic Research Working Paper* No. 22476.

Puschmann, T. (2017). Fintech. *Business & Information Systems Engineering*, *59*(1), 69–76.

Riedl, A., & Smeets, P. (2017). Why do investors hold socially responsible mutual funds? *The Journal of Finance*, *72*(6), 2505–2550.

Schwienbacher, A. (2018). Entrepreneurial risk-taking in crowdfunding campaigns. *Small Business Economics*, *51*(4), 843–859.

Thakor, A. V. (2020). Fintech and banking: What do we know? *Journal of Financial Intermediation*, *41*, 100833.

UNEP. (2023). *Global landscape of climate finance 2023*. United Nations Environment Programme.

Weber, C., & Dorband, I. I. (2019). The importance of project selection in green finance: Evidence from the Clean Development Mechanism. *Applied Economics*, *51*(50), 5402–5416.

Zhang, D., Zhang, Z., & Managi, S. (2019). A bibliometric analysis on green finance: Current status, development, and future directions. *Finance Research Letters*, *29*, 425–430.

Chapter 12
Quantum Strategies in Finance:
Portfolio Optimization and Risk Assessment

S. Ida Evangeline
https://orcid.org/0000-0003-2997-7897
Government College of Engineering, Tirunelveli, India

Mohammad Zahid
Rajiv Academy for Technology and Management, Mathura, India

Swati Gupta
Canterbury Institute of Management, Australia

ABSTRACT

Quantum computing is poised to revolutionize financial intelligence by offering unprecedented computational power for solving complex problems in portfolio optimization and risk assessment. As financial markets become increasingly data-driven and interconnected, classical computational methods struggle to handle the exponential growth of financial data and the complexity of optimization challenges. Novel quantum algorithms, such as quantum approximate optimization algorithm, variational quantum Eigensolver and quantum enhanced Monte Carlo simulations, offer new ways of asset allocation, risk modelling and predictive analytics. In this chapter, we discuss how quantum computing can be used to optimize portfolio management strategies via efficient solutions to constrained optimization problems and subsequently enhanced risk and return tradeoffs. Furthermore, quantum machine learning techniques improve risk assessment models by providing better credit risk analysis, liquidity risk forecasting, and modeling volatility.

DOI: 10.4018/979-8-3373-2893-5.ch012

1. INTRODUCTION

As financial markets become more complex and depend more on data, we need better ways to employ computers to optimize portfolios and analyze risk. Old financial models that have always employed classical computing approaches don't work well with a lot of data. Financial transactions are getting more and more complicated, therefore institutions need to use more advanced computer approaches for risk analysis, portfolio optimization, and improving predictive analytics (Raj et al. 2024). Quantum computing can accomplish a lot of parallel computing and tackle very difficult optimization issues. This indicates that the financial industry can alter. This chapter talks about how quantum computing can help with financial intelligence, such managing portfolios and figuring out hazards.

1.1 A look at how quantum computing is used in finance

Quantum computing, which uses ideas from quantum mechanics like superposition, entanglement, and quantum parallelism, could change how we model money. Quantum computers process data using qubits, which can exist in multiple states simultaneously. On the other hand, classical computers can only work with binary data. This skill lets them solve optimization problems with many dimensions faster than classical ones (Barral et al. 2025). In finance, quantum computing is most useful for portfolio optimization, risk modeling, and high-frequency trading. Being able to quickly process large amounts of data gives you an edge over your competitors in these areas. Hedge funds and asset management firms are among the numerous financial institutions investing in quantum computing research to enhance their decision-making processes. The Quantum Approximate Optimization Algorithm (QAOA) and the Variational Quantum Eigensolver (VQE) are two quantum algorithms that businesses can use to make their investment portfolios more accurate and less risky (Di Meglio et al. 2024).

1.2 The importance of portfolio optimization and risk assessment

Making smart financial choices depends a lot on portfolio optimization. This means picking asset allocations that give you the best returns with the least amount of risk. Traditional models, like the Markowitz Mean-Variance Optimization framework, have trouble dealing with the complexities of real-world finance, such as transaction costs, liquidity restrictions, and non-linear asset dependencies. Quantum computing can help with these issues by making it easier to find the best portfolios (Salo et al. 2024). Risk assessment is also a part of financial management. This means correctly modeling changes in the market, credit risks, and other systemic uncertainties. Quantum machine learning can be used to make quantum-enhanced risk assessment models that can help with predicting volatility, analyzing credit risk, and predicting liquidity risk. As financial markets become more connected and less stable, the need for strong risk assessment tools grows (Abate et al. 2024).

1.3 Constraints of traditional computational methodologies

Even though classical computational methods are used a lot, they have built-in problems when it comes to dealing with the huge amounts of financial data and complicated optimization problems. Traditional numerical methods often use approximation methods that take a lot of time and money to compute. Monte Carlo simulation is a common method for risk analysis, but it doesn't work well when looking at financial systems with a lot of dimensions. Similarly, combinatorial optimization problems like asset allocation and derivative pricing need a lot of processing power, which can lead to inefficient execution. The second big problem is scalability, which means that financial data is still growing and classical algorithms don't work well when the amount of data grows. Also, classical machine learning models are strong, but they need a lot of feature engineering and data preprocessing. Quantum machine learning models, on the other hand, can find patterns and correlations more quickly (Zhou, 2025).

1.4 Objectives and structure of the chapter

This chapter aims to provide a thorough analysis of the revolutionary effects of quantum computing on portfolio optimization and risk evaluation in financial markets. It begins with a simple explanation of the ideas behind quantum computing and why they are better than classical methods. The next step is to look at quantum-enhanced portfolio optimization methods like Monte Carlo simulations, quantum annealing, and hybrid quantum-classical models. The chapter then talks about quantum risk assessment strategies and shows how they can be used to model credit risk, predict liquidity, and predict volatility. We will look at real-life examples of banks and other financial institutions using quantum-driven strategies to better understand how they work in practice, what problems they face, and what the future holds. We will also talk about the problems with quantum hardware right now and how hard it is to add quantum solutions to the current financial system. The chapter concludes with an examination of the future of quantum finance, encompassing quantum cryptography, quantum cloud computing, and the potential for fully autonomous quantum trading systems. This chapter seeks to clarify the influence of quantum computing on financial intelligence through a methodical examination, providing insights for researchers, financial professionals, and policymakers.

2. SOME BASIC IDEAS ABOUT USING QUANTUM COMPUTING IN FINANCE

Quantum computers are useful in finance because they can solve hard problems more quickly than regular computers. Quantum computing uses quantum mechanics to do things on a scale that has never been seen before. This is not the same as classical computing, which uses bits that can be either 0 or 1 to process information. This difference is very important for financial modeling because the data is getting more complicated, the optimization problems are getting more dimensions, and the risk assessment scenarios are getting more complicated, which traditional methods don't usually work for. Quantum computing is a brand-new way to encode and process financial data, and it gives us new ways to solve these problems. In this part, we'll talk about the basic ideas behind quantum computing, why it's better than classical computing, and the best quantum hardware and software that are available right now. This will help us learn more about how quantum computing affects making financial decisions (Naik et al. 2025), (Irfan, Mohammed, Kassim, & Ofori, 2024).

2.1 Basic ideas behind quantum computing (superposition, entanglement, quantum gates)

Ideas from quantum mechanics, like superposition, entanglement, and quantum gates, are what quantum computing is based on. Superposition allows quantum bits, or qubits, to be in more than one state at the same time, rather than just one binary state. Entanglement is another important feature. It tells you how strongly correlated qubits are, which means that the state of one qubit changes the state of another qubit right away, even if they are very far apart. This interconnectedness lets quantum algorithms do a lot of calculations at once, which makes it faster to solve problems in financial modeling. Quantum circuits are made up of quantum gates. They use unitary transformations to change qubits. For quantum algorithms that deal with optimization and risk assessment, quantum gates can do probabilistic and reversible calculations. In contrast to classical logic gates, which only do deterministic operations, this is not the case. Quantum computing's fundamental principles are well-suited for tackling complex financial problems that require the simultaneous analysis of large datasets and the intricate relationships between financial variables (Lu & Yang, 2024).

2.2 Quantum vs. classical computing: significant advantages for financial modeling

Classical computing has improved its processing power, but it still can't keep up with the growing needs of financial modeling. Some financial applications that need to solve high-dimensional optimization problems that are too hard to do on regular hardware are portfolio optimization, option pricing, and risk assessment. Monte Carlo simulations and linear programming are two examples of approximation methods that classical methods use. These methods are hard on computers and take a long time to run. But it can make some of the most important financial algorithms run much faster by using its ability to do parallel computation and look at many solutions at once (Chang et al. 2024). Quantum machine learning (QML) improves predictive analytics in finance by helping it find complex patterns in financial data that classical machine learning models might miss. Quantum computing is a disruptive technology that can change how financial intelligence and decision-making are done (Dolu-Surabhi, 2024).

2.3 The current state of quantum hardware and software development

There are a lot of good things that could come from quantum computing, but it is still in the early stages of being used. One of the biggest problems is still making quantum hardware. This is because current quantum processors are noisy and prone to decoherence, which makes them less reliable for computing Irfan et al. (2024). Researchers are looking into different types of hardware, like superconducting qubits, trapped ions, and photonic quantum computing, to make systems more stable and able to grow. IBM, Google, and Rigetti are among of the biggest tech companies that have created quantum processors with more and more qubits. However, rectifying errors is a huge problem that needs to be overcome before quantum advantage can be used in real life. Researchers and banks can use IBM Quantum Experience and Google's Quantum AI to test out quantum algorithms on early-stage quantum hardware. Qiskit, Cirq, and PennyLane are quantum programming languages that let financial researchers make and test quantum algorithms to find out what they can do. Hybrid quantum-classical approaches, where quantum algorithms run on classical processors, are also becoming a useful way to use quantum computing power because current hardware isn't powerful enough. As qubit coherence, error correction, and algorithmic efficiency continue to improve with advancing quantum technology, quantum technology will begin to be adopted in financial applications, enabling more sophisticated and scalable quantum-driven financial intelligence systems (Dwivedi et al. 2024).

3. WAYS TO MAKE QUANTUM PORTFOLIOS BETTER

Portfolio optimization is one of the most important parts of managing money. It means using advanced methods to arrange assets in the best way to make the most money while lowering risk. The Markowitz mean-variance framework and other traditional portfolio optimization models use classical computing techniques to figure out the best way to spread out assets. Classical approaches are useful, but they don't work on massive systems. This is because in complicated financial markets, high-dimensional optimization problems involve variables and constraints that grow exponentially. Despite these constraints, quantum computing presents a substantial chance to transcend them by employing quantum algorithms that can concurrently handle large datasets, thereby providing more efficient and accurate optimization methodologies (Qu et al. 2024).

3.1 Issues with conventional portfolio optimization (scalability, complexity)

When dealing with large, complex financial datasets, traditional portfolio optimization methods have a lot of trouble with computing power. It is hard for classical models to optimize portfolios with thousands of assets since the expenses of doing so grow up quickly. But you can't optimize a portfolio in real time because linear programming and numerical approximation methods, such Monte Carlo simulations, take too long to identify the optimum answers. Also, real financial markets include problems that standard models don't do a good job of showing, such as transaction costs, liquidity constraints, and nonlinear asset relationships. The previously described constraints highlight the need for more advanced computational methods that can effectively tackle extensive combinatorial optimization problems in finance (Lim & Rebentrost, 2024).

3.2 Quantum Monte Carlo simulations for evaluating portfolio risk

Quantum Monte Carlo simulations are a strong alternative to standard Monte Carlo methods for figuring out how risky a portfolio is. Unlike classical Monte Carlo simulations, which utilize random sampling to guess probability distributions, quantum-enhanced Monte Carlo algorithms use quantum superposition and interference to speed up the simulation process. This helps banks and other financial institutions quickly figure out how risky something is, which makes it easier to make decisions when things are unclear (Matsakos & Nield, 2024).

3.3 Quantum annealing for combinatorial optimization in selecting a portfolio

Quantum annealing is a specific method for using quantum computers to solve problems with many possible solutions. This makes it great for choosing a portfolio. It is NP hard to pick the ideal mix of assets while taking into consideration things like risk tolerance, diversification, and sector allocation. Classical computers have a hard time accomplishing it quickly. Quantum annealing, which is done with quantum processors like the ones built by D-Wave, employs quantum tunneling and entanglement to look at many possible portfolio settings at the same time. This is a much better technique to get the best answers than the old-fashioned brute-force methods, which take a lot longer to locate the best ones. Quantum annealing is very helpful for cases where traditional optimization approaches like genetic algorithms and simulated annealing get trapped in local minima. Financial companies that use quantum annealing to pick their portfolios have already experienced good outcomes (Chou et al. 2024).

3.5 Hybrid quantum-classical techniques for financial optimization

Quantum hardware isn't very good right now, but hybrid quantum-classical methods are a viable way to leverage quantum computing to make financial processes better. An interesting example is quantum-inspired classical algorithms, which leverage quantum concepts like tensor networks and variational circuits to speed up classical calculations, even when quantum computers aren't available. Quantum cloud computing platforms like IBM Quantum and Google Quantum AI also let financial professionals test quantum algorithms on quantum processors that they can access through the cloud. These platforms make it straightforward to incorporate quantum solutions to current financial systems and transition to quantum hardware as it gets better (Valecha et al. 2024), (Irfan, Mohammed, Kassim, & Ofori, 2024).

Quantum computing fixes the flaws with standard portfolio optimization methods that make them slow. This opens up new approaches to allocate assets, analyze risk, and make financial decisions. Quantum hardware is still in its early stages, but quantum algorithms and hybrid methods are moving quickly. This makes it likely that quantum-driven portfolio optimization will become the standard in financial markets.

4. MODELS THAT EMPLOY QUANTUM TECHNOLOGIES TO FIGURE OUT HOW RISKY SOMETHING IS

Risk assessment is a key part of making financial decisions because it helps organizations deal with the unknown, cut losses, and make sensible choices about their strategies. Classical statistical approaches are used in traditional risk models, but they don't necessarily work well with the financial markets, which are becoming more complicated and interconnected. Because financial data is growing so quickly and the global economy is continually changing, we need better analytical tools that can swiftly and reliably process vast amounts of data. Quantum computing also changes the way we think about risk by making calculations faster, better at predicting the future, and able to apply more advanced modeling methods. This section talks about how crucial risk modeling is in finance and how quantum computing is transforming how we think about credit risk, liquidity risk, and volatility. It also talks about the norms and regulations that must be followed when quantum-enhanced risk models are utilized in the financial sector (Nguyen, 2025).

4.1 The importance of risk modeling in finance

Banks and other financial organizations need to undertake good risk modeling to keep their assets safe, keep their risk under control, and meet the restrictions set by the government. Institutions need to build solid risk assessment frameworks since market volatility, credit defaults, and liquidity crises are substantial threats. Stress testing and value at risk are two common approaches to figure out how much money you might lose. They employ facts from the past and procedures based on chance. But these strategies don't work well when the market changes a lot or when there are nonlinear linkages between financial assets. Classical models have problems with massive, high-dimensional financial datasets since they can't manage them adequately. Machine learning and artificial intelligence have made forecasts more accurate. Quantum computing can help with these issues, though. It can do risk assessments faster and more correctly, which can assist build financial plans that are less likely to change (Joshi, 2025).

4.2 Quantum computing for figuring out credit risk

Credit risk analysis, which looks at how likely it is that borrowers won't pay back their debts, is a key aspect of controlling financial risk. Using things like their income, debt-to-equity ratios, and prior payment behavior, traditional credit risk models work out how likely someone is to pay back a loan. They use statistical approaches like logistic regression, decision trees, and Monte Carlo simulations. But these strategies cost a lot to use, especially on large and varied financial datasets. Quantum computing speeds up matrix operations and makes pattern recognition more efficient, which makes it possible to analyze credit risk. Quantum-enhanced Monte Carlo simulation is one example of how banks and other financial organizations might get better at figuring out how hazardous different assets are. This makes it faster to verify credit. Quantum machine learning algorithms may also look at how different financial indicators are related to one other in sophisticated ways. This makes credit scoring models better at guessing how likely someone is to pay back a loan. Quantum computing can assist banks and other financial organizations in gaining insights into the risk profiles of borrowers, enhancing their lending strategies, and mitigating the likelihood of credit defaults (Chandrasekar & Wisetsri, 2025).

4.3 Quantum machine learning for predicting liquidity risk

A key fear in financial markets is liquidity risk, which is the chance that an organization won't be able to satisfy its short-term obligations. Traditional liquidity risk models use time-series analysis, stochastic differential equations, and network models to guess when cash flow will shift and when there will be a lack of liquidity. These models do have difficulties with unexpected liquidity crises and nonlinear market behavior that might happen when something happens outside of the market, like a recession or a change in rules. Quantum machine learning (QML) is a more advanced approach to figure out how likely it is that there will be a liquidity risk. Using QML in liquidity risk management can help banks and other financial organizations make their liquidity strategies stronger and more flexible. This helps them deal with problems in the industry (Vashishth et al. 2025), (Irfan, Dias, Rastogi, & Zebende, 2025).

4.4 Quantum algorithms for modeling volatility

Market volatility, which illustrates how much the prices of financial assets move, is particularly significant for managing risk and portfolios. Two examples of classic volatility models that use historical price data to forecast future volatility trends are generalized autoregressive conditional heteroskedasticity and stochastic volatility models. But these models don't always work effectively when the market changes suddenly or when the government changes, or when asset values don't follow a straight line. Quantum algorithms are better than volatility modeling because they make calculations faster and let you run more accurate probabilistic simulations. You can quickly find volatility surfaces with quantum-assisted Monte Carlo methods, and you can also get better results when you price options and calculate out risk. Quantum Boltzmann machines, which are another type of quantum neural network, may also uncover multidimensional correlations in financial data to predict complex volatility patterns. Quantum computing can provide financial analysts with deeper understanding of market dynamics, enabling more educated risk management decisions and improved trading tactics (Wang & Kan, 2024).

4.5 Regulatory issues and problems with compliance in quantum risk modeling

When banks and other financial organizations start utilizing quantum computers for risk modeling, they will have to deal with new rules and regulations. Basel III, Dodd-Frank, and MiFID II are all instances of standards that say exactly how to handle risk. These standards say that financial models must be clear, accountable, and easy to understand. Quantum algorithms are wonderful for doing a lot of math, but quantum-based risk models are hard to understand because they use probabilities and aren't particularly easy to understand. Hybrid quantum-classical models that are clear and use quantum advances must be made to follow the rules. You should also think about how quantum computing will affect security, since quantum cryptography may be necessary to keep sensitive financial data safe from emerging cyber attacks. Regulatory organizations will need to create new guidelines for employing quantum computing in financial risk modeling as it gets better. This will let institutions exploit its influence without infringing any global financial norms (Zhou, 2025).

Quantum computing has a transformative chance to change financial risk assessment by strengthening predictive analytics, improving computational efficiency, and enabling sophisticated modeling methodologies. Even though there aren't many computers and people have to follow the regulations, more work on quantum algorithms and hybrid techniques is making it possible for the future of financial risk management to be stronger and more adaptable.

5. REAL-WORLD EXAMPLES AND CASE STUDIES

Quantum computing is no longer just a theory; it's becoming a reality as banks and other financial institutions research into and employ quantum tactics. Hedge funds, investment banks, and asset management organizations are still looking into quantum technologies. They are utilizing quantum-enhanced algorithms to make trading, risk assessment, and portfolio management better. People that are early adopters of quantum computing realize how powerful it is since it can manage data that classical models can't, discover the best solutions for high dimensions that conventional models can't, and find market inefficiencies faster than ever before. The reason finance is utilizing quantum computing is that it needs better tools for making judgments in markets that are getting more intricate and unstable. Strategic relationships between quantum research companies and technology providers are helping big banks and other financial institutions lay the groundwork for quantum-powered financial intelligence (Purohit et al. 2024), (Irfan, Kadry, Sharif, & Khan, 2023).

Hedge funds and asset management organizations are among the first to investigate quantum computing's possibilities due to their utilization of complex mathematical models and predictive analytics. These businesses are especially interested in employing quantum algorithms to improve their portfolios, set prices for derivatives, and trade at high speeds. Quantum-inspired computing, which exploits quantum principles to make conventional algorithms better, is already being utilized to make trading and arbitrage methods better. Recently, some hedge funds have started adopting quantum annealing methods to handle massive combinatorial optimization issues. This helps them get to the best asset allocations faster than other models. On the other hand, asset management businesses are looking into how quantum machine learning could help them make better predictions about market patterns and risk scenarios (Bhasin et al. 2024).

Several large banks have begun to implement quantum methods by collaborating with technology firms specializing in quantum computing. Goldman Sachs, JPMorgan Chase, and HSBC are just a handful of the financial services companies that are partnering with quantum research labs to build and test quantum algorithms that could help with managing risk and pricing complicated financial instruments. For example, JPMorgan Chase and IBM are working together to study quantum algorithms that can be used to price options and optimize portfolios. HSBC has also looked into how quantum computing could help find fraud and figure out how risky it is to lend money. On the other hand, these groups know that full-scale quantum advantage is still a few years away. However, early-stage quantum applications will offer minor enhancements that can already confer a competitive advantage (Shafranova et al. 2024).

There have been some excellent advances, but banks still have a lot of difficulties to fix before they can deploy quantum computing. The first concern is that the quantum technology we have now is noisy and likely to decohere, which makes it hard to scale up and address the massive financial problems it is designed to. It is also still challenging to incorporate quantum algorithms to current financial systems since it is hard to alter classical models so that they can function with quantum models. People who were early adopters have also had problems understanding quantum models since they work in a way that is very different from how classical computers work. This has made it harder to check the models and obey the regulations. However, lessons gathered from these early deployments demonstrate that in the medium future, hybrid quantum-classical techniques can provide a more practical answer by allowing financial institutions to utilize the advantage of quantum computing while dealing with its existing limitations (Coccia, 2024).

The financial sector is exploring how quantum computing, artificial intelligence, and blockchain technology can collaborate to enhance risk assessment and trade security. Quantum machine learning can help AI trading algorithms by making it easier and faster to discover patterns in financial data. Combining quantum computing with AI could make forecasting models stronger, which would assist traders and asset managers better understand how the market is likely to move. Quantum cryptographic approaches can enhance blockchain technology, which is what makes decentralized financial transactions possible. They can also make things safer and thwart new quantum threats. . It is also still challenging to incorporate quantum algorithms to current financial systems since it is hard to alter classical models so that they can function with quantum models. People who were early adopters have also had problems understanding quantum models since they work in a way that is very different from how classical computers work. This has made it harder to check the models and obey the regulations. Financial institutions and quantum technology providers are still working together to make the financial markets more efficient, predictable, and resilient (Coccia & Roshani, 2024).

6. ISSUES AND CONSTRAINTS OF QUANTUM COMPUTING IN FINANCE

Quantum computing in banking has a lot of promise, but it also has a number of huge issues and limits that make it hard for people to use it a lot. However, actual implementation has not yet been achievable due to the current state of quantum hardware, algorithmic restrictions, and regulatory issues. Quantum solutions, on the other hand, have their own challenges that need to be fixed. When banks look into quantum solutions, they need to find a balance between being new and being useful. Moving from conventional to quantum-driven financial intelligence is not easy; it requires changes in technology, financial modeling, regulatory compliance, and risk management. These issues must be resolved for quantum computing to fulfill its promise of transforming portfolio optimization, risk assessment, and trading (Yamini et al. 2024).

One of the main reasons quantum computing isn't used more in banking is because of the hardware that is available right now. Quantum processors are improving swiftly, but they still have trouble scaling up, which makes it challenging to execute large-scale financial calculations with full dependability. Most quantum systems still don't have enough qubits to address really hard financial problems since only a few quantum algorithms are better than classical ones. But most quantum systems still don't have enough qubits to figure out really hard money problems. This is because just a few quantum algorithms have been able to show that they can do better than classical ones. Also, the times that a qubit may stay in a quantum state before it is disturbed, called coherence times, are still small. This makes it hard to undertake really deep and complicated calculations. Because of these constraints, most real-world financial applications would need to use hybrid quantum-classical solutions instead of purely quantum ones. Hardware companies are still working on improving superconducting qubit technology, trapped ion systems, and other novel quantum architectures so that quantum computing can actually help the banking sector (Sotelo et al. 2024).

One of the major difficulties with quantum computing in banking is that quantum systems need to be able to fix mistakes and cut down on noise. Changes in temperature, electromagnetic interference, and hardware problems are all examples of things that can easily mess up a quantum computation. These things can lead to inaccuracies that make financial models and forecasts less reliable. To make their computations right, quantum computers have to apply sophisticated error correcting methods. Classical computers, on the other hand, can use stable binary logic operations to help them. Presently, existing quantum error correction techniques, including the surface code, are unable to transform many physical qubits that are excessively large into a single reliable logical qubit. This means that running effective quantum algorithms in finance demands more resources. Until scalable quantum hardware provides powerful error correction mechanisms, quantum-driven financial models will still have problems with accuracy and dependability (Bhasin et al. 2024).

Banks and other financial institutions have a lot of work to do to make classical financial models work with quantum computers, in addition to fixing hardware problems. However, most standard financial models, such Monte Carlo simulations for figuring out risk or mean variance optimization for picking a portfolio, were built for classical computers and can't be directly used with quantum algorithms. You need to know a lot about both finance and quantum mechanics, as well as how to construct new math representations for quantum processing, in order to update these models. We need to change some of the underlying assumptions underpinning financial modeling in order to encode financial data into quantum states. This can be done via amplitude encoding, variational quantum algorithms, or quantum annealing. Also, hybrid methods that mix classical and quantum computing need to be able to work with both the old and new quantum financial systems. Until standardized methods for converting financial models to quantum frameworks are developed, industry adoption will remain delayed and inconsistent (Memon et al. 2024).

Legal, ethical, and regulatory constraints make it even tougher to deploy quantum computers for financial intelligence. In financial markets, there are strong laws about being open, responsible, and managing risk. Quantum algorithms are based on chance, which makes them tougher to explain. This is because the results from quantum models are often hard to interpret from a standard financial point of view. The Securities and Exchange Commission (SEC) and the European Central Bank (ECB) are two examples of regulatory authorities that need financial models to be easy to understand and check. People are worried that quantum-driven decision-making won't be able to meet these standards. Quantum computing is a cybersecurity threat because quantum algorithms can break conventional cryptographic methods that protect financial transactions. People are already talking about post-quantum cryptography, in fact. This is to keep private financial information safe against quantum attacks on encryption methods like RSA and elliptic curve cryptography. Quantum financial intelligence also raises ethical concerns with the utilization of highly advanced predictive models for trading. Quantum algorithms for high-frequency trading and arbitrage tactics could give some traders an unfair edge, make the system more risky, and draw more attention from regulators (Palaniappan et al. 2024).

There are a lot of issues that need to be worked out before quantum computing can be employed in banking. However, advancements in hardware, algorithm development, and adjusting to new norms can help. As quantum technology gets better, banks and other financial institutions need to be proactive and collaborate with quantum researchers, politicians, and regulatory agencies to make sure that quantum solutions are used safely and effectively. To fully utilize quantum-driven financial intelligence, we must address hardware scalability, enhance error correction, develop quantum-compatible financial models, and navigate complex regulations. There are still a lot of problems to solve, but the progress made so far is a good sign that quantum computing will play a bigger and bigger role in the creation of future financial markets (Abdikhakimov, 2024).

7. WHAT WILL HAPPEN IN QUANTUM FINANCE IN THE FUTURE

As technology gets better and quantum computing becomes easier to employ in banking, it will transform the way finance operates in big ways. Quantum systems are still extremely new, but constant progress in hardware, algorithms, and regulations is paving the way for a new era of quantum-powered financial intelligence. Quantum computing will not only help with modeling finances and figuring out risks, but it will also revolutionize the way the market works, how transactions are made, and how financial security works. Investing in quantum research by institutions is speeding up the process of financial companies working with quantum technology providers. These relationships will let us learn new things that will change the way money works in the future (Zhou, 2025).

One key reason why quantum financial apps will become popular is that quantum hardware is getting better. The challenges with qubit coherence, error rates, and computational stability are steadily getting better as more scalable quantum processors are produced. IBM, Google, and Rigetti are all working on getting more qubits and better techniques to rectify mistakes so that computers will be more dependable. Banks and other financial institutions will be able to solve optimization issues, assess risk, and handle large volumes of financial data much faster and more accurately than they could before with the emergence of fault-tolerant quantum computing. The time it takes to go from experimental quantum applications to a full quantum financial system will get shorter as quantum technology gets better. Investment banks, hedge funds, and regulatory agencies will all find high-performance quantum computing to be valuable (Dong et al. 2024).

Quantum cryptography is predicted to play a significant role in enhancing the security of our finances, alongside its computing capabilities. Banks and other financial institutions are already exploring toward post-quantum cryptographic solutions to protect sensitive data because quantum assaults on classical encryption technologies are becoming more widespread. Shor's algorithm and other quantum algorithms can swiftly defeat major encryption standards like RSA and elliptic curve cryptography and factor enormous integers. This makes current encryption protocols not very strong. In response, scientists are developing encryption methods that are resistant to quantum computers, such as lattice-based cryptography and quantum key distribution. These technologies harness the laws of quantum physics to build security systems that are very hard to break. Adding quantum cryptography to financial networks will make transactions private, make cross-border payments safer, and protect financial institutions from new cyber threats. As quantum cryptography protocols become more common, they will set the new norm for safe financial communications and data protection (Bhasin et al. 2024).

The future of trading systems will also be affected by quantum progress, and the idea of fully autonomous quantum trading platforms is becoming more and more realistic. Machine learning and AI have already transformed the financial markets by making it possible to trade with algorithms. This kind of trading uses sophisticated patterns in the market to make trades very quickly. The next phase is quantum computing, which can do things that classical computer can't, including look at big datasets, uncover arbitrage possibilities, and make trading techniques better. Quantum-enhanced trading algorithms will be able to manage more than one market situation at a time, but classical models won't be able to discover inefficiencies that occurs in microseconds. As quantum trading systems get better, they could eventually lead to fully automated trading platforms that make judgments based on current market conditions without any human input. This upgrade makes trading a lot more efficient, but it also raises concerns about the fairness and openness of the market, as well as the possibility of systemic dangers from quantum-powered trade domination (Chang et al. 2024).

More people will be able to use quantum finance as quantum cloud computing gets better. This will help banks and other financial organizations of all sizes test and use quantum solutions without needing to buy quantum gear for their own offices. IBM Quantum, Microsoft Azure Quantum, and Google's Quantum AI are all quantum cloud platforms that already include quantum processors that financial companies may use to test algorithms and add quantum capabilities to their workflows. Cloud-based quantum computing services will get better, and those who work in finance will be able to get to quantum resources whenever they need them. This will make it easier for people to learn about quantum finance and use it more quickly. Quantum cloud solutions are becoming more prevalent, and they will revolutionize how financial companies predict, manage risk, and invest. This is true even for smaller and mid-sized companies that seek to compete with quantum-powered analytics (Mishra et al. 2024).

Quantum computing will impact the financial industry a lot as it grows better. This is because of better hardware, security protocols, trading methods, and access to the cloud. It won't happen overnight, but as quantum technology gets better, it will change the way people make financial decisions. In a market that is full with data and hard to understand, banks and other financial firms who actively participate in quantum research, hire quantum experts, and get ready for the quantum future will have an edge. Quantum computing will profoundly affect how we think about risk management, trading, and financial security in the long run, even though there are still concerns with regulatory adaption, ethical issues, and computational stability. These developments were unimaginable until recently (Thakkar et al. 2024).

8. FINAL THOUGHTS

The application of quantum computing in financial intelligence is one of the biggest changes in finance today. Banks and other financial institutions can transform how they optimize portfolios, assess risk, and trade by applying quantum mechanics. This fixes some of the main flaws with conventional computational models. Quantum computing is transforming how people make judgments in markets that are particularly unstable by speeding up intricate calculations, improving asset allocation, and improving predictive analytics. But quantum finance is still a new industry that needs to work out some technological, regulatory, and infrastructure issues before it can be used by a lot of people. We use quantum algorithms like QAOA, VQE, and quantum enhanced Monte Carlo to prove that quantum computing is better for financial modeling than classical computing. But quantum hardware still has some problems. Quantum hardware's error correction methods aren't perfect yet, and it's not easy to make classical financial models work in quantum models that are both strong and fast.

For quantum finance to progress, it must establish an equilibrium between innovative concepts and pragmatic reasoning. Quantum computing could transform how we predict finances, manage risk, and trade, but the sector needs to be prudent and progressively apply quantum advances to existing systems. The most likely approach to switch will be to use both quantum and classical systems. Quantum computers will do the hardest parts of financial analysis, while classical computers will be employed for stability and ease of understanding. To proceed from proof-of-concept experiments to fully functional quantum-driven financial applications, quantum hardware will also need to keep getting better, such as by making qubits more coherent and scalable. Financial institutions must also prepare for the cybersecurity implications of quantum computing on quantum cryptography to be ready for the moment when quantum decryption is feasible. The financial industry needs to stay adaptable and constantly be ready to use new technology as quantum research advances further. It also needs to think about how quantum adoption will change things in the future.

The progress of quantum finance has significant implications for scholars, financial professionals, and legislators. Researchers have the chance to help make new technologies that revolutionize the way we think about computational finance by studying quantum algorithms and how they are used in financial markets. The entire potential of quantum finance will be achieved through the research of the integration of quantum machine learning, quantum-enhanced optimization, and hybrid computational models. Financial professionals need to stay up to date on the newest advances in quantum technology so they know how they will effect trading, risk management, and portfolio management. Companies who do quantum research, test out early-stage quantum solutions, and train their workers will have an edge over their competitors as quantum technology gets better. Lawmakers also need to make sure that quantum-driven financial models are secure, open, and responsible by creating laws. Quantum computing is changing how we think about money, which makes it hard for regulators to understand algorithms, figure out the moral implications of autonomous trading, and handle quantum-enhanced financial intelligence.

Quantum computing is more than just a theory in finance; it's already affecting how things function and will keep doing so for many years to come. There are still certain issues that need to be worked out, but quantum technology is making progress, which means it will someday be utilized to make financial decisions. But for quantum finance to work for everyone, banks, researchers, and regulators need to work together to make sure that the good things happen while keeping an eye on the bad things. As quantum computing becomes more ubiquitous, this will make financial markets more open, safe, and efficient. As quantum finance grows, people who understand its promise and know how to deal with its complexities will be best prepared to do well in the age of quantum-driven financial intelligence.

REFERENCES

Abate, G., Basile, I., & Ferrari, P. (2024). The integration of environmental, social and governance criteria in portfolio optimization: An empirical analysis. *Corporate Social Responsibility and Environmental Management, 31*(3), 2054–2065.

Abdikhakimov, I. (2024). The Interplay of Quantum Computing, Blockchain Systems, and Privacy Laws: Challenges and Opportunities. Elita. uz-Elektron Ilmiy Jurnal, 2(1), 1-12.

Barral, D., Cardama, F. J., Díaz-Camacho, G., Faílde, D., Llovo, I. F., Mussa-Juane, M., & Gómez, A. (2025). Review of distributed quantum computing: From single qpu to high performance quantum computing. *Computer Science Review*, *57*, 100747.

Bhasin, N. K., Kadyan, S., & Santosh, K., HP, R., Changala, R., & Bala, B. K. (2024). Enhancing Quantum Machine Learning Algorithms for Optimized Financial Portfolio Management. In 2024 Third International Conference on Intelligent Techniques in Control, Optimization and Signal Processing (INCOS) (pp. 1-7). IEEE.

Chandrasekar, V., & Wisetsri, W. (2025). The Prospects for Applications of Quantum Computing in the Financial Sector. Shaping Cutting-Edge Technologies and Applications for Digital Banking and Financial Services, 106.

Chang, Y. J., Wang, W. T., Chen, H. Y., Liao, S. W., & Chang, C. R. (2024). A novel approach for quantum financial simulation and quantum state preparation. *Quantum Machine Intelligence*, *6*(1), 24.

Chou, Y. H., Wu, C. H., Huang, P. S., Kuo, S. Y., Jiang, Y. C., Kuo, S. Y., & Chang, C. R. (2024, June). Hybrid quantum annealing with innovative trend ratio model for portfolio optimization. In *2024 IEEE Congress on Evolutionary Computation (CEC)* (pp. 1-8). IEEE.

Coccia, M. (2024). Technological trajectories in quantum computing to design a quantum ecosystem for industrial change. *Technology Analysis and Strategic Management*, *36*(8), 1733–1748.

Coccia, M., & Roshani, S. (2024). Path-breaking directions in quantum computing technology: A patent analysis with multiple techniques. *Journal of the Knowledge Economy*, •••, 1–34.

Di Meglio, A., Jansen, K., Tavernelli, I., Alexandrou, C., Arunachalam, S., Bauer, C. W., & Zhang, J. (2024). Quantum computing for high-energy physics: State of the art and challenges. *PFX Quantum : a Physical Review Journal*, *5*(3), 037001.

Dolu-Surabhi, S. N. (2024). Advancing Financial Decision-Making through Quantum Computing and Cloud-Based AI Models: A Comparative Analysis of Predictive Algorithms. *Journal of Artificial Intelligence and Big Data Disciplines*, *1*(1), 27–37.

Dong, Y., Zheng, H., & Zhu, J. (2024). A narrative review on quantum finance theory. *International Journal of Quantum Information*, *22*(06), 2450016.

Dwivedi, K., Haghparast, M., & Mikkonen, T. (2024). Quantum software engineering and quantum software development lifecycle: A survey. *Cluster Computing*, *27*(6), 7127–7145.

Irfan, M., Dias, R., Rastogi, R., & Zebende, G. F. (2025). *Generative AI insights for financial decision making*. IGI Global.

Irfan, M., Elmogy, M., Gupta, S., Khalifa, F., & Dias, R. T. (2024). *AI-driven decentralized finance and the future of finance*. IGI Global USA.

Irfan, M., Hussainey, K., Bukhari, S. A. C., & Nam, Y. (2024). *Issues of sustainability in AI and new-age thematic investing*. IGI Global.

Irfan, M., Kadry, S., Sharif, M., & Khan, H. U. (2023). *Fintech applications in Islamic finance: AI, machine learning, and blockchain techniques*. IGI Global.

Irfan, M., Mohammed, M., Kassim, S., & Ofori, K. S. (2024). *The future of indigenous inclusivity: Unlocking finance for economic development*. IGI Global.

Joshi, S. (2025). Review of Gen AI models for financial risk management. International Journal of Scientific Research in Computer Science. *Engineering and Information Technology*, *11*(1), 709–723.

Lim, D., & Rebentrost, P. (2024). A quantum online portfolio optimization algorithm. *Quantum Information Processing*, *23*(3), 63.

Lu, Y., & Yang, J. (2024). Quantum financing system: A survey on quantum algorithms, potential scenarios and open research issues. *Journal of Industrial Information Integration*, •••, 100663.

Matsakos, T., & Nield, S. (2024). Quantum Monte Carlo simulations for financial risk analytics: Scenario generation for equity, rate, and credit risk factors. *Quantum : the Open Journal for Quantum Science*, *8*, 1306.

Memon, Q. A., Al Ahmad, M., & Pecht, M. (2024). Quantum computing: Navigating the future of computation, challenges, and technological breakthroughs. *Quantum Reports*, *6*(4), 627–663.

Mishra, A. K., Tyagi, A. K., & Arowolo, M. O. (2024). Future Trends and Opportunities in Machine Learning and Artificial Intelligence for Banking and Finance. In *Applications of Block Chain technology and Artificial Intelligence: Lead-ins in Banking, Finance, and Capital Market* (pp. 211–238). Springer International Publishing.

Naik, A. S., Yeniaras, E., Hellstern, G., Prasad, G., & Vishwakarma, S. K. L. P. (2025). From portfolio optimization to quantum blockchain and security: A systematic review of quantum computing in finance. *Financial Innovation*, *11*(1), 1–67.

Nguyen, P. N. (2025). Quantum technology: A financial risk assessment. *Digital Finance*, •••, 1–40.

Palaniappan, V., Ishak, I., Ibrahim, H., Sidi, F., & Zukarnain, Z. A. (2024). A Review on High Frequency Trading Forecasting Methods: Opportunity and Challenges for Quantum based Method. *IEEE Access : Practical Innovations, Open Solutions*.

Purohit, A., Kaur, M., Seskir, Z. C., Posner, M. T., & Venegas-Gomez, A. (2024). Building a quantum-ready ecosystem. *IET Quantum Communication*, *5*(1), 1–18.

Qu, D., Matwiejew, E., Wang, K., Wang, J., & Xue, P. (2024). Experimental implementation of quantum-walk-based portfolio optimization. *Quantum Science and Technology*, *9*(2), 025014.

Raj, K. B., Mehta, K., Siddi, S., Sharma, M. K., Sharma, D. K., Adhav, S., & Gonzáles, J. L. (2024). Optimizing Financial Transactions and Processes Through the Power of Distributed Systems. Meta Heuristic Algorithms for Advanced Distributed Systems, 289-303.

Salo, A., Doumpos, M., Liesiö, J., & Zopounidis, C. (2024). Fifty years of portfolio optimization. *European Journal of Operational Research*, *318*(1), 1–18.

Shafranova, K., Navolska, N., & Koldovskyi, A. (2024). Navigating the digital frontier: A comparative examination of Central Bank Digital Currency (CBDC) and the Quantum Financial System (QFS). *SocioEconomic Challenges*, *8*(1), 90–111.

Sotelo, R., Corbelletto, D., Dri, E., Giusto, E., & Montrucchio, B. (2024). Quantum Computing in Finance: The Intesa Sanpaolo Experience. *IEEE Engineering Management Review*.

Thakkar, S., Kazdaghli, S., Mathur, N., Kerenidis, I., Ferreira–Martins, A. J., & Brito, S. (2024). Improved financial forecasting via quantum machine learning. *Quantum Machine Intelligence*, *6*(1), 27.

Valecha, K., Yeole, A., Salian, A., & Mathur, S. (2024). Empirical Analysis of Classical and Quantum Algorithms for Portfolio Optimization: Enhancing Financial Decision-Making Through Quantum Computing. In *2024 International Conference on Sustainable Communication Networks and Application (ICSCNA)* (pp. 1085-1090). IEEE.

Vashishth, T. K., Sharma, V., Kaushik, V., Singh, A., & Kaushik, S. (2025). Exploring Quantum Challenges and Opportunities of Quantum Machine Learning Adoption in Finance. Machine Learning and Modeling Techniques in Financial Data Science, 437-460.

Wang, G., & Kan, A. (2024). Option pricing under stochastic volatility on a quantum computer. *Quantum : the Open Journal for Quantum Science*, *8*, 1504.

Yamini, B., Nithyanandhan, R., Sudha, K., Nithya, T., Vijayakumar, K., & Subramanian, R. S. (2024). Maximizing the Revolutionary Potential of Quantum Computing: Challenges, Opportunities, and Future Directions. In 2024 10th International Conference on Communication and Signal Processing (ICCSP) (pp. 756-761). IEEE.

Zhou, J. (2025). Quantum Finance: Exploring the Implications of Quantum Computing on Financial Models. *Computational Economics*, •••, 1–30.

Chapter 13
Pioneering Quantum Computing in Financial Services:
Early Adopters and Their Strategies

Rismawati Rismawati
https://orcid.org/0000-0001-8046-6764
Universitas Muhammadiyah Palopo, Indonesia

ABSTRACT

Quantum computing is set to transform financial services through improved risk assessment, portfolio optimization, fraud detection, and high-frequency trading. Early adopters, such as prominent banks, hedge funds, and regulatory agencies, are diligently investigating quantum algorithms to surmount the constraints of classical computers in financial modeling and decision-making. This book analyzes the strategies of JPMorgan Chase, Goldman Sachs, and HSBC, as well as the impact of quantum annealing, Shor's algorithm, and quantum machine learning on the evolution of financial markets. Furthermore, it addresses the obstacles of hardware scalability, regulatory structures, cybersecurity threats, and workforce adjustment in the quantum age. The research underscores the significance of quantum cloud computing and AI-quantum integration in maintaining the competitiveness of financial institutions. As quantum technology advances, financial services must establish quantum-ready infrastructures to ensure future operations.

DOI: 10.4018/979-8-3373-2893-5.ch013

OVERVIEW OF QUANTUM COMPUTING IN FINANCIAL SERVICES

1.1 Comprehending Quantum Computing: Fundamentals of quantum mechanics, qubits, and superposition in computation.

Quantum computing signifies a revolutionary advancement in computer technology, utilizing the principles of quantum mechanics to address intricate issues at unparalleled velocities (Memon et al., 2024)(Yazdi2024). In contrast to classical computers that utilize bits—binary units representing either 0 or 1—quantum computers employ quantum bits, or qubits, which can concurrently exist in various states due to the laws of superposition and entanglement. These quantum features facilitate exponential growth in processing capacity, unlocking dramatic opportunities for financial services.

Principles of Quantum Mechanics and Computing

Quantum computing is fundamentally based on quantum mechanics, a field of physics that elucidates the behavior of particles at atomic and subatomic scales. This paradigm presents essential concepts such wave-particle duality, quantum uncertainty, and probability-driven results, which starkly differ from deterministic classical computing models (Ghose & Patra, 2023). Quantum mechanics provides computing benefits via two fundamental concepts: Superposition — In contrast to classical bits, which can only represent a single value (0 or 1) at any moment, qubits can simultaneously embody both 0 and 1. This enables quantum computers to simultaneously process numerous possibilities, hence enhancing computational performance dramatically (Outeiral et al. 2021).

Entanglement is a distinct quantum phenomena in which two or more qubits become interdependent, so that the state of one qubit instantaneously influences the state of another, irrespective of the distance separating them (Meng et al. 2023). This characteristic facilitates highly effective parallel processing, hence augmenting problem-solving capacities in intricate simulations and optimizations.

Qubits and Their Function in Computation

The qubit, the essential unit of quantum computation, distinguishes itself from classical bits not only by its capacity for superposition but also by its capability to do intricate calculations via quantum interference. When integrated with entanglement, qubits facilitate quantum algorithms to investigate numerous computational avenues concurrently, thereby diminishing the time needed to resolve issues such as risk assessment, financial modeling, and portfolio optimization (Yazdi, 2024; Saxena et al., 2023).

Contemporary quantum computers utilize various methodologies for the generation of stable qubits, such as superconducting circuits (utilized by IBM and Google), trapped ions (adopted by IonQ), and topological qubits (developed by Microsoft). Each method seeks to enhance the coherence and error rectification of quantum systems, hence ensuring reliability in intricate financial calculations.

Consequences for Financial Services

The incorporation of quantum computing in financial services is poised to transform domains including option pricing, fraud detection, asset allocation, and cryptography (Paramesha et al. 2024). Conventional financial models, dependent on Monte Carlo simulations and linear algebra methods, can necessitate substantial processing resources. Quantum computing, capable of processing extensive datasets and concurrently addressing optimization challenges, has the potential to transform risk assessment, algorithmic trading, and secure transactions.

As financial institutions investigate quantum computing applications, comprehending its fundamental principles is essential for realizing its disruptive potential in the business (Gill & Buyya, 2024). The subsequent sections will explore the early adopters of quantum technology in banking and the techniques they utilize to leverage this advanced innovation.

1.2 The Necessity of Quantum Computing in Finance: Constraints of classical computing in financial modeling and risk evaluation.

The financial sector functions within a complex and rapidly evolving landscape, necessitating the real-time processing, analysis, and action upon substantial volumes of data. Classical computing has facilitated financial modeling and risk assessment for decades, allowing institutions to do asset pricing, risk management, and portfolio optimization. As financial markets become more sophisticated and interconnected, the shortcomings of classical computers are becoming increasingly evident. Quantum computing is a transformative advancement, providing computational capabilities that can address these challenges with more efficiency and precision (Gill et al. 2022; Gill & Buyya, 2024).

Constraints of Classical Computing in Financial Modeling

Conventional financial modeling predominantly depends on classical algorithms, which may falter in handling the vast volume and intricacy of contemporary financial data. Principal constraints encompass:

1. Exponential Growth of Computational Complexity — Numerous financial models, including Monte Carlo simulations employed for option pricing, become computationally impractical as the number of variables escalates. Classical computers are required to process scenarios in a sequential manner, hence complicating real-time decision-making.
2. Inefficiency in Portfolio Optimization — Portfolio optimization, especially for large-scale institutional investors, entails balancing risk and return across numerous assets. Classical computing employs linear programming and convex optimization methods, necessitating considerable time and computational resources to determine optimal asset allocations.
3. Challenges in High-Frequency Trading (HFT) — Classical computers face difficulties in real-time data processing and predictive analytics, constraining the efficacy of algorithmic trading techniques reliant on microsecond-level decision-making.

Constraints of Classical Computing in Risk Evaluation

Risk assessment is a critical component of financial services, especially for banks, investment organizations, and insurance companies. Nonetheless, classical computing encounters substantial obstacles in domains such as:

1. Inability to Manage Large-Scale Simulations — Financial institutions depend on stress testing and scenario analysis to anticipate potential hazards. Classical computing requires hours, if not days, to simulate intricate, high-dimensional risk scenarios across global markets.
2. Cybersecurity and Cryptographic Vulnerabilities — Conventional encryption techniques, including RSA and ECC, are increasingly susceptible as computational power progresses. Financial institutions must ready themselves for the post-quantum era, in which classical encryption may prove inadequate for security.
3. Inadequate Predictive Abilities for Market Volatility — Conventional risk models, like Value at Risk (VaR) and Credit Risk assessment, frequently rely on historical data and linear regressions, rendering them less proficient in forecasting severe occurrences such as financial crises.

How Quantum Computing Mitigates These Constraints

Quantum computing provides innovative answers to these difficulties via parallel computation, sophisticated optimization techniques, and superior data processing capabilities (Gad, 2022). Principal benefits comprise:

- Exponential Acceleration in Simulations — Quantum computing can markedly diminish the duration necessary for Monte Carlo simulations, rendering real-time financial risk evaluations more attainable.
- Enhanced Portfolio Optimization — Quantum methods, like the Quantum Approximate Optimization Algorithm (QAOA), provide rapid optimization of extensive portfolios, optimizing returns while mitigating risk.
- Augmented Fraud Detection and Cybersecurity - Quantum computing can fortify encryption methods, enabling financial institutions to remain proactive against cyber attacks while enhancing fraud detection via sophisticated pattern recognition.

As financial markets progress, organizations utilizing quantum computing will acquire a competitive advantage in risk management, decision-making, and secure transactions (Saxena et al., 2023; Claudiu et al., 2023). The subsequent section examines how early adopters are employing quantum methods to transform financial services.

1.3 Initial Applications in Financial Services: Examination of the testing of quantum computing in portfolio optimization, fraud detection, and high-frequency trading.

The incorporation of quantum computing in financial services has transitioned from theory to practice, with numerous financial institutions and technology companies actively testing quantum algorithms to improve decision-making, optimize portfolios, and more effectively identify fraudulent activity. Although quantum computing is nascent, its prospective applications in finance are already exhibiting considerable promise. This section emphasizes several of the most promising applications in portfolio optimization, fraud detection, and high-frequency trading (HFT) (Palaniappan et al. 2024).

Quantum Computing for Portfolio Optimization

Portfolio optimization is a critical difficulty in asset management, necessitating financial institutions to equilibrate risk and return across a diverse range of investments (Kanaparthi, 2024). Conventional approaches depend on classical computer algorithms like Markowitz's mean-variance optimization model, which grow computationally intensive as the asset count rises. Quantum computing mitigates these constraints by means of:

- Quantum Approximate Optimization Algorithm (QAOA) - Employed to efficiently address combinatorial optimization challenges, rendering it suitable for asset allocation in extensive portfolios.
- Quantum Annealing — Utilized to improve multi-asset portfolio strategies, specifically in reducing risk exposure and transaction expenses.
- Real-time Market Adaptation — Quantum algorithms can analyze financial data at unparalleled velocities, facilitating more agile and responsive portfolio modifications in turbulent markets.

Prominent financial institutions, including Goldman Sachs and JPMorgan Chase, are partnering with quantum computing organizations to create models that enhance portfolio management efficiency (Szczesny & Gryncewicz, 2024)

Quantum Computing in Fraud Detection

Fraud detection is an essential domain in which financial institutions must scrutinize extensive datasets in real time to discover dubious actions. Conventional machine learning methods for fraud detection sometimes encounter difficulties with high-dimensional data, resulting in false positives and inefficiency (Sharma et al. 2024). Quantum computing improves fraud detection by:

- Quantum Machine Learning (QML) — Quantum-enhanced algorithms boost anomaly detection by swiftly and accurately identifying intricate fraud patterns.
- Pattern Recognition in Extensive Datasets - Quantum computing can concurrently evaluate substantial volumes of transactional data, therefore decreasing the time required for fraud detection.
- Augmented Predictive Analytics — Quantum models can forecast emerging fraud strategies by analyzing historical and real-time transaction data with more efficiency.

Institutions like HSBC and BBVA are presently investigating quantum methodologies to enhance fraud detection systems.

Quantum Computing in High-Frequency Trading (HFT)

High-frequency trading (HFT) depends on performing several deals per second to exploit micro-market inefficiencies. Conventional high-frequency trading tactics rely on robust classical computing frameworks; nevertheless, as market complexity escalates, (Zaharudin et al. 2022) Quantum computing is emerging as a transformative force in:

- Ultra-Fast Trade Execution — Quantum parallel computing enables organizations to assess numerous trading scenarios concurrently, enhancing execution speed and efficiency.
- Advanced Market Prediction Models - Quantum algorithms improve the precision of predictive trading models by examining correlations among several asset classes.
- Real-Time Risk Mitigation — Quantum-enhanced trading platforms can evaluate risk exposure with unmatched rapidity, facilitating more informed and accurate trading decisions.

Companies like Citadel Securities and Renaissance Technologies are significant entities investigating the influence of quantum computing on algorithmic trading methods. The financial sector is on the brink of a quantum revolution, with early adopters rigorously evaluating quantum algorithms in portfolio management, fraud detection, and high-frequency trading. As quantum technology and software progress, the forthcoming improvements are expected to transform the operations of financial services. The subsequent chapters will examine the tactics of financial organizations leading these quantum innovations and their ramifications for the wider financial ecosystem.

THE INITIAL PARTICIPANTS: PRINCIPAL FINANCIAL INSTITUTIONS AND THEIR QUANTUM STRATEGIES

2.1 Global Financial Institutions and Quantum Implementation: Case Studies of JPMorgan, Goldman Sachs, and HSBC's Quantum Initiatives.

The financial sector is pioneering the implementation of quantum computing, with international banks spearheading the exploration of quantum solutions for risk assessment, portfolio optimization, fraud detection, and cryptographic security (Ukpabi et al. 2023; Pfaendler et al., 2024). Institutions including JPMorgan Chase,

Goldman Sachs, and HSBC have commenced research and development initiatives to incorporate quantum computing into their financial operations, acknowledging its potential to improve efficiency and decision-making.

JPMorgan Chase: Innovating Quantum Algorithms for Financial Applications

JPMorgan Chase has been a leading proponent of quantum computing in the financial services sector. The bank partners with IBM's Quantum Network and D-Wave to create quantum algorithms for optimization and risk assessment (Saxena et al., 2023). Principal initiatives encompass:

JPMorgan has evaluated quantum-enhanced techniques, including the Quantum Approximate Optimization Algorithm (QAOA), to enhance asset allocation efficiency in portfolio optimization.

- Quantum Algorithms for Option Pricing — The bank has investigated quantum Monte Carlo techniques to enhance derivative pricing, markedly decreasing computing complexity.
- Cryptographic Security in the Post-Quantum Era – JPMorgan is conducting research on quantum-resistant cryptographic methods to safeguard financial transactions from impending quantum threats.

PMorgan Chase intends to utilize IBM's superconducting quantum processors to develop commercial applications that surpass classical models in financial modeling.

Goldman Sachs: Progressing Quantum Computing for Derivatives Valuation

Goldman Sachs has concentrated on incorporating quantum computing into its trading and risk management functions. The bank partners with Google Quantum AI and IBM Quantum to create apps that improve its trading tactics (Saxena et al., 2023; Mosteanu and Faccia, 2021). Among its prominent quantum initiatives are: Goldman Sachs is evaluating quantum-enhanced algorithms to better the precision and efficiency of pricing intricate financial transactions, especially derivatives. The firm is utilizing quantum algorithms to improve risk modeling and stress testing, yielding enhanced insights into financial market volatility.

Quantum Acceleration in Trading Strategies – The bank has investigated quantum-assisted machine learning models to enhance its high-frequency trading (HFT) activities. Goldman Sachs' quantum research seeks to diminish Monte Carlo simulation runtimes from days to minutes, so enhancing real-time trading judgments. (Rayhana et al., 2024; Liu et al., 2022; Lo et al., 2024).

HSBC: Utilizing Quantum Computing for Fraud Detection and Risk Management

HSBC has adopted a strategic approach to quantum implementation, emphasizing fraud detection, cybersecurity, and risk management. The bank is collaborating with Cambridge Quantum Computing (CQC) and IBM Quantum to investigate quantum applications in: HSBC is evaluating quantum-enhanced pattern recognition and anomaly detection models to improve the accuracy of fraud detection and transaction security.

The bank is investing in post-quantum cryptography algorithms to protect sensitive financial data from potential quantum cyber threats. HSBC is incorporating quantum methodologies into its compliance frameworks to enhance regulatory stress testing and scenario analysis. HSBC's policy is consistent with its overarching digital transformation initiative, guaranteeing that its risk assessment and fraud detection functions stay robust against emerging threats.

JPMorgan Chase, Goldman Sachs, and HSBC are leading the deployment of quantum computing in the financial sector. Their strategic partnerships with prominent quantum technology companies illustrate the increasing significance of quantum computing in improving financial modeling, trading, risk management, and cybersecurity (Jhessim and Santigie-Sankoh2025). As quantum technology advances, these early adopters are establishing the groundwork for extensive industry transformation, positioning themselves ahead of rivals in the quantum-enhanced financial sector.

2.2 Hedge Funds and High-Frequency Trading: The utilization of quantum computing by hedge funds for arbitrage possibilities.

Hedge funds are among the most zealous implementers of breakthrough technology, perpetually pursuing a competitive advantage in financial markets. The emergence of quantum computing has offered a revolutionary possibility for hedge funds, especially in high-frequency trading (HFT) and arbitrage methods (Zhang et al., 2024). Utilizing quantum algorithms, hedge funds can implement swifter, more precise, and more efficient trading decisions, surpassing conventional computational models.

The Influence of Quantum Computing on Arbitrage Strategies

Arbitrage—capitalizing on price discrepancies of identical assets across many markets—depends significantly on rapidity and accuracy. Conventional high-frequency trading firms employ classical supercomputers to detect mispricings in only fractions of a second; but, when trade volumes escalate and market inefficiencies diminish, classical algorithms find it increasingly challenging to sustain profitability. Quantum computing provides a substantial benefit by:

1. Concurrent Processing of Complex Market Data - Quantum algorithms evaluate various arbitrage opportunities across worldwide exchanges simultaneously, markedly decreasing latency.
2. Augmenting Predictive Analytics — Quantum-enhanced machine learning algorithms optimize trade execution timing by discerning trends in price fluctuations.
3. Minimizing Execution Risk — Quantum optimization algorithms offer enhanced risk-adjusted arbitrage solutions, reducing potential losses from market volatility.

Prominent Hedge Funds Investigating Quantum Computing

Numerous hedge funds have commenced investments in quantum computer research, establishing collaborations with technology companies to secure early access to quantum capabilities. Prominent participants encompass: • Renaissance Technologies - Renaissance Technologies, recognized for its supremacy in algorithmic trading, is investigating quantum algorithms to improve statistical arbitrage and signal processing in financial markets.

Citadel Securities, a frontrunner in high-frequency trading, is investing in quantum computing to enhance market-making tactics and reduce transaction execution delays. D.E. Shaw Group — This quantitative hedge fund is utilizing quantum Monte Carlo simulations to enhance risk assessment and asset pricing models. Quantum Algorithms Revolutionizing High-Frequency Trading

Multiple quantum algorithms are undergoing evaluation to enhance hedge fund trading strategies:

- Quantum Approximate Optimization Algorithm (QAOA) – Facilitates the optimization of multi-asset arbitrage schemes by identifying the most lucrative trade routes.
- Variational Quantum Eigensolver (VQE) - Employed in portfolio optimization to mitigate arbitrage execution risk.
- Quantum-Enhanced Monte Carlo Simulations — Augments trade execution models through improved scenario analysis and market volatility forecasts.

The Prospects of Quantum Computing in Hedge Fund Trading

With the progression of quantum computing, hedge funds that include quantum capabilities into their trading models will attain enhanced execution speeds, more prediction accuracy, and greater profitability in arbitrage trading. The competition for quantum dominance in financial markets is actively progressing, with early adopters in the hedge fund sector strategizing to lead the forthcoming era of algorithmic trading.

2.3 Central Banks and Regulatory Interest: The function of quantum computing in risk simulations and monetary policy projections.

Central banks and financial regulators are essential for preserving economic stability, reducing systemic risk, and formulating monetary policy. As financial markets get more intricate and interrelated, conventional computational models encounter constraints in forecasting macroeconomic results, evaluating systemic risk, and reacting to market disturbances. Quantum computing provides a transformative method for risk simulations and monetary policy forecasting, allowing central banks to make better informed decisions with enhanced precision and speed (Vashishth et al. 2025)(Mosteanu and Faccia 2021).

Quantum Computing in Risk Simulations

Central banks have a paramount duty to perform stress tests and systemic risk simulations to assess the robustness of financial institutions and economic systems. Traditional computing techniques, such Monte Carlo simulations and econometric modeling, necessitate significant time and processing resources, rendering real-time risk assessment difficult. Quantum computing mitigates these inefficiencies by:

1. Augmenting Stress Testing — Quantum Monte Carlo simulations may analyze intricate financial scenarios at an exponentially accelerated rate compared to traditional models, hence enhancing the precision of stress tests for banks and financial organizations.
2. Enhancing Systemic Risk Analysis - Quantum computing facilitates more effective modeling of interbank lending networks and liquidity flows, assisting central banks in identifying possible contagion hazards prior to their escalation.
3. Enhancing Forecasting Models — Through the utilization of quantum-enhanced machine learning, central banks may concurrently examine historical and real-

time data, thereby improving prediction accuracy for economic recessions and financial crises.

Institutions such as the European Central Bank (ECB) and the Federal Reserve have commenced investigations into the potential of quantum computing for enhancing financial stability models and detecting vulnerabilities inside global financial systems.

Quantum Computing in Monetary Policy Forecasting Monetary policy choices, including interest rate determination and inflation management, necessitate the analysis of extensive datasets that span consumer behavior, employment patterns, and global trade flows. Conventional economic models, including dynamic stochastic general equilibrium (DSGE) models, encounter difficulties due to the complexity and non-linearity of financial markets. Quantum computing provides solutions by:

- Enhancing Macro-Economic Simulations – Quantum algorithms may concurrently process numerous economic possibilities, hence augmenting the efficacy of policy simulations.
- Improving Decision-Making Frameworks — Quantum-enhanced AI can discern patterns in economic data that classical models cannot detect, enabling central banks to formulate more informed monetary policy decisions.
- Enhancing Currency and Inflation Management — Quantum computing facilitates advanced predictive modeling of inflationary pressures and foreign exchange variations, hence optimizing central bank interventions.

Regulatory and Security Considerations

As quantum computing advances, financial authorities must confront concerns such as:

- Post-Quantum Cryptography — Facilitating the transition of financial institutions to quantum-resistant encryption to safeguard against prospective cyber threats.
- Ethical and Policy Implications — Formulating protocols for the judicious application of quantum computing in financial decision-making.
- Market Stability Concerns — Assessing the influence of quantum-driven financial techniques on market volatility and systemic concerns.

Central banks and financial authorities acknowledge the revolutionary capacity of quantum computing in risk management, economic forecasting, and the formulation of monetary policy. Through the integration of quantum-powered simulations and predictive analytics, regulators may bolster financial stability and adeptly manage economic uncertainty. As quantum technology advances, its influence on global financial policy will increasingly intensify.

QUANTUM ALGORITHMS AND THEIR APPLICATIONS IN FINANCE

3.1 Shor's Algorithm and Its Cryptographic Implications: Possible risks and prospects in financial security.

Cryptographic security underpins contemporary financial systems, guaranteeing safe transactions, data integrity, and secrecy in banking and capital markets. The advent of quantum computing poses a considerable threat and an opportunity for financial security (Wang et al., 2024; Mittal et al., 2021; Seth et al., 2022). Central to this disruption is Shor's Algorithm, a quantum algorithm proficient at compromising prevalent encryption techniques such as RSA (Rivest-Shamir-Adleman) and ECC (Elliptic Curve Cryptography).

Comprehending Shor's Algorithm

Formulated by mathematician Peter Shor in 1994, Shor's Algorithm illustrates the capability of a quantum computer to quickly factor big integers, addressing a challenge that classical computers find difficult due to its exponential complexity. The security of RSA encryption, which safeguards the majority of financial transactions, depends on the challenge of factoring big prime numbers—a process that traditional computers would require millions of years to accomplish (Overmars & Venkatraman, 2021)(Imam et al., 2021). Nonetheless, quantum computing can accomplish this in mere minutes or hours, so compromising standard encryption.

The fundamental components of Shor's Algorithm comprise:

1. Quantum Fourier Transform (QFT) — An essential subroutine enabling quantum computers to effectively detect periodicities in modular exponentiation.
2. Exponential Speedup in Factoring — In contrast to traditional factoring techniques like trial division or the General Number Field Sieve (GNFS), Shor's Algorithm significantly decreases computational time exponentially.
3. Potential to Undermine Public-Key Cryptography — Given that public-key encryption depends on the impracticality of prime factorization, Shor's Algorithm may render the majority of current cryptographic systems outdated.

Threats to Financial Stability

The capacity of quantum computers to compromise RSA and ECC encryption poses multiple threats to financial institutions:

- Threat to Digital Transactions — Online banking, credit card transactions, and secure communications networks depend on encryption technologies susceptible to quantum assaults.
- Exposure of Sensitive Financial Data — Financial organizations retain extensive quantities of encrypted client information, which may become accessible when quantum computers attain adequate computational capacity.
- Escalated Cybersecurity Threats — Cybercriminals may leverage quantum computing to circumvent existing cryptographic safeguards, resulting in possible intrusions into stock exchanges, central banking systems, and payment networks.

Prospects: Post-Quantum Cryptography

Notwithstanding the hazards, financial institutions and technology companies are creating quantum-resistant encryption techniques to safeguard financial transactions in a post-quantum landscape.

Lattice-Based Cryptography employs intricate geometric frameworks to generate encryption keys that are resistant to decryption by quantum computers. Hash-Based Cryptography — Guarantees the security of digital signatures against quantum decoding. Quantum Key Distribution (QKD) employs principles of quantum mechanics to facilitate unbreakable encryption, utilizing quantum entanglement and Heisenberg's uncertainty principle to identify any eavesdropping efforts.

Shor's Algorithm signifies a significant upheaval and a cautionary alert for the financial sector. Quantum computing poses a risk to current encryption models while simultaneously fostering the advancement of next-generation cryptographic standards (Bhat et al. 2023). Financial institutions must ready themselves for the shift to post-quantum encryption to secure assets, safeguard sensitive information, and guarantee the enduring security of digital financial systems. With the progression of quantum computing, it is imperative to invest proactively in quantum-resistant security frameworks to uphold trust and stability in worldwide financial systems.

3.2 Quantum Annealing for Portfolio Optimization: Applications in asset allocation and risk mitigation.

Portfolio optimization represents a highly computationally demanding challenge within the financial services sector. Investors and asset managers must equilibrate risk and return, allocate resources effectively, and execute real-time decisions in highly turbulent markets. Traditional optimization techniques, including mean-variance optimization (MVO) and Monte Carlo simulations, have difficulties in efficiently handling huge datasets (Liang, 2025). Quantum annealing, a distinct quantum computing method, provides an innovative solution for intricate portfolio optimization challenges.

What is quantum annealing?

Quantum annealing is a quantum computing technique aimed at resolving combinatorial optimization issues by identifying the optimal solution from a multitude of options. In contrast to gate-based quantum computing, which necessitates fault-tolerant qubits, quantum annealing is more feasible in the short term, as it functions on specialized hardware tailored for optimization tasks. D-Wave Systems, a pioneer in quantum annealing, has collaborated with financial institutions to investigate potential uses in asset allocation and risk management.

Quantum Annealing in Portfolio Optimization

Asset allocation necessitates the optimization of a portfolio in accordance with diverse limitations, such as anticipated return, risk tolerance, and regulatory mandates (Arcuri et al. 2023). Conventional methods employ quadratic programming or exhaustive computing, both of which become inefficient with an increasing number of assets.

Quantum annealing improves asset allocation through:

1. Effectively Addressing Large-Scale Optimization Challenges — Quantum annealers investigate several portfolio configurations concurrently, markedly decreasing the time needed to identify optimal allocations.
2. Simultaneously Analyzing Multiple Market Variables — Quantum models more efficiently incorporate real-time market data, historical patterns, and risk parameters compared to classical models.
3. Minimizing Computational Expenses - In contrast to conventional supercomputers, quantum annealers utilize less energy and handle financial data with more efficiency.

Risk Management Utilizing Quantum Annealing

Risk management is essential in finance, as investors want to reduce exposure to market volatility, credit risk, and systemic financial disruptions. Conventional risk assessment depends on Value at Risk (VaR) models, necessitating extensive simulations. Quantum annealing enhances risk management by:

- Improving Stress Testing — Quantum-augmented models evaluate possible losses during extreme market situations with increased precision.
- Enhancing Hedging Strategies — Quantum algorithms determine optimal hedge positions, minimizing exposure to unfavorable market fluctuations.
- Real-Time Market Scenario Simulation — Quantum computers can concurrently process hundreds of market situations, enhancing real-time risk evaluation.

Implementation of Quantum Annealing in Finance

Prominent financial institutions, including as JPMorgan Chase, Goldman Sachs, and BBVA, have partnered with D-Wave and other quantum computing companies to evaluate quantum annealing in portfolio management. Preliminary findings suggest enhanced efficiency in:

- Developing optimum portfolios with intricate limitations
- Reducing downside risk while optimizing returns
- Minimizing the computational duration necessary for extensive investment decisions

Quantum annealing signifies a substantial advancement in portfolio optimization and risk management. As financial markets grow increasingly intricate, conventional computational techniques will find it challenging to maintain relevance. Quantum-enhanced portfolio strategies will enable asset managers to execute swifter, more precise, and more lucrative investment decisions. Although quantum annealing remains nascent, its prospective influence on financial services is indisputable, rendering it an essential technology for forthcoming investment strategies.

3.3 Quantum Machine Learning in Fraud Detection: Augmenting prediction efficacy in transaction surveillance.

Fraud detection is an essential aspect of financial security, given that financial institutions handle billions of transactions each day. Conventional fraud detection systems utilize machine learning (ML) and rule-based algorithms to detect irregularities in transaction patterns. Nonetheless, these technologies frequently encounter challenges related to false positives, constraints in real-time processing, and the escalating intricacy of financial fraud schemes. Quantum machine learning (QML) provides a transformative method that markedly improves pattern recognition, anomaly detection, and real-time transaction surveillance in the prevention of financial fraud.

Quantum Machine Learning and Fraud Detection

Quantum machine learning amalgamates quantum computing with classical machine learning frameworks to enhance data processing velocity and efficacy. In contrast to classical computers that evaluate transaction data in a linear fashion, quantum computers simultaneously analyze numerous fraud detection situations, hence enhancing the speed and precision of fraudulent activity detection.

The primary benefits of QML in fraud detection encompass:

1. Improved Pattern Recognition — Quantum algorithms may process extensive datasets more effectively, revealing concealed correlations among fraudulent transactions that standard machine learning models may overlook.
2. Real-Time Transaction Monitoring – Quantum models can concurrently analyze extensive volumes of financial data, thereby minimizing the duration needed to identify suspicious activities.
3. Reduced False Positives – By utilizing quantum-enhanced support vector machines (QSVMs) and variational quantum classifiers (VQCs), quantum machine learning (QML) enhances fraud detection precision while decreasing false alerts.

Quantum Algorithms Revolutionizing Fraud Detection

A variety of quantum algorithms have been evaluated in applications for fraud detection:

Quantum Neural Networks (QNNs) utilize quantum circuits to enhance anomaly detection in financial transactions, surpassing traditional deep learning models.

Quantum Boltzmann Machines (QBMs) — Employed for fraud classification, QBMs enhance fraud detection models by adeptly understanding intricate transactional patterns. Quantum k-Means Clustering enhances unsupervised fraud detection by aggregating analogous fraudulent behaviors, hence enhancing detection accuracy.

Practical Implementation of Quantum Machine Learning in Financial Security

Prominent banks and financial technology companies are diligently exploring QML to improve fraud prevention. JPMorgan Chase is investigating quantum-enhanced anomaly detection in financial transactions to mitigate fraud-related losses. HSBC has collaborated with quantum computing companies to create fraud risk models utilizing QML to enhance client protection.

BBVA is evaluating quantum-based classification algorithms to enhance its fraud detection capabilities. Obstacles and Future Opportunities. Notwithstanding its potential, the incorporation of QML in fraud detection encounters numerous challenges:

- Restricted Quantum Hardware Accessibility - Presently, quantum computers remain in nascent developmental phases, constraining extensive use.
- Integration with Classical Systems — Hybrid quantum-classical models must be established to facilitate the seamless application of fraud detection.
- Cybersecurity Considerations — Financial institutions must address possible security issues associated with quantum-enhanced cyber threats as they use quantum computing.

Quantum machine learning signifies a transformative advancement in fraud detection, providing expedited, more precise, and more sophisticated transaction monitoring for financial organizations. As quantum computing technology progresses, QML will become increasingly essential in safeguarding global financial systems, mitigating fraud-related losses, and bolstering trust in digital financial transactions. Initial efforts by the banking sector in quantum fraud detection will influence the future of fraud prevention and cybersecurity in the quantum age.

OBSTACLES AND HINDRANCES TO QUANTUM IMPLEMENTATION IN FINANCE

4.1 Hardware and Scalability Obstacles: The existing constraints of quantum processors in financial modeling.

Quantum computing has arisen as a disruptive technology capable of revolutionizing financial modeling, risk assessment, and trading methods. Nonetheless, its extensive implementation in finance encounters considerable obstacles, especially regarding hardware constraints and scalability (Mzukwa, 2024; Allioui & Mourdi,

2023). Notwithstanding swift progress, contemporary quantum processors remain nascent and fail to satisfy the high-performance requirements of financial applications.

1. The Intricacy of Quantum Hardware

Quantum computers function fundamentally differently from classical computers, utilizing qubits rather than conventional binary bits. In contrast to traditional bits, which are limited to the values of 0 or 1, qubits can occupy several states concurrently owing to superposition and entanglement. Nonetheless, these benefits are presently obstructed by hardware constraints, including:

- Qubit Stability and Decoherence - Qubits exhibit significant sensitivity to ambient noise and necessitate intense cooling (approaching absolute zero) to preserve coherence. Even slight perturbations can induce errors in quantum computing.
- Error Rates and Fault Tolerance — Present quantum processors exhibit elevated error rates attributable to qubit instability. Techniques for error correction, including quantum error correction (QEC), necessitate supplementary qubits, hence posing a hurdle to scalability.
- Brief Qubit Lifespan – Numerous quantum systems encounter difficulties in sustaining quantum coherence over prolonged durations, constraining their capacity to execute intricate financial computations that necessitate protracted processing times.

2. Scalability Obstacles in Financial Modeling

Financial modeling necessitates substantial computer power to evaluate extensive datasets and perform intricate simulations, including Monte Carlo simulations, portfolio optimization, and credit risk analysis (Roger, 2024). Despite the potential for exponential speedup in quantum computing, certain scalability challenges hinder its practical application at present:

- Restricted Qubit Quantity — The most sophisticated quantum computers currently possess qubit counts between 50 and several hundred, which is inadequate for extensive financial models. Estimates indicate that hundreds, or potentially millions, of qubits will be necessary for viable financial applications.
- Quantum Hardware Infrastructure — Quantum computers necessitate highly specialized conditions, such as cryogenic cooling systems and vacuum chambers, rendering them costly and challenging to incorporate into current financial infrastructures.

- Absence of Commercially Viable Quantum Processors — Despite substantial advancements by businesses such as IBM, Google, D-Wave, and Rigetti Computing, fully operational and error-free quantum computers suitable for commercial finance applications remain many years from realization.

3. Surmounting Hardware and Scalability Obstacles

Financial institutions investing in quantum computing are partnering with quantum hardware businesses to tackle these difficulties. Several of the more promising solutions encompass:

- Hybrid Quantum-Classical Approaches — Numerous firms are investigating hybrid models that integrate classical supercomputers with quantum processors to capitalize on the advantages of quantum computing while alleviating hardware constraints.
- Progress in Qubit Technology - Investigations into topological qubits, trapped ions, and superconducting qubits seek to enhance qubit stability and diminish error rates.
- Cloud-Based Quantum Computing — Corporations like as IBM and Microsoft provide quantum computing services through the cloud, allowing financial institutions to explore quantum algorithms without the need for real hardware investment.

Quantum computing possesses substantial potential for financial modeling, risk assessment, and trading; yet, considerable hardware and scalability issues persist (Vashishth et al. 2025). The financial sector must address these constraints by implementing hybrid quantum-classical models and investing in quantum-capable infrastructures. As hardware technology progresses and quantum processors achieve more scalability, financial institutions will be more equipped to utilize quantum computing for practical financial applications.

4.2 Regulatory and Security Concerns: The ramifications of quantum cryptography and the necessity for novel compliance frameworks.

With the progression of quantum computing, financial organizations encounter substantial legal and security problems, especially concerning data protection, cybersecurity, and compliance frameworks. The advent of quantum algorithms that can compromise current encryption standards presents a significant risk to the security of financial transactions, requiring the advancement of post-quantum cryptography and revised regulatory frameworks.

1. The Peril of Quantum Computing to Financial Security

A primary concern surrounding quantum computing is its potential to compromise classical encryption systems. Contemporary banking systems depend on RSA (Rivest-Shamir-Adleman) and ECC (Elliptic Curve Cryptography) to secure transactions, digital signatures, and client information. Nonetheless, the advent of Shor's Algorithm enables quantum computers to factor big prime numbers at an exponentially accelerated rate compared to classical computers, hence rendering current encryption techniques obsolete.

Significant security issues presented by quantum computing encompass:

- Compromised Encryption — Sensitive financial information, encompassing consumer transactions and interbank communications, may be susceptible to cyberattacks if not migrated to quantum-resistant encryption.
- Threats to Blockchain and Digital Currencies – Numerous blockchain protocols, such as Bitcoin and Ethereum, depend on cryptographic hash functions that quantum computers may exploit, resulting in vulnerabilities in digital asset security.
- Threats to Secure Messaging and Identity Verification - Quantum attacks may undermine secure communication channels and authentication mechanisms, heightening the danger of fraud and identity theft in financial services.

2. The Necessity for Post-Quantum Cryptography

To address quantum security threats, financial organizations and regulators must use post-quantum cryptography (PQC) solutions capable of resisting quantum attacks. Various cryptographic methodologies are in development (Hasan et al. 2024), including:

- Lattice-Based Cryptography — Employs intricate mathematical frameworks to generate encryption keys that are resistant to quantum decryption efforts.
- Hash-Based Cryptography — Guarantees the security of digital signatures against quantum decoding efforts.
- Quantum Key Distribution (QKD) utilizes quantum mechanics concepts to generate unbreakable encryption keys by identifying any eavesdropping attempts.

- Governments and financial authorities, such as the National Institute of Standards and Technology (NIST) and the European Central Bank (ECB), are diligently developing post-quantum cryptography standards to protect financial systems.

Regulatory Challenges and Compliance Frameworks

The integration of quantum computing in banking necessitates that regulatory authorities revise current compliance frameworks to tackle emerging security and privacy issues. Principal regulatory challenges encompass:

• Absence of Standardized Quantum Security Policies - Existing finance regulations fail to address the hazards posed by quantum computing.

• Cross-Border Compliance Challenges — Financial organizations operating internationally must comply with various regulatory norms, complicating the implementation of quantum security measures.

• Ethical and Privacy Concerns - The capacity of quantum computers to decrypt historical transactions and stored financial information prompts ethical inquiries regarding data privacy and the security of historical records.

4. Readying for a Quantum-Resilient Financial System

To mitigate these issues, financial institutions must undertake proactive measures, including:

- Investing in Quantum-Resistant Encryption — Financial institutions must partner with cybersecurity firms to use post-quantum encryption techniques.
- Regulatory Collaboration — Governments, financial regulators, and industry leaders must collaborate to develop quantum-safe compliance frameworks.
- Financial organizations should investigate hybrid cryptographic models, wherein traditional encryption is augmented with quantum-resistant algorithms until quantum computing reaches full maturity.

Quantum computing offers unparalleled opportunities and considerable security threats for the banking sector. Financial institutions must implement post-quantum cryptography measures, collaborate with regulators to develop new compliance frameworks, and invest in quantum-resilient cybersecurity technologies to facilitate a secure transition. By implementing preemptive measures now, the financial sector can ensure data integrity, transaction security, and regulatory compliance in the quantum age.

4.3 Ethical and Workforce Disruptions: The influence of quantum computing on financial analysts and data scientists.

The integration of quantum computing in financial services poses significant technological and regulatory obstacles, as well as substantial ethical and workforce consequences (Boretti, 2024 & Neway, 2024). As quantum algorithms improve risk assessment, trading techniques, fraud detection, and portfolio optimization, financial professionals—especially analysts, data scientists, and quantitative traders—must adapt to a swiftly evolving technical environment. This transition prompts apprehensions regarding job displacement, skill evolution, and ethical obligations in the quantum age.

1. Ethical Issues in Quantum Financial Applications

The capacity of quantum computing to handle extensive data at unparalleled velocities presents ethical challenges in financial services, including:

- Market Manipulation Risks — Quantum algorithms may confer an inequitable advantage to early adopters in high-frequency trading (HFT), heightening the risk of market manipulation and information asymmetry.
- Bias in Quantum-Enhanced AI Models – Quantum machine learning (QML) models employed for credit scoring, loan approvals, and risk assessment may perpetuate existing biases if not meticulously constructed.
- Data Privacy and Ethical AI Utilization - The capacity of quantum computing to undermine conventional encryption techniques engenders apprehensions over data privacy, surveillance, and the potential exploitation of consumer information.

Financial institutions and authorities must establish ethical rules and governance methods to guarantee equitable, transparent, and accountable quantum-driven financial processes.

2. Workforce Disruptions and Labor Market Transformations

The incorporation of quantum computing into financial services will result in substantial alterations to the workforce, especially affecting financial analysts, data scientists, and quantitative researchers. The foremost challenges encompass:

- Automation of Conventional Financial Positions - A multitude of responsibilities undertaken by financial analysts, risk managers, and actuaries—such as portfolio optimization, risk modeling, and fraud detection—will progressively be automated via quantum-enhanced AI.

- Demand for Professionals with Quantum Expertise – With the increasing acceptance of quantum computing, there will be a significant demand for experts in quantum programming, quantum cryptography, and quantum-enhanced artificial intelligence.
- Requirement for Ongoing Upskilling – Present financial experts must reskill and enhance their expertise by acquiring knowledge in quantum algorithms, hybrid quantum-classical computing, and sophisticated financial modeling methodologies (Irfan, Mohammed, Kassim, & Ofori, 2024).

3. Equipping the Financial Workforce for the Quantum Era

To alleviate workforce disruptions and facilitate a seamless transition, financial institutions must:

- Invest in Quantum Education and Training - Organizations should provide quantum literacy programs, workshops, and certifications for staff to maintain competitiveness.
- Foster Collaboration Between Quantum Scientists and Financial Experts – Forming interdisciplinary teams that integrate finance, quantum computing, and AI skills will be essential for closing knowledge gaps.
- Implement a Hybrid Strategy for Quantum Integration - Merging classical and quantum computing techniques in financial modeling will enable experts to progressively acclimate to quantum technologies.

The emergence of quantum computing in finance will transform the industry's workforce, alter financial modeling methodologies, and present new ethical challenges. Quantum technology poses hazards like job displacement, market imbalances, and privacy issues, however it simultaneously offers possibilities for financial professionals to acquire new skills and foster innovation (How & Cheah, 2024). Organizations that prioritize workforce transformation, ethical AI frameworks, and regulatory engagement will spearhead the quantum-driven financial future, assuring equity, security, and sustainability in global financial markets.

THE PROSPECTS OF QUANTUM COMPUTING IN FINANCIAL SERVICES

5.1 Quantum Cloud Computing for Financial Institutions: Utilizing quantum computing as a service for banks and fintech companies.

The incorporation of quantum computing into financial services is progressing rapidly; yet, the substantial expense and technical intricacy of quantum hardware pose obstacles to widespread implementation (Awan et al. 2022). Quantum cloud computing, offering Quantum Computing as a Service (QCaaS), has emerged as a feasible alternative for banks, financial businesses, and fintech organizations to address these difficulties. This strategy enables financial organizations to utilize quantum computing capabilities through cloud-based platforms, eliminating the necessity for direct investment in quantum hardware.

1. What constitutes Quantum Cloud Computing?

Quantum cloud computing allows financial organizations to utilize quantum computers remotely, analogous to how standard cloud computing offers access to high-performance classical computing resources. Prominent technology companies, such as IBM Quantum, Google Quantum AI, Microsoft Azure Quantum, and Amazon Braket, provide QCaaS platforms enabling financial institutions to explore quantum algorithms and implement them in practical financial scenarios.

2. Advantages of Quantum Cloud Computing for Financial Institutions

The implementation of QCaaS offers numerous benefits for banks and fintech companies, including:

- Economical Access to Quantum Technology — Financial institutions can utilize cloud-based quantum computing on a pay-as-you-go model rather than investing in costly quantum hardware.
- Scalability and Flexibility — Financial institutions and fintech enterprises can conduct quantum experiments and simulations without requiring specialist internal quantum expertise or infrastructure.
- Integration with Classical Systems - Quantum cloud systems facilitate hybrid models that merge classical machine learning with quantum algorithms, enhancing risk management, fraud detection, and portfolio optimization Irfan et al. (2024).

- Expedited Research and Development — QCaaS allows financial institutions to evaluate quantum applications in real-time trading, derivatives pricing, and asset management without the necessity of awaiting the commercial availability of full-scale quantum computers.

Applications of Quantum Cloud Computing in Finance

Financial organizations are utilizing quantum cloud computing in various critical domains:

• Portfolio Optimization - Quantum techniques, like the Quantum Approximate Optimization Algorithm (QAOA), are being evaluated using cloud services to improve investing strategies.

• Fraud Detection and Cybersecurity — Financial institutions employ quantum-enhanced machine learning models via QCaaS systems to boost the precision of fraud detection and fortify encryption methods.

• Monte Carlo Simulations for Risk Analysis — Cloud-based quantum computing facilitates real-time simulations for risk evaluation, enabling institutions to react more efficiently to market volatility.

4. Challenges and Considerations in the Adoption of Quantum Cloud Technology

Notwithstanding its advantages, quantum cloud computing poses problems, including:

- Data Security Risks - Financial institutions must safeguard sensitive financial data during processing by external quantum cloud providers.
- Latency and Computational Constraints - Although QCaaS offers access to quantum processors, existing hardware restrictions imply that not all quantum algorithms yield a prompt benefit over traditional computing.
- Regulatory and Compliance Issues — Financial authorities must formulate explicit standards for quantum-enhanced decision-making and the secure implementation of quantum cloud computing in financial markets.

Quantum cloud computing is reducing entry barriers for financial organizations, allowing them to investigate quantum-driven solutions without substantial infrastructure expenditures (Rishiwal et al. 2025). As QCaaS providers augment their capabilities, banks and fintech companies will progressively incorporate quantum-enhanced analytics, risk management, and trading techniques into their operations. Despite existing problems, quantum cloud computing signifies a vital advancement towards a more efficient, safe, and data-centric financial sector in the quantum age.

5.2 AI and Quantum Synergy in Trading: Integrating quantum computing with AI for predictive analytics and autonomous trading.

The integration of artificial intelligence (AI) with quantum computing is poised to transform financial markets, especially in predictive analytics, algorithmic trading, and autonomous decision-making. AI has already revolutionized financial trading with advanced data-driven techniques, while the incorporation of quantum computing offers significant enhancements in computational efficiency, pattern recognition, and risk assessment (Boretti, 2024; Yazdi, 2024).

1. The Function of Artificial Intelligence in Financial Trading

Artificial intelligence has significantly transformed financial markets via high-frequency trading, market prediction models, and sentiment analysis. Conventional AI models depend on conventional machine learning and deep learning methodologies to discern trade trends and enhance decision-making. Nonetheless, these models encounter difficulties in real-time processing of extensive datasets, particularly when addressing non-linear correlations and intricate market swings (Ahmed et al. 2023) (Han et al. 2024), (Irfan, Mohammed, Kassim, & Ofori, 2024).

- AI-driven trading tactics encompass: • Neural Networks and Deep Learning — Employed to discern trends in historical price fluctuations.
- Reinforcement Learning - Utilized in autonomous trading algorithms that adjust to market dynamics.
- Natural Language Processing (NLP) - Evaluates news sentiment and social media trends to forecast market fluctuations.

2. The Enhancement of AI in Trading using Quantum Computing

Quantum computing possesses the capacity to significantly enhance AI algorithms, rendering financial predictions more precise, expeditious, and adept at concurrently analyzing multifaceted market conditions. Quantum computing enhances AI-driven trading primarily through Quantum Machine Learning (QML), which accelerates deep learning model training and optimizes feature selection for market prediction.

Quantum Pattern Recognition — Quantum algorithms can concurrently evaluate extensive datasets, enhancing anomaly detection and fraud prevention in trading methods. Accelerated Portfolio Optimization — AI-driven portfolio management leverages quantum-enhanced optimization techniques to more efficiently analyze numerous investment situations. Integrating quantum algorithms like the Quantum

Approximate Optimization Algorithm (QAOA) and Variational Quantum Eigensolver (VQE) with AI-enhanced market forecasting enables traders to make judgments with unparalleled speed and enhanced precision (Devi et al. 2024)(Boretti, 2024).

3. The Ascendancy of Autonomous Quantum Trading

The use of quantum AI with algorithmic trading facilitates the development of entirely autonomous trading systems that can execute real-time judgments with limited human involvement. Possible advantages encompass:

- Ultra-Fast Execution — Quantum-enhanced AI models may respond to market changes instantaneously, minimizing latency in high-frequency trading.
- Risk-Optimized Trading — Quantum AI improves risk-adjusted profits by concurrently simulating thousands of market scenarios (Irfan, Dias, Rastogi, & Zebende, 2025).
- Enhanced Market Prediction Accuracy — AI-driven quantum analytics refine sentiment analysis and technical trading methodologies.

4. Challenges and Ethical Considerations

Despite the obvious advantages of AI-quantum synergy in trading, problems persist:

- Regulatory Oversight - Autonomous quantum trading engenders apprehensions over market manipulation, transparency, and adherence to financial regulations.
- Computational Limitations - Quantum computers are nascent, characterized by restricted qubit stability and elevated error rates.
- Ethical Concerns - The application of quantum AI in finance could exacerbate disparities between organizations with access to quantum resources and smaller enterprises, leading to potential market imbalances.

The integration of AI and quantum computing signifies the forthcoming advancement in predictive analytics and algorithmic trading, allowing financial institutions to conduct more intelligent, rapid, and lucrative transactions (Saxena et al., 2023; Boretti, 2024). Despite ongoing hurdles including regulatory, ethical issues, and hardware constraints, the future of autonomous quantum trading is poised to transform global financial markets, providing a remarkable competitive edge to early adopters of quantum-AI integration.

5.3 Preparing for a Quantum Future: Actions financial institutions must undertake to establish quantum-ready infrastructures.

As quantum computing progresses towards practical applications, financial institutions must undertake proactive measures to guarantee their quantum preparedness. The shift to quantum-enabled financial services necessitates substantial technological, strategic, and regulatory preparations to harness the advantages of quantum computing while minimizing hazards. Institutions that proactively prepare will secure a competitive edge in risk management, trading, fraud detection, and encryption security.

1. Developing Quantum-Resilient Cybersecurity

A primary worry for financial institutions is the risk that quantum computing presents to existing cryptographic security techniques. As quantum computers attain sufficient capacity to compromise conventional encryption techniques, organizations must adopt quantum-resistant cryptographic alternatives. Essential steps encompass:

- Implementing Post-Quantum Cryptography (PQC) — Utilizing lattice-based, hash-based, and multivariate cryptographic algorithms to safeguard financial transactions.
- Quantum Key Distribution (QKD) — Utilizing quantum physics to establish highly secure encryption for data transport (Irfan, Kadry, Sharif, & Khan, 2023).

2. Regulatory Compliance for Quantum Security — Collaborating with governmental and regulatory entities to establish secure frameworks prepared for quantum technology.
   2. Cultivating Proficiency in Quantum Computing

For the successful integration of quantum computing into financial operations, banks and fintech companies must engage in quantum literacy and worker development. Actions involve:

- Engaging Quantum Specialists — Attracting professionals in quantum computing, cryptography, and quantum AI research to create financial applications.
- Training Current Employees — Offering quantum computing educational programs for financial analysts, risk managers, and IT specialists.

- Establishing Collaborations with Quantum Technology Enterprises — Partnering with prominent quantum firms such IBM Quantum, Google Quantum AI, D-Wave, and Rigetti Computing to utilize quantum computing capabilities.

3. Exploring Quantum Cloud Services

Quantum hardware is costly and intricate to sustain; however, Quantum Computing as a Service (QCaaS) enables institutions to evaluate quantum algorithms without possessing quantum processors (Mittal et al., 2024). Steps to incorporate QCaaS encompass:

- Executing Pilot Programs — Evaluating quantum algorithms for portfolio optimization, risk assessment, and fraud detection using cloud-based quantum platforms.
- Formulating Hybrid Quantum-Classical Models — Employing quantum computing to enhance current financial AI and machine learning frameworks.
- Gradual Scaling of Quantum Adoption — Progressing from limited quantum experiments to comprehensive integration within essential financial operations.

4. Formulating a Quantum Strategy and Roadmap

Financial institutions must create long-term quantum strategies that correspond with their business objectives to maintain a competitive edge. This encompasses:

- Evaluating Quantum Readiness - Performing internal assessments to ascertain how quantum computing can improve current banking services.
- Investing in Quantum Research and Development (R&D) - Allocating resources to investigate novel quantum applications in trading, risk modeling, and cybersecurity.
- Establishing Regulatory and Ethical Frameworks — Ensuring responsible quantum adoption by addressing ethical issues pertaining to market manipulation, data privacy, and security.

Preparing for the quantum future necessitates early adoption, deliberate investments, and a dedication to workforce development (How & Cheah, 2023; Bhasin and Tripathi, 2021). Financial institutions that adopt quantum computing at this juncture will be strategically positioned to use its transformative capabilities, so securing long-term stability, efficiency, and competitive superiority in the swiftly changing financial environment.

REFERENCES

Ahmed, S. F., Alam, M. S. B., Hassan, M., Rozbu, M. R., Ishtiak, T., Rafa, N., ... & Gandomi, A. H. (2023). Deep learning modelling techniques: current progress, applications, advantages, and challenges. Artificial Intelligence Review, 56(11), 13521-13617. DOI: 10.1007/s10462-023-10466-8

Allioui, H. & Mourdi, Y. (2023). Exploring the full potentials of IoT for better financial growth and stability: A comprehensive survey. Sensors. DOI: 10.3390/s23198015

Arcuri, M. C., Gandolfi, G., & Laurini, F. (2023). Robust portfolio optimization for banking foundations: a CVaR approach for asset allocation with mandatory constraints. Central European Journal of Operations Research, 31(2), 557-581. DOI: 10.1007/s10100-022-00821-5

Awan, U., Hannola, L., Tandon, A., Goyal, R. K., & Dhir, A. (2022). Quantum computing challenges in the software industry. A fuzzy AHP-based approach. Information and Software Technology, 147, 106896. DOI: 10.1016/j.infsof.2022.106896

Bhasin, A., & Tripathi, M. (2021). Quantum computing at an inflection point: Are we ready for a new paradigm. [HTML]. *IEEE Transactions on Engineering Management, 70*(7), 2546–2557. DOI: 10.1109/TEM.2021.3103904

Bhat, J. R., AlQahtani, S. A., & Nekovee, M. (2023). FinTech enablers, use cases, and role of future internet of things. Journal of King Saud University-Computer and Information Sciences, 35(1), 87-101. DOI: 10.1016/j.jksuci.2022.08.033

Boretti, A. (2024). Technical, economic, and societal risks in the progress of artificial intelligence driven quantum technologies. Discover Artificial Intelligence. DOI: 10.1007/s44163-024-00171-y

Claudiu, B., Cosmin, E., Otniel, D., & Andrei, A. (2023, May). Enhancing the financial sector with quantum computing: A comprehensive review of current and future applications. In International Conference on Informatics in Economy (pp. 195-203). Singapore: Springer Nature Singapore. DOI: 10.1007/978-981-99-6529-8_17

Devi, P., Desai, S. S., Kumar, R., Naruka, M. S., & Tripathi, V. (2024, December). A Strategic Innovations for Stock Market Optimization by Using Data Science & Explainable AI in High Frequency Trading. In 2024 International Conference on IoT Based Control Networks and Intelligent Systems (ICICNIS) (pp. 1510-1515). IEEE. DOI: 10.1109/ICICNIS64247.2024.10823313

Gad, A. G. (2022). Particle swarm optimization algorithm and its applications: a systematic review. Archives of computational methods in engineering. DOI: 10.1007/s11831-021-09694-4

Ghose, P., & Patra, S. (2023). An interdisciplinary approach to cognitive modelling: A framework based on philosophy and modern science. http://doi.org/ jgu.edu.inDOI: 10.17304/ijil.vol20.3.4

Gill, S. S., Kumar, A., Singh, H., Singh, M., Kaur, K., Usman, M., & Buyya, R. (2022). Quantum computing: A taxonomy, systematic review and future directions. Software: Practice and Experience, 52(1), 66-114. https://onlinelibrary.wiley.com/doi/10.1002/spe.3039

Han, H., Liu, Z., Barrios Barrios, M., Li, J., Zeng, Z., Sarhan, N., & Awwad, E. M. (2024). Time series forecasting model for non-stationary series pattern extraction using deep learning and GARCH modeling. Journal of Cloud Computing, 13(1), 2. DOI: 10.1186/s13677-023-00576-7

Hasan, K. F., Simpson, L., Baee, M. A. R., Islam, C., Rahman, Z., Armstrong, W., ... & McKague, M. (2024). A framework for migrating to post-quantum cryptography: Security dependency analysis and case studies. IEEE Access, 12, 23427-23450. DOI: 10.1109/ACCESS.2024.3360412

How, M. L. & Cheah, S. M. (2023). Business Renaissance: Opportunities and challenges at the dawn of the Quantum Computing Era. Businesses. DOI: 10.3390/businesses3040036

How, M. L. & Cheah, S. M. (2024). Forging the future: Strategic approaches to quantum ai integration for industry transformation. Ai. DOI: 10.3390/ai5010015

Imam, R., Areeb, Q. M., Alturki, A., & Anwer, F. (2021). Systematic and critical review of rsa based public key cryptographic schemes: Past and present status. IEEE access. DOI: 10.1109/ACCESS.2021.3129224

Irfan, M., Dias, R., Rastogi, R., & Zebende, G. F. (2025). *Generative AI insights for financial decision making*. IGI Global.

Irfan, M., Elmogy, M., Gupta, S., Khalifa, F., & Dias, R. T. (2024). *AI-driven decentralized finance and the future of finance*. IGI Global USA.

Irfan, M., Hussainey, K., Bukhari, S. A. C., & Nam, Y. (2024). *Issues of sustainability in AI and new-age thematic investing*. IGI Global.

Irfan, M., Kadry, S., Sharif, M., & Khan, H. U. (2023). *Fintech applications in Islamic finance: AI, machine learning, and blockchain techniques*. IGI Global.

Irfan, M., Mohammed, M., Kassim, S., & Ofori, K. S. (2024). *The future of indigenous inclusivity: Unlocking finance for economic development*. IGI Global.

Jhessim, E., & Santigie-Sankoh, T. (2025). Quantum computing in financial security: A risk management framework for systemically important financial institutions. World Journal of Advanced Research and Reviews, 25(1), 1963-1967. DOI: 10.30574/wjarr.2025.25.1.0235

Kanaparthi, V. K. (2024). Navigating uncertainty: enhancing markowitz asset allocation strategies through out-of-sample analysis. FinTech. mdpi.commdpi.comDOI: 10.3390/fintech3010010

Liang, J. (2025). Machine learning in asset pricing and portfolio optimization. https://theses.gla.ac.uk/84858/ gla.ac.uk

Liu, Q., Jiao, Y., & Guo, S. (2022). GARCH pricing and hedging of VIX options. [HTML]. *Journal of Futures Markets*. Advance online publication. DOI: 10.1002/fut.22318

Lo, S., Baird, S. G., Schrier, J., Blaiszik, B., Carson, N., Foster, I., ... & Aspuru-Guzik, A. (2024). Review of low-cost self-driving laboratories in chemistry and materials science: the "frugal twin" concept. Digital Discovery, 3(5), 842-868. DOI: 10.1039/d3dd00223c

Memon, Q. A., Al Ahmad, M., & Pecht, M. (2024). Quantum computing: navigating the future of computation, challenges, and technological breakthroughs. Quantum Reports. DOI: 10.3390/quantum6040039

Meng, X., Hu, X., Tian, Y., Dong, G., Lambiotte, R., Gao, J., & Havlin, S. (2023). Percolation theories for quantum networks. Entropy, 25(11), 1564. DOI: 10.3390/e25111564

Mittal, S., Koushik, P., Batra, I., & Whig, P. (2024). AI-Driven Inventory Management for Optimizing Operations With Quantum Computing. In Quantum Computing and Supply Chain Management: A New Era of Optimization (pp. 125-140). IGI Global. DOI: 10.4018/979-8-3693-4107-0.ch009

Mosteanu, N. R., & Faccia, A. (2021). Fintech frontiers in quantum computing, fractals, and blockchain distributed ledger: Paradigm shifts and open innovation. Journal of Open Innovation: Technology, Market, and Complexity, 7(1), 19. DOI: 10.3390/joitmc7010019

Mzukwa, A. (2024). Exploring Next-Generation Architectures for Advanced Computing Systems: Challenges and Opportunities. Journal of Advanced Computing Systems. DOI: 10.69987/JACS..2024.40601

Neway, A. S. (2024). Beyond the bit: A guide to quantum computing and its impact. ISBN 9798-300-628 3-38

Outeiral, C., Strahm, M., Shi, J., Morris, G. M., Benjamin, S. C., & Deane, C. M. (2021). The prospects of quantum computing in computational molecular biology. Wiley Interdisciplinary Reviews: Computational Molecular Science, 11(1), e1481. DOI: 10.1002/wcms.1481

Overmars, A. & Venkatraman, S. (2021). New semi-prime factorization and application in large rsa key attacks. Journal of Cybersecurity and Privacy. DOI: 10.3390/jcp1040033

Palaniappan, V., Ishak, I., Ibrahim, H., Sidi, F., & Zukarnain, Z. A. (2024). A Review on High Frequency Trading Forecasting Methods: Opportunity and Challenges for Quantum based Method. IEEE Access. DOI: 10.1109/ACCESS.2024.3418458

Paramesha, M., Rane, N. L., & Rane, J. (2024). Artificial intelligence, machine learning, deep learning, and blockchain in financial and banking services: A comprehensive review. Partners Universal Multidisciplinary Research Journal, 1(2), 51-67. pumrj.comDOI: 0.5281/zenodo.12826933

Pfaendler, S. M. L., Konson, K., & Greinert, F. (2024). Advancements in quantum computing—viewpoint: Building adoption and competency in industry. Datenbank-spektrum. DOI: 10.1007/s13222-024-00467-4

Rayhana, R., Bai, L., Xiao, G., Liao, M., & Liu, Z. (2024). Digital twin models: Functions, challenges, and industry applications. [HTML]. *IEEE Journal of Radio Frequency Identification*. Advance online publication. DOI: 10.1109/JR-FID.2024.3387996

Rishiwal, V., Agarwal, U., Yadav, M., Tanwar, S., Garg, D., & Guizani, M. (2025). A New Alliance of Machine Learning and Quantum Computing: Concepts, Attacks, and Challenges in IoT Networks. [HTML]. *IEEE Internet ofThings Journal*. Advance online publication. DOI: 10.1109/JIOT.2025.3535414

Roger, J. D. D. (2024). AI-Driven Financial Modeling Techniques: Transforming Investment Strategies. The Journal of Applied Business and Economics. https://dx .doi.Org/http://dx.doi.org/10.14453/aabf1.vl8i4.09

Saxena, A., Mancilla, J., Montalban, I., & Pere, C. (2023). Financial Modeling Using Quantum Computing: Design and manage quantum machine learning solutions for financial analysis and decision making. ISBN 978-1-80461-842-4

Seth, B., Dalal, S., Jaglan, V., Le, D. N., Mohan, S., & Srivastava, G. (2022). Integrating encryption techniques for secure data storage in the cloud. [HTML]. *Transactions on Emerging Telecommunications Technologies*, *33*(4), e4108. DOI: 10.1002/ett.4108

Sharma, R., Mehta, K., & Sharma, P. (2024). Role of Artificial Intelligence and Machine Learning in Fraud Detection and Prevention. In Risks and Challenges of AI-Driven Finance: Bias, Ethics, and Security (pp. 90-120). IGI Global. DOI: 10.4018/979-8-3693-2185-0.ch005

Szczesny, B., & Gryncewicz, W. (2024). Between 0 and 1. Exploring the Algorithmic Restraints and the Potential of Quantum Computing in the Financial Sector. *European Conference on Artificial Intelligence*.]DOI: 10.1007/978-3-031-78468-2_4

Ukpabi, D., Karjaluoto, H., Bötticher, A., Nikiforova, A., Petrescu, D., Schindler, P., ... & Lehmann, L. (2023). Framework for understanding quantum computing use cases from a multidisciplinary perspective and future research directions. Futures, 154, 103277. DOI: 10.1016/j.futures.2023.103277

Vashishth, T. K., Sharma, V., Kaushik, V., Singh, A., & Kaushik, S. (2025). Exploring Quantum Challenges and Opportunities of Quantum Machine Learning Adoption in Finance. Machine Learning and Modeling Techniques in Financial Data Science, 437-460. DOI: 10.4018/979-8-3693-8186-1.ch017

Wang, J., David, L. K., Cisse, I. I., & Angel, V. (2024). Quantum computing and its implications for Asian innovation ecosystems. [HTML] [REMOVED HYPERLINK FIELD]. *Asian Journal of Technology Innovation*, 1–50. DOI: 10.1080/19761597.2024.2420920

Wang, S., Asif, M., Shahzad, M. F., & Ashfaq, M. (2024). Data privacy and cybersecurity challenges in the digital transformation of the banking sector. [HTML]. *Computers & Security*. Advance online publication. DOI: 10.1016/j.cose.2024.104051

Yazdi, M. (2024). Application of Quantum Computing in Reliability Analysis. In *Advances in Computational Mathematics for Industrial System Reliability and Maintainability* (pp. 139–154). Springer Nature Switzerland. DOI: 10.1007/978-3-031-53514-7_8

Zaharudin, K. Z., Young, M. R., & Hsu, W. H. (2022). High-frequency trading: Definition, implications, and controversies. Journal of Economic Surveys, 36(1), 75-107. DOI: 10.1111/joes.12434

Zhang, M., Lu, T., & Shi, C. (2024). Navigating the Factor Zoo: The Science of Quantitative Investing. DOI: 10.4324/9781003480204

Compilation of References

Abate, G., Basile, I., & Ferrari, P. (2024). The integration of environmental, social and governance criteria in portfolio optimization: An empirical analysis. *Corporate Social Responsibility and Environmental Management*, *31*(3), 2054–2065.

Abbas, A., Ambainis, A., Augustino, B., Bärtschi, A., Buhrman, H., Coffrin, C., Cortiana, G., Dunjko, V., Egger, D. J., Elmegreen, B. G., Franco, N., Fratini, F., Fuller, B., Gacon, J., Gonciulea, C., Gribling, S., Gupta, S., Hadfield, S., Heese, R., & Zoufal, C. (2024). Challenges and opportunities in quantum optimization [Review]. *Nature Reviews. Physics*, *6*(12), 718–735. DOI: 10.1038/s42254-024-00770-9

Abbasi, M., Cardoso, F., Váz, P., Silva, J., & Martins, P. (2025). A Practical Performance Benchmark of Post-Quantum Cryptography Across Heterogeneous Computing Environments [Article]. *Cryptography*, *9*(2), 32. Advance online publication. DOI: 10.3390/cryptography9020032

Abdikhakimov, I. (2024). The Interplay of Quantum Computing, Blockchain Systems, and Privacy Laws: Challenges and Opportunities. Elita. uz-Elektron Ilmiy Jurnal, 2(1), 1-12.

Abohashima, Z., Elhosen, M., Houssein, E. H., & Mohamed, W. M. (2020). *Classification with Quantum Machine Learning: A Survey* (Version 1). arXiv. DOI: 10.48550/ARXIV.2006.12270

Adamowicz, M. (2022). Green deal, green growth and green economy as a means of support for attaining the sustainable development goals. *Sustainability*, *14*(10), 5901.

Adeola, O., Adeleye, I., Muhammed, G., Olajubu, B. J., Oji, C., & Ibelegbu, O. (2022). Savings groups in Nigeria. In *Transforming Africa: How savings groups foster financial inclusion, resilience and economic development* (pp. 193–216). Emerald Publishing Limited.

Ahluwalia, M. S., & Patel, U. (2021). *Getting to net zero: an approach for India at CoP-26*. Centre for Social and Economic Progress.

Ahmed, M. (2026). Quantum Computing: Transforming the Landscape of Financial Markets. In *Emerging Trends and Innovations in Financial Services: A Futurology Perspective* (pp. 263-276). IGI Global Scientific Publishing.

Ahmed, S. F., Alam, M. S. B., Hassan, M., Rozbu, M. R., Ishtiak, T., Rafa, N., ... & Gandomi, A. H. (2023). Deep learning modelling techniques: current progress, applications, advantages, and challenges. Artificial Intelligence Review, 56(11), 13521-13617. DOI: 10.1007/s10462-023-10466-8

Ajagbe, S. A., Majola, S., & Mudali, P. (2025, December). Comparative analysis of machine learning algorithms for money laundering detection. *Discover Artificial Intelligence*, *05*(01). Advance online publication. DOI: 10.1007/s44163-025-00397-4

Al Ghatrifi, M. O. M., Al Amairi, J. S. S., & Thottoli, M. M. (2023). Surfing the technology wave: An international perspective on enhancing teaching and learning in accounting. *Computers and Education: Artificial Intelligence*, *4*, 100144.

Alashetty, A., Vani, M. P., Anitha, E., & Satyamurty, C. V. (2025). Introduction of quantum computing. In *Quantum machine learning in industrial automation* (pp. 277–304). Springer Nature Switzerland.

Albareti, F. D., Ankenbrand, T., Bieri, D., Hänggi, E., Lötscher, D., Stettler, S., & Schöngens, M. (2022). A structured survey of quantum computing for the financial industry. arXiv preprint arXiv:2204.10026.

Alcazar, J., Cadarso, A., Katabarwa, A., Mauri, M., Peropadre, B., Wang, G., & Cao, Y. (2022). Quantum algorithm for credit valuation adjustments [Article]. *New Journal of Physics*, *24*(2), 023036. Advance online publication. DOI: 10.1088/1367-2630/ac5003

Alexander, P. A., Graham, S., & Harris, K. R. (1998). A Perspective on Strategy Research: Progress and Prospects. *Educational Psychology Review*, *10*(2), 129–154. DOI: 10.1023/A:1022185502996

Ali, S., Wadho, S. A., Talpur, K. R., Talpur, B. A., & Alshudukhi, K. S. (2025, December). Next-Generation Quantum Security: The Impact of Quantum Computing on Cybersecurity—Threats, Mitigations, and Solutions. *Computers & Electrical Engineering*, *128*. Advance online publication. DOI: 10.1016/j.compeleceng.2025.110649

Alkurdi, A., Al Amosh, H., & Khatib, S. F. (2024). The mediating role of carbon emissions in the relationship between the board attributes and ESG performance: European evidence. *EuroMed Journal of Business*, *19*(4), 1016–1041.

Allioui, H. & Mourdi, Y. (2023). Exploring the full potentials of IoT for better financial growth and stability: A comprehensive survey. Sensors. DOI: 10.3390/s23198015

Alonso-Conde, A. B., & Rojo-Suárez, J. (2020). On the effect of green bonds on the profitability and credit quality of project financing. *Sustainability*, *12*(16), 6695.

Al-Zubi, Z., Shaban, O. S., & Alnaser, N. (2014). The effect of business intelligence tools on raising the efficiency of modern management accounting. *International Review of Management and Business Research*, *3*(1), 68.

Anakpo, G., Xhate, Z., & Mishi, S. (2023). The policies, practices, and challenges of digital financial inclusion for sustainable development: The case of the developing economy. *FinTech*, *2*(2), 327–343.

Arcuri, M. C., Gandolfi, G., & Laurini, F. (2023). Robust portfolio optimization for banking foundations: a CVaR approach for asset allocation with mandatory constraints. Central European Journal of Operations Research, 31(2), 557-581. DOI: 10.1007/s10100-022-00821-5

Arner, D. W., Buckley, R. P., Zetzsche, D. A., & Veidt, R. (2020). Sustainability, FinTech and financial inclusion. *European Business Organization Law Review*, *21*(1), 7–35.

Asni, F., Zulkifli, M. I., & Yusli, Y. (2024). Acceptance of zakat institutions in Malaysia towards micro credit–Qard Hasan financing through zakat fund (MCZF) for post-pandemic Asnaf entrepreneurs. *Journal of Islamic Accounting and Business Research*.

Atadoga, A., Ike, C. U., Asuzu, O. F., Ayinla, B. S., Ndubuisi, N. L., & Adeleye, R. A. (2024). The intersection of Ai and Quantum Computing in financial markets: A critical review. Comput. Sci. IT Res. j., 5(2), 461–472.

Awan, U., Hannola, L., Tandon, A., Goyal, R. K., & Dhir, A. (2022). Quantum computing challenges in the software industry. A fuzzy AHP-based approach. Information and Software Technology, 147, 106896. DOI: 10.1016/j.infsof.2022.106896

Ayanzadeh, R., Alavisamani, N., Das, P., & Qureshi, M. (2023). FrozenQubits: Boosting Fidelity of QAOA by Skipping Hotspot Nodes. International Conference on Architectural Support for Programming Languages and Operating Systems - ASPLOS

Aziz, S., Ahmed, I., Khan, K., & Khalid, M. (2024). Emerging trends and approaches for designing net-zero low-carbon integrated energy networks: A review of current practices. *Arabian Journal for Science and Engineering*, *49*(5), 6163–6185.

Baaquie, B. E. (2022). Quantum Computations and Option Pricing. In *Looking Beyond the Frontiers of Science: Dedicated to the 80th Birthday of K.K. Phua* (pp. 159-179). World Scientific Publishing Co. https://doi.org/DOI: 10.1142/9789811263699_0027

Baaquie, B. E. (2013). Financial modeling and quantum mathematics. *Computers & Mathematics with Applications (Oxford, England)*, *65*(10), 1665–1673. DOI: 10.1016/j.camwa.2013.01.025

Badmus, O., Rajput, S., Arogundade, J., & Williams, M. (2024). AI-driven business analytics and decision making. *World Journal of Advanced Research and Reviews*, *24*(1), 616–633.

Baiardi, A., Christandl, M., & Reiher, M. (2023). Quantum computing for molecular biology. *ChemBioChem*, *24*(13), e202300120. PMID: 37151197

Bansal, S., Mani, S. P., Gupta, H., & Maurya, S. (2023). Sustainable development of the green bond markets in India: Challenges and strategies. *Sustainable Development*, *31*(1), 237–252.

Baratta, A., Cimino, A., Longo, F., Solina, V., & Verteramo, S. (2023). The impact of ESG practices in industry with a focus on carbon emissions: Insights and future perspectives. *Sustainability*, *15*(8), 6685.

Barral, D., Cardama, F. J., Díaz-Camacho, G., Faílde, D., Llovo, I. F., Mussa-Juane, M., & Gómez, A. (2025). Review of distributed quantum computing: From single qpu to high performance quantum computing. *Computer Science Review*, *57*, 100747.

Bauer, B., Wecker, D., Millis, A. J., Hastings, M. B., & Troyer, M. (2016). Hybrid Quantum-Classical Approach to Correlated Materials. *Physical Review X*, *6*(3), 031045. DOI: 10.1103/PhysRevX.6.031045

Beck, T., & Demirguc-Kunt, A. (2008). Access to finance: An unfinished agenda. *The World Bank Economic Review*, *22*(3), 383–396.

Bhasin, N. K., Kadyan, S., & Santosh, K., HP, R., Changala, R., & Bala, B. K. (2024). Enhancing Quantum Machine Learning Algorithms for Optimized Financial Portfolio Management. In 2024 Third International Conference on Intelligent Techniques in Control, Optimization and Signal Processing (INCOS) (pp. 1-7). IEEE.

Bhasin, A., & Tripathi, M. (2021). Quantum computing at an inflection point: Are we ready for a new paradigm. [HTML]. *IEEE Transactions on Engineering Management*, *70*(7), 2546–2557. DOI: 10.1109/TEM.2021.3103904

Bhat, J. R., AlQahtani, S. A., & Nekovee, M. (2023). FinTech enablers, use cases, and role of future internet of things. Journal of King Saud University-Computer and Information Sciences, 35(1), 87-101. DOI: 10.1016/j.jksuci.2022.08.033

Bhattacharyya, A., & Nanda, A. (2022). Green finance, fintech and environmental performance: Evidence from China. *Economic Modelling*, *114*, 105925.

Bhutta, U. S., Tariq, A., Farrukh, M., Raza, A., & Iqbal, M. K. (2022). Green bonds for sustainable development: Review of literature on development and impact of green bonds. *Technological Forecasting and Social Change*, *175*, 121378.

Boretti, A. (2024). Technical, economic, and societal risks in the progress of artificial intelligence driven quantum technologies. Discover Artificial Intelligence. DOI: 10.1007/s44163-024-00171-y

Bouland, A., van Dam, W., Joorati, H., Kerenidis, I., & Prakash, A. (2020). Prospects and challenges of quantum finance.

Bremner, M., Devitt, S., & Zerenturk, E. (2024). *Quantum algorithms and applications*. Office of the NSW Chief Scientist & Engineer.

Brest, P., & Born, K. (2013). When can impact investing create real impact? *Stanford Social Innovation Review*, *11*(4), 22–31.

Broby, D. (2022). The use of predictive analytics in finance. *The Journal of Financial Data Science*, *8*, 145–165.

Buchak, G., Matvos, G., Piskorski, T., & Seru, A. (2018). Fintech, regulatory arbitrage, and the rise of shadow banks. *Journal of Financial Economics*, *130*(3), 453–473.

Bunescu, L., & Vârtei, A. M. (2024a). Modern finance through quantum computing-A systematic literature review. *PLoS One*, *19*(7), e0304317. PMID: 39024227

Capellaro, C., Martín-Cuevas, R., Calleja, G., Halffmann, P., & Sharma, S. (2025). Application of Quantum Computing in the Energy Industry, Decarbonization, and Sustainability. In *Quantum Technology Applications, Impact, and Future Challenges* (pp. 09-36). CRC Press. https://doi.org/DOI: 10.1201/9781003537243-2

Carrera Vazquez, A., & Woerner, S. (2021). Efficient State Preparation for Quantum Amplitude Estimation [Article]. *Physical Review Applied*, *15*(3), 034027. Advance online publication. DOI: 10.1103/PhysRevApplied.15.034027

Cerezo, M., Verdon, G., Huang, H.-Y., Cincio, L., & Coles, P. J. (2022). Challenges and opportunities in quantum machine learning. *Nature Computational Science*, *2*(9), 567–576. DOI: 10.1038/s43588-022-00311-3 PMID: 38177473

Chambers-Jones, C. (2021). AI, big data, quantum computing, and financial exclusion: Tempering enthusiasm and offering a human-centric approach to policy. *FinTech. Artificial Intelligence and Law*, •••, 193–210.

Chandrasekar, V., & Wisetsri, W. (2025). The Prospects for Applications of Quantum Computing in the Financial Sector. Shaping Cutting-Edge Technologies and Applications for Digital Banking and Financial Services, 106.

Chang, Y. J., Wang, W. T., Chen, H. Y., Liao, S. W., & Chang, C. R. (2024). A novel approach for quantum financial simulation and quantum state preparation. *Quantum Machine Intelligence*, *6*(1), 24.

Chan, R. (2021). Ensuring impactful performance in green bonds and sustainability-linked loans. *TheADELAIDE LAW REVIEW*, *42*(1), 221–258.

Cheng, M., & Qu, Y. (2020). Does bank FinTech reduce credit risk? Evidence from China. *Pacific-Basin Finance Journal*, *63*, 101398.

Chen, L., Msigwa, G., Yang, M., Osman, A. I., Fawzy, S., Rooney, D. W., & Yap, P. S. (2022). Strategies to achieve a carbon neutral society: A review. *Environmental Chemistry Letters*, *20*(4), 2277–2310. PMID: 35431715

Chen, M. A., Wu, Q., & Yang, B. (2019). How valuable is fintech innovation? *Review of Financial Studies*, *32*(5), 2062–2106.

Chen, Y., & Zhao, Z. J. (2021). The rise of green bonds for sustainable finance: Global standards and issues with the expanding Chinese market. *Current Opinion in Environmental Sustainability*, *52*, 54–57.

Cherepovitsyn, A., Solovyova, V., & Dmitrieva, D. (2023). New challenges for the sustainable development of the rare-earth metals sector in Russia: Transforming industrial policies. *Resources Policy*, *81*, 103347.

Chien, F., Ngo, Q. T., Hsu, C. C., Chau, K. Y., & Iram, R. (2021). Assessing the mechanism of barriers towards green finance and public spending in small and medium enterprises from developed countries. *Environmental Science and Pollution Research International*, *28*(43), 60495–60510. PMID: 34156623

Choi, M., Eom, C., & Kang, H.-G. (2023, February 01). Quantum Finance and Its Implications. *Asian Review of Financial Research*, *36*(01), 103–129. DOI: 10.37197/ARFR.2023.36.1.4

Choustova, O. (2004). Bohmian mechanics for financial processes. *Journal of Modern Optics*, *51*(6–7), 1111. DOI: 10.1080/09500340408233645

Chou, Y. H., Wu, C. H., Huang, P. S., Kuo, S. Y., Jiang, Y. C., Kuo, S. Y., & Chang, C. R. (2024, June). Hybrid quantum annealing with innovative trend ratio model for portfolio optimization. In *2024 IEEE Congress on Evolutionary Computation (CEC)* (pp. 1-8). IEEE.

Chung, D., Lee, S., Choi, D., & Lee, J. (2022, October 01). Alternative Tower Field Construction for Quantum Implementation of the AES S-Box. *IEEE Transactions on Computers*, *71*(10), 2553–2564. DOI: 10.1109/TC.2021.3135759

Claudiu, B., Cosmin, E., Otniel, D., & Andrei, A. (2024). Enhancing the Financial Sector with Quantum Computing: A Comprehensive Review of Current and Future Applications. *22nd International Conference on Informatics in Economy, IE 2023. 367.* Bucharest: Springer Science and Business Media Deutschland GmbH. https://doi.org/DOI: 10.1007/978-981-99-6529-8_17

Claudiu, B., Cosmin, E., Otniel, D., & Andrei, A. (2024). *Enhancing the Financial Sector with Quantum Computing: A Comprehensive Review of Current and Future Applications*. Smart Innovation, Systems and Technologies.

Coccia, M. (2024). Technological trajectories in quantum computing to design a quantum ecosystem for industrial change. *Technology Analysis and Strategic Management, 36*(8), 1733–1748.

Coccia, M., & Roshani, S. (2024). Path-breaking directions in quantum computing technology: A patent analysis with multiple techniques. *Journal of the Knowledge Economy*, •••, 1–34.

Columbus Chinnappan, C., Thanaraj Krishnan, P., Elamaran, E., Arul, R., & Sunil Kumar, T. (2025). Quantum computing: Foundations, architecture and applications. *Engineering Reports*, *7*(8), e70337.

Compston, H., & Bailey, I. (2016). Climate policy strength compared: China, the US, the EU, India, Russia, and Japan. *Climate Policy*, *16*(2), 145–164.

Corley-Coulibaly, M., Grasselli, G., & Postolachi, I. (2023). *Promoting and enforcing compliance with labour provisions in trade agreements: Comparative analysis of Canada, European Union and United States approaches and practices*. ILO.

Cuomo, M. T., & Foroudi, P. (2025). Tools and Techniques for Quantum Business. In M. T. Cuomo & P. Foroudi, *Quantum Level Business Model: A New Managerial Perspective* (Vol. 3, pp. 83–104). Springer Nature Switzerland. DOI: 10.1007/978-3-031-92052-3_5

D'Angelo, V., Cappa, F., & Peruffo, E. (2023). Green manufacturing for sustainable development: The positive effects of green activities, green investments, and non-green products on economic performance. *Business Strategy and the Environment*, *32*(4), 1900–1913.

Dai, X., & Zhang, Y. (2011). Additivity Of quantum channel capacity. *Proceedings - 2011 International Conference on Intelligence Science and Information Engineering, ISIE 2011*, 199–201. DOI: 10.1109/ISIE.2011.102

Darbyshire, P. (2005). Quantum physics meets classical finance. *Physics World*, *18*(5), 25–29. DOI: 10.1088/2058-7058/18/5/36

De Jong, A., Nguyen, T. T., Nguyen, T. V., & Sila, V. (2022). How does green finance impact green innovation? *Journal of Financial and Quantitative Analysis, 57*(3), 863–893.

de Lima Marquezino, F., Portugal, R., & Lavor, C. (2019). Shor's algorithm for integer factorization. In *SpringerBriefs in Computer Science* (pp. 57–77). Springer., DOI: 10.1007/978-3-030-19066-8_4

Dehn, V., & Wellens, T. (2024). A hybrid quantum-classical approach to warm-starting optimization. *Proceedings of SPIE - the International Society for Optical Engineering*.

Demiralay, S., Gencer, H. G., & Bayraci, S. (2022). Carbon credit futures as an emerging asset: Hedging, diversification and downside risks. *Energy Economics, 113*, 106196.

Devi, P., Desai, S. S., Kumar, R., Naruka, M. S., & Tripathi, V. (2024, December). A Strategic Innovations for Stock Market Optimization by Using Data Science & Explainable AI in High Frequency Trading. In 2024 International Conference on IoT Based Control Networks and Intelligent Systems (ICICNIS) (pp. 1510-1515). IEEE. DOI: 10.1109/ICICNIS64247.2024.10823313

Devikar, R. N., Patil, D. V., & Prakash, V. C. (2020). A hybrid computing approach to improve convergence time for scalable network. *Sadhana, 45*(1), 225. DOI: 10.1007/s12046-020-01454-7

Dey, N., Ghosh, M., & Chakrabarti, A. (2022). Quantum solutions to possible challenges of blockchain technology. In *Quantum and Blockchain for Modern Computing Systems: Vision and Advancements: Quantum and Blockchain Technologies: Current Trends.*

Di Meglio, A., Jansen, K., Tavernelli, I., Alexandrou, C., Arunachalam, S., Bauer, C. W., & Zhang, J. (2024). Quantum computing for high-energy physics: State of the art and challenges. *PFX Quantum : a Physical Review Journal, 5*(3), 037001.

Dixit, S. (2022). AI-powered risk modeling in quantum finance: Redefining enterprise decision systems.

Dolu-Surabhi, S. N. (2024). Advancing Financial Decision-Making through Quantum Computing and Cloud-Based AI Models: A Comparative Analysis of Predictive Algorithms. *Journal of Artificial Intelligence and Big Data Disciplines, 1*(1), 27–37.

Dong, Y., Zheng, H., & Zhu, J. (2024). A narrative review on quantum finance theory. *International Journal of Quantum Information, 22*(6). Advance online publication. DOI: 10.1142/S0219749924500163

Dorfleitner, G., Hornuf, L., Schmitt, M., & Weber, M. (2017). *FinTech in Germany*. Springer.

Dörn, S. (2009). Quantum algorithms for graph and algebra problems [Article]. *Recent Patents on Computer Science*, *2*(2), 124–130. DOI: 10.2174/1874479610902020124

Dri, E., Aita, A., Giusto, E., Ricossa, D., & Corbelletto, D. (2023, April). A More General Quantum Credit Risk Analysis Framework. *Entropy (Basel, Switzerland)*, *25*(04). Advance online publication. DOI: 10.3390/e25040593 PMID: 37190381

Dwivedi, K., Haghparast, M., & Mikkonen, T. (2024). Quantum software engineering and quantum software development lifecycle: A survey. *Cluster Computing*, *27*(6), 7127–7145.

Economist Intelligence Unit. (2019). A whole new world: How technology is driving the evolution of intelligent banking. Temenos. https://impact.economist.com/perspectives/financial-services/whole-new-world-how-technology-driving-evolution-intelligent-banking

Egger, D. J., Gambella, C., Marecek, J., McFaddin, S., Mevissen, M., Raymond, R., Simonetto, A., Woerner, S., & Yndurain, E. (2020). Quantum Computing for Finance: State-of-the-Art and Future Prospects [Article]. *IEEE Transactions on Quantum Engineering*, *1*, 3101724. Advance online publication. DOI: 10.1109/TQE.2020.3030314

Egger, D. J., Gambella, C., Marecek, J., McFaddin, S., Mevissen, M., Raymond, R., Simonetto, A., Woerner, S., & Yndurain, E. (2020). Quantum computing for finance: State-of-the-art and future prospects. *IEEE Transactions on Quantum Engineering*, *1*, 1–24.

Ekert, A., Hayden, P. M., & Inamori, H. (2002). Basic concepts in quantum computation. In *Coherent atomic matter waves: 27 July–27 August 1999* (pp. 661–701). Springer Berlin Heidelberg.

Elmisery, A. M., Sertovic, M., Zayin, A., & Watson, P. (2025). Cyber Threats in Financial Transactions—Addressing the Dual Challenge of AI and Quantum Computing. *arXiv preprint arXiv:2503.15678*.

Elmisery, A. M., Sertovic, M., Zayin, A., & Watson, P. (2025a). *Cyber Threats in Financial Transactions—Addressing the Dual Challenge of AI and Quantum Computing* (Version 1). arXiv. DOI: 10.48550/ARXIV.2503.15678

Elyashiv, T. (2025). Quantum revolution investment scenario examples, or putting theory to practice. In *Investing in revolutions: Creating wealth from transformational technology waves* (pp. 187–221). Apress.

Eswaran, U., Eswaran, V., Murali, K., & Eswaran, V. (2025). Quantum Computing Applications. In *Quantum Computing: the Future of Information Processing* (pp. 42–61). CRC Press., DOI: 10.1201/9781003499459-3

Faccia, A. (2024). Quantum Fintech. In *Artificial Intelligence and beyond for Finance* (Vol. 15, pp. 235–263). World Scientific Publishing Co., https://www.scopus.com/inward/record.uri?eid=2-s2.0-85206039703&partnerID=40&md5=ab840cf89e262e04a8c7afeadcadefaa

Fay, M. (2012). *Inclusive green growth: The pathway to sustainable development*. World Bank Publications.

Filipović, S., Lior, N., & Radovanović, M. (2022). The green deal–just transition and sustainable development goals Nexus. *Renewable & Sustainable Energy Reviews, 168*, 112759.

Fisher, P. F. (1993). Algorithm and implementation uncertainty in viewshed analysis. *International Journal of Geographical Information Systems*, *7*(4), 331–347. DOI: 10.1080/02693799308901965

Friede, G., Busch, T., & Bassen, A. (2015). ESG and financial performance: Aggregated evidence from more than 2000 empirical studies. *Journal of Sustainable Finance & Investment*, *5*(4), 210–233.

Fu, J., Xu, M., Qian, H., & Li, Z. (2024). Theoretical and Experimental Performance Analysis on Error-Bounded Quantum Search Process. *Journal of Systems Science and Complexity*. Advance online publication. DOI: 10.1007/s11424-024-4062-7a

Gabor, T., Zielinski, S., Roch, C., Feld, S., & Linnhoff-Popien, C. (2020). The U Q platform: A u nifed approach to q uantum annealing. *5th International Conference on Computer and Communication Systems, ICCCS 2020* (pp. 115-119). Shanghai: Institute of Electrical and Electronics Engineers Inc. https://doi.org/DOI: 10.1109/ICCCS49078.2020.9118547

Gabr, D. H., & ElBannan, M. A. (2025). Is it worth it to go green? ESG disclosure, carbon emissions and firm financial performance in emerging markets. *Review of Accounting and Finance*, *24*(2), 193–217.

Gad, A. G. (2022). Particle swarm optimization algorithm and its applications: a systematic review. Archives of computational methods in engineering. DOI: 10.1007/s11831-021-09694-4

Galatsanos-Dueck, J. (2024). *Re-imagining Drug Discovery with Quantum Computing: A Framework and Critical Benchmark Analysis for achieving Quantum Economic Advantage*. Massachusetts Institute of Technology.

Gatti, S. (2023). *Project finance in theory and practice: designing, structuring, and financing private and public projects*. Elsevier.

Ghelani, D., Hua, T. K., & Koduru, S. K. R. (2022). Cyber security threats, vulnerabilities, and security solutions models in banking. *Authorea Preprints*.

Ghose, P., & Patra, S. (2023). An interdisciplinary approach to cognitive modelling: A framework based on philosophy and modern science. http://doi.org/ jgu.edu. inDOI: 10.17304/ijil.vol20.3.4

Ghosh, D. (2024). Quantum Computing for Real-Time Decision Making in Supply Chain Operations. In *Quantum Computing and Supply Chain Management: A New Era of Optimization* (pp. 176–186). IGI Global.

Gill, S. S., Kumar, A., Singh, H., Singh, M., Kaur, K., Usman, M., & Buyya, R. (2022). Quantum computing: A taxonomy, systematic review and future directions. Software: Practice and Experience, 52(1), 66-114. https://onlinelibrary.wiley.com/doi/10.1002/spe.3039

Girasa, R., & Scalabrini, G. J. (2022). *Regulation of innovative technologies: blockchain, artificial intelligence and quantum computing*. Springer Nature.

Global Sustainable Investment Alliance. (2021). *Global Sustainable Investment Review 2020*. Retrieved from http://www.gsi-alliance.org/wp-content/uploads/2021/08/GSIR-20201.pdf

Gomber, P., & Haferkorn, M. (2013). High-Frequency-Trading: High-Frequency-Trading Technologies and Their Implications for Electronic Securities Trading. *Business & Information Systems Engineering*, *5*(2), 97–99. DOI: 10.1007/s12599-013-0255-7

Gomber, P., Kauffman, R. J., Parker, C., & Weber, B. W. (2018). On the fintech revolution: Interpreting the forces of innovation, disruption, and transformation in financial services. *Journal of Management Information Systems*, *35*(1), 220–265.

Gómez, A., Leitao, Á., Manzano, A., Musso, D., Nogueiras, M. R., Ordóñez, G., & Vázquez, C. (2022). A survey on quantum computational finance for derivatives pricing and VaR. *Archives of Computational Methods in Engineering*, *29*(6), 4137–4163.

Gonzalez, E. D., Sijariya, R., Singh, A. K., & Garg, V. (2025). Integrating Climate Change, Social Responsibility and Electronic Financial Inclusion: A Pathway to Sustainable Development. In *Climate Change and Social Responsibility* (pp. 147-164). Emerald Publishing Limited.

Griffin, P., & Sampat, R. (2021). Quantum Computing for Supply Chain Finance. *2021 IEEE International Conference on Services Computing, SCC 2021* (pp. 456-459). Online: Institute of Electrical and Electronics Engineers Inc. https://doi.org/DOI: 10.1109/SCC53864.2021.00066

Guo, Z., Song, T., & Lin, G. (2024). Portfolio optimization based on quantum linear algorithm. *Physica Scripta*, *99*(8), 85107.

Habib, A., Oláh, J., Khan, M. H., & Luboš, S. (2025). Does integration of ESG disclosure and green financing improve firm performance: Practical applications of stakeholders' theory. *Heliyon*, *11*(4). PMID: 40028513

Hamood, M. M., Atia, T. S., & Moosa, A. A. (2025). Performance evaluation of post quantum digital signature algorithms over WDM optical communication system [Article]. *Journal of Optical Communications*. https://doi.org/DOI: 10.1515/joc-2025-0104

Han, H., Liu, Z., Barrios Barrios, M., Li, J., Zeng, Z., Sarhan, N., & Awwad, E. M. (2024). Time series forecasting model for non-stationary series pattern extraction using deep learning and GARCH modeling. Journal of Cloud Computing, 13(1), 2. DOI: 10.1186/s13677-023-00576-7

Hanif, M. W., & Zheng, S. (2025). Assessing the economic impact of green finance and renewable energy use on environmental sustainability in high-polluting sectors. *Renewable Energy*, *247*, 123017.

Hasan, K. F., Simpson, L., Baee, M. A. R., Islam, C., Rahman, Z., Armstrong, W., ... & McKague, M. (2024). A framework for migrating to post-quantum cryptography: Security dependency analysis and case studies. IEEE Access, 12, 23427-23450. DOI: 10.1109/ACCESS.2024.3360412

Hegade, N. N., Paul, K., Ding, Y., Sanz, M., Albarrán-Arriagada, F., Solano, E., & Chen, X. (2021). Shortcuts to adiabaticity in digitized adiabatic quantum computing. *Physical Review Applied*, *15*(2), 024038.

Hellstern, G., & Yeniaras, E. (2025). *Quantum Leap in Finance: Economic Advantages, Security, and Post-Quantum Readiness* (Version 1). arXiv. DOI: 10.48550/ARXIV.2508.21548

He, Q., Li, W., Zhang, P., & Guo, C. (2024). Corporate governance, policy robustness and carbon neutrality in the digital economy: Insights from the natural resource exploitation sector. *Resources Policy*, *88*, 104477.

Herbert, S. (2022). Quantum Monte Carlo Integration: The Full Advantage in Minimal Circuit Depth [Article]. *Quantum : the Open Journal for Quantum Science, 6*, 823. Advance online publication. DOI: 10.22331/Q-2022-09-29-823

Herman, D., Googin, C., Liu, X., Galda, A., Safro, I., Sun, Y., Pistoia, M., & Alexeev, Y. (2022). A survey of quantum computing for finance.

Hodson, M., Ruck, B., Ong, H., Garvin, D., & Dulman, S. (2019). Portfolio rebalancing experiments using the quantum alternating operator ansatz. *arXiv preprint arXiv:1911.05296.*

Hornuf, L., & Schwienbacher, A. (2018). Market mechanisms and funding dynamics in equity crowdfunding. *Journal of Corporate Finance, 50*, 556–574.

How, M. L. & Cheah, S. M. (2024). Forging the future: Strategic approaches to quantum ai integration for industry transformation. Ai. DOI: 10.3390/ai5010015

How, M. L., & Cheah, S. M. (2023). Business Renaissance: Opportunities and challenges at the dawn of the Quantum Computing Era. *Businesses, 3*(4), 585–605.

How, M.-L., & Cheah, S.-M. (2023). Business Renaissance: Opportunities and Challenges at the Dawn of the Quantum Computing Era. *Businesses, 3*(4), 585–605. DOI: 10.3390/businesses3040036

Hughes, C., Isaacson, J., Perry, A., Sun, R. F., & Turner, J. (2021). What is a qubit? In *Quantum computing for the quantum curious* (pp. 7–16). Springer International Publishing.

Hu, M., Sima, Z., Chen, S., & Huang, M. (2023). Does green finance promote low-carbon economic transition? *Journal of Cleaner Production, 427*, 139231.

Hyvönen, T. (2022). Data analytics in financial forecasting: Practitioner perspectives. *Journal of Accounting and Organizational Change, 18*(3), 456–475.

Hyvönen, T., Lepistö, L., & Mäki, S. (n.d.). Data analytics and financial forecasting: A field study from Finnish enterprises (*Vol. 72, Issue 2*). *SSRN*. https://ssrn.com/abstract=4244157

Imam, R., Areeb, Q. M., Alturki, A., & Anwer, F. (2021). Systematic and critical review of rsa based public key cryptographic schemes: Past and present status. IEEE access. DOI: 10.1109/ACCESS.2021.3129224

Inakoti, R. K., Stephen, M. J., & Reddy, P. V. G. D. P. (2025). Enhancing Quantum Cryptography with Machine and Deep Learning A Hybrid Approach for Secure and Scalable Post-Quantum Security [Article]. *Journal of Theoretical and Applied Information Technology*, *103*(11), 4972–4988. https://www.scopus.com/inward/record.uri?eid=2-s2.0-105009299729&partnerID=40&md5=60b6b1301acf7594bb490a6b31326489

Ingber, L. (2021). Hybrid classical-quantum computing: Applications to statistical mechanics of financial markets. In Kwilinski, A. (Ed.), *E3S Web of Conferences* (Vol. 307). EDP Sciences., DOI: 10.1051/e3sconf/202130704001

Irfan, M., Dias, R., Rastogi, R., & Zebende, G. F. (2025). *Generative AI insights for financial decision making*. IGI Global.

Irfan, M., Elhoseny, M., Kassim, S., & Metawa, N. (2023). *Advanced machine learning algorithms for complex financial applications*. IGI Global.

Irfan, M., Elmogy, M., Gupta, S., Khalifa, F., & Dias, R. T. (2024). *AI-driven decentralized finance and the future of finance*. IGI Global USA.

Irfan, M., Elmogy, M., Majid, M. S., & El-Sappagh, S. (2023). *The impact of AI innovation on financial sectors in the era of Industry 5.0*. IGI Global.

Irfan, M., Hussainey, K., Bukhari, S. A. C., & Nam, Y. (2024). *Issues of sustainability in AI and new-age thematic investing*. IGI Global.

Irfan, M., Kadry, S., Sharif, M., & Khan, H. U. (2023). *Fintech applications in Islamic finance: AI, machine learning, and blockchain techniques*. IGI Global.

Irfan, M., Mohammed, M., Kassim, S., & Ofori, K. S. (2024). *The future of indigenous inclusivity: Unlocking finance for economic development*. IGI Global.

Irofti, P., Pătraşcu, A., & Băltoiu, A. (2021). Fraud detection in networks. In *Studies in Computational Intelligence* (Vol. 911, pp. 517–536). Springer Science and Business Media Deutschland GmbH., DOI: 10.1007/978-3-030-52067-0_23

Jain, N., Khandelwal, A., & Girish Chandra, M. (2023). Efficient and Flexible Annealer-Gate Hybrid Model for Solving Large-Scale Portfolio Optimization. Proceedings - 2023 IEEE International Conference on Quantum Computing and Engineering, QCE 2023

Jhessim, E., & Santigie-Sankoh, T. (2025). Quantum computing in financial security: A risk management framework for systemically important financial institutions. World Journal of Advanced Research and Reviews, 25(1), 1963-1967. DOI: 10.30574/wjarr.2025.25.1.0235

Jonas, N., & Christian, M. (2025). Transforming South African agriculture: The role of credit in supporting value chain sustainability. *Agriculture*, *15*(6), 620.

Joshi, S. (2025). Review of Gen AI models for financial risk management. International Journal of Scientific Research in Computer Science. *Engineering and Information Technology*, *11*(1), 709–723.

Judijanto, L. (2025). Exploring the potential of quantum computing in revolutionising risk management and digital financial security. *International Journal of Finance & Economics*, *2*(6), 685–693.

Kakran, S., Rathore, J. S., Sidhu, A., & Kumar, A. (2024). Solar energy advances and CO2 emissions: A comparative review of leading nations' path to sustainable future. *Journal of Cleaner Production*, •••, 143598.

Kanaparthi, V. K. (2024). Navigating uncertainty: enhancing markowitz asset allocation strategies through out-of-sample analysis. FinTech. mdpi.commdpi.comDOI: 10.3390/fintech3010010

Kaneko, K., Miyamoto, K., Takeda, N., & Yoshino, K. (2020). Quantum pricing with a smile: Implementation of local volatility model on quantum computer.

Kasirajan, V. (2021). *Fundamentals of quantum computing*. Springer International Publishing.

Kedia, U., Joshi, S., Pandey, T. N., & Shukla, P. (2025). The Applications of Quantum Machine Learning in Today's World. In *Intelligent Systems Reference Library* (Vol. 274, pp. 171–191). Springer Science and Business Media Deutschland GmbH., DOI: 10.1007/978-3-031-89905-8_9

Khairy, S., Shaydulin, R., Cincio, L., Alexeev, Y., & Balaprakash, P. (2020). Learning to optimize variational quantum vircuits to solve combinatorial problems. AAAI 2020 - 34th AAAI Conference on Artificial Intelligence

Khang, A. (Ed.). (2025). *Shaping cutting-edge technologies and applications for digital banking and financial services*. Productivity Press.

Khang, A., Rath, K. C., Madapana, K., Rao, J., & Panda, L. P. (2025). Quantum computing and portfolio optimization in finance services. In *Shaping Cutting-Edge Technologies and Applications for Digital Banking and Financial Services* (pp. 27–45). Taylor and Francis., DOI: 10.4324/9781003501947-2

Khurana, S., & Nene, M. (2023). Implementation of Database Search with Quantum Computing: Grover's Algorithm vs Linear Search. *1st IEEE International Conference on Ambient Intelligence, Knowledge Informatics and Industrial Electronics, AIKIIE 2023.* Ballari: Institute of Electrical and Electronics Engineers Inc. https://doi.org/DOI: 10.1109/AIKIIE60097.2023.10389962

Khurshid, A., Rauf, A., Qayyum, S., Calin, A. C., & Duan, W. (2023). Green innovation and carbon emissions: The role of carbon pricing and environmental policies in attaining sustainable development targets of carbon mitigation—evidence from Central-Eastern Europe. *Environment, Development and Sustainability*, *25*(8), 8777–8798.

Kim, S. M. (2021). *Payment methods and finance for international trade*. Springer.

Kiss, T., & Popovics, S. (2021). Evaluation on the effectiveness of energy policies–Evidence from the carbon reductions in 25 countries. *Renewable & Sustainable Energy Reviews*, *149*, 111348.

Koc, B., Yildirak, K., & Yokus, A. (2025). A New Perspective for Financial Option Pricing with New Dynamic Solutions of the Black-Scholes Equation. *Computational Economics*. Advance online publication. DOI: 10.1007/s10614-025-11055-3

Komiyama, T., & Suzuki, T. (2024). QUBO formulation using inequalities for problems with complex constraints. *7th International Conference on High Performance Computing in Asia-Pacific Region, HPC Asia 2024* (pp. 55-61). Nagoya: Association for Computing Machinery. https://doi.org/DOI: 10.1145/3635035.3635042

KPMG. (2022, Aug). *Quantum is coming — and bringing new cybersecurity threats with it.* Retrieved Aug 13, 2025, from https://kpmg.com: https://kpmg.com/xx/en/our-insights/ai-and-technology/quantum-and-cybersecurity.html

Kumar, B., Kumar, L., Kumar, A., Kumari, R., Tagar, U., & Sassanelli, C. (2024). Green finance in circular economy: A literature review. *Environment, Development and Sustainability*, *26*(7), 16419–16459. PMID: 37362997

Kuo, S.-Y., Lee, K.-L., Shen, J.-Y., Chou, Y.-H., & Kuo, S.-Y. (2025). *Quantum Annealing for Bi-objective Weighted Portfolio Optimization in Real-world Financial Markets. 2025 Genetic and Evolutionary Computation Conference Companion, GECCO 2025 Companion*. Association for Computing Machinery, Inc., DOI: 10.1145/3712255.3734282

Kurvits, E. (2022). The role of stakeholders in a transition toward advanced corporate sustainability: A representation of the European wind power industry and the case of Vestas Wind Systems A/S. *IIIEE Master Thesis.*

Labatt, S., & White, R. R. (2011). *Carbon finance: the financial implications of climate change*. John Wiley & Sons.

Lamichhane, P., & Rawat, D. B. (2025). Quantum Machine Learning: Recent Advances, Challenges, and Perspectives. *IEEE Access : Practical Innovations, Open Solutions, 13*, 94057–94105. DOI: 10.1109/ACCESS.2025.3573244

Leclerc, L., Ortiz-Gutiérrez, L., Grijalva, S., Albrecht, B., & Cline, J. R. (2023, October). Financial risk management on a neutral atom quantum processor. *Physical Review Research, 05*(04). Advance online publication. DOI: 10.1103/PhysRevResearch.5.043117

Lecompte, T., Qi, F., Yuan, X., Tzeng, N. F., Najafi, M. H., & Peng, L. (2023). Machine-Learning-Based Qubit Allocation for Error Reduction in Quantum Circuits [Article]. *IEEE Transactions on Quantum Engineering, 4*, 3101414. Advance online publication. DOI: 10.1109/TQE.2023.3301899

Lee, W. B., & Constantinides, A. G. (2023). Computational Results for a Quantum Computing Application in Real-Life Finance. Proceedings - 2023 IEEE International Conference on Quantum Computing and Engineering, QCE 2023

Lee, X., Saito, Y., Cai, D., & Asai, N. (2021). Parameters Fixing Strategy for Quantum Approximate Optimization Algorithm. Proceedings - 2021 IEEE International Conference on Quantum Computing and Engineering, QCE 2021

Liang, J. (2025). Machine learning in asset pricing and portfolio optimization. https://theses.gla.ac.uk/84858/ gla.ac.uk

Li, H., Xing, T., Wei, S., Liu, Z., Zhang, J., & Long, G. L. (2023). BQ-Bank: A Quantum Software for Finance and Banking. *Quantum Engineering, 2023*(1), 7810974.

Li, H., Xing, T., Wei, S., Liu, Z., Zhang, J., & Long, G.-L. (2023). BQ-Bank: A quantum software for finance and banking. *Quantum Engineering, 2023*, 1–10.

Li, J., Wang, D., & Qin, M. (2024). Understanding the role of mineral resources and inflation in promoting sustainable development under the inflation reduction act. *Resources Policy, 90*, 104757.

Lim, D., & Rebentrost, P. (2024). A quantum online portfolio optimization algorithm. *Quantum Information Processing, 23*(3).

Lim, D., & Rebentrost, P. (2024). A quantum online portfolio optimization algorithm: D. Lim, P. Rebentrost. *Quantum Information Processing, 23*(3), 63.

Lindenberg, N. (2014). *Definition of Green Finance*. German Development Institute.

Lin, G., Guo, Z., & Song, T. (2025). Power Law Amplitude Estimation for Option Pricing with NISQ Devices [Article]. *Advanced Quantum Technologies, 8*(6), 2400411. Advance online publication. DOI: 10.1002/qute.202400411

Linghu, K., Qian, Y., Wang, R., Hu, M. J., Li, Z., Li, X., Xu, H., Zhang, J., Ma, T., Zhao, P., Liu, D. E., Hsieh, M. H., Wu, X., Du, Y., Tao, D., Jin, Y., & Yu, H. (2024). Quantum Circuit Architecture Search on a Superconducting Processor [Article]. *Entropy (Basel, Switzerland), 26*(12), 1025. Advance online publication. DOI: 10.3390/e26121025 PMID: 39766654

Linton, O., & Mahmoodzadeh, S. (2018). Implications of High-Frequency Trading for Security Markets. *Annual Review of Economics, 10*(1), 237–259. DOI: 10.1146/annurev-economics-063016-104407

Liu, C., Lee, W. B., & Constantinides, A. G. (2025, April). Quantum Testing of Recommender Algorithms on GPU-Based Quantum Simulators. *Computers, 14*(04). Advance online publication. DOI: 10.3390/computers14040137

Liu, H., Yao, P., Latif, S., Aslam, S., & Iqbal, N. (2022). Impact of Green financing, FinTech, and financial inclusion on energy efficiency. *Environmental Science and Pollution Research International, 29*(13), 18955–18966. PMID: 34705207

Liu, J., Lim, K. H., Wood, K. L., Huang, W., Guo, C., & Huang, H.-L. (2021). Hybrid quantum-classical convolutional neural networks. *Science China. Physics, Mechanics & Astronomy, 64*(9), 290311. DOI: 10.1007/s11433-021-1734-3

Liu, Q., Jiao, Y., & Guo, S. (2022). GARCH pricing and hedging of VIX options. [HTML]. *Journal of Futures Markets*. Advance online publication. DOI: 10.1002/fut.22318

Lo, S., Baird, S. G., Schrier, J., Blaiszik, B., Carson, N., Foster, I., ... & Aspuru-Guzik, A. (2024). Review of low-cost self-driving laboratories in chemistry and materials science: the “frugal twin” concept. Digital Discovery, 3(5), 842-868. DOI: 10.1039/d3dd00223c

Lu, Y., & Yang, J. (2024). Quantum financing system: A survey on quantum algorithms, potential scenarios and open research issues. *Journal of Industrial Information Integration, 41*. Advance online publication. DOI: 10.1016/j.jii.2024.100663

Machkour, B., & Abriane, A. (2020). Industry 4.0 and its Implications for the Financial Sector. *Procedia Computer Science, 177*, 496–502. DOI: 10.1016/j.procs.2020.10.068

Maheshwari, D., Garcia-Zapirain, B., & Sierra-Sosa, D. (2022). Quantum Machine Learning Applications in the Biomedical Domain: A Systematic Review. *IEEE Access : Practical Innovations, Open Solutions, 10*, 80463–80484. DOI: 10.1109/ACCESS.2022.3195044

Maino, A. (2022). *Financing the energy transition: The role, opportunities and challenges of green bonds*. Oxford Institute for Energy Studies.

Malhotra, J., Chavan, O., & Thakur, P. (2025). Grover Algorithm: Enhancing the Search Mechanism. *4th OPJU International Technology Conference on Smart Computing for Innovation and Advancement in Industry 5.0, OTCON 2025*. Raigarh: Institute of Electrical and Electronics Engineers Inc. https://doi.org/DOI: 10.1109/OTCON65728.2025.11071106

Mandung, F., Sahari, S., & Amra, W. (2025). Understanding How Companies Utilize Technological Innovation for Competitive Advantage: A Qualitative Inquiry. *Golden Ratio of Data in Summary, 5*(1), 144–154.

Martín-Guerrero, J. D., & Lamata, L. (2022). Quantum Machine Learning: A tutorial. *Neurocomputing, 470*, 457–461. DOI: 10.1016/j.neucom.2021.02.102

Matsakos, T., & Nield, S. (2024). Quantum Monte Carlo simulations for financial risk analytics: Scenario generation for equity, rate, and credit risk factors. *Quantum : the Open Journal for Quantum Science, 8*, 1306.

Mazumder, A. R., Sen, A., & Sen, U. (2024). Benchmarking Metaheuristic-Integrated QAOA Against Quantum Annealing. *Science and Information Conference, SAI 2024. 1018 LNNS*, pp. 651 - 666. London: Springer Science and Business Media Deutschland GmbH. https://doi.org/DOI: 10.1007/978-3-031-62269-4_42

Mazumder, A. R., Sen, A., & Sen, U. (2024). *Benchmarking Metaheuristic-Integrated QAOA Against Quantum Annealing*. Lecture Notes in Networks and Systems.

McKinsey & Company. (2025). *Quantum computing in financial services: Value creation outlook 2035*. McKinsey & Company. https://www.mckinsey.com/industries/financial-services/our-insights

Memon, Q. A., Al Ahmad, M., & Pecht, M. (2024). Quantum computing: navigating the future of computation, challenges, and technological breakthroughs. Quantum Reports. DOI: 10.3390/quantum6040039

Memon, Q. A., Al Ahmad, M., & Pecht, M. (2024). Quantum computing: Navigating the future of computation, challenges, and technological breakthroughs. *Quantum Reports, 6*(4), 627–663.

Meng, X., Hu, X., Tian, Y., Dong, G., Lambiotte, R., Gao, J., & Havlin, S. (2023). Percolation theories for quantum networks. Entropy, 25(11), 1564. DOI: 10.3390/e25111564

Mentes, M. (2023). RETRACTED ARTICLE: Sustainable development economy and the development of green economy in the European Union. *Energy, Sustainability and Society*, *13*(1), 32.

Meo, M. S., & Abd Karim, M. Z. (2022). The role of green finance in reducing CO2 emissions: An empirical analysis. *Borsa Istanbul Review*, *22*(1), 169–178.

Migliorelli, M. (2021). What do we mean by sustainable finance? Assessing existing frameworks and policy risks. *Sustainability*, *13*(2), 975.

Millett, S. M. (2003). The future of scenarios: Challenges and opportunities. *Strategy and Leadership*, *31*(2), 16–24. DOI: 10.1108/10878570310698089

Mina, M.-Z., & Simion, E. (2022). A Multifunctional Modular Implementation of Grover's Algorithm. *14th International Conference on Innovative Security Solutions for Information Technology and Communications, SecITC 2021. 13195 LNCS*, pp. 228 - 247. Virtual: Springer Science and Business Media Deutschland GmbH. https://doi.org/DOI: 10.1007/978-3-031-17510-7_16

Mironowicz, P. H., A. S., Mandarino, A., Yilmaz, A. E., & Ankenbrand, T. (2024). *Applications of Quantum Machine Learning for Quantitative Finance* (Version 1). arXiv. DOI: 10.48550/ARXIV.2405.10119

Mishra, A. K., & Tyagi, A. K. Richa, & Patra, S. R. (2024). Introduction to machine learning and artificial intelligence in Banking and finance. In *Applications of block chain technology and artificial intelligence: Lead-ins in Banking, finance, and capital market* (pp. 239-290). Cham: Springer International Publishing.

Mishra, A. K., Tyagi, A. K., & Arowolo, M. O. (2024). Future Trends and Opportunities in Machine Learning and Artificial Intelligence for Banking and Finance. In *Applications of Block Chain technology and Artificial Intelligence: Lead-ins in Banking, Finance, and Capital Market* (pp. 211–238). Springer International Publishing.

Mishra, L., & Kaushik, V. (2023). Application of blockchain in dealing with sustainability issues and challenges of financial sector. *Journal of Sustainable Finance & Investment*, *13*(3), 1318–1333. DOI: 10.1080/20430795.2021.1940805

Mishra, S., Agarwal, O., & Patel, S. K. (2024). Quantum Decryption using Shor's Algorithm. *7th IEEE Pune Section International Conference, PuneCon 2024.* Pune: Institute of Electrical and Electronics Engineers Inc. https://doi.org/DOI: 10.1109/PuneCon63413.2024.10895777

Mittal, S., Koushik, P., Batra, I., & Whig, P. (2024). AI-Driven Inventory Management for Optimizing Operations With Quantum Computing. In Quantum Computing and Supply Chain Management: A New Era of Optimization (pp. 125-140). IGI Global. DOI: 10.4018/979-8-3693-4107-0.ch009

Miyamoto, K. (2021). Quantum algorithms for Monte Carlo integration using pseudo-random numbers. Proceedings - 2021 IEEE International Conference on Quantum Computing and Engineering, QCE 2021

Miyamoto, K., & Shiohara, K. (2020). Reduction of qubits in a quantum algorithm for Monte Carlo simulation by a pseudo-random-number generator [Article]. *Physical Review. A*, *102*(2), 022424. Advance online publication. DOI: 10.1103/PhysRevA.102.022424

Mohamed, B. S., Kumar, M. S., & Srinivasagan, K. G. (2022). Quantum computing and quantum cryptography. In *Privacy and Security Challenges in Cloud Computing* (pp. 171–189). CRC Press.

Mohd, S., Dasgupta, M., Akter, F., Arunachalam, M. P., Sharma, S., & Prasanna, C. K. L. (2025). Quantum Computing Applications in Financial Modeling and Portfolio Optimization. *1st International Conference on Advances in Computer Science, Electrical, Electronics, and Communication Technologies, CE2CT 2025*, 868–872. DOI: 10.1109/CE2CT64011.2025.10939675

Mosteanu, N. R., & Faccia, A. (2021). Fintech frontiers in quantum computing, fractals, and blockchain distributed ledger: Paradigm shifts and open innovation. Journal of Open Innovation: Technology, Market, and Complexity, 7(1), 19. DOI: 10.3390/joitmc7010019

Mosteanu, N. R., & Faccia, A. (2021). Fintech frontiers in quantum computing, fractals, and blockchain distributed ledger: Paradigm shifts and open innovation. *Journal of Open Innovation*, *7*(1), 19.

Mugel, S., Lizaso, E., & Orus, R. (2020). Use Cases of Quantum Optimization for Finance.

Murali, P., Baker, J. M., Abhari, A. J., Chong, F. T., & Martonosi, M. (2019). Noise-Adaptive Compiler Mappings for Noisy Intermediate-Scale Quantum Computers. International Conference on Architectural Support for Programming Languages and Operating Systems - ASPLOS

Mwakalila, E. (2025). Impact of government domestic borrowing on monetary policy rate pass-through in Tanzania. *Journal of Policy Modeling*, *47*(1), 150–165.

Mzukwa, A. (2024). Exploring Next-Generation Architectures for Advanced Computing Systems: Challenges and Opportunities. Journal of Advanced Computing Systems. DOI: 10.69987/JACS..2024.40601

Naik, A. S., Yeniaras, E., Hellstern, G., Prasad, G., & Vishwakarma, S. K. L. P. (2025). From portfolio optimization to quantum blockchain and security: A systematic review of quantum computing in finance. *Financial Innovation*, *11*(1). Advance online publication. DOI: 10.1186/s40854-025-00751-6

Narayan, S. (2025). Preparing for Quantum Transformation: Strategic Implications for Business and Finance in Asia. In Endress, T., & Badir, Y. F. (Eds.), *Business and Management in Asia: Finance and Investments in the Digital Age* (pp. 221–238). Springer Nature Singapore., DOI: 10.1007/978-981-96-3452-1_14

Natraj, N., Sundaravadivazhagan, B. R. S., Anandaram, H., & Patchala, S. (2025). Quantum Computing in Industry: Unveiling Applications and Opportunities. In *Quantum Computing and Artificial Intelligence: The Industry Use Cases* (pp. 305 - 330). wiley. https://doi.org/DOI: 10.1002/9781394242399.ch12

Navaretti, G. B., Calzolari, G., Mansilla-Fernandez, J. M., & Pozzolo, A. F. (2018). Fintech and banks. Friends or foes? *European Economy*, *2018*(3), 9–30.

Neway, A. S. (2024). Beyond the bit: A guide to quantum computing and its impact. ISBN 9798-300-628 3-38

Nguyen, P. N. (2025). Quantum technology: A financial risk assessment. *Digital Finance*, •••, 1–40.

Nguyen, T., Sipola, T., & Hautamäki, J. (2024). *Machine Learning Applications of Quantum Computing: A Review*. DOI: 10.48550/ARXIV.2406.13262

Nisa, C., Subhan, M. N., Hendratni, T. W., & Oentarjo, Y. (2024). The nexus between rural bank performance and growth of regional gross domestic product in Depok, West Java. *Dinasti International Journal of Economics, Finance & Accounting (DIJEFA), 5*(1).

Olorunyomi, T. D. (2024). Business Intelligence tools in financial analysis: Opportunities and challenges. *Journal of Financial Reporting and Accounting*, *22*(1), 78–95.

Onabowale, O. (2024). Energy policy and sustainable finance: Navigating the future of renewable energy and energy markets. *World Journal of Advanced Research and Reviews*, *25*, 2235–2252.

Orús, R., Mugel, S., & Lizaso, E. (2019). Quantum computing for finance: Overview and prospects. *Rev. Phys.*, *4*(100028), 100028.

Orús, R., Mugel, S., & Lizaso, E. (2019, November). Quantum computing for finance: Overview and prospects. *Reviews in Physics*, *04*. Advance online publication. DOI: 10.1016/j.revip.2019.100028

Outeiral, C., Strahm, M., Shi, J., Morris, G. M., Benjamin, S. C., & Deane, C. M. (2021). The prospects of quantum computing in computational molecular biology. Wiley Interdisciplinary Reviews: Computational Molecular Science, 11(1), e1481. DOI: 10.1002/wcms.1481

Overmars, A. & Venkatraman, S. (2021). New semi-prime factorization and application in large rsa key attacks. Journal of Cybersecurity and Privacy. DOI: 10.3390/jcp1040033

Owusu-Antwi, D., & Gokhale, P. (2023). Low-level Circuit Optimization for the Quantum Approximate Optimization Algorithm. *IET Conference Proceedings*

Ozili, P. K. (2022). Green finance research around the world: A review of literature. *International Journal of Green Economics*, *16*(1), 56–75.

Palaniappan, V., Ishak, I., Ibrahim, H., Sidi, F., & Zukarnain, Z. A. (2024). A Review on High Frequency Trading Forecasting Methods: Opportunity and Challenges for Quantum based Method. IEEE Access. DOI: 10.1109/ACCESS.2024.3418458

Palaniappan, V., Ishak, I., Ibrahim, H., Sidi, F., & Zukarnain, Z. A. (2024). A Review on High Frequency Trading Forecasting Methods: Opportunity and Challenges for Quantum based Method. *IEEE Access : Practical Innovations, Open Solutions*.

Paramesha, M., Rane, N. L., & Rane, J. (2024). Artificial intelligence, machine learning, deep learning, and blockchain in financial and banking services: A comprehensive review. Partners Universal Multidisciplinary Research Journal, 1(2), 51-67. pumrj.comDOI: 0.5281/zenodo.12826933

Patel, A. (2025). ADVANCING FINANCIAL PREDICTION THROUGH QUANTUM MACHINE LEARNING. *International Journal of Intelligent Data and Machine Learning*, *2*(02), 1–7.

Pattanayak, S. (2021). Quantum Machine Learning with Python: Using Cirq from Google Research and IBM Qiskit. In *Quantum Machine Learning with Python: Using Cirq from Google Research and IBM Qiskit.* Apress Media LLC. DOI: 10.1007/978-1-4842-6522-2

Perez, K. (2024). *Green Money: How to Reduce Waste, Build Wealth, and Create a Better Future for All.* John Wiley & Sons.

Perissi, I., & Jones, A. (2022). Investigating European Union decarbonization strategies: Evaluating the pathway to carbon neutrality by 2050. *Sustainability, 14*(8), 4728.

Peyvandi, M., Hajinezhad, A., & Moosavian, S. F. (2023). Investigating the intensity of GHG emissions from electricity production in Iran using renewable sources. *Results in Engineering, 17,* 100819.

Pfaendler, S. M. L., Konson, K., & Greinert, F. (2024). Advancements in quantum computing—viewpoint: Building adoption and competency in industry. Datenbank-spektrum. DOI: 10.1007/s13222-024-00467-4

Philippon, T. (2016). The fintech opportunity. *National Bureau of Economic Research Working Paper*, No. 22476.

Phillipson, F., & Bhatia, H. S. (2020). Portfolio Optimisation using the D-Wave quantum annealer.

Pistoia, M., Ahmad, S. F., Ajagekar, A., Buts, A., Chakrabarti, S., Herman, D., ... & Yalovetzky, R. (2021, November). Quantum machine learning for finance ICCAD special session paper. In 2021 IEEE/ACM international conference on computer aided design (ICCAD) (pp. 1-9). IEEE.

Possati, L. M. (2024). Quantum technologies: A hermeneutic technology assessment approach. *NanoEthics, 18*(1), 2.

Prakash, M. S., Gupta, P., & Gupta, S. (2024). EVALUATION AND SIGNIFICANCE OF GREEN FINANCE. *NOLEGEIN-Journal of Financial Planning and Management, 7*(1), 34–47.

Prasad, N. S., Gangopadhyay, A., Prabakaran, R., Mishra, N., & Prasad, D. S. (2024). Utilizing Anomaly Detection Methods for Identifying Fraudulent Activities in Credit Card Transactions. *1st IEEE International Conference on Advances in Computing, Communication and Networking, ICAC2N 2024* (pp. 1641 - 1646). Greater Noida: Institute of Electrical and Electronics Engineers Inc. https://doi.org/DOI: 10.1109/ICAC2N63387.2024.10895602

Prodan, A., Manta, V.-I., & Tudorache, A.-G. (2021). The performance impact of the graph topology in Ibm's Quantum devices on Grover's search algorithm. *25th International Conference on System Theory, Control and* (pp. 327 - 333). Iasi: Institute of Electrical and Electronics Engineers Inc. https://doi.org/DOI: 10.1109/ICSTCC52150.2021.9607230

Purohit, A., Kaur, M., Seskir, Z. C., Posner, M. T., & Venegas-Gomez, A. (2024). Building a quantum-ready ecosystem. *IET Quantum Communication*, *5*(1), 1–18.

Putranto, D. S. C., Wardhani, R. W., Ji, J., & Kim, H. (2024). A Deep Inside Quantum Technology Industry Trends and Future Implications. *IEEE Access : Practical Innovations, Open Solutions*, *12*, 115776–115801. DOI: 10.1109/ACCESS.2024.3444779

Qamruzzaman, M., & Karim, S. (2024). Unveiling the synergy: Green finance, technological innovation, green energy, and carbon neutrality. *PLoS One*, *19*(10), e0308170. PMID: 39378193

Qian, Y., & Liu, Y. (2024). Improve carbon emission efficiency: What role does the ESG initiatives play? *Journal of Environmental Management*, *367*, 122016. PMID: 39106795

Qu, D., Matwiejew, E., Wang, K., Wang, J., & Xue, P. (2024). Experimental implementation of quantum-walk-based portfolio optimization. *Quantum Science and Technology*, *9*(2), 025014.

Quynh, D. T. (2023). The impact of dashboards on risk management and decision-making in finance. *Journal of Risk Management in Financial Institutions*, *16*(2), 123–138.

Ragel, R. G., & Parameswaran, S. (2011). A hybrid hardware—Software technique to improve reliability in embedded processors. *ACM Transactions on Embedded Computing Systems*, *10*(3), 1–16. DOI: 10.1145/1952522.1952529

Rahimi, M., & Asadi, F. (2023). Oncological Applications of Quantum Machine Learning. *Technology in Cancer Research & Treatment*, *22*, 15330338231215214. DOI: 10.1177/15330338231215214 PMID: 38105500

Raj, K. B., Mehta, K., Siddi, S., Sharma, M. K., Sharma, D. K., Adhav, S., & Gonzáles, J. L. (2024). Optimizing Financial Transactions and Processes Through the Power of Distributed Systems. Meta Heuristic Algorithms for Advanced Distributed Systems, 289-303.

Ralston, P. A. S., Graham, J. H., & Hieb, J. L. (2007). Cyber security risk assessment for SCADA and DCS networks. *ISA Transactions*, *46*(4), 583–594. DOI: 10.1016/j.isatra.2007.04.003 PMID: 17624350

Raman, R., Ray, S., Das, D., & Nedungadi, P. (2025). Innovations and barriers in sustainable and green finance for advancing sustainable development goals. *Frontiers in Environmental Science*, *12*, 1513204.

Ramesh, J. V. N., Singh Kadyan, J., Kadyan, S., Hussein, O. M., Teltumbade, G. R., & Valavan, M., P. (2025). Enhancing Corporate Tax Compliance and Fraud Detection Using Principal Component Analysis and Auto-Encoder. *2025 Fifth International Conference on Advances in Electrical, Computing, Communication and Sustainable Technologies (ICAECT)*, 1–6. DOI: 10.1109/ICAECT63952.2025.10958987

Rapp, H. P., Schneider, S., & AG, D. B. (2021). Economic-technological revolution through Quantum 2.0. *Germany Monitor.*

Rastogi, R., & Iqbal, M. I. (2024). Data security and privacy in RegTech. In *Integrating RegTech solutions for Industry 4.0* (pp. 185–198). IGI Global.

Rastogi, R., & Iqbal, M. I. (2024). Data security and privacy in RegTech. In *Integrating RegTech Solutions for Industry 4.0* (pp. 185–198). IGI Global.

Rath, M., & Date, H. (2025, December). Quantum powered credit risk assessment: A novel approach using Hybrid Quantum-Classical Deep Neural Network for Row-Type Dependent Predictive Analysis. *EPJ Quantum Technology*, *12*(01). Advance online publication. DOI: 10.1140/epjqt/s40507-025-00323-8

Rayhana, R., Bai, L., Xiao, G., Liao, M., & Liu, Z. (2024). Digital twin models: Functions, challenges, and industry applications. [HTML]. *IEEE Journal of Radio Frequency Identification*. Advance online publication. DOI: 10.1109/JRFID.2024.3387996

Raza, S. A., Syed, D., Rizwan, S., & Ahmed, M. (2025). Trends of AI in financial services and its applications. In *The global evolution, changing landscape and future of financial markets: From traditional to digital* (pp. 33–46). Emerald Publishing Limited.

Rebentrost, P., Gupt, B., & Bromley, T. R. (2018). Quantum computational finance: Monte Carlo pricing of financial derivatives [Article]. *Physical Review. A*, *98*(2), 022321. Advance online publication. DOI: 10.1103/PhysRevA.98.022321

Rebentrost, P., & Lloyd, S. (2024). Quantum Computational Finance: Quantum Algorithm for Portfolio Optimization [Article]. *KI - Kunstliche Intelligenz, 38*(4), 327-338. *Article, 150502*. Advance online publication. DOI: 10.1007/s13218-024-00870-9

Reyad, H. M., Zariyawati, M. A., Ong, T. S., & Muhamad, H. (2022). The impact of macroeconomic risk factors, the adoption of financial derivatives on working capital management, and firm performance. *Sustainability*, *14*(21), 14447.

Riedl, A., & Smeets, P. (2017). Why do investors hold socially responsible mutual funds? *The Journal of Finance*, *72*(6), 2505–2550.

Rietsche, R., Dremel, C., Bosch, S., Steinacker, L., Meckel, M., & Leimeister, J. M. (2022). Quantum computing. *Electronic Markets*, *32*(4), 2525–2536.

Rishiwal, V., Agarwal, U., Yadav, M., Tanwar, S., Garg, D., & Guizani, M. (2025). A New Alliance of Machine Learning and Quantum Computing: Concepts, Attacks, and Challenges in IoT Networks. [HTML]. *IEEE Internet of Things Journal*. Advance online publication. DOI: 10.1109/JIOT.2025.3535414

Roger, J. D. D. (2024). AI-Driven Financial Modeling Techniques: Transforming Investment Strategies. The Journal of Applied Business and Economics. https://dx.doi.Org/http://dx.doi.org/10.14453/aabf1.vl8i4.09

Rotimi, F., Olubiyo, S., Agbonlahor, M., & Adeogun, S. (2024). Determinants of loan repayment among agricultural beneficiaries of public funded credit scheme in Ekiti State, Nigeria. *Journal of Contemporary African Studies*, *42*(1), 88–103.

Sabani, M., Galanis, I., Savvas, I., & Garani, G. (2021). Implementation of Shor's Algorithm and Reliability of Quantum Computing Devices. *25th Pan-Hellenic Conference on Informatics, PCI 2021* (pp. 392 - 396). Virtul: Association for Computing Machinery. https://doi.org/DOI: 10.1145/3503823.3503895

Saito, Y., Xie, N., Shin, J., Lee, X., & Cai, D. (2023). Iterative Refinement Quantum Amplitude Estimation. *16th IEEE International Symposium on Embedded Multicore/Many-Core Systems-on-Chip, MCSoC 2023* (pp. 202-209). Singapore: Institute of Electrical and Electronics Engineers Inc. https://doi.org/DOI: 10.1109/MCSoC60832.2023.00038

Sakuma, T. (2025). Quantum differential machine learning. *Quantum Economics and Finance*, *2*(1), 3–12.

Salo, A., Doumpos, M., Liesiö, J., & Zopounidis, C. (2024). Fifty years of portfolio optimization. *European Journal of Operational Research*, *318*(1), 1–18.

Samonte, M. J. C., Asuncion, K. D. R., Castillo, J. J. A. G., & Santos, H. H. I. (2025). *Quantum-Resistant Cryptographic Algorithms for Blockchain Integration in Financial Services. Smart Innovation*. Systems and Technologies.

Sawaya, N. P. D., Schmitz, A. T., & Hadfield, S. (2023). Encoding trade-offs and design toolkits in quantum algorithms for discrete optimization: Coloring, routing, scheduling, and other problems [Article]. *Quantum : the Open Journal for Quantum Science*, *7*. Advance online publication. DOI: 10.22331/Q-2023-09-14-1111

Saxena, A., Mancilla, J., Montalban, I., & Pere, C. (2023). Financial Modeling Using Quantum Computing: Design and manage quantum machine learning solutions for financial analysis and decision making. ISBN 978-1-80461-842-4

Schwienbacher, A. (2018). Entrepreneurial risk-taking in crowdfunding campaigns. *Small Business Economics*, *51*(4), 843–859.

Sengar, A., Vijayaraghavan, A., & Hwang, J. (2023). A Comparative Analysis of Hybrid Quantum Neural Networks in Binary Credit Defaulting Tasks. *IEEE MIT Undergraduate Research Technology Conference, URTC 2023 - Proceedings*. DOI: 10.1109/URTC60662.2023.10535032

Seth, B., Dalal, S., Jaglan, V., Le, D. N., Mohan, S., & Srivastava, G. (2022). Integrating encryption techniques for secure data storage in the cloud. [HTML]. *Transactions on Emerging Telecommunications Technologies*, *33*(4), e4108. DOI: 10.1002/ett.4108

Shafranova, K., Navolska, N., & Koldovskyi, A. (2024). Navigating the digital frontier: A comparative examination of Central Bank Digital Currency (CBDC) and the Quantum Financial System (QFS). *SocioEconomic Challenges*, *8*(1), 90–111.

Shan, B., & Shang, Z. (2023). Quantum computing simulated annealing algorithm applying in portfolio optimization problem. Proceedings of the 2nd International Conference on Public, Digital Economy and Internet Technology, ICPDI 2023, September 1–3, 2023, Chongqing, China.

Sharif, A., Saqib, N., Dong, K., & Khan, S. A. R. (2022). Nexus between green technology innovation, green financing, and CO2 emissions in the G7 countries: The moderating role of social globalisation. *Sustainable Development*, *30*(6), 1934–1946.

Sharma, R., Mehta, K., & Sharma, P. (2024). Role of Artificial Intelligence and Machine Learning in Fraud Detection and Prevention. In Risks and Challenges of AI-Driven Finance: Bias, Ethics, and Security (pp. 90-120). IGI Global. DOI: 10.4018/979-8-3693-2185-0.ch005

Sharma, R. C., & Kohli, D. (2024). Embracing digital transformation for sustainable development: The synergy between learning organizations, human resource management, and service quality. *Journal of Chinese Human Resource Management*, *14*(3), 3–17.

Sharma, R., Mehta, K., & Yu, P. (Eds.). (2024). *Fostering innovation in venture capital and startup ecosystems*. IGI Global.

Shi, J., Yuan, B., Lu, Y., Zhang, S., & Li, X. (2025). Quantum Option Profit and Loss Encoding for Risk Assessment. *IEEE Transactions on Emerging Topics in Computational Intelligence*. Advance online publication. DOI: 10.1109/TETCI.2025.3593781

Shipalana, P. (2022). *Green finance mechanisms in developing countries: Emerging practice*. South African Institute of International Affairs.

Shishlov, I., & Censkowsky, P. (2022). Same but different? Understanding divergent definitions of and views on climate finance. In *Handbook of international climate finance* (pp. 16–39). Edward Elgar Publishing.

Shrivastava, P., Soni, K. K., & Rasool, A. (2019). Evolution of Quantum Computing Based on Grover's Search Algorithm. 2019 10th International Conference on Computing, Communication and Networking Technologies, ICCCNT 2019

Shunza, J., Akinyemi, M., & Yinka-Banjo, C. (2023, December). Application of quantum computing in discrete portfolio optimization. *Journal of Management Science and Engineering*, *08*(04), 453–464. DOI: 10.1016/j.jmse.2023.02.001

Sindayigaya, J. M. (2025). Real-Time Threat Mitigation in Financial IT Infrastructures Using Quantum Computing. *International Journal of Electronics and Telecommunications*, *71*(02), 583–589. DOI: 10.24425/ijet.2025.153578

Singhania, M., & Saini, N. (2023). Institutional framework of ESG disclosures: Comparative analysis of developed and developing countries. *Journal of Sustainable Finance & Investment*, *13*(1), 516–559.

Sinha, U., & Ghosh, D. (2025). Interference in quantum mechanics. *Journal of the Indian Institute of Science*, •••, 1–21.

Sotelo, R., Corbelletto, D., Dri, E., Giusto, E., & Montrucchio, B. (2024). Quantum Computing in Finance: The Intesa Sanpaolo Experience. *IEEE Engineering Management Review*.

Statista. (2021). *Projected worldwide market size of quantum computing from 2020 to 2030*. Statista Digital Economy Compass 2021. https://www.statista.com/statistics/1242930/global-quantum-computing-market-size/

Steane, A. M. (1999). Efficient fault-tolerant quantum computing. *Nature*, *399*(6732), 124–126.

Stockman, D. (2013). The great deformation: The corruption of capitalism in America. Hachette UK.

Susskind, L., Chun, J., Gant, A., Hodgkins, C., Cohen, J., & Lohmar, S. (2022). Sources of opposition to renewable energy projects in the United States. *Energy Policy*, *165*, 112922.

Szczesny, B., & Gryncewicz, W. (2024). Between 0 and 1. Exploring the Algorithmic Restraints and the Potential of Quantum Computing in the Financial Sector. In M. Hernes, J. Wątróbski, & A. Rot (Eds.), *Lecture Notes in Networks and Systems: Vol. 1218 LNNS* (pp. 42–51). Springer Science and Business Media Deutschland GmbH. DOI: 10.1007/978-3-031-78468-2_4

Szczesny, B., & Gryncewicz, W. (2023). Quantum Advantage Applied - Research on Probability of Success. *13th International Conference on Advanced Computer Information Technologies, ACIT 2023*, (pp. 468 - 472). Wroclaw. https://doi.org/DOI: 10.1109/ACIT58437.2023.10275418

Taghizadeh-Hesary, F., Yoshino, N., & Phoumin, H. (2021). Analyzing the characteristics of green bond markets to facilitate green finance in the post-COVID-19 world. *Sustainability*, *13*(10), 5719. DOI: 10.3390/su131 05719

Tao, Z., & Chao, J. (2023). Financial Fraud and Anomaly Detection Techniques: A Literature Review. *4th International Conference on Computer Science and Management Technology, ICCSMT 2023* (pp. 634 - 641). Xi'an: Association for Computing Machinery. https://doi.org/DOI: 10.1145/3644523.3644639

Thakkar, S., Kazdaghli, S., Mathur, N., Kerenidis, I., & Ferreira–Martins, A. J. (2024, June). Improved financial forecasting via quantum machine learning. *Quantum Machine Intelligence*, *06*(01). Advance online publication. DOI: 10.1007/s42484-024-00157-0

Thi, H. L., & Nguyen, T. (2024). *Variational Quantum Algorithms in Anomaly Detection, Fraud Indicator Identification, Credit Scoring, and Stock Price Prediction*. Lecture Notes in Networks and Systems.

Tripathy, S. S., Koul, N., & Patel, H. (2022). Comparative Study between Quantum and Classical Methods: Few Observations from Portfolio Optimization Problem. *2022 International Conference on Trends in Quantum Computing and Emerging Business Technologies, TQCEBT 2022*. DOI: 10.1109/TQCEBT54229.2022.10041475

Tueno, A., Boehm, D., & Choe, S. H. (2022). Integrating and Evaluating Quantum-safe TLS in Database Applications. In S. Sural & H. Lu (Eds.), *Lecture Notes in Computer Science (including subseries Lecture Notes in Artificial Intelligence and Lecture Notes in Bioinformatics): Vol. 13383 LNCS* (pp. 259–278). Springer Science and Business Media Deutschland GmbH. DOI: 10.1007/978-3-031-10684-2_15

Ukpabi, D., Karjaluoto, H., Bötticher, A., Nikiforova, A., Petrescu, D., Schindler, P., ... & Lehmann, L. (2023). Framework for understanding quantum computing use cases from a multidisciplinary perspective and future research directions. Futures, 154, 103277. DOI: 10.1016/j.futures.2023.103277

UNEP. (2023). *Global Landscape of Climate Finance 2023*. United Nations Environment Programme. ADDITONAL READING.

Vaishnavi, A., & Pillai, S. (2021). Cybersecurity in the Quantum Era-A Study of Perceived Risks in Conventional Cryptography and Discussion on Post Quantum Methods. *1st International Conference on Advances in Computational Science and Engineering, ICACSE 2020. 1964*. Coimbatore, Tamilnadu, Virtual: IOP Publishing Ltd. https://doi.org/DOI: 10.1088/1742-6596/1964/4/042002

Valecha, K., Yeole, A., Salian, A., & Mathur, S. (2024). Empirical Analysis of Classical and Quantum Algorithms for Portfolio Optimization: Enhancing Financial Decision-Making Through Quantum Computing. In *2024 International Conference on Sustainable Communication Networks and Application (ICSCNA)* (pp. 1085-1090). IEEE.

Vanishvili, M., & Katsadze, I. (2022). Bank financing of green economy: Review of modern research. *Scientific Collection. InterConf*, (18 (95)), 120–143.

Vashishth, T. K., Sharma, V., Kaushik, V., Singh, A., & Kaushik, S. (2025). Exploring Quantum Challenges and Opportunities of Quantum Machine Learning Adoption in Finance. Machine Learning and Modeling Techniques in Financial Data Science, 437-460.

Vashishth, T. K., Sharma, V., Kaushik, V., Singh, A., & Teotia, S. (2025). Exploring Quantum Challenges and Opportunities of Quantum Machine Learning Adoption in Finance. In *Machine Learning and Modeling Techniques in Financial Data Science* (pp. 437–460). IGI Global., DOI: 10.4018/979-8-3693-8186-1.ch017

Virmani, D., Anuradha, R., Bani Ahmad, A. Y. A., Kumar, P. S., Ravuri, A., Poshamallu, G., & Mircetic, D. (2025). Evaluating Quantum Computing's Potential for Financial Engineering Optimisation. In *Recent Trends in Engineering and Science for Resource Optimization and Sustainable Development* (pp. 40–43). CRC Press., DOI: 10.1201/9781003596721-10

Volz, U. (2018). Fostering green finance for sustainable development in Asia. In *Routledge handbook of banking and finance in Asia* (pp. 488–504). Routledge.

Vorathammathorn, S., Binhar, M., Patamawisut, N., Chanchuphol, S., Prechaprapranwong, P., Hansomboon, J., & Sarochawikasit, R. (2025). Understanding Noise-Adaptive Transpilation Techniques Using the SupermarQ Benchmark. Proceedings - 2025 International Conference on Quantum Communications, Networking, and Computing, QCNC 2025

Walker, T., Davis, F., & Schwartz, T. (2022). Big Data in Finance: An Overview. In *Big Data in Finance: Opportunities and Challenges of Financial Digitalization* (pp. 03-09). Springer International Publishing. https://doi.org/DOI: 10.1007/978-3-031-12240-8_1

Wang, J., & Tian, B. (2024). Research and Application of Quantum Computing Algorithm for Asset Portfolio Optimization. Proceedings - 2024 3rd International Conference on Data Analytics, Computing and Artificial Intelligence, ICDACAI 2024

Wang, L., & Lee, R. S. T. (2022). The Design and Implementation of Quantum Finance Software Development Kit (QFSDK) for AI Education. *2022 20th International Conference on Information Technology Based Higher Education and Training, ITHET 2022*. DOI: 10.1109/ITHET56107.2022.10031712

Wang, P., Zhu, Q., Wu, H., Li, X., & Yang, S. (2024). The Equity Fund Risk Predictions Via Quantum-Classical Hybrid Neural Networks. *13th International Conference on Computer Engineering and Networks, CENet 2023. 1126 LNEE*, pp. 320 - 331. Wuxi: Springer Science and Business Media Deutschland GmbH. https://doi.org/DOI: 10.1007/978-981-99-9243-0_32

Wang, G., & Kan, A. (2024). Option pricing under stochastic volatility on a quantum computer. *Quantum : the Open Journal for Quantum Science*, *8*, 1504.

Wang, J., David, L. K., Cisse, I. I., & Angel, V. (2024). Quantum computing and its implications for Asian innovation ecosystems. [HTML] [REMOVED HYPERLINK FIELD]. *Asian Journal of Technology Innovation*, 1–50. DOI: 10.1080/19761597.2024.2420920

Wang, M. L. (2023). Effects of the green finance policy on the green innovation efficiency of the manufacturing industry: A difference-in-difference model. *Technological Forecasting and Social Change*, *189*, 122333.

Wang, S., Asif, M., Shahzad, M. F., & Ashfaq, M. (2024). Data privacy and cybersecurity challenges in the digital transformation of the banking sector. [HTML]. *Computers & Security*. Advance online publication. DOI: 10.1016/j.cose.2024.104051

Wang, S., Czarnik, P., Arrasmith, A., Cerezo, M., Cincio, L., & Coles, P. J. (2024). Can Error Mitigation Improve Trainability of Noisy Variational Quantum Algorithms? [Article]. *Quantum : the Open Journal for Quantum Science, 8*. Advance online publication. DOI: 10.22331/q-2024-03-14-1287

Wang, S., Sun, L., & Iqbal, S. (2022). Green financing role on renewable energy dependence and energy transition in E7 economies. *Renewable Energy*, *200*, 1561–1572.

Wang, X., & Wang, Q. (2021). Research on the impact of green finance on the upgrading of China's regional industrial structure from the perspective of sustainable development. *Resources Policy*, *74*, 102436.

Wang, Y., Guo, C. H., Chen, X. J., Jia, L. Q., Guo, X. N., Chen, R. S., & Wang, H. D. (2021). Carbon peak and carbon neutrality in China: Goals, implementation path and prospects. *China Geology*, *4*(4), 720–746.

Wang, Y., Hanif, N., Arshed, N., Hussain, M., Arshad, Z., & Usman, M. (2024). Synergizing social sustainability and technological innovation for carbon neutrality in OECD economies. *Sustainable Development*, *32*(6), 6614–6628.

Wasan, P., Kumar, A., & Luthra, S. (2021). Green finance barriers and solution strategies for emerging economies: The case of India. *IEEE Transactions on Engineering Management*, *71*, 414–425.

Wilkens, S., & Moorhouse, J. (2023, January). Quantum computing for financial risk measurement. *Quantum Information Processing*, *22*(01). Advance online publication. DOI: 10.1007/s11128-022-03777-2

Woerner, S., & Egger, D. J. (2019). Quantum risk analysis. npj Quantum Information, 5(1), 15.

Woerner, S., & Egger, D. J. (2019, Dec 01). Quantum risk analysis. *npj Quantum Information, 05*(01). https://doi.org/DOI: 10.1038/s41534-019-0130-6

Wolf, M. O., Ewen, T., & Turkalj, I. (2023). Quantum Architecture Search for Quantum Monte Carlo Integration via Conditional Parameterized Circuits with Application to Finance. Proceedings - 2023 IEEE International Conference on Quantum Computing and Engineering, QCE 2023

World Economic Forum. (2025). *Quantum technologies: Key strategies and opportunities for financial services leaders*. World Economic Forum. https://www.weforum.org/stories/2025/07/banking-quantum-era-fraud-detection-risk-forecasting-financial-services/

Wu, Y. A., Ng, A. W., Yu, Z., Huang, J., Meng, K., & Dong, Z. Y. (2021). A review of evolutionary policy incentives for sustainable development of electric vehicles in China: Strategic implications. *Energy Policy*, *148*, 111983.

Xiao, J. J., & Tao, C. (2021). Consumer finance/household finance: The definition and scope. *China Finance Review International*, *11*(1), 1–25.

Xiao, Y., Ma, D., Zhang, F., Zhao, N., Wang, L., Guo, Z., & Xiao, Y. (2023). Spatiotemporal differentiation of carbon emission efficiency and influencing factors: From the perspective of 136 countries. *The Science of the Total Environment*, *879*, 163032. PMID: 36965718

Xie, Y. (2024). The interactive impact of green finance, ESG performance, and carbon neutrality. *Journal of Cleaner Production*, *456*, 142269.

Xu, P., Zhang, J., & Mehmood, U. (2023). How do green Investments, foreign direct investment, and renewable energy impact CO2 emissions? Measuring the role of education in E-7 nations. *Sustainability*, *15*(19), 14052.

Yamini, B., Nithyanandhan, R., Sudha, K., Nithya, T., Vijayakumar, K., & Subramanian, R. S. (2024). Maximizing the Revolutionary Potential of Quantum Computing: Challenges, Opportunities, and Future Directions. In 2024 10th International Conference on Communication and Signal Processing (ICCSP) (pp. 756-761). IEEE.

Yang, Q., Du, Q., Razzaq, A., & Shang, Y. (2022). How volatility in green financing, clean energy, and green economic practices derive sustainable performance through ESG indicators? A sectoral study of G7 countries. *Resources Policy*, *75*, 102526.

Yazdi, M. (2024). Application of Quantum Computing in Reliability Analysis. In *Advances in Computational Mathematics for Industrial System Reliability and Maintainability* (pp. 139–154). Springer Nature Switzerland. DOI: 10.1007/978-3-031-53514-7_8

Yu, S., Wang, X., Liu, J., & Wei, F. (2023). Role of mining waste trade on green development in China: Policy implications for circular economy. *Resources Policy*, *86*, 104147.

Zafar, A. (2025). Quantum Computing in Finance: Regulatory Readiness, Legal Gaps, and the Future of Secure Tech Innovation. *European Journal of Risk Regulation*. Advance online publication. DOI: 10.1017/err.2025.10050

Zaharudin, K. Z., Young, M. R., & Hsu, W. (2022). High-frequency trading: Definition, implications, and controversies. *Journal of Economic Surveys*, *36*(1), 75–107. DOI: 10.1111/joes.12434

Zaidi, S. A. H., Hussain, M., & Zaman, Q. U. (2021). Dynamic linkages between financial inclusion and carbon emissions: Evidence from selected OECD countries. *Resources. Environmental Sustainability*, *4*, 100022.

Zhang, M., Lu, T., & Shi, C. (2024). Navigating the Factor Zoo: The Science of Quantitative Investing. DOI: 10.4324/9781003480204

Zhang, L., Saydaliev, H. B., & Ma, X. (2022). Does green finance investment and technological innovation improve renewable energy efficiency and sustainable development goals. *Renewable Energy*, *193*, 991–1000.

Zhao, L., Chau, K. Y., Tran, T. K., Sadiq, M., Xuyen, N. T. M., & Phan, T. T. H. (2022). Enhancing green economic recovery through green bonds financing and energy efficiency investments. *Economic Analysis and Policy*, *76*, 488–501.

Zheng, G. W., Siddik, A. B., Masukujjaman, M., & Fatema, N. (2021). Factors affecting the sustainability performance of financial institutions in Bangladesh: The role of green finance. *Sustainability*, *13*(18), 10165.

Zhou, J. (2025). Quantum finance: Exploring the implications of quantum computing on financial models. *Computational Economics*, •••, 1–30.

Zhou, J. (2025). Quantum Finance: Exploring the Implications of Quantum Computing on Financial Models. *Computational Economics*. Advance online publication. DOI: 10.1007/s10614-025-10894-4

About the Contributors

Mohammad Irfan is a Professor at the School of Business and Commerce, Chandigarh University, Uttar Pradesh, Unnao, India. He earned his Ph.D. from the Central University of Haryana and holds an MBA in Finance, an M.Com in Accounts and Law, and an MA in Economics. A UGC-JRF/SRF/NET qualifier in Management and Commerce, he also holds certifications from NSE (NCFM) and BSE. With more than sixteen years of teaching and research experience, Dr. Irfan's expertise includes Security Analysis and Portfolio Management (SAPM), Artificial Intelligence, Machine Learning, Blockchain, Cryptocurrency, Financial Engineering, FinTech, Green Finance, and Alternative Finance. He has authored over 109 Scopus-indexed research papers in reputed journals such as The Journal of Economic Cooperation and Development (Q2), International Journal of Business Excellence, Montenegrin Journal of Economics (Q2), Cogent Business & Management (Q2), and Journal of Islamic Monetary Economics and Finance. His work has received 734+ citations with an H-index of 15. He has also published 12 books with Springer and IGI Global and is listed among the World's Top 2% Scientists.

Gilney Figueira Zebende, He is currently a full professor at the State University of Feira de Santana. He has experience in Physics, with an emphasis on Condensed Matter Physics, working mainly on the following topics: dfa, long-range correlation, dcca, dcca cross-correlation coefficient, rho_dcca coefficient and quantum finance. How AI and Eduction coming togather to resolve the current generation need abd challenges. Dr. Gilney has citaions on his research work 3114+

Adel Sarea is the winner of Emerald Literati Award 2014 (UK). He possesses over 100 publications indexed in [SCOPUS, SSCI, ESCI, ABDC, ABS], and he has more than a decade of teaching experience. He has been bestowed with many awards and been summoned as the keynote speaker on several occasions. He serves on the editorial team of several international journals published by Elsevier, Emerald, and Taylor & Francis. He is a member of the Accounting and Finance Association of

Australia and New Zealand (AFAANZ). In 2015, Prof Sarea has been appointed as a recognized Ph.D. supervisor by Brunel University London. In 2021, he has been entitled as the senior editor of the International Journal of Emerging Markets at Emerald Publishing (UK); associate editor, Heliyon Business and Economics (Elsevier); consulting editor, Journal of Education for Business (Taylor & Francis); associate editor, International Journal of Islamic and Middle Eastern Finance and Management (Emerald); associate editor, ISRA International Journal of Islamic Finance (Emerald); associate editor, Asian Journal of Accounting Research (Emerald); associate editor, Journal of Islamic Accounting and Business Research (Emerald); guest editor, Journal of Financial Reporting and Accounting (Emerald); and associate editor, MENA Journal of Cross-Cultural Management-Inderscience (UK) with 4114+ citations

Muhammad Shahbaz research focuses on a range of important topics, including development economics, energy economics, environmental economics, and tourism economics. He is a prolific author, having published over 500 research papers in peer-reviewed international journals such as Energy Economics, Energy Policy, Journal of Banking & Finance, Economic Modeling, Quantum Finance and Applied Economics. His accumulated impact factor is an impressive 2193. Dr. Shahbaz is widely recognized as one of the World's top authors in the Economics category, as compiled by IDEAS. He has also been named among the top 5 active researchers from developing countries by David McKenzie, Chief Economist at the World Bank. In 2019, Dr. Shahbaz was awarded Scientist of the Year by the Turkish Presidency, and he was also recognized as a distinguished scientist by Dozce University of Turkey in the same year. Additionally, Dr. Shahbaz has been recognized as a highly cited author in the category of economics, business, and social sciences for both 2020 and 2021. According to the AD Scientific Index for economics and econometrics, he is ranked # 43 in the world ranking and #1 in China and Asia based on H-Index ranking in 2023. Overall, Dr. Shahbaz's impressive accomplishments and contributions to the field of economics make him a highly respected and influential figure in his field.

***

Benedict Valentine Arulanandam Asst Professor and Head of Praxis, Industry and Community Engagement UCSI University, Malaysia Email: BenedictValentine@ucsiuniversity.edu.my

Nitesh Behare is an accomplished author with a wealth of knowledge and 16 years of experience in the academic field. He currently holds the position of Associate Professor at the Balaji Institute of International Business (BIIB), Sri Balaji

University Pune (SBUP). Throughout his career, Dr. Behare has made significant contributions to the academic world through the publication of numerous research papers and book chapters, establishing himself as a recognized authority in his field.

Sashwat Dixit is an MBA student at Pranveer Singh Institute of Technology (PSIT), Kanpur, specializing in finance. Her academic interests lie in areas such as financial markets, investment analysis, and the integration of emerging technologies in financial services. He has actively engaged in research work during her postgraduate studies and aspires to contribute to the field of finance through innovative research and practical applications. With a keen interest in contemporary financial challenges, Sashwat is focused on building expertise that bridges theoretical knowledge with real-world financial decision-making.

Sneha Awasthi is an MBA student at Pranveer Singh Institute of Technology (PSIT), Kanpur, specializing in finance. Her academic interests lie in areas such as financial markets, investment analysis, and the integration of emerging technologies in financial services. She has actively engaged in research work during her postgraduate studies and aspires to contribute to the field of finance through innovative research and practical applications. With a keen interest in contemporary financial challenges, Sneha is focused on building expertise that bridges theoretical knowledge with real-world financial decision-making.

Samuel Mores Geddam is an accomplished academician and researcher with over 14 years of experience in higher education, currently serving as Assistant Professor at St. Joseph's University, Bengaluru. Specializing in Human Resources, Business Analytics, and General Management, he is recognized for his pioneering work on Smart Human Augmentation through AI using the Technology Acceptance Model. A member of the ORCID Researcher Advisory Council, Dr. Samuel has published extensively on AI adoption, sustainable development, and organizational behavior, with his work featured on Scopus and Web of Science. Renowned for his expertise in SPSS, AMOS, R, NVIVO, and Tableau, he actively mentors students and professionals through workshops on advanced research methodologies, driving innovation and impactful academic initiatives.

S. Ida Evangeline, presently working as an Assistant Professor in the Department of Electrical and Electronics Engineering at the Government College of Engineering, Tirunelveli, Tamilnadu, India. She obtained her Bachelor's in Electrical and Electronics Engineering from Manonmaniam Sundaranar University in 2003, and Master's in Power Systems Engineering from Anna University, Chennai, Tamilnadu, India in 2005. She completed her PhD degree in 2023 at Anna University, Chennai, Tamilnadu, India. She has published six research papers in international journals. Her current research interests include optimal power flow, renewable energy, soft computing, machine learning, and deep learning.

Ashok Kaushal, Rotor dynamics; Modal testing and analysis; Finite element method; Vibration analysis and machine dynamics; Machinery monitoring and diagnostics; Product Development product development

Early Ridho Kismawadi, S.E.I, MA is a lecturer at the Department of Islamic Banking, Faculty of Islamic Economics and Business IAIN Langsa, Aceh, Indonesia, he has been a lecturer since 2013, he has completed a doctoral program in 2018 majoring in Sharia economics at the State Islamic University of North Sumatra. He was appointed head of the Islamic economics Law study program (2023) Islamic banking study program (2020) and Islamic financial management study program (2019) at Langsa State Islamic Institute (IAIN Langsa), Aceh, Indonesia. His research interests include financial economics, applied econometrics, Islamic economics, banking, and finance. He has published articles in national and international journals. In addition, he is also a reviewer of several reputable international journals such as Finance Research Letters, Financial Innovation, Cogent Business &; Management, Journal of Islamic Accounting and Business Research. He has also presented his papers at various local and international seminars. Dr. Early Ridho Kismawadi, S.E.I, MA, can be contacted at kismawadi@iainlangsa.ac.id.

Sandeep Kumar is an assistant professor at Institute of Business Management, GLA University, Mathura, Utter Pradesh. He received his Ph.D. degree from from Haryana School of Business, Guru Jambheshwar University of Science and Technology, Hisar, Haryana (India). His Eleven research papers have been published in National and International journals. His research papers have been accepted and presented in National and International conferences held in India.

Sanjeev Kumar Is a Professor in Lovely Professional University Punjab India. He received Undergraduate in Hotel Management from Osmania University, Postgraduate in Tourism Management from Madurai Kamaraj University. He completed Doctor of Philosophy in Hospitality Management in 2019 from Amity University Jaipur India. His research areas lies in food Service Industry, his research focuses on Alcoholic beverages, Event management and Sustainable Management Practices, Metaverse, AI Machine Learning and Artificial Intelligence. He published more than 80 research papers, articles and chapters in Scopus Indexed, UGC Approved and peer reviewed Journals and books. Dr. Sanjeev Kumar participated and acted as resource person in various National and International conferences, seminars, session chair, research workshops and industry talks and his work has been widely cited. Dr. Sanjeev also edited more than 20 books with various International

Publishers such as IGI Global, Cambridge Scholars, Emerald, CABI, Bentham Science, Taylor & Francis. Dr Sanjeev is an active researcher and has published numerous research articles in prestigious National and International journals and books.

Mohammed Majeed is a Senior Lecturer (PhD) at Tamale Technical University (TaTU). He is the current HoD for Logistics and procurement management and former HoD for Marketing. Dr Majeed is a reviewer to many reputable business and management journals. He holds PhD in Marketing, Doctor of Business Administration (DBA), Certified Business Consultant (CBC), Certified Global Business Analyst (CGBA) Mphil and MBA in Marketing, Postgraduate Diploma in Management Studies, and HND Marketing. He has published with Emerald, IGI Global, Taylor and Francis, Cogent, Wiley, Springer, Palgrave McMillan, CRC press and Bentham Science publishers. My current research interests include digital marketing, green/sustainability marketing, consumer research and co-creation

Jamshid Pardaev is an associate professor working in the Department of Finance and Tourism at Termez University of Economics and Service, Termez, Uzbekistan.

Bhagyashri Patil is currently working as an Assistant Professor of Finance at School of Business, MBA Indira University, Pune. She has completed her Ph.D. in Finance from Kavayitri Bahinabai Chaudhari North Maharashtra University, Jalgaon. With nearly eight years of academic experience, she has made substantial contributions to teaching in the domains of behavioral finance, financial laws, accounting and financial management, and personal financial planning. Her research in domain behavioral finance has been published in reputed academic journals. Currently, she is focusing her research on Climate FinTech, ESG integration, sustainable finance and behavioral finance and sustainability. She is known for her student-centric teaching methodologies, which have consistently led to high levels of student engagement and academic performance. She is also an active mentor, guiding students in both their academic development and career planning.

Prabhakar K. is an accomplished academician and seasoned professional with over 15 years of teaching experience across undergraduate (UG), postgraduate (PG), and postgraduate diploma (PGD) programs. He currently serves as the Head of the Department of Management at St. Joseph's University, Karnataka. He holds an MBA with dual specialization in Marketing and Human Resource Management from Visvesvaraya Technological University, Karnataka. He earned his Ph.D. in Management from the University of Technology, Jaipur. In addition, Dr. Prabhakar has qualified both NET and KSET, demonstrating his academic excellence.Before transitioning into academia, he gained valuable corporate experience at IBM, which has enriched his teaching with practical industry insights. His passion for continuous learning, teaching, and research has made him an inspiring figure among students and peers alike. Dr. Prabhakar has actively participated in over 100 workshops and Faculty Development Programs (FDPs) at both national and international levels. He has presented 35 research papers at various conferences in India and abroad, including Thailand, and has authored five textbooks in the field of management. He is frequently invited as a resource person, subject matter expert, board/external examiner, and has contributed to curriculum design and academic evaluation processes at multiple institutions.Driven by a strong commitment to education, Dr. Prabhakar is passionate about transforming student lives and making education more impactful and meaningful.

Ravikumar R. Natarajan is an experienced academician with over 12+ years of teaching and research expertise across institutions in India, the UAE, and the Maldives. He currently serves as an Assistant Professor at Marwadi University, Rajkot, specializing in Machine Learning, Recommender Systems, and AI-driven applications in healthcare and security. He holds a Ph.D. in Machine Learning and Recommender Systems from Amity University, Jaipur, a Master of Engineering in CSE from VMRF University, Salem, and a Bachelor of Engineering in CSE from Anna University. He also has a MiniMBA from the Swiss eLearning Institute. Dr. Ravikumar has authored more than 20 IEEE conference papers, multiple SCIE/Scopus-indexed journal articles, and co-authored a book on Artificial Intelligence. He has also published 9 patents and contributed several book chapters in emerging domains such as Federated Learning, Blockchain, and Digital Twins. He actively mentors students through initiatives like the Research Activities Club (RAC) and Student Research Internship Training (SRIT), promoting innovation and research culture.

R. Rajeshkanna is an accomplished academic with over 16 years of experience in the field of computer science and information technology. He holds a Ph.D. from Bharathiar University, Coimbatore, and an M.Phil from Vinayaka Missions University, Salem. He also earned his MCA from Periyar University, Salem. Currently, Dr. Rajeshkanna serves as an Assistant Professor in the Department of Computer Science at CHRIST (Deemed to be University), Bangalore, a position he has held since July 2022. Prior to this, he was the Professor and Head of the Department of Information Technology at Dr. N.G.P Arts & Science College (Autonomous), Coimbatore. His tenure at this institution, spanning from January 2020 to June 2022, followed a series of progressive roles, including Associate Professor and Head of the Department, and earlier, as an Assistant Professor. Dr.

Rajeshkanna has made significant academic contributions through his research and scholarly activities. He has published 35 papers in reputed international journals with high impact factors and has contributed 16 book chapters through IGI Global Publications.

Rismawati is a distinguished academic and consultant with a robust focus on sustainability reporting. She currently holds the position of lecturer and Head of the Quality Assurance Institute at Universitas Muhammadiyah Palopo, where she has been pivotal in ensuring the quality of university processes and outputs since February 2020. Additionally, she serves as an Assurer for Sustainability Reporting at the National Center for Sustainability Reporting in Jakarta, specializing in the evaluation of sustainability reports for mining companies across Indonesia. Her academic qualifications are extensive, comprising a Bachelor's degree in Economics and Accounting, a Master's degree in Accounting Science, and a Doctorate in Accounting from Universitas Brawijaya, Malang. Rismawati is also a certified specialist in sustainability reporting, risk management, and tax planning, holding several prestigious certifications including Certified Sustainability Reporting Specialist (CSRS), Certified Risk Management Practitioner (CRMP), Certified Management Accountant (CMA) and Certified Enterprise Risk Analysis (CERA). In her professional capacity, she has provided consultancy services in financial management and tax compliance for companies such as PT. Reski Barito Timur and PT. Helay Raya. Furthermore, she has authored multiple publications on Social Accounting, Sustainability Accounting, Management Accounting and CSR, contributing significantly to the academic community. Her interests in reading, writing, and travel reflect her commitment to lifelong learning and professional growth in her field.

Ruchika Rastogi is currently working as a Professor in the Department of Business Administration, Pranveer Singh Institute of Technology, Kanpur. She has been teaching Managerial Economics, Strategic Management & Operations Management at Post Graduate Level since 2009. She has published several research articles in Scopus and UGC Care indexed journals. She has published one book titles as 'international Logistics Management'. Her areas of research are Behavioural Economic & Marketing. She has conducted Research Development Programs at different institute of India.

Mandakini Garg is an Associate Professor in the Department of Business Administration at Pranveer Singh Institute of Technology (PSIT), Kanpur. She specializes in the field of finance, with her research focusing on emerging trends, financial innovation, and strategic applications of technology in financial services.

She has published extensively in reputed national and international journals, contributing to the academic discourse on finance and management. Her scholarly work reflects a strong engagement with contemporary issues such as quantum finance, financial inclusion, risk management, and corporate strategy.

Rui Manuel Teixeira Santos Dias. Postdoctoral degree in Econophysics at the State University of Feira de Santana (BR), Department of Exact Sciences. Doctor of Finance at the University of Évora - Institute of Research and Advanced Training (PT). Diploma of Advanced Studies in Doctoral Studies (DEA), at the University of Extremadura (ES), in the scientific area of Financial Economics.

Aarthi S is a dedicated Assistant Professor in Computer Science with over six years of teaching experience. She is currently pursuing her Ph.D. at Marwadi University, Gujarat, and holds an M.Phil. and MCA from Bharathiar University, Tamil Nadu. Throughout her academic career, Aarthi has specialized in programming languages such as C++, Java, and C, and contributed to research in recommender systems and AI-related data privacy. She has published journal articles, contributed to book chapters, and actively participated in technical workshops. Known for her student mentorship and engagement in academic events, Aarthi remains committed to fostering innovation and excellence in computer science education.

Christo Selvan, Dean of the School of Business at St. Joseph's University, is a distinguished academic leader with 23 years of experience in business education across India and Malaysia. He has spearheaded exponential growth in student and faculty strength, elevated national rankings, and fostered global collaborations with institutions like ACCA, Sunway University, and IMA CMA. A prolific researcher in Financial Accounting, IFRS, and HRM, he publishes in Clarivate and Scopus-indexed journals and serves as a reviewer for top international publications. Dr. Selvan also designs innovative academic programs and leads impactful international conferences, shaping future leaders through excellence and global engagement.

Syed Muhammad Abdul Rehman Shah holds a Ph.D. in Islamic Banking and Finance from International Islamic University Islamabad, where his thesis focused on the Monetary Policy Transmission Mechanism in Islamic versus Conventional banks. He also earned an M.S. in Islamic Banking and Finance from the same university, with a thesis on Capital Structure Decisions in the Islamic banking industry. His other degrees include an M.Sc in Economics from Quaid-i-Azam University Islamabad, an M.A in Islamic Studies from the University of Sargodha, and the Al-shahadat-ul-Almia fil Uloom ill Arbia-wal-Islamia (Dars-e-Nizami) from the HEC-recognized institute DMG Bhera District Sargodha, Pakistan. Dr. Shah has over 14 years of experience teaching at the university level and conducting research with national and international institutions. His publication record includes 33 research papers and 8 book chapters for publishers like Springer, IGI Global and Routledge. He is fluent in English, Urdu, Arabic, and Persian. Since September 2025, Dr. Shah has been a faculty member at the Department of Islamic Economics, Allama Iqbal Open University Islamabad. Before that, he served for 14 years as a full-time faculty member at the Department of Basic Sciences and Humanities at the University of Engineering and Technology (UET) Taxila, where he taught subjects like Engineering Economics, Professional and Social Ethics, and Islamic Studies. He also works as a part-time faculty member at NUST Business School, International Islamic University, Riphah International University and Quaid-i-Azam University, teaching courses such as Islamic Law of Business Contracts, Islamic Banking and Finance, Financial Management, and Corporate Finance. Dr. Shah has presented his research at numerous international conferences, including events at Kazguu University in Astana, Kazakhstan; Marmara University in Istanbul, Turkey; Ibn Sina University in Khartoum, Sudan; and conferences organized by Bank Indonesia in Surabaya and Jakarta. He also delivered a lecture series at Al-Azhar University in Cairo, Egypt, and has conducted online lectures and symposiums on Islamic economics and finance. Beyond his academic work, Dr. Shah is a sought-after media commentator, providing expert analysis on national budget discussions and exploring the philosophical thought of Allama Iqbal Lahori and Maulana Rumi for public audiences.

Parag Shukla [M.Com, PGDMM, UGC- NET and SET] is a PhD Scholar and working as an Assistant Professor in the Faculty of Commerce at the M.S.University of Baroda, Department of Commerce and Business Management, Gujarat, India. He received his Bachelors and Masters Degree with specialization in Marketing Management from the M.S.University of Baroda, India. His area of research is in the field of Retailing. His experience includes content analysis with the television and media research industry. He currently teaches courses of management in various under graduate and post graduate levels in the University. He has presented and published several research papers in different areas of Retailing and Marketing in various National and International refereed Journals and conference proceedings. He has also received other accolades in his research papers from various academia. Mr. Shukla is the recipient of the Best Business Academic of the Year Award [BBAY] where he won the Silver Medal for his research paper in 68th International All India Commerce Conference, which is widely recognized in Indian Education and Retail Industry.

Divyanshi Singh is an MBA student at Pranveer Singh Institute of Technology (PSIT), Kanpur, specializing in finance. Her academic interests lie in areas such as financial markets, investment analysis, and the integration of emerging technologies in financial services. She has actively engaged in research work during her postgraduate studies and aspires to contribute to the field of finance through innovative research and practical applications. With a keen interest in contemporary financial challenges, Sneha is focused on building expertise that bridges theoretical knowledge with real-world financial decision-making.

Shraddha Verma is an Assistant Professor in the School of Management at Chandigarh University with over 13 years of academic and research experience. She holds an MBA, PGDM, and M.Com, and specializes in Finance and Human Resource Management. Dr. Verma has published extensively in reputed journals including Scopus, Web of Science, ABDC, and UGC-CARE, and authored a textbook on Research Methodology. She has also contributed book chapters, delivered invited talks, and presented papers at national and international conferences. Her research interests include risk management, project finance, financial modeling, fintech innovations, and talent management. She is a member of professional bodies such as LMA, AIMA, AOM, CMA, and AIMS, and has also been granted a patent on AI-based Virtual and Augmented Reality systems.

Index

Q

www.ingramcontent.com/pod-product-compliance
Lightning Source LLC
LaVergne TN
LVHW080906300926
849162LV00003B/573
* 9 7 9 8 3 3 7 3 2 8 9 3 5 *